PEOPLE'S
COMPANION
to the
BREVIARY
VOLUME II

Revised and Expanded Edition
of the
New Companion to the Breviary with
Seasonal Supplement

The Liturgy of the Hours with Inclusive Language

CONTENTS

Volume II

HOW TO USE THIS BOOK

This *People's Companion to the Breviary* contains the four-week psalter and seasonal prayers for Advent, Christmas, Epiphany, Lent, Easter, Sundays of the Year, and Special Feasts and Commemorations. A calendar indicates the proper week of the psalter to use for the years from 1997–2020.

Each **Psalm** follows a given antiphon. The **Antiphon** from the four-week Psalter or from the Season is generally prayed before and after the psalm. Three Psalms are used for each office. If two or more people are praying together, the verses of the psalms are alternated, i.e., one person or a group of persons prays a verse, then another person or group prays the following verse.

After the psalms, a suggested **Reading** is given for silent meditation or faith sharing among those praying together. Other readings may be substituted. The **Responsory** is begun by the leader and the group repeats the prayer as indicated by the parts printed in bold print.

After the antiphon for the **Canticle** is prayed, one may use the Canticle of Zechariah (on the last page) or the Canticle of Mary (on the inside back cover). Traditionally the Canticle of Zechariah is prayed in the morning and the Canticle of Mary is prayed in the evening, but the office chosen may dictate the preference of the group.

The **Intercessions** are begun by the leader and the group prays the response together. It is suggested that those praying add their own petitions after reading the intercessions given.

The **Prayer** can be prayed by the leader or in unison.

WEEK I

SUNDAY, EVENING PRAYER I

Ant 1 Let my prayer rise as incense before you.

Psalm 141:1-9

I call upon you, O God; make
  haste to help me;
give ear to my voice, when I call
  to you.
Let my prayer rise as incense
  before you,
and the lifting up of my hands as
  an evening sacrifice!

Set a guard over my mouth, O
  God,
keep watch over the door of my
  lips!
Do not incline my heart to evil,
that I not busy myself with
  wicked deeds
in company with those who work
  iniquity;
let me not partake of their
  dainties!

Let a good person strike or
  rebuke me in kindness,
but let the oil of wickedness
  never anoint my head;
for my prayer is constantly
  against wicked deeds.

When those who do evil are given
  over to those who condemn
  them,
then they shall learn that your
  word is true.—

***Glory to you, Source of all
  Being, Eternal Word and Holy
  Spirit,**

**As it was in the beginning is
  now and will be forever. Amen.**

As a rock which one holds and
  shatters on the ground,
so shall their bones be strewn at
  the mouth of the grave.

But my eyes are turned toward
  you, O God;
in you I seek refuge; leave me not
  defenseless!
Keep me from the trap which evil
  lays before me,
and from the snares of my own
  wickedness. **Glory*...**

**Ant 2 You are my refuge, O
  God; my portion in the land of
  the living.**

Psalm 142

I cry out with my voice to you, O
  God,
with my voice I make supplication
  to you.
I pour out my complaints before
  you,
before you I place all my troubles.
When my spirit is faint, you, O
  God, know my way!

In the path where I walk
hidden traps surround me.
I look to the right and watch,
but no one takes notice of me;
no human refuge remains for me,
no one cares for my soul.

I cry out to you, O God;
I say, you are my refuge,
my portion in the land of the
  living.
Give heed to my cry;
for I am brought low, indeed!

Deliver me from those who would hurt me;
for they are too strong for me!
Bring me out of my distress,
that I may give thanks to your name!
Let your holy ones surround me;
for you will deal graciously with me. **Glory*...**

Ant 3 Every tongue will proclaim the glory of God.

Cant: Phil 2:6–11

Though he was in the form of God,
Jesus did not count equality with God
something to be grasped at.

But emptied himself—

taking the form of a slave,
being born in human likeness.

Being found in human estate,
he humbled himself and became obedient,
obediently accepting death,
even death on a cross!

Therefore God has highly exalted him
and bestowed on him the name above every other name.

So that at the name of Jesus
every knee should bow,
in heaven, on the earth,
and under the earth,
and every tongue proclaim
to the glory of God:
Jesus Christ is Lord! **Glory*...**

READING

We can apply...what Christ says about the narrow gate to the sensitive part of the human person, and what he says about the constricting way to the spiritual or rational part. Since he proclaims that few find it, we ought to note the cause: Few there are with the knowledge and desire to enter into this supreme nakedness and emptiness of spirit. As this path on the high mount of perfection is narrow and steep, it demands travelers who are neither weighed down by the lower part of their nature nor burdened in the higher part. This is a venture in which God alone is sought and gained; thus only God ought to be sought and gained.

John of the Cross, *The Ascent of Mount Carmel*, II.7:3, (3)

RESPONSORY

In love and thanksgiving, we praise you, Holy God. **—In love...**
Your name is written in our hearts; **—we praise...**
Glory to you, Source of all Being, Eternal Word and Holy Spirit.
    —In love...

CANTICLE OF MARY

Ant. Forever I will sing your praise.

INTERCESSIONS

Heaven and earth will pass away, but your word will remain, O God;
> —let this promise of eternal life in you give meaning to our lives and energize us in your service.

You bless your people with a variety of talents, O God;
> —give us the courage to develop our gifts for your glory and the good of all.

Jesus, you foresaw the stark reality of the future, and you encouraged your followers to have patience;
> —help us to live the gospel so faithfully that our lives will be a beacon of hope to others.

We are your children and you look upon us with love.
> —help us to refrain from judging others negatively and to temper justice with mercy.

Prayer is your invitation to realize our union with you;
> —awaken us to your presence in us; teach us what it means to pray always.

PRAYER: Most loving God, you pursue creation with your love and rescue us with your mercy. Look upon us, your people, this evening with tenderness and compassion. Especially do we pray for all world leaders. May they all find strength in your love and courage in your wisdom. We ask this through the holy name of Jesus. Amen.

MORNING PRAYER

Ant. 1 As morning breaks I call upon your name, O God.

Psalm 63:1–9

O God, you are my God, I long for you;
my soul thirsts for you;
My body seeks for you
as in a dry and weary land without water.
So I have looked upon you in the sanctuary,—

beholding your power and your glory.

For your constant love is better than life,
So I will bless you as long as I live;
I will lift up my hands and call on your name.

My soul feasts on you and my mouth praises you,
as I think of you upon my bed,
and meditate on you in the watches of the night;—

for you have been my help,
In the shadow of your wings I sing
  for joy.
My soul clings to you; your hand
  upholds me.   **Glory*...**

**Ant. 2 Not fearing the flames the
three young men cried out with
one voice: Blessed be God,
(alleluia).**

Cant: Daniel 3:57–88, 56

All you works of God, praise our
  God.
Praise and exalt God above all
  forever.
All you angels, sing God's praise,
you heavens and waters above.
Sun and moon, and stars of
  heaven,
sing praise with the heavenly
  hosts.

Every shower and dew, praise our
  God.
Give praise all you winds.
Praise our God, you fire and heat,
cold and chill—dew and rain.
Frost and chill, praise our God.
Praise God, ice and snow.
Nights and days, sing hymns of
  praise,
light and darkness,
lightnings and clouds.

Let all the earth bless our God.
Praise and exalt God above all
  forever.
Let all that grows from the earth
  give praise
together with mountains and hills.
Give praise you springs,
you seas and rivers,
dolphins and all water creatures.
Let birds of the air,—

beasts wild and tame,
together will all living peoples,
praise and exalt God above all
  forever.

O Israel praise our God.
Praise and exalt God above all
  forever.
Give praise, you priests,
servants of the Most High,
spirits and souls of the just.
Holy ones of humble heart,
sing your hymns of praise.
Hananiah, Azariah, Mishael,
  praise our God.
Praise and exalt God above all
  forever.

Let us bless our God, Holy
  Mystery,
Source of All Being, Word, and
  Spirit.
Let us praise and exalt God above
  all forever.
Blessed are you, O God, in the
  firmament of heaven.
Praiseworthy and glorious and
  exalted above all forever.

**Ant. 3 Let the people of Zion
rejoice, (alleluia).**

Psalm 149

Sing a new song to our God,
Give praise in the assembly of the
  faithful.
Let Israel be glad in its maker,
let Zion's heirs exult in the Most
  High.
Let them praise God's name with
  dancing,
and make music with timbrel and
  harp.

For you take delight in your
  people, O God.—

You adorn the humble with victory.
Let the faithful exult in their glory, in their rest, let them sing for joy.
Let the praises of God be on their lips
and two-edged swords in their hands,
to wreak vengeance on all that is wicked,
and chastisement on all injustice;
to bind what is evil in chains
and oppression in fetters of iron;
to carry out the sentence pre-ordained;
this is glory for all God's faithful ones. **Glory*...**

READING

[I], John looked, and there was a great multitude that no one could count, from every nation, from all tribes and peoples and languages, standing before the throne and before the Lamb, robed in white, with palm branches in their hands. They cried out in a loud voice, saying, "Salvation belongs to our God who is seated on the throne, and to the Lamb!" And all the angels stood around the throne and around the elders and the four living creatures, and they fell on their faces before the throne and worshipped God, singing, "Amen! Blessing and glory and wisdom and thanksgiving and honor and power and might be to our God forever and ever! Amen."

Rev 7:9–12

RESPONSORY

Christ, living word in our midst, hear our morning prayer.
    —**Christ...**
You are the light of the world; —**hear our...**
Glory to you, Source of all Being, Eternal Word and Holy Spirit.
    —**Christ...**

CANTICLE OF ZECHARIAH

Ant. Most gracious God, may you bless us all our days.

INTERCESSIONS

The earth is your masterpiece, O God, and you have made us its stewards;
    —give us eyes to see your handiwork in every creature.
Creator is your name, and all that comes from your hand is good;
    —cleanse our hearts and enlighten our minds that our
        choices may enhance and magnify your work in our world.
Your measuring rod is love;
    —give us a love that takes us out of and beyond ourselves.

Jesus, you know the strengths and weaknesses of the human heart;
>—share with us your patience and compassion; remind us that another may carry a cross beyond our imagining.

Death is our last chance on earth to say yes to you, O God;
>—make us one with your will day by day.

PRAYER: O loving God we take delight in your people and all of creation. Together we unite our hearts and voices to sing your praise. Be with us this day and help us to treat each other and all living creatures with respect and appreciation. Grant this in the name of Jesus who is our way, our truth, and our life. Amen.

DAYTIME PRAYER

Ant. 1 O God, to whom shall we go? You alone are our refuge.
Psalm 118
I

We give thanks to you, for you are good,
and your steadfast love endures forever.
Let the descendants of Israel say:
"Your steadfast love endures forever."
Let the descendants of Aaron say:
"Your steadfast love endures forever."
Let those who fear you say:
"Your steadfast love endures forever."

In my distress, I called to you;
you answered me and set me free.
With you at my side I do not fear.
What can anyone do against me?
You are at my side to help me:
I shall withstand all evildoers.

It is better to take refuge in you,
than to trust in people:—

it is better to take refuge in you
than to trust in our leaders.
>**Glory***...

Ant. 2 God's holy hand has raised me up, (alleluia).
II

All wickedness surrounded me;
in your name I crushed it.
It surrounded me, surrounded me on every side;
in your name I cut it off.
It surrounded me like bees;
it blazed like a fire among thorns.
In your name I crushed it.

I was pushed hard, and was falling
but you came to help me.
You are my strength and my song;
you are my salvation.

O God, you have triumphed;
your reign is exalted.
You have triumphed over all;
I shall not die, I shall live
and recount your wondrous deeds.
You have chastened me sorely,—

but have not given me over to death. **Glory*...**

Ant. 3 Our God has let the light of the Most High to shine upon us, (alleluia).

III

Open to me the gates of justice,
that I may enter and give thanks.
This is your gate, O God;
the just shall enter through it.
I thank you for you have answered me
you alone are my salvation.

The stone which the builders rejected
has become the cornerstone.
This is your doing, O God,
it is marvelous in our eyes.—

This is the day which you have made;
let us rejoice and be glad in it.

Save us, we beseech you, O God!
O God, grant us success.
Blessed are those who enter
in your holy name.
For you O God, are our God,
and you have given us light.

Let us go forward in procession with branches,
up to your holy altar.
You are my God, I thank you.
You are my God, I praise you.
We give thanks to you for you are good;
and your steadfast love endures forever. **Glory*...**

PRAYER: Most holy God, we rejoice in your gift of life as shared with us in the paschal mystery. On this day of remembrance, help us to enter more deeply into the mystery of your life lived among us, your people. We ask this in the name of Jesus who lived as one of us and through your Spirit who enlivens us. Amen.

EVENING PRAYER II

Ant. 1 God's reign will last forever.

Psalm 110:1-5, 7

God's revelation to the Anointed One:
"Sit at my side:
till I put injustice beneath your feet."

God will send forth from Zion
your scepter of power:
rule in the midst of your foes.

Your people will give themselves freely
on the day you lead your host
upon the holy mountains.
From the womb of the morning
your youth will come like dew.

God has sworn an oath that will not be changed.
"You are a priest forever,
after the order of Melchizedek."

The Anointed standing at your side,—

will shatter rulers on the day of wrath.

Drinking from your streams by the wayside
shall the Chosen One be refreshed. **Glory*...**

Ant. 2 Tremble, O earth, at the presence of your God.

Psalm 114

When Israel went forth from Egypt,
Jacob's heirs from an alien people,
Judah became God's sanctuary,
Israel, the dominion of the Most High.

The sea looked and fled,
Jordan turned back on it's course.
The mountains skipped like rams,
the hills like yearling lambs.

What ails you, O sea, that you flee?
O Jordan, that you turn back?
Mountains, that you skip like rams,
hills, like yearling lambs?

Tremble, O earth, at the presence of God,
at the presence of the God of your ancestors,
who turns the rock into a pool,
the flint into a spring of water. **Glory*...**

Ant. 3 All power is yours, O God, creator of all.

Cant: Rev 19:1, 5–7

Salvation, glory, and power belong to you,
your judgments are honest and true.

All of us, your servants, sing praise to you,
we worship you reverently, both great and small.

You, our almighty God, are Creator of heaven and earth.
Let us rejoice and exult, and give you glory.

The wedding feast of the Lamb has begun,
And the bride has made herself ready. **Glory*...**

READING

Blessed be the God...of our Lord Jesus Christ, the [God] of mercies and the God of all consolation, who consoles us in all our affliction, so that we may be able to console those who are in any affliction with the consolation with which we ourselves are consoled by God. For just as the sufferings of Christ are abundant for us, so also our consolation is abundant through Christ. If we are being afflicted, it is for your consolation and salvation; if we are being consoled, it is for your consolation, which you experience when you patiently endure the same sufferings that we are also suffering. Our hope for you is unshaken; for we know that as you share in our sufferings, so also you share in our consolation.

2 Cor 1:3–7

RESPONSORY

Incline my heart to praise your goodness all the days of my life.
  —**Incline...**
For my prayer is always before you; —**all the...**
Glory to you, Source of all Being, Eternal Word and Holy Spirit.
  —**Incline...**

CANTICLE OF MARY

Ant. You fill us with goodness and mercy.

INTERCESSIONS

Spirit of God, you lead each of us in a direction that is life-giving
and fruitful;
  —help us to silence all that would deafen us to your call.
As the possibilities of science continue to expand;
  —remind us of our creaturehood and give us humble hearts.
Life is your gift to us, O God, and your love for us gives meaning
to your gift;
  —show yourself to those who are tempted to despair.
Jesus, you knew the cares of family life;
  —encourage and strengthen heads of families who face the
    special challenges of our culture.
Jesus you healed on the Sabbath and were persecuted for it;
  —be with our present day prophets who make unpopular
    decisions for the cause of justice and truth.

PRAYER: You, O God, are our place of refuge; you continue to
call us forth to be your people in a world of division
and distress. Help us to be people of faith, joy, and love
in the midst of chaos. This we ask through the
intercession of Jesus, Mary, and Joseph, who imaged
community in a captive and oppressed land. Amen.

MONDAY

MORNING PRAYER

Ant 1 Give heed to my words, O God, and listen to my morning prayer.

Psalm 5:1–9, 11–12

Give ear to my words, O God,
give heed to my groaning.
Attend to the sound of my cry,
O God, Most High.

For it is you to whom I pray.
In the morning you hear my
  voice;
I prepare a sacrifice for you,
watching and waiting.

You are not a God delighting in
  evil;
no sinner is your companion.
The boastful may not stand before
  you,
before your holy face.

You hate all that is evil;
you destroy all that is false.
The deceitful and the bloodthirsty
you chastise, O God.

But I through the abundance of
  your love
will enter your holy house.
I will worship at your holy temple,
filled with awe.

Lead me, O God, in your justice;
there are those who seek to
  seduce me,
make clear your way before me.

For there is no truth in their
  mouth,
their heart is destruction,
their throat is a wide-open grave,
all flattery their speech.

Let all be glad who take refuge in
  you,
forever, sing out their joy.
Shelter those who love your
  name;
May they ever exult in you.

For you it is, who bless the just;
you cover them with favor,
  as with a shield. **Glory*...**

Ant. 2 We sing your praises from generation to generation.

Cant: 1 Chron 9:10b–13

Blessed may you be,
O God of Israel,
from eternity to eternity.

Yours, O God, are grandeur and
  power,
majesty, splendor, and glory.

For all in heaven and on earth is
  yours;
yours, O God, is the sovereignty;
you are exalted as head over all.

Riches and honor are from you;
you have dominion over all.
In your hands are power and
  might;
it is yours to give grandeur and
  strength to all.

Therefore, our God, we give you
  thanks
and we praise the majesty of
  your name. **Glory*...**

Ant. 3 You are the Alpha and the Omega, the first and the last, the beginning and the end.

Psalm 29

O give to God, you heavenly
  beings,
give to God glory and power;
give glory to God's holy name.
Worship your God in holy array.

For God's voice is heard on the
  waters,
thundering on many waters;
the voice of God is powerful,
God's voice, full of splendor.

Your voice shatters the cedars,—

it shatters the cedars of Lebanon;
you make Lebanon skip like a calf
and Sirion like a young wild ox.

Your voice, O God flashes flames
  of fire.
Your voice shakes the wilderness
  of Kadesh;
it makes the oak trees whirl,
and strips the forests bare.

The God of glory thunders!
In your temple all cry: "Glory!"
You sit enthroned over the flood;
you sit, our sovereign forever.

May you give strength to your
  people,
and bless your people with peace.
  Glory*...

READING

Do as perfectly as you can the tasks of your every day life, even the
most trivial. It is quite simple. Follow our Lord [Jesus] like a little child.
I skip after him as best I can. I put my trust in him and abandon all
care.

The Beatification of Father Titus Brandsma, Carmelite, p. 46, (12)

RESPONSORY

Shelter us, O God, in the safety of your dwelling place. **—Shelter...**
Your name is forever blessed; **—in the...**
Glory to you, Source of all Being, Eternal Word and Holy Spirit.
  —Shelter...

CANTICLE OF ZECHARIAH

Ant. You are faithful to your word, forever.

INTERCESSIONS

O God, you bow to our weakness and need;
  —deliver us from temptation and guide us in the way of truth.
Your Spirit prays in us for what we know not how to ask;
  —let that same Spirit draw us to a maturity worthy of you.
Jesus, you drew your disciples to yourself and taught them
eternal truths;

—bless the young people who must live in our streets,
    jobless and tempted to crime and despair.
Our minds and hearts are pulled in many directions;
    —let the words of your gospel unify and direct our lives.
The sick and the poor were drawn to you;
    —help us to find ways to care for all who are terminally ill.

PRAYER: O Holy God, you continue to bless us with your gifts of
    creation. We give thanks to you for your kindness to
    your people and take delight in the gifts we share to
    bring about the fullness of your life in our world. All
    praise to you, Most Blessed Trinity, living in us and
    among us through all generations. Amen.

DAYTIME PRAYER

**Ant. 1 Teach us to love you and
our neighbor, so as to fulfill
your law.**
Psalm 19:7-14

Your law, O God, is perfect,
reviving the soul.
Your testimony is to be trusted,
making the simple wise.

Your precepts are right,
rejoicing the heart.
Your command is pure,
giving light to the eyes.

The fear of God is holy,
enduring forever.
God's ordinances are true,
and all of them just.

More to be desired are they than
    gold,
more than the purest gold,
and sweeter are they than honey,
than drippings from the comb.

By them your servant finds
    instruction;
great reward is in their keeping.
But who can detect all one's
    errors?—

From hidden faults acquit me.

Restrain me from presumptuous
    sins,
let them not have rule over me!
Then shall I be blameless,
and clean from serious sin.

Let the words of my mouth,
the thoughts of my heart,
be acceptable in your sight,
O God, my rock and my
    redeemer. **Glory*...**

**Ant. 2 Judge me, O God,
according to your law.**

Psalm 7
I

O God, in you I take refuge;
Save me from my pursuers and
    rescue me,
lest they tear me to pieces like a
    lion,
dragging me off with none to
    rescue me.

O God, if I have done this,
if my hands have done wrong,
if I have paid my friend with evil
or plundered without cause,—

then let my foes pursue me and
  seize me,
let them trample my life to the
  ground
and lay my soul in the dust.

Let the assembly of nations
  gather round you,
taking your seat above them on
  high.
For you, O God, are judge of the
  peoples.

Judge me, O God, according to
  my justice,
and according to the integrity
  that is mine.
Put an end to the evil of the
  wicked;
and make the just stand firm,
you who test the mind and heart,
you, our most just God!
  Glory*...

**Ant. 3 Search me, O God, and
know my heart; cleanse me
from all sin.**

II

God is the shield that protects
  me,
who saves the upright of heart.—

God is a just judge
slow to anger;
challenging the wicked every day,
those who are slow to repent.

God sharpens the sword,
bends the bow that is strung,
prepares deadly weapons for
  wickedness,
and barbs the arrows with fire.
Behold those who are pregnant
  with malice,
who conceive evil and bring forth
  lies.

They dig a pitfall, dig it deep;
and fall into the trap they have
  made.
Their malice will recoil on
  themselves;
on their own heads their violence
  will fall.

I will give thanks to you, God,
for your justice;
and will sing to your name,
  O Most High.   **Glory*...**

PRAYER: As we pause to remember your fidelity to us, O Source
of Life, continue to abide with us this day. We give
thanks for all people working for justice and peace, and
we ask you, O God, to come in power to give your
people courage and strength. We ask this through the
intercession of Jesus and all who have given their lives
in the cause of justice. Amen.

EVENING PRAYER

Ant. 1 Teach us how to act justly, and to walk humbly with one another.

Psalm 11

In God I have taken my refuge.
How can you say to my soul:
"Fly like a bird to the mountains.

See the wicked bending the bow;
they have fitted their arrows on
  the string
to shoot the upright in the dark.
If the foundations are destroyed,
what can the righteous do?"

But you are in your holy temple,
you, whose throne is in heaven.
Your eyes look down on the
  world;
your gaze tests mortal flesh.

God tests the just and the
  wicked,
scorned by the lovers of violence.
God will chastise those who do
  evil;
a scorching wind shall be their
  lot.

You are just and love justice;
the upright shall behold your
  face. **Glory*...**

Ant. 2 Create in me an upright spirit that I may serve you in others.

Psalm 15

Who shall visit in your tent,
and dwell on your holy
  mountain?

They who walk blamelessly,
and do what is right,
who speak the truth from their
  hearts;—

and do not slander with their
  tongues;

they who do no wrong to each
  other,
nor cast reproaches on their
  neighbors,
who pray the godless to repent,
and honor those who fear the
  Most High;

they who keep their pledge, come
  what may;
who take no profit from injustice,
nor accept bribes against the
  innocent.
Such as these will stand firm
  forever. **Glory*...**

Ant. 3 We are your people, chosen before the foundation of the world.

Cant: Ephesians 1:3–10

Praised be the God
of our Lord Jesus Christ,
who has blessed us in Christ
with every spiritual blessing in
  the heavens.

God chose us in him
before the foundation of the
  world,
that we should be holy
and blameless in God's sight.

We have been predestined
to be God's children through
  Jesus Christ,
such was the purpose of God's
  will,
that all might praise the glorious
  favor
bestowed on us in Christ.

In Christ and through his blood,
we have redemption,—

the forgiveness of our sins,
according to the riches of God's
  grace lavished upon us.

For God has made known to us
in all wisdom and insight,
the mystery of the plan set forth
  in Christ.

A plan to be carried out in Christ,
in the fullness of time,
to unite all things in Christ,
things in heaven and things on
  earth. **Glory*...**

READING

If love is the soul of Christian existence, it must be at the heart of
every other Christian virtue. Thus, for example, *justice* without love is
legalism; *faith* without love is ideology; *hope* without love is self-
centeredness; *forgiveness* without love is self-abasement; *fortitude*
without love is recklessness; *generosity* without love is extravagance;
care without love is mere duty; *fidelity* without love is servitude. Every
virtue is an expression of love. No virtue is really a virtue unless it is
permeated, or informed, by love (1 Cor 13).

Richard P. McBrien, Catholicism: Study Edition, p. 977, (14)

RESPONSORY

Look upon us graciously, O God, and have mercy on us. **—Look...**
For you are our source of love; **—have...**
Glory to you, Source of all Being, Eternal Word and Holy Spirit.
  —Look...

CANTICLE OF MARY

Ant. I long for you, God of my life.

INTERCESSIONS

Jesus, you loved the land of your birth;
  —bless all nations torn by war and division.
You were filled with the Holy Spirit, the very Wisdom of God;
  —enlighten and guide all who labor to discover insights
    toward our spiritual and physical healing and growth.
Many believed in you because of your miracles;
  —let our love for you and for one another be the sign that
    draws others to you.
You welcomed outcasts and dined with them;
  —teach us how to reverently minister to those who are
    rejected today.
Your gospel is a call to life;
  —bring its message of peace to those who are dying.

PRAYER: Most loving God, you love justice. Help us to be open to your ways of mercy, compassion, and truth that we may call forth in ourselves and in one another your ways of wisdom and truth. We ask this through the Holy Spirit of Wisdom living in you through all eternity. Amen.

TUESDAY
MORNING PRAYER

Ant. 1 Blessed are the pure of heart, for they shall see God.

Psalm 24

Yours is the earth and its fullness,
the world and all who dwell there;
for you have founded it upon the
  seas,
and established it upon the rivers.

Who shall climb your mountain, O
  God?
Who shall stand in your holy
  place?
Those with clean hands and pure
  hearts,
who do not desire what is vain,
who have not sworn so as to
  deceive their neighbors.

They shall receive blessings from
  the Most High,
and reward from the God who
  saves them.
Such are those who seek after the
  Holy One;
who seek the face of the God of
  their ancestors.

O gates, lift up your heads;
grow higher, ancient doors.
Let enter the God of glory!

Who is this God of glory?
The One who is mighty and
  valiant,
valiant against all injustice.

O gates, lift up your heads;
grow higher, ancient doors.
Let enter the God of glory!

Who is this God of glory?
You, the God of hosts,
You, O God, are the God of glory.
  Glory*...

Ant. 2 Turn to me, O God, and show me your face.

Cant: Tobit 13:1b–8

Blessed be God who lives forever,
whose realm lasts for all ages.

For you scourge, O God, and then
  have mercy;
you cast down to the depths of the
  nether world,
and bring up from the great abyss.
No one can escape your hand.

Praise God, you Israelites, before
  the Gentiles,
for though you are scattered
  among them,
you have seen God's greatness
  even there.

Exalt God before every living
  being,
because you, O God, are the Most
  High,
our God forever and ever.

God has scourged you for your
  iniquities,—

but will again have mercy on you all.
Gathering you from all the Gentiles
among whom you have been scattered.

When you turn back to God with all your heart,
to do only what is right,
then God will turn back to you,
God's face will no longer be hidden.

So now consider what has been done for you,
and give praise with full voice.
Bless the God of righteousness,
and exalt the Ruler of the ages.

In the land of my exile I praise you, O God,
and show your power and majesty to a sinful nation.
"Turn back, you sinners! do what is right:
perhaps God may look with favor upon you
and show you mercy.

As for me, I exult in my God,
and my spirit rejoices.
Let all speak of God's majesty,
and sing God's praises in Jerusalem." **Glory*...**

Ant. 3 Blessed are those who hear your word and keep it.

Psalm 33

Rejoice in God, O you just;
praise is fitting for loyal hearts.
We give thanks to you with the lyre,
make melody with ten-stringed harps.
Let us sing a song that is new,
and play skillfully, full of gladness.

For your words, O God are faithful
and all your works to be trusted.
You love justice and righteousness,
and fill the earth with your steadfast love.

By your word the heavens were made,
by the breath of your mouth all the stars.
You gather the waters of the oceans;
you store up the depths of the seas.

Let all the earth fear you, O God,
all who live in the world, stand in wonder.
For you spoke; and it came to be.
You commanded; it sprang into being.

You frustrate the designs of the nations,
you upset the plans of the peoples.
Your own designs stand forever,
the plans of your heart to all generations.

Happy are they whose God you are,
the peoples you have chosen for your heritage.
From the heavens you look forth,
and see all the peoples of the earth.

From the place where you dwell you gaze
on all the dwellers of this earth,
you who fashion the hearts of them all
and observe all their deeds.

Rulers are not saved by their armies,
nor leaders preserved by their strength.—

A vain hope for safety are our
  weapons;
despite their power they cannot
  save.

Look on those who reverence you,
on those who hope in your love,
to deliver their souls from death,
and keep them alive in famine.

Our souls are waiting for you;
you are our help and our
  shield.
In you do our hearts find joy;
we trust in your holy name.

Let your love be upon us, O God,
as we place all our hope in you.
Glory*...

READING

Humanly speaking a genuine gift is given freely, out of love and not
out of necessity; its reception is occasion for gratitude and joy. In the
divine freedom to be present to all creatures, empowering them to
birth and rebirth in the midst of the antagonistic structures of reality,
the Spirit is intelligible as the first gift, freely given and giving. Her
loving in the world is gracious and inviting, never forcing or using
violence but respectfully calling to human freedom, as is befitting a
gift.

Elizabeth Johnson, *She Who Is*, p. 143, (2)

RESPONSORY

You call us each by name, for we are blessed in you. **—You call...**
Faithful to your promise; **—for we are...**
Glory to you, Source of all Being, Eternal Word and Holy Spirit.
    —You call...

CANTICLE OF ZECHARIAH

Ant. You are our God and holy is your name.

INTERCESSIONS

Jesus, you enabled your disciples to hear your call and to follow
you;
    —enable all Christians to discern the promptings of your
      Spirit and to respond wholeheartedly.
Through your death and rising, we have become your body; your
Spirit lives on in us;
    —awaken us to our responsibility as your people; let us meet
      each other with openness and good will.
Your apostle Paul prayed for an end to division within his
community;

—teach us positive ways to heal our differences and to
cultivate peace of mind for ourselves and our children.
Jesus, our Savior, you were taught and nourished by the words
of Scripture;
—may our hearing of the word of God today help us to bring
quality of life to those who are imprisoned, the oppressed,
and the disabled.
O God, time after time you spoke to your people and drew them
to conversion of heart;
—grant us the ability to read the signs of the times, that we
may hear your call to a change of heart as individuals and
as a people.

PRAYER: Most compassionate God, touch our hearts this
morning with your mercy and love. Help us to be a
source of love and light to those who are suffering this
day. May all who die today experience the joy of being
in your presence. Grant this through the intercession
of all who suffered persecution for the sake of justice.
Amen.

DAYTIME PRAYER

Ant. 1 The just shall praise you with upright hearts.

Psalm 119:1–8

Blessed are they whose way is
blameless,
who follow your law, O God!
Blessed are they who do your will,
who seek you with all their hearts,
who never do anything wrong,
but walk in your ways.

You have laid down your precepts
to be diligently kept.
O that my ways may be firm
in obeying your statutes.
Then I shall not be put to shame
as I heed your commands.

I will praise you with an upright
heart
as I learn your decrees.—

I will obey your statutes;
do not forsake me. **Glory*...**

Ant. 2 My heart rejoices in your saving grace, O God.

Psalm 13

How long, O God? Will you forget
me forever?
How long will you hide your face?
How long must I bear pain in my
soul,
and sorrow in my heart day and
night?
How long shall my oppressors
prevail?

Look at me, answer me, my God!
Lighten my eyes lest I sleep the
sleep of death,—

lest my oppressors say: "I have overcome you";
lest they rejoice to see me shaken.

As for me, I trust in your merciful love.
My heart rejoices in your salvation;
I will sing to you for your goodness,
because you are gracious to me. **Glory*...**

Ant. 3 Give us your wisdom that we may follow your way.

Psalm 14

Fools say in their hearts:
"There is no God!"
They are corrupt, their deeds, depraved;
there are none that do good.

But you look down from heaven,
upon the peoples of the earth,—

to see if any are wise,
if any seek God.

All seem to have gone astray,
depraved, every one;
there are none that do good,
no, not even one.

Do evildoers have no knowledge?
They eat up God's people
as though they were eating bread;
do they never call upon the Most High God?

There they shall be in great terror,
for God is with the just.
You may mock the hope of the poor,
but their refuge is the Most High God.

O that Israel's salvation might come from Zion!
When God delivers the people from bondage,
then Jacob shall rejoice and Israel be glad. **Glory*...**

PRAYER: Gentle God, you remind us that you are our faithful friend, and that you will deliver us from bondage. Look upon us, your people, and deliver us from the chains that keep us from the fullness of life. We pray this in love and confidence in Jesus' name. Amen.

EVENING PRAYER

Ant. 1 Only in you, O God, will my soul be at rest.

Psalm 20

May God answer in time of trouble!
May the name of our God protect you.

Send your help, O God, from your sanctuary,
and give your support from Zion.
May you remember all our offerings
and receive our sacrifice with favor.

May you give us our heart's desire
and fulfill every one of our plans.–

May we ring out our joy at your
victory
and rejoice in your name, O God.
May you grant all our prayers.

Now I know that you, O God,
will give victory to your anointed;
you will reply from your holy
heaven
with the help of your hand.

Some trust in chariots or horses,
but we trust in your holy name.
They will collapse and fall,
but we shall rise and stand firm.

Give victory to your Anointed,
give answer on the day we call.
Glory*...

**Ant. 2 To know you, O God, is
to possess eternal life.**

Psalm 21:2-8, 14

O God, your strength gives joy to
your people;
how your saving help makes them
glad!
You have granted them the desire
of their hearts;
you have not refused the prayer of
their lips.

You came to meet them with
goodly blessings,
you have set blessings on their
heads.
They asked you for life and this
you have given,
length of days forever and ever.

Your saving help has given them
glory.—

Splendor you bestow upon them.
You grant your blessings to them
forever.
You gladden them with the joy of
your presence.

They put their trust in you:
through your steadfast love, they
shall stand firm.
O God, we exult in your strength;
we shall sing and praise your
goodness. **Glory*...**

**Ant. 3 O God, you have made us
in your own image.**

Cant: Rev 4:11, 5:9, 10, 12

Worthy are you, O God, our God,
to receive glory and honor and
power.

For you have created all things;
by your will they came to be and
were made.

Worthy are you to take the scroll
and to open its seals,

For you were slain, and by your
blood,
you purchased for God
saints of every race and tongue,
of every people and nation.

You have made of them a kindom,
and priests to serve our God,
and they shall reign on the earth.

Worthy is the Lamb who was slain
to receive power and riches,
wisdom and strength,
honor and glory and praise.
Glory*...

READING

As happiness lies in the ultimate perfection we all hope for, so there is
virtuous, contented rest in having accomplished the purpose for which

we begin a good work, and we should not linger in the task but take heart in the promise of satisfaction and joy in the happy conclusion that we trust our [God] will give to the good work begun.

Francisco de Osuna, *The Third Spiritual Alphabet*, p. 35, (1)

RESPONSORY

In you, Word of God, I place my trust and love.—**In you...**
For you are our redeemer; —**I place...**
Glory to you, Source of all Being, Eternal Word and Holy Spirit.
   —**In you...**

CANTICLE OF MARY

Ant. My soul will sing your praises.

INTERCESSIONS

O God, you are ever calling us to greater freedom, to walk in the light, to grow and to deepen our lives;
   —give us the desire and the courage to respond fully to your
      goodness; make our lives pleasing to you.
Your compassion is boundless; you uphold your gift of freedom to us;
   —deliver us from timidity and all that would keep us from
      turning to you.
Jesus, you respected those who worked with their hands; some became your disciples;
   —preserve the dignity of those who work for others; deliver
      them from harassment of any kind.
You prayed with your people and read to them from the Scriptures;
   —may all who lend their gifts to liturgical service enrich
      our lives and be blessed in their sharing.
You promised to be with us till the end of time;
   —may the words of your gospel keep hope alive in our hearts.

PRAYER: At the close of our day, we turn to you, our God, and with hearts of gratitude, we ask you to remember our deeds of goodness and to have mercy upon our shortcomings. May all who have died this day find peace in you and may all the sorrowing find comfort in those around them and in your compassionate heart. We ask this mindful of your mercy and forgiveness. Amen.

WEDNESDAY

MORNING PRAYER

Ant 1 You are the light of the world.

Psalm 36

Sin speaks to the wicked
in the depths of their hearts.
There is no fear of God
before their eyes.

They so flatter themselves in their
own eyes
that they know not their own
guilt.
In their mouths are mischief and
deceit.
They no longer act wisely or good.

They plot the defeat of goodness
as they lie on their beds.
They set their feet on evil ways,
and do not spurn what is evil.

But your steadfast love extends to
the heavens,
your faithfulness to the skies.
Your justice is like the mountain,
your judgments like the great
deep.

To both human and beast you
give salvation.
How precious is your love.
The children of this earth
take refuge in the shadow of your
wings.

They feast on the riches of your
house;
and drink from the stream of your
delight.
In you is the fountain of life
and in your light we see light.

Keep on loving those who know
you,
giving salvation to upright hearts.
Let the foot of the proud not
crush me
nor the hand of the wicked drive
me away.

There the evildoers like prostrate!
Thrust down, they are unable to
rise. **Glory*...**

**Ant. 2 Let all creation bow
down before you.**

Cant: Judith 16:1, 13–15

Strike up the instruments,
a song to my God with timbrels,
chant to the Most High with
cymbals.
Sing a new song,
exalt and acclaim God's name.

A new hymn I will sing to you.
O God, great are you and
glorious,
wonderful in power and
unsurpassable.

Let your every creature serve you;
for you spoke, and they were
made,
you sent forth your spirit, and
they were created;
no one can resist your word.

The mountains to their bases,
and the seas, are shaken;
the rocks, like wax, melt before
your glance.
But to those who fear you,
you are very merciful. **Glory*...**

Ant. 3 We sing praise to you, Most High.

Psalm 47

Clap your hands, all you peoples,
shout to God with songs of joy!
For the Most High we must fear,
great ruler over all the earth!

O God, you subdue evil
    oppression,
and challenge unjust nations.
You chose our heritage for us,
gave it to us out of love.

You go up with shouts of joy;
O God, with trumpet blast.—

We sing praise to you, sing
    praise,
sing praise to you, Most High.

For your realm is all the earth.
We sing to you our hymns of
    praise!
Your reign is over all the nations;
Over all the peoples of this earth.

The leaders of the peoples gather
with the people of Abraham's
    God.
May all leaders of the earth pay
    heed,
to God who reigns over all.
    Glory*...

READING

My [God], you are my hope; you the glory; you the joy; you my
blessedness. You are the thirst of my spirit; you the life of my soul, you
the jubilation of my heart. Where above you could my wonder lead me,
my God? You are the beginning and the consummation of all the good,
and in you all those who are glad have, as it were, a dwelling-place
together. You are the praise in my heart and mouth. You glow altogether
red in the spring-like loveliness of the festival of your love. May your
most outstanding divinity magnify and glorify you because you are the
source of light and the fountain of life forever.

                    Gertrud the Great of Helfta, *Spiritual Exercises*, p. 101, (7)

RESPONSORY

Living source of light and wisdom, be with us always. **—Living...**
In you we find new life; **—be with...**
Glory to you, Source of all Being, Eternal Word and Holy Spirit.
    —Living...

CANTICLE OF ZECHARIAH

Ant. You are faithful to your promise, God of all the ages.

INTERCESSIONS

O God, you know our coming and our going, and you bless our
every effort to live justly;
    —help us to remember your faithfulness and that our
        inspiration and strength is your gift.

You have power over all that you have created;
—enable warring nations to redeem the wounds of the past
and to discover creative ways to peace.
Jesus, you were rejected by your own people;
—direct each of us to a milieu that is receptive of our gifts.
Love is patient and kind, but a stressful world can thin our
resources;
—have mercy on parents who are overworked and fearful;
guide and protect teen-agers who run away from home.
Mindful that you call us to be a light in darkness, we pray;
—be with us in our poverty and need.

PRAYER: O God, source of our light, you are ever with us to
reveal the way of truth and justice. Be with us this day
as we struggle to ease the burdens of our sisters and
brothers. We ask this in Jesus who is our way, our
truth, and our life. Amen.

DAYTIME PRAYER

**Ant. 1 Your law is written on
my heart.**
Psalm 119:9–16

How shall the young remain
sinless?
By living according to your word.
I have sought you with all my
heart;
let me not stray from your
commands.

I carry your word in my heart
lest I sin against you.
Blessed are you, O God;
teach me your statutes.

With my lips I have recounted
all the decrees of your mouth.
I delight to do your will
as though all riches were mine.

I will meditate on your precepts
and fix my eyes on your ways.
I will delight in your statutes;—

I will not forget your word.
Glory*...

**Ant. 2 You are a light to my
eyes, a lamp for my feet.**

Psalm 17

O God, hear a cause that is just,
attend to my cry.
Give ear to my prayer
from lips free of deceit.

If you should try my heart
or visit me by night;
if you should test me,
you will find no deceit in me;
my tongue has not deceived.

Because of the word of your
mouth
I have avoided the ways of the
violent.
My steps have held fast to your
paths,
my feet have not slipped.

I call upon you, for you will hear
me.
Turn your ear to me; hear my
words.
Show your steadfast love,
to all who seek refuge
in the shelter of your hand.

Keep me as the apple of your eye.
Hide me in the shadow of your
wings
from the wicked who seek to
destroy. **Glory*...**

**Ant. 3 You are my portion, the
God of my life.**

II

They close their hearts to pity;
with their mouths they speak
arrogantly.
They track me down, surrounding
me;
setting their eyes to cast me to
the ground—

as though they were a lion eager
to tear,
as a young lion lurking in
ambush.

Arise, O God, confront them,
strike them down!
Deliver my life from the wicked;
by your hand, O God, rescue me
from evildoers,
from those whose portion is of
this world.

May they be filled from the
abundance of your storehouse;
may their children have more
than enough;
may their wealth extend to their
offspring.

As for me, in my justice I shall
see your face;
when I awake, I shall be filled
with the sight of your glory.
Glory*...

PRAYER: God of wisdom, enlighten us with your spirit that we
may work to bring about your love and justice within
our hearts and in the hearts of all your people.
Strengthen us with insight to be faithful to your word
revealed among us. Grant this through the
intercessions of all those who faithfully heard your
word and kept it. Amen.

EVENING PRAYER

**Ant. 1 You are my dwelling
place, in you I take my rest.**

Psalm 27

O God, you are my light and my
help;
whom shall I fear?
You are the stronghold of my life;
before whom shall I be afraid?

When evildoers assail me
uttering slanders against me,
it is they, my enemies and foes,
who shall stumble and fall.

Though an army encamp against
me
my heart shall not fear.
Though war break out against me
yet will I trust.

One thing I have asked of you,
for this will I seek,
that I may dwell in your holy
  house
all the days of my life,
to behold the beauty of your
  countenance
and the holiness of your temple.

In your shelter you will hide me
in the day of trouble;
you will conceal me under the
  cover of your tent,
you will set me high upon a rock.

And now my head shall be raised
above my foes who surround me;
and I will offer in your tent
sacrifices with songs of joy.
I will sing and make music to my
  God. **Glory*...**

**Ant. 2 It is you, O God that I
seek.**

II

Hear my voice when I cry aloud,
be gracious to me and give
  answer!
You say to me: "Seek my face,
Seek the face of your God."

"Your face, O God, I do seek."
Hide not your face from me.
Do not dismiss me in anger;
you have been my help.

Do not cast me off or forsake me,
O God, my help!
Though father and mother
  forsake me,
You, O God, will receive me.

Teach me your way, O God;
lead me on a level path.
Give me not up to the will of
  evildoers;
who bear false witness and
  breathe out violence.

I believe I shall see your goodness
in the land of the living.
Hope in God, be strong and take
  heart.
Hope in God, the Most High!
  Glory*...

**Ant. 3 Jesus is the image of the
invisible God.**

Cant: Colossians 1:12–20

Let us give thanks to God
for having made us worthy
to share the inheritance of the
  saints in light.

God has delivered us
from the power of darkness
and transferred us
into the kindom of God's beloved
  Son, Jesus,
in whom we have redemption,
the forgiveness of our sins.

Jesus is the image of the invisible
  God,
the first-born of all creation;
in him all things were created,
in heaven and on earth,
things visible and invisible.

All things were created through
  him;
all were created for him.
He is before all else that is.
In him all things hold together.

He is the head of the body, the
  church!
He is the beginning,
the firstborn from the dead,
that in everything, he might be
  above all others.

In him all the fullness of God was
  pleased to dwell,
and through him, to reconcile all
  things to himself,—

whether on earth or in heaven,
making peace by the blood of his
   cross. **Glory*...**

READING

Certainly when [I] lie in jail thinking of these things, thinking of war and
peace, and the problems of human freedom...and the apathy of great
masses of people who believe that nothing can be done, I am all the
more confirmed in my faith in the little way of St. Thérèse. We do the
minute things that come to hand, we pray our prayers, and beg also for
an increase of faith—and God will do the rest.

The Dorothy Day Book, p. 59, (21)

RESPONSORY

Hold me gently, O God, in the palm of your hand. **—Hold...**
In you I find my rest; **—in the...**
Glory to you, Source of all Being, Eternal Word and Holy Spirit.
   —Hold...

CANTICLE OF MARY

**Ant. You have done great things for us and holy is your
         name.**

INTERCESSIONS

Faith, hope, and love are the things that last;
   —O God, make us good stewards of what we have, and grant
      us the help we need to be a sign of your kindom.
You created our bodies as temples of the Holy Spirit;
   —send your healing to victims of rape, incest, and every
      form of violence that destroys and deforms.
You call each one of us to be holy;
   —help us to reflect the divine imprint of your creativity in our
      lives.
You bless those who bear insult and persecution;
   —give wise advocates to those who are falsely accused; make
      us humble and just in our speech.
In the many voices that cry out for attention, help us to recognize
you and to pray;
   —"Speak, O God, for your servant is listening."

PRAYER: In the evening we come to you, O God, to thank you for
            the blessings of this day. May we be ever mindful of
            your love in the midst of life's joys and burdens, and

may all your people experience your peace this night.
This we ask placing ourselves in your care, Most
Blessed Trinity. Amen.

THURSDAY

MORNING PRAYER

Ant. 1 In the early hours of the morning, my heart will sing your praise.

Psalm 57

Have mercy on me, have mercy,
for in you my soul takes refuge.
In the shadow of your wings I take
refuge
till the storms of destruction pass
by.

I cry to God the Most High,
to God who has always been my
help.
May you send from heaven and
save me
and shame those who trample
upon me.
O God, send your truth and your
love.

My soul lies down among lions,
who greedily devour the peoples of
the earth.
Their teeth are spears and arrows,
their tongues a sharpened sword.

Be exalted, O God, above the
heavens;
let your glory be over all the earth!

They laid a snare for my steps,
my soul was bowed down.
They dug a pit in my path
but they fell in it themselves.

My heart is steadfast, O God,
my heart is steadfast.
I will sing and make melody!—

Awake, my soul,
awake, lyre and harp!
I will awake the dawn!

I will give thanks to you among the
peoples,
I will praise you among the
nations
for your love reaches to the
heavens
your faithfulness to the skies.

Be exalted, O God, above the
heavens!
let your glory be over all the earth!
Glory*...

Ant. 2 You are the bread of life; you are the cup of salvation.

Cant: Jeremiah 31:10–14

Hear the word of God, O nations,
proclaim it on distant coasts and
say:
God who scattered Israel, now
gathers them together,
and guards them as shepherds
guard their flocks.

God will ransom the chosen
people
and redeem them from the hands
of their conquerors.

Shouting, they shall mount the
heights of Zion,
they shall come streaming to God's
blessings:
the grain, the wine, and the oil,–

the sheep and the oxen;
they themselves shall be like
  watered gardens,
never again shall they languish.

Then the young shall make merry
  and dance,
old men and women as well.
I will turn their mourning into joy,
I will console and gladden them
  after their sorrows.
I will lavish choice portions upon
  them,
and my people shall be filled with
  my blessings,
says our God. **Glory*....**

Ant. 3 Let us build the city of God!

Psalm 48

O God, you are great and worthy
  to be praised
in your holy city.
Your holy mountain rising in
  beauty,
is the joy of all the earth.

Mount Zion, in the far north,
your holy city!
Within its citadels,
you show yourself its stronghold.

For invaders assembled together,
together they advanced.—

As soon as they saw it, they were
  astounded;
in panic they took to flight.

Trembling took hold of them there,
like the anguish of a woman giving
  birth;
By the east wind you have
  shattered the ships of Tarshish.

As we have heard, so we have seen
in the city of our God,
in the city of the Most High
which God establishes forever.

O God, we ponder your love
in the midst of your temple.
Your praise, like your name
reaches to the ends of the earth.

With justice your hands are filled.
Let Mount Zion be glad!
The people of Judah rejoice
because of your judgments.

Walk through Zion, walk all round
  it;
number its towers.
Review its ramparts,
examine its citadels;

that you may tell the next
  generation
that this is our God,
our God forever and ever.
You will always be our guide.
      Glory*...

READING

It is with the moral infirmities we may see in one another—our defects of character or temperament, our faults, our failings—that I think we should try to be watchful to exercise charity in thought, word, and deed. It is so easy and so natural to criticize; yet we cannot do so even interiorly without detriment to our soul. Such thoughts consented to, certainly retard our progress in the perfection of charity, if they do not offend God.

Mother Aloysius Rogers, OCD, *Fragrance from Alabaster*, p. 18, (6)

RESPONSORY

I have seen the glory of God, in the land of the living. —**I have...**
You are with us always; —**in the...**
Glory to you, Source of all Being, Eternal Word and Holy Spirit.
—**I have...**

CANTICLE OF ZECHARIAH

Ant. In love let us ponder your word forever.

INTERCESSIONS

O God, the path to holiness includes times of emptiness and darkness;
—let us realize that you are with us as you walked with
Jesus on his journey toward the cross.
Holy, holy, holy are you, O God; the whole earth is full of your glory;
—help us to live compatibly with our environment.
The voice of God said, "Whom shall I send, and who will go for us";
—with your help, may I answer: "Here I am! Send me."
Jesus, you healed many who were sick with various diseases;
—be with all healers and health care personnel as they give
of themselves to care for us.
Jesus, you have called us to preach the good news by the
statement of our lives;
—help us to live the truth with compassion.

PRAYER: Most gracious God and Father, you are with us as we
make our journey throughout this day. Help us to
look lovingly upon all people and events that come
into our lives today and to walk gently upon our land.
Grant this through Jesus who lives and walks among
us ever present at each moment. Amen.

DAYTIME PRAYER

Ant. 1 I am a sojourner on earth; teach me your ways.

Open my eyes that I may behold the wonders of your law.

Psalm 119:17–24

Bless your servant that I may live and obey your word.—

I am a sojourner on earth;
hide not your commands from me!—

My soul is consumed with longing
forever, for your decrees.

You rebuke the insolent,
who turn from your commands.
Relieve me of their scorn and
  contempt
for I have kept your word.

Though others sit plotting against
  me
I ponder on your statutes.
Your will is my delight;
your decrees are my counselors.
    Glory*...

**Ant. 2 Lead me in your truth,
  and guide me in the path of
  salvation.**
             Psalm 25

To you, O God, I lift up my soul.
In you, I trust, let me not be put to
  shame;
let not the wicked exult over me.
Those who wait on you shall not
  be put to shame;
but only those who wantonly
  break faith.

Make me know your ways, O God;
Teach me your paths.
Lead me in your truth, and teach
  me,
for you are God, my savior.
For you I wait all the day long.

Remember your mercy, O God,
and your steadfast love,
which you have given from of old.
Remember not the sins of my
  youth, or my transgressions;
But in your goodness, remember
  me
according to your steadfast love!

You, O God, are good and
  upright.—
You instruct sinners in your way.
You lead the humble in the right
  path;
you teach your way to the poor.

All your ways are loving and
  constant
for those who keep your covenant
  and your decrees.
For your name's sake, O God,
pardon my guilt, for it is great.
    Glory*...

**Ant. 3 Say but the word, and I
  shall be healed.**
               II

Those who fear you, O God,
you will instruct in the way they
  should choose.
They shall abide in prosperity,
and their children shall possess
  the land.
Your friendship is for those who
  revere you;
make known to them your
  covenant.

My eyes are ever turned toward
  you,
for you rescue my feet from the
  snare.
Turn to me and be gracious to me;
for I am lonely and afflicted.

Relieve the troubles of my heart
and bring me out of my distress.
See my affliction and my troubles,
and forgive all my sins.

See how many are my faults,
with what violence they pursue
  me.
Preserve my life and deliver me;
let me not be put to shame,—

for I take refuge in you.
May integrity and uprightness
  preserve me:
for my hope is in you.

Redeem Israel, O God, from all its
  troubles. **Glory*...**

PRAYER: To you, O God, we lift up our hearts at this midday
prayer. We ask you to remember us and all those who
are troubled at this time. Help us to reach out in
justice and charity to those in need among us. Grant
this through the intercessions of all who served you in
serving your poor. Amen.

EVENING PRAYER

**Ant. 1 You heal my affliction;
you restore my soul to life!**
Psalm 30

I will praise you, O God, you have
  rescued me
and have not let evil triumph over
  me.

O God, I cried to you for help
and you have healed me.
You have raised my soul from the
  dead,
restored me to life from among
  those gone down to the grave.

We sing praises to you, we your
  people,
and give thanks to your holy
  name.
For your anger lasts but a
  moment,
your favors for a lifetime.
At night there may be weeping,
but joy comes with the morning.

I said to myself in my prosperity,
"Nothing will ever disturb me."
By your favor, O God,
you have made me strong as a
  mountain;
when you hide your face, I am
  dismayed.

O God, to you I cried,
to you I make supplication:
"What profit is there in my death,
if I go down to the grave?
Can dust praise you, or tell of your
  faithfulness?"

Hear, O God, and be gracious to
  me!
O God be my help!
You have turned my mourning
  into dancing;
you have removed my sackcloth
  and clothed me with gladness,
that I may praise you with full
  voice,
and give thanks to you forever.
  Glory*...

**Ant. 2 In the integrity of my
heart, I lay my guilt before you.**

Psalm 32

Happy are they whose faults are
  forgiven,
whose sins are covered.
Happy are they to whom our God
  imputes no guilt,
in whose spirits there is no deceit.

When I declared not my sin,
my body wasted away—

with groanings all the day long.
For day and night your hand was
heavy upon me;
my strength was dried up as by
the heat of summer.

When I acknowledged my sin to
you,
and did not hide my guilt;
I said: "I will confess my sins to
you, O God."
Then you did forgive me the guilt
of my sin.

So let all who acclaim you offer
prayers;
in times of distress, the rush of
the flood waters will not reach
them.
For you are a hiding place for me,
you preserve me from trouble;
you surround me with deliverance.

I will instruct you and teach you
the way you should go;
I will counsel you with my eye
upon you.
Be not like a horse or a mule,
without understanding,
which must be curbed with bit and
bridle else it will not keep you.

Many are the sorrows of the
wicked;
but faithful love surrounds those
who trust in you.
We rejoice in you and are glad.
Let all the upright in heart rejoice
and shout for joy.
   Glory*...

**Ant. 3 Behold the Lamb of God,
who takes away the sins of the
world.**
   **Cant: Rev 11: 17–18;
      12:10b–12a**

We praise you, God Almighty,
who is and who was.
You have assumed your great
power,
you have begun your reign.

The nations have raged in anger,
but then came your day of wrath
and the moment to judge the
dead;
the time to reward your servants
the prophets
and the holy ones who revere you,
the great and the small alike.

Now have salvation and power
come,
your reign, O God, and the
authority of your Anointed One.
For the accusers of our loved ones
have been cast out,
who night and day accused them.

By the blood of the Lamb have
they been defeated,
and by the testimony of your
servants;
love for life did not deter them
from death.
So rejoice, you heavens,
and you that dwell therein!
   Glory*...

READING

Jesus gives [his disciples] a simple, clear example of what discipleship
is all about: service. Washing one another's feet, feeding the hungry,
clothing the naked—here is the core of the Eucharist, our great miracle
of love.... God's table is large, as large as creation. All are invited, all are

to have access to the necessity of food and the miracle of love. Both are essential to the fullness of life. Without food, the body languishes and dies; without love, our souls wither and are filled with despair. The leftovers in our lives? What are they and who will get them? So many people can live off our leavings if we would only share. This is hardly sufficient. Disciples of Christ give abundantly in imitation of the Master who gave his very self.

Robert F. Morneau, *Ashes to Easter*, p. 107, p. 108, (2)

RESPONSORY

You gather us together in the bosom of your love. **—You...**
As a mother hen, **—in the...**
Glory to you, Source of all Being, Eternal Word and Holy Spirit. **—You...**

CANTICLE OF MARY

Ant. In you I rejoice all the days of my life.

INTERCESSIONS

Jesus, in the days of your ministry, many traveled far to listen to you;
   —keep alive our search for truth and our efforts to live by it.
You tell us not to be afraid;
   —let your Spirit guide the oppressed as they seek ways to freedom.
You call us "salt of the earth";
   —make us your true followers, one with the suffering of the world, and calling down God's blessing on your people.
You withdrew to lonely places, praying in the night;
   —remind us that you are with us in light or darkness, joy or sorrow—the abiding guest of our hearts.
Spirit of God, source of our deepest desires for good;
   —show us ways to be light for the world.

PRAYER: You, Mother and God, are our safety in times of distress. Show us your ways of peace that we may gather one another into your loving embrace, into your dwelling place. May you be with us this night and may all those in darkness walk in your light. Grant this, Spirit of Comfort, through Jesus, our brother. Amen.

FRIDAY

MORNING PRAYER

Ant 1 Create in me a clean heart, O God.
Psalm 51

Have mercy on me, O God,
according to your steadfast love;
in your abundant mercy blot out
   my sins.
Wash me thoroughly from my
   offenses,
and cleanse me from my sin!

For I know my offenses,
and my sin is ever before me.
Against you, you alone, have I
   sinned,
and done what is evil in your
   sight,
so you are justified in your
   sentence
and blameless in your judgment.
Behold, I was brought forth in a
   sinful world.

For you desire truth in my
   innermost being;
teach me wisdom in the depths of
   my heart.
O purify me, and I shall be clean;
O wash me, I shall be whiter than
   snow.
Fill me with joy and gladness;
let the bones you have broken
   rejoice.
Hide your face from my guilt,
and blot out all my offenses.

Create in me a clean heart,
put a steadfast spirit within me.
Cast me not from your presence,
take not your spirit from me.
Give me again the joy of your
   salvation,
with a willing spirit uphold me.

Then I will teach transgressors
   your ways
and sinners will return to you.
Deliver me from death,
O God of my salvation,
and my tongue will sing out your
   saving help.

Open my lips and my mouth will
   sing your praises.
For you take no delight in
   sacrifice;
were I to give a burnt offering,
you would not be pleased.
A broken spirit you accept;
a contrite heart, you will not
   despise.

In your goodness, show favor to
   Zion;
rebuild the walls of Jerusalem.
Then you will delight in just
   sacrifices,
in gifts offered on your altar.
   Glory*...

Ant. 2 You are our God, there is no other besides you.

Cant: Isaiah 45:15–25

Truly you are a God who is
   hidden,
the God of Israel, the savior!
They are put to shame and
   disgraced,
the makers of idols are put to
   confusion.

Israel, you are saved by the Most
   High,
with everlasting salvation!
You shall never be put to shame
   or disgraced for all eternity.

For thus says the Most High,
the creator of the heavens,
who is God,
the designer and maker of the
  earth,
who established it,
not creating it as chaos,
but designing it to be lived in.

I am God, and there is no other.
I have not spoken in secret,
in a land of darkness;
I have not said to the
  descendants of my people,
"Look for me in chaos."
I, your God, speak the truth,
I declare what is right.

Come and assemble, gather
  together,
you survivors of the nations!
They are without knowledge who
  bear wooden idols
and pray to gods that cannot
  save.

Come here and declare in counsel
  together!
Who declared this from the
  beginning
and foretold it from of old?
Was it not I, your God?
There is no other besides me,
a just and saving God!

Turn to me and be saved,
all you ends of the earth,
for I am God; there is no other!
By myself I have sworn,
uttering my just decree—

and my word which cannot be
  changed.

To me every knee shall bend;
by me every tongue shall swear,
saying, "Only in you, our God, are
  justice and righteousness.

You, O God, shall be the
  vindication and the glory
of all the descendants of Israel."
  Glory*...

**Ant. 3 We are your people, the
sheep of your pasture.**

Psalm 100

All the earth cries out to you with
  shouts of joy, O God,
Serving you with gladness;
coming before you, singing for
  joy.

You, Creator of all, are God.
You made us, we belong to you,
we are your people, the sheep of
  your pasture.

We enter your gates with
  thanksgiving,
and your courts with songs of
  praise!
We give you thanks and bless
  your name.

Indeed, how good you are,
enduring, your steadfast love.
You are faithful to all generations.
  Glory*...

READING

...Ask grace not instruction, desire not understanding, the groaning of prayer not diligent reading, the Spouse not the teacher, God not [people], darkness not clarity, not light but the fire that totally inflames and carries us into God by ecstatic unctions and burning affections.

This fire is God, and [God's] furnace is in Jerusalem; and Christ enkindles it in the heat of his burning passion...

Bonaventure, The Soul's Journey into God, p. 115, (1)

RESPONSORY

You are the Good Shepherd, have compassion on us. **—You are...**
In you we find mercy; **—have...**
Glory to you, Source of all Being, Eternal Word and Holy Spirit.
     —You are...

CANTICLE OF ZECHARIAH

Ant. You teach us the way of peace.

INTERCESSIONS

O God, you are Truth itself;
    —give us discerning hearts that we may live full and creative
        lives.
Jesus, you walked among the outcasts of your day, healing them
and drawing them to yourself;
    —help us to walk in your ways that those who are shunned
        by society may know your love and healing through us.
Jesus, you bless with a hundredfold our endeavors to serve you;
    —give us the generosity to enable and support one another.
Spirit of God, you pray within us for needs we hardly know;
    —make our prayer one with yours that we may be one with
        you.
Eternal Shepherd, every person and the future of us all is
precious to you;
    —bless those who are tempted to take negative or destructive
        paths this day.

PRAYER: Forgiving God, look not upon our sins but upon our
         desire to serve you and one another. Dispel our
         darkness, and help us to embrace our failings in
         loving union with your goodness. Heal us this day,
         and may we be a source of strength and courage for
         others. Grant this through the intercession of all
         those who fill up what is wanting in the sufferings of
         Christ. Amen.

DAYTIME PRAYER

Ant. 1 I cling to your will, O God.

Psalm 119:25–32

My soul cleaves to the dust;
revive me according to your word!
I told of my ways and you
  answered me;
teach me your statutes.

Make me understand the way of
  your precepts
and I will ponder on your wonders.
My soul pines with sorrow;
strengthen me by your word.

Keep me from the way of
  falsehood;
and teach me your law!
I have chosen the way of
  faithfulness,
I set your decrees before me.

I cling to your will, O God;
let me not be put to shame!
I will run in the way of your
  commands;
when you enlighten my
  understanding. **Glory*...**

**Ant. 2 I trust in God without
  wavering.**

Psalm 26

Judge me, O God, for I walk in the
  way of integrity,
I trust in you without wavering.

Examine me, O God, and try me;
test my heart and my mind,
for your steadfast love is before
  me,
and I walk to you in faithfulness.

I do not sit with the wicked,
nor conspire with those who cause
  trouble;—

I avoid the company of evildoers;
and those who speak falsehood.

I wash my hands in innocence,
and gather around your altar,
singing a song of thanksgiving,
and telling of all your wonders.

I love the house where you live,
the place where your glory dwells.
Do not sweep me away with
  sinners,
nor my life with those who
  oppress,
who plot evil deeds,
whose hands are full of bribes.

As for me, I walk the path of
  integrity.
Redeem me, and be gracious to
  me.
My foot stands on level ground;
I will bless you in the assembly.
  Glory*...

**Ant. 3 I call to you, O God, hear
  the sound of my voice.**

Psalm 28:1–3, 6–9

To you, O God, I call,
my rock, be not deaf to me.
If you turn your ear away from me,
I become like those in the grave.

Hear the voice of my pleading
as I cry to you for help,
as I lift up my hands in prayer
to your holy sanctuary.

Do not take me away with the
  wicked,
with those who are workers of evil,
who speak peace with their
  neighbors,
while evil is in their hearts.

I bless you, for you have heard
the voice of my supplication.
You are my strength and my
  shield;
in you my heart trusts.
I am helped, and my heart exults,
with my song I give you thanks.

You are the strength of your
  people,
you are the refuge of your
  anointed.
Save your people; and bless your
  heritage;
be their shepherd and carry them
  forever. **Glory*...**

PRAYER: Jesus, our Redeemer, you brought us into life by dying
upon the cross. May we search for new ways to
alleviate suffering among all creatures that your name
be glorified and that peace may find a home in us. We
ask this in the name of all creation that groans for your
salvation to be realized within its being. Amen.

EVENING PRAYER

**Ant. 1 Be gracious to me, O
God, for I have sinned.**

Psalm 41

Blessed are they who consider
  the poor!
O God, you deliver them in the
  day of trouble;
you guard them and give them
  life;
they are called blessed in the
  land;
you do not give them up to
  temptation.
You sustain them on their
  sickbeds;
you heal them of all their
  infirmities.

As for me, I said: "O God, be
  gracious to me,
heal me, for I have sinned against
  you."
Some could say of me in malice:
"When will you die and your
  name perish?"—

They come to see me, uttering
  empty words,
while their hearts gather
  mischief;
and spread it abroad.
They whisper about me,
  imagining the worst of me.

They say, "A deadly thing has
  come upon you;
you will not rise from where you
  lie."
Even my friend in whom I
  trusted,
who ate of my bread, has turned
  against me.

But you, O God, be gracious to
  me.
Raise me up in your great mercy.
By this I shall know that you are
  pleased with me,
that evildoers have not
  triumphed.
You have upheld me in my
  integrity,—

and set me in your presence
forever.

Blessed are you, God of Israel,
from everlasting to everlasting.
Amen. Amen. **Glory*...**

Ant. 2 In the stillness we will hear your voice.

Psalm 46

God is our refuge and strength,
a helper in time of trouble.
We shall not fear though the
earth should rock,
though the mountains fall into
the depths of the sea,
though its waters rage and foam,
though the mountains tremble
with its tumult.

There is a river whose streams
gladden the city of God,
the holy place of the Most High.
God is within, it shall not be
moved;
God will help it at the dawning of
the day.
Nations rage, sovereignties are
shaken;
at the sound of God's voice, the
earth melts away.

The God of hosts is with us;
the God of our ancestors is our
refuge.

Come, behold the works of our
God,
who has wrought wonders on the
earth.
Making wars cease to the ends of
the earth;
breaking the bow, snapping the
spear,
burning the chariots with fire.
"Be still, and know that I am God,
I am exalted among the nations,
I am exalted on the earth!"

The God of hosts is with us;
the God of our ancestors is our
refuge. **Glory*....**

Ant. 3 You are the ruler of all the ages, O God.

Cant: Rev 15:3–4

Great and wonderful are your
works,
God the Almighty One!
Just and true are your ways,
Ruler of all the ages!

Who shall refuse you honor,
or the glory due your name?

For you alone are holy,
all nations shall come and
worship in your presence.
Your judgments are clearly seen.
Glory*...

READING

I asked the earth, the sea and the deeps, heaven, the sun, the moon
and the stars.... My questioning of them was my contemplation, and
their answer was their beauty.... They do not change their voice, that is
their beauty, if one person is there to see and another to see and to
question.... Beauty appears to all in the same way, but is silent to one
and speaks to the other.... They understand it who compare the voice
received on the outside with the truth that lies within.

The Confessions of St. Augustine (adapted), pp. 234–35, (48)

RESPONSORY

In the spirit of Jesus, we give praise to our God. **—In the...**
For our sins are forgiven; **—we give...**
Glory to you, Source of all Being, Eternal Word and Holy Spirit.
   —In the...

CANTICLE OF MARY

Ant. Your covenant is one of mercy and forgiveness.

INTERCESSIONS

The law of God is perfect, refreshing the soul;
   —let your love, O God, be our law of life and perfect guide.
Your forgiveness of humankind flows from generation to
generation;
   —heal the nations that continue to seek vengeance; teach us
      all how to forgive in the name of Jesus.
Jesus, you stayed in desert places, strengthened there by God.
   —In time of pain or trouble, help us to find God in the solitude
      of our hearts.
You are our hope in life and in death;
   —help us to live our belief in you for the strength and courage
      of all in need of your truth.
Spirit of God, your gifts abound in humankind;
   —bless the poor whose creativity is buried by a raw search
      for survival.

PRAYER: Jesus, you heal the sick and brokenhearted. Let your
            mercy be upon us so that we may be a sign of your
            mercy in our world. We thank you for your forgiveness
            and for bringing us to this time of our lives. May all
            those who died find rest in you. Grant this through the
            intercession of all who died forgiving those who
            oppressed them. Amen.

SATURDAY

MORNING PRAYER

Ant. 1 Before the dawn, O God, hear my call for help.

Psalm 119: 145–152

With all my heart, I cry to you;
answer me, O God.
I cry to you; save me,
that I may observe your will.

I rise before dawn and cry for help;
I hope in your words.
My eyes watch throughout the
night
meditating on your promises.

Hear my voice in your steadfast
love;
in your justice preserve my life.
Those who persecute me draw
near;
they are far from your law.

But you, O God, are near at hand,
all your commands are true.
Long have I known that your will
endures forever. **Glory*...**

Ant. 2 Bring me to your holy mountain, the place of your dwelling.

Cant: Exodus 15:1–4a, 8–13, 17–18

I will sing to you, O God, for you
are gloriously triumphant;
horse and rider you have cast into
the sea.

You are my strength and my
courage,
you are my salvation.
You are my God, I praise you;
God of my ancestors, I extol you.

Pharaoh's chariots and army you
cast into the sea.
At a breath of your anger the
waters piled up,
the floods stood up in a heap;
the floods congealed in the midst
of the sea.

The enemy boasted, "I will pursue
and overtake them;
I will divide the spoils and have
my fill of them;
I will draw my sword; my hand
shall destroy them!"
When your wind blew, the sea
covered them;
they sank as lead in the mighty
waters.

Who is like you, among the gods?
Who is like you, majestic in
holiness,
terrible in glorious deeds, worker
of wonders?
You stretched out your hand, the
earth swallowed them!

In your love you led the people
you redeemed;
you guided them to your holy
dwelling.
You bring them in and plant them
on your mountain,
the place you have made for your
abode,
the sanctuary which your hands
have established.
You, O God, will reign forever and
ever. **Glory*...**

**Ant. 3 O praise God all you
  nations.**
                Psalm 117

Praise our God, all you nations!
Acclaim the Most High, all you
  peoples!

For great is your love for us;
and your faithfulness endures
  forever. **Glory*...**

READING

Mindful now of our own rich tradition of meditation and contemplative
prayer and eager to learn what is "true and holy" in other religions, the
time is right for us to learn from one another, from whatever culture
and religion, all that is helpful in moving toward a simpler life, a
deeper life, and a more authentic life in which the inner experience of
God is primary and energizing and centering!

Pascaline Coff, OSB, "Many Mansions," (4)

RESPONSORY

Your love is round about me; in you I find my life. **—Your love...**
Forever I will sing your praise; **—in you...**
Glory to you, Source of all Being, Eternal Word and Holy Spirit.
    —Your love...

CANTICLE OF ZECHARIAH

Ant. You are the light of my salvation.

INTERCESSIONS

O God, your son Jesus prayed that we all may be one;
    —help us to love one another as you love us.
All of creation cries out for healing;
    —make us instruments of your peace.
You are the Center of all that is;
    —teach us to listen to your life within us.
Many do not know your love and care for us;
    —let our lives bear witness to your unending mercy.
You call us to live in freedom and happiness;
    —give hope and peace of heart to all in prison or bondage
of any kind.

PRAYER: You give and sustain our lives, O God, and in you we
              find our sanctuary. May all displaced people find a
              place of sanctuary and safety in our hearts and

homes this day, and may all those who seek you find you in the living word among us. Grant this through Jesus who lives and reigns among us. Amen.

DAYTIME PRAYER

Ant. 1 Incline my heart to your decrees.

Psalm 119:33–40

Teach me the way of your
  precepts
and I will keep them to the end.
Give me understanding,
that I may keep your law
and observe it with all my heart.

Guide me in the path of your
  commandments,
for there is my delight.
Incline my heart to your will
and not to love of profit.

Turn my eyes from what is vain;
by your ways, give me life.
Keep the promise you have made
to those who reverence you.

Turn away the reproach which I
  dread;
for your decrees are good.
Behold, I long for your precepts;
in your justice, give me life!
  Glory*...

Ant. 2 O taste and see the goodness of our God!

Psalm 34

I will bless you, O God, at all
  times,
your praise always on my lips.
My soul makes its boast in you;
the afflicted shall hear and be
  glad.
Glorify our God with me.—

Together let us praise God's
  name.

I sought you, and you answered
  me;
and delivered me from all my
  fears.
Look towards the Most High, and
  be radiant;
let your faces not be ashamed.
These poor ones cried; you heard
  them,
and saved them from all their
  troubles.

Your angel, O God, is encamped
around those who revere you, to
  deliver them.
Taste and see that God is good!
Happy are they who take refuge
  in you.

May all the saints revere you, O
  God.
Those who revere you, have no
  want!
Young lions suffer want and
  hunger;
but those who seek you lack no
  blessing. **Glory*...**

Ant. 3 Blessed are those who seek after peace.

II

Come, children, listen to me,
I will teach you to reverence the
  Most High.
Who among you longs for life
and many days to enjoy
  prosperity?

Keep your tongue from evil,
your lips from speaking deceit.
Turn aside from evil and do good;
seek peace and pursue it.

God's eyes are turned to the
  righteous,
God's ears toward their cry.
God's face turns away from evil,
that it not be remembered on
  earth.

When the just cry, the Most High
  hears,
and delivers them from their
  troubles.
God is close to the
  brokenhearted;—

saving those whose spirits are
  crushed.

Many are the afflictions of the
  just;
they will be delivered from them
  all.
God will keep guard over all their
  bones,
not one of them shall be broken.

Evil shall be its own destruction;
oppression shall be condemned.
You redeem the lives of your
  servants;
those who take refuge in you
  shall not be condemned.
  Glory*...

PRAYER: Most provident God, you graciously give us all good
             gifts. Teach us to care for our earth: to till our soil
             responsibly, to keep our air pure, to free our waters
             from pollution, to harvest the warmth of our sun, and
             to respect the rights of all species. May we willingly
             share the gifts of your goodness with one another. We
             ask this of you, God of our universe. Amen.

WEEK II

SUNDAY, EVENING PRAYER I

Ant. 1 Your word, O God, is a light for my path.

Psalm 119:105–112

O God, your word is a lamp to my
  feet
and a light for my path.
I have sworn an oath and
  confirmed it
to observe your commandments.

I am sorely afflicted:
give me life according to your
  word!
Accept my offerings of praise,
and teach me your decrees.

Though I hold my life in my
  hands,
I do not forget your law.
Though the wicked try to ensnare
  me,
I do not stray from your precepts.

Your will is my heritage forever,
the joy of my heart.
I incline my heart to carry out
  your will forever, to endless
  ages. **Glory*...**

Ant. 2 I have given you as a covenant to the people.

Psalm 16

Preserve me, O God, for in you I
  take refuge.—

*Glory to you, Source of all Being, Eternal Word, and Holy Spirit.

As it was in the beginning is now and will be forever. Amen.

I say to you: "You are my God;
I have no good apart from you."
All my delight is in your saints;
the faithful who dwell in your
  land.

Those who choose other gods
  increase their sorrows;
their offerings of blood I will not
  pour out
or take their names upon my lips.

You are my portion and my cup;
you are my fortune, my prize.
The lines have fallen for me in
  pleasant places;
I have been given a welcome
  heritage.

I will bless you who give me
  counsel;
in the night my heart instructs
  me.
I keep you always before me;
because you are near, I shall
  stand firm.

Therefore my heart is glad, and
  my soul rejoices;
even my body rests securely.
For you do not give me up to
  death,
or let your faithful see the grave.

You will show me the path of life;
in your presence there is fullness
  of joy,
in your hands, happiness forever.
  Glory*...

Ant. 3 For me to live is Christ and to die is gain.

Cant: Phil 2:6–11

Though he was in the form of
  God,
Jesus did not count equality with
  God
something to be grasped at.

But emptied himself
taking the form of a slave,
being born in human likeness.

Being found in human estate,
he humbled himself and became
  obedient,—

obediently accepting death, even
  death on a cross!

Therefore God has highly exalted
  him
and bestowed on him the name
above every other name.

So that at the name of Jesus
every knee should bow,
in heaven, on the earth,
and under the earth,
and every tongue proclaim
to the glory of God:
Jesus Christ is Lord! **Glory*...**

READING

[O loving God], help us to be masters of the weapons that threaten to
master us. Help us to use science for peace and plenty, not for war and
destruction. Show us how to use atomic power to bless our children's
children, not to blight them. Save us from the compulsion to follow our
adversaries in all that we most hate, confirming them in their hatred
and suspicion of us. Resolve our inner contradictions, which now grow
beyond belief and beyond bearing. They are at once a torment and a
blessing; for if you had not left us the light of conscience, we would not
have to endure them. Teach us to be long-suffering in anguish and
insecurity, teach us to wait and trust. Grant light, grant strength and
patience to all who work for peace...grant us prudence in proportion to
our power, wisdom in proportion to our science, humaneness in
proportion to our wealth and might. And bless our earnest will to help
all races and peoples to travel, in friendship with us, along the road to
justice, liberty and lasting peace.... (Merton's Prayer for Peace)

Thomas Merton, *Nonviolent Alternative*, (59)

RESPONSORY

We call to you in our need, O God, for you hear the cry of the poor.
  —We call...
You will not leave us orphans; **—for you...**
Glory to you, Source of all Being, Eternal Word and Holy Spirit.
  —We call...

CANTICLE OF MARY

Ant. Be mindful of your mercy to us, O loving God.

INTERCESSIONS

O God, you grieve for all that afflicts us;
—give those who struggle with addictions the courage and
perseverance they need.
You are father and mother to us, and we bask in your love;
—inspire persons of integrity and compassion to care for
children who are separated from their parents.
You bless those who employ the talents you have given them;
—give all in research the insight they need to develop the good
you desire for us.
Jesus, you loved the land and fields of flowers;
—bless farmers and all who are stewards of the soil.
You taught your followers to travel lightly through life;
—call our consumer culture to a change of heart—to values
that lead to life.

PRAYER: O God, we long to love you with all our heart and mind
and soul, but we know we are divided. Give us a single
heart. Make us one as you are one with Jesus and your
Holy Spirit. Amen.

MORNING PRAYER

**Ant. 1 You are members of the
household of God.**

Psalm 118

We give thanks to you, for you are
good,
and your steadfast love endures
forever.

Let the descendants of Israel say:
"Your steadfast love endures
forever."
Let the descendants of Aaron say:
"Your steadfast love endures
forever."
Let those who fear you say:
"Your steadfast love endures
forever."

In my distress, I called to you;
you answered me and set me free.
With you at my side, I do not fear.
What can anyone do against me?
You are at my side to help me:
I shall withstand all evildoers.

It is better to take refuge in you,
than to trust in people:
it is better to take refuge in you
than to trust in our leaders.

All wickedness surrounded me;
in your name I crushed it.
It surrounded me like bees;
it blazed like a fire among thorns.
In your name I crushed it.

I was pushed hard, and was falling
but you came to help me.
You are my strength and my song;
you are my salvation.

O God, you have triumphed;
your reign is exalted.
You have triumphed over all;
I shall not die, I shall live
and recount your wondrous deeds.
You have chastened me sorely,
but have not given me over to
    death.

Open to me the gates of justice,
that I may enter and give thanks.
This is your gate, O God;
the just shall enter through it.
I thank you for you have answered
    me
you alone are my salvation.

The stone which the builders
    rejected
has become the cornerstone.
This is your doing, O God;
it is marvelous in our eyes.
This is the day which you have
    made;
let us rejoice and be glad in it.

Save us, we beseech you, O God!
O God, grant us success.
Blessed are those who enter in
    your holy name.
For you O God, are our God,
and you have given us light.

Let us go forward in procession
    with branches,
up to your holy altar.
You are my God, I thank you.
You are my God, I praise you.
We give thanks to you for you are
    good;
and your steadfast love endures
    forever.   **Glory*...**

**Ant. 2 How glorious is your name
over all the earth.**

Cant: Daniel 3:52–57

Blessed are you, God of our
    ancestors,
praiseworthy and exalted above all
    forever.

Blessed be your holy and glorious
    name,
praiseworthy and exalted above all
    for all ages.

Blessed are you in the temple of
    your glory,
praiseworthy and exalted above all
    forever.

Blessed are you on the throne of
    your kindom,
praiseworthy and exalted above all
    forever.

Blessed are you who look into the
    depths
from your throne upon the
    cherubim,
praiseworthy and exalted above all
    forever.

Blessed are you in the firmament of
    heaven,
praiseworthy and glorious forever.

Blessed are you by all your works.
We praise and exalt you above all
    forever.   **Glory*...**

**Ant. 3 Let us praise God's infinite
greatness.**

Psalm 150

We praise you, O God, in your holy
    sanctuary;
we praise you in your mighty
    heavens.—

We praise you for your powerful deeds;
we praise you according to your greatness.

We praise you with trumpet sound;
We praise you with lute and harp!
We praise you with strings and pipe!

We praise you with sounding cymbals,
We praise you with clashing cymbals!
Let everything that breathes, give praise to you, O God.
Glory*...

READING

I will sprinkle clean water upon you, and you shall be clean from all your uncleanness, and from all your idols I will cleanse you. A new heart I will give you, and a new spirit I will put within you; and I will remove from your body the heart of stone and give you a heart of flesh. I will put my spirit within you, and make you follow my statutes and be careful to observe my ordinances. Then you shall live in the land that I gave to your ancestors; and you shall be my people and I will be your God.

Ezek 36:25–28

RESPONSORY

Our hearts are restless, O God, till they rest in you. **—Our...**
Searching and waiting; **—till they...**
Glory to you, Source of all Being, Eternal Word and Holy Spirit.
—Our...

CANTICLE OF ZECHARIAH

Ant. May you give light to those who sit in darkness.

INTERCESSIONS

God revealing, forgiving, ever recreating us;
   —we thank you for your abiding care, and we pray for those who do not know your love.
You are a God of the living, and your Spirit brings us joy;
   —let our lives bear witness to the resurrection of Jesus.
Minorities, countries, the earth itself—all cry out for liberation as never before;
   —Spirit of God, flood our lives with the wisdom to make all things new.
You raise up prophets today;
   —open our hearts, our church, and our world to their message.

Jesus, your message calls for the new wineskins of openness to your word;

—help us to free ourselves from what is merely familiar and comfortable.

PRAYER: O God, on this first day of the week, we join all creation and people of all ages in praising you. Your kindness and forgiveness flow like a river through the centuries refreshing our faith, our hope and our love. May you be forever praised throughout all the ages. Amen.

DAYTIME PRAYER

Ant. 1 You restore my soul in your living waters.

Psalm 23

O God, you are my shepherd;
I shall not want.
You make me to lie in green
  pastures.
You lead me to restful waters,
to restore my soul.

You guide me in paths of
  righteousness
for the sake of your name.
Even though I walk through the
  valley of the shadow of death,
I fear no evil;
for you are with me;
your crook and your staff
give me comfort.

You prepare a table before me
in the presence of my foes;
you anoint my head with oil,
my cup overflows.

Surely goodness and mercy shall
  follow me
all the days of my life;
and I shall dwell in your holy
  house forever and ever. **Glory*...**

Ant. 2 Lead a life worthy of God, who calls you to glory.

Psalm 76

In Judah you are made known, O
  God,
your name is great in Israel.
Your abode is established in
  Jerusalem,
your dwelling place in Zion.
There you broke the flashing
  arrows,
the shield, the sword, the weapons
  of war.

You, O God, are glorious,
more majestic than the mountains.
The stouthearted were stripped of
  their spoil;
they sank into sleep;
all the provokers of war
were unable to use their hands.
At your rebuke, O God, our God,
both rider and horse lay stunned.
    Glory*...

Ant. 3 Do not let the sun go down on your anger, for God is a forgiving God.

II

You, you alone, strike terror.
When your anger is aroused,
who can stand before you?
From heaven you utter judgment;
the earth feared and stood still,—

when you arose to give judgment
to save the oppressed of the earth.

Our anger will serve to praise you;
its residue gird you round.
We fulfill the vows made before
    you;
you whom we revere,
who cut short the lives of leaders,
who strike terror in unjust rulers.
    Glory*...

PRAYER: O God, you have created us to be free. Only through the power of your love do you reign over us. Help us to be worthy of the gift of freedom, and teach us to respect all creation as the work of your hands. We ask this, Creator God, giver of all good gifts, through Jesus who taught us the way. Amen.

EVENING PRAYER II

Ant. 1 You are a priestly people according to the order of Melchizedeck.

Psalm 110:1–5, 7

God's revelation to the Anointed
    One:
"Sit at my side:
till I put injustice beneath your
    feet."

God will send forth from Zion
your scepter of power:
rule in the midst of your foes.

Your people will give themselves
    freely
on the day you lead your host
upon the holy mountains.
From the womb of the morning
your youth will come like dew.

God has sworn an oath that will
    not be changed.—

"You are a priest forever,
after the order of Melchizedek."

The Anointed standing by your
    side,
will shatter rulers on the day of
    wrath.

Drinking from your streams by
    the wayside
shall the Chosen One be
    refreshed. **Glory*...**

Ant. 2 The heavens belong to you, but the earth has been given to us.

Psalm 115

Not to us, O God, not to us,
but to your name give glory
for the sake of your love and your
    truth!
Why should the nations say,
"Where is their God?"

But you are in the heavens;
you do whatever you please.
Their idols are silver and gold,
the work of human hands.

They have mouths, but cannot
    speak;
eyes, but cannot see;
they have ears, but cannot hear;
noses, but cannot smell.

They have hands, but cannot feel;
feet, but cannot walk.
No sound comes from their
    throats.
Those who make them are like
    them;
so are all who trust in them.

Descendants of Abraham, trust in
    God,
who is your help and your shield.
Descendants of Sarah, trust in
    God,
who is your help and your shield.
You who fear, trust in God,
who is your help and your shield.

You remember us and will bless
    us,
blessing the descendants of
    Abraham,
blessing the descendants of
    Sarah.
God will bless those who fear,
the little no less than the great.

May God give you increase,—

you and all your children.
May you be blessed by the Most
    High,
who made heaven and earth!

The heavens belong to God,
but the earth has been given to
    us.
The dead do not praise you,
nor those who go down into
    silence.
But we who live, bless you,
both now and forever. Amen.
    Glory*...

**Ant. 3 We come to join in your
holy banquet, O God.**

Cant: Rev 19:1, 5–7

Salvation, glory, and power
    belong to you,
your judgments are honest and
    true.

All of us, your servants, sing
    praise to you,
we worship you reverently, both
    great and small.

You, our almighty God, are
    Creator of heaven and earth.
Let us rejoice and exult, and give
    you glory.

The wedding feast of the Lamb
    has begun,
And the bride has made herself
    ready. **Glory*...**

READING

But we must always give thanks to God for you, brothers and sisters
beloved by the [Lord Jesus], because God chose you as the first fruits
for salvation through sanctification by the Spirit and through belief in
the truth. For this purpose [God] called you through our proclamation of
the good news, so that you may obtain the glory of our Lord Jesus
Christ.

2 Thess 2:13–14

RESPONSORY

How can we repay you, O God, for your goodness to us?
  —How can...
We will sing your praise; **—for your...**
Glory to you, Source of all Being, Eternal Word and Holy Spirit.
  —How can...

CANTICLE OF MARY

Ant. My spirit rejoices in God, my Savior.

INTERCESSIONS

Rain and clouds are your gifts of life and beauty to us, O God;
  —teach us how to use and preserve the waters of the earth.
You surround us with beauty on earth and in the sky;
  —bless those who have lost the gift of sight.
You are always with us, silently guiding and encouraging us;
  —help us to quiet our lives with moments for listening to your
    voice in our hearts.
You love justice, and all your ways are true;
  —give us the insight and courage to face our prejudices and
    blind spots.
Jesus is your supreme gift to us;
  —let the words of his gospel be woven into our daily lives,
    coming easily to mind for our inspiration and your glory.

PRAYER: God of mystery, God of love, send your Spirit into our
hearts with gifts of wisdom and peace, fortitude and
charity. We long to love and serve you. Faithful God,
make us faithful. This we ask through the intercession
of all your saints. Amen.

MONDAY

MORNING PRAYER

**Ant 1 When from this exile
shall we behold you face to
face?**

Psalm 42

Like the deer that yearns
for flowing streams,—

so my soul is longing
for you, my God.

My soul is thirsting for God,
the living God.
When shall I come and see,
the face of God?

My tears have become my food,
by night and day,
while I hear it said all day,
"Where is your God?"

These things will I remember
as I pour out my soul:
how I led the throng,
to the house of God,
with shouts of gladness and
  songs of thanksgiving,
the multitude keeping festival.

Why are you cast down my soul,
why disquieted within me?
Hope in God; I will again praise
  you,
my help and my God.

My soul is cast down within me,
therefore I think of you
from the land of Jordan and of
  Hermon,
from Mount Mizar.

Deep calls to deep,
in the thunder of your waters;
all your waves and your billows
have swept over me.

By day you will send me
your steadfast love;
and at night your song is with
  me,
a prayer to the God of my life.

I will say to you my rock:
"Why have you forgotten me?
Why do I go mourning
because of oppression?"

As with a deadly wound,
my adversaries taunt me,
saying to me all the day long:
"Where is your God?"

Why are you cast down, my soul,
why disquieted within me?
Hope in God; for I shall praise
  again,
my savior and my God.
  Glory*...

**Ant. 2 Worker of wonders,
  show forth your splendor!**

Cant: Sirach 36:1–5, 10–13

Come to our aid, O God of the
  universe,
and put all the nations in dread
  of you!
Raise your hand toward the
  heathen,
that they may realize your power.

As you have used us to show
  them your holiness,
so now use them to show us your
  glory.
Thus they will know, as we know,
that there is no God but you.

Give new signs and work new
  wonders;
show forth the splendor of the
  works of your hands.

Gather all the tribes of Jacob,
that they may inherit the land as
  of old.
Show mercy to the people called
  by your name;
Israel, whom you named your
  first-born.

Take pity on your holy city,
Jerusalem, your dwelling place.
Fill Zion with your majesty,
your temple with your glory.
  Glory*...

Ant. 3 The courts of heaven ring with the praise of our God.

Psalm 19a

The heavens tell of your glory, O God,
and the firmament proclaims your handiwork.
Day unto day pours forth the story
and night unto night reveals its knowledge.

No speech, no word, no voice is heard;—

yet their voice goes out to all the earth,
their words to the end of the world.

In them you set a tent for the sun;
it comes forth like a bridegroom leaving his chamber,
rejoices like a champion running its course.

Its rising is from the end of the heavens,
and its course to the end of them;
there is nothing concealed from its heat. **Glory*...**

READING

I saw that [God] is everything which is good, as I understand. And in this [God] showed me something small, no bigger than a hazelnut, lying in the palm of my hand, as it seemed to me, and it was as round as a ball. I looked at it with the eye of my understanding and thought: What can this be? I was amazed that it could last, for I thought that because of its littleness it would suddenly have fallen into nothing. And I was answered in my understanding: It lasts and always will, because God loves it; and thus everything has being through the love of God.

Julian of Norwich, *Showings*, p. 183, (1)

RESPONSORY

You are present to us, O God, in all creation. **—You are...**
Enriching our lives; **—in all...**
Glory to you, Source of all Being, Eternal Word and Holy Spirit.
—You are...

CANTICLE OF ZECHARIAH

Ant. Blessed be God who has visited us and saved us.

INTERCESSIONS

O God, you ask us to keep your words in our minds and hearts and so we pray:
—give us the grace to hear you in turmoil and in silence.
Help us to recognize our sinfulness and to be grateful for your gifts of grace;
—give us the strength and courage to act in humility and truth.

God of wisdom and source of all that is sacred;
 —help teachers to value and nourish the wisdom and goodness
  of children.
Jesus, you came to serve and not to be served;
 —bless all who serve us daily, in inclement weather, in
  dangerous jobs, and at work that is tedious or monotonous.
We are blessed by the words of your gospel;
 —make us aware of the ways we shield ourselves from its
  challenge to us.

PRAYER: O God, you have made us in your image and we long to
see your face. Quiet our minds and enkindle our hearts
that walking the way of your truth we may leave the
imprint of your goodness throughout the world. Grant
this in the name of Jesus. Amen.

DAYTIME PRAYER

**Ant. 1 Make love your aim, and
desire every spiritual gift.**

Psalm 119:41–48

O God, let your love come upon
  me,
your salvation according to your
  promise;
Then I have answer for those who
  taunt me
for I trust in your word.

Take not truth from my mouth,
for my hope is in your decrees.
I shall always keep your law
forever and ever.

I shall walk in the path of
  freedom
for I have sought your precepts.
I will speak of your will before
  rulers
and shall not be put to shame;

for my delight is in your
  commandments;
these I have loved.—

I revere your precepts,
and will ponder on your statutes.
Glory*...

**Ant. 2 My delight is to do your
will, O God.**

Psalm 40:2–14, 17–18

I waited patiently for you, O God
and you stooped down to me;
and heard my cry.

You drew me from the desolate
  pit,
out of the miry clay,
and set my feet upon a rock,
making my steps secure.

You put a new song in my mouth,
a song of praise to you.
Many shall see and fear
and place their trust in you.

Happy are we who have placed
our trust in you, O God,
who do not turn to the proud,
to those who follow false gods!

For us you have multiplied, O
  God, my Creator,
your wondrous deeds and plans;
none can compare with you!
Were I to proclaim and tell of
  them,
they are more than can be
  numbered.

Sacrifice and offering you do not
  desire;
but you have given me an open
  ear.
Burnt offering and sin offering
  you have not required.

Therefore, I said, "Here I am;
In the scroll of the book it is
  written of me:
my delight is to do your will;
your law is within my heart."
  Glory*...

**Ant. 3 Your mercy is from age
  to age toward those who
  revere you.**
  II

Your deliverance I have
  proclaimed
in the great assembly.
I have not restrained my lips,
as you well know, O God.

I have not concealed your saving
  help within my heart;
but have spoken of your
  faithfulness, and your salvation;
I have not hidden your steadfast
  love nor your faithfulness
from the great assembly.

O God, you will not withhold
your mercy from me.
Your steadfast love and
  faithfulness always surround
  me.

For evils without number have
  encompassed me;
My sins have overtaken me,
till I cannot see.
They are more than the hairs of
  my head;
my heart fails me.

Be pleased, O God, to deliver me!
O God, make haste to help me!

May all who seek you rejoice and
  be glad;
May all who love your salvation
say evermore: "Great is our God!"

As for me, I am poor and needy;
but you take thought of me.
You are my help, my deliverer;
O God, do not delay.
  Glory*...

PRAYER: God of justice, God of mercy, bless all those who are
surprised with pain this day from suffering caused by
their own weakness or that of others. Let what we
suffer teach us to be merciful; let our sins teach us to
forgive. This we ask through the intercession of Jesus
and all who died forgiving those who oppressed them.
Amen.

EVENING PRAYER

Ant. 1 O God, how great is your wisdom, so far beyond my understanding.

Psalm 139:1–18, 23–24

O God, you have searched me
  and you know me,
you know when I sit and when I
  stand;
you discern my thoughts from
  afar.
You mark when I walk or lie
  down,
with all my ways you are
  acquainted.

Before a word is on my tongue,
behold, O God, you know the
  whole of it.
Behind and before you besiege
  me,
You lay your hand upon me.
Such knowledge is too wonderful
  for me:
too high, beyond my reach.

O where can I go from your spirit,
or where can I flee from your
  presence?
If I climb to heaven, you are
  there!
If I lie in the grave, you are there!

If I take the wings of the morning
and dwell in the depths of the
  sea,
even there your hand shall lead
  me,
your hand shall hold me fast.

If I say: "Let darkness cover me,
and the light around me be
  night,"
even darkness is not dark to
  you,—

and the night is as bright as the
  day;
for darkness is as light to you.
  Glory*...

Ant. 2 You search the mind and probe the heart, giving to each as we deserve.

II

For it was you who formed my
  inmost parts,
knit me together in my mother's
  womb.
I praise you for the wonder of my
  being,
for the wonder of all your works.

Already you knew me well;
my body was not hidden from
  you,
when I was being made in secret
and molded in the depths of the
  earth.

Your eyes beheld my unformed
  substance;
in your book they all were
  written,
the days that you had formed for
  me
when none of them yet were.

How precious to me are your
  thoughts!
How vast the sum of them!
If I count them, they are more
  than the sand.
When I awake, I am still with you.

Search me, O God, and know my
  heart!
O test me and know my thoughts!
See that I follow not the wrong
  way,—

and lead me in the way of life eternal. **Glory*...**

Ant. 3 May Christ dwell in our hearts through faith that we may be rooted in love.

Cant: Ephesians 1:3–10

Praised be the God
of our Lord Jesus Christ,
who has blessed us in Christ
with every spiritual blessing in
the heavens.

God chose us in him
before the foundation of the
world,
that we should be holy
and blameless in God's sight.

We have been predestined
to be God's children through
Jesus Christ,—

such was the purpose of God's
will,
that all might praise the glorious
favor
bestowed on us in Christ.

In Christ and through his blood,
we have redemption,
the forgiveness of our sins,
according to the riches of God's
grace lavished upon us.

For God has made known to us
in all wisdom and insight,
the mystery of the plan set forth
in Christ.

A plan to be carried out in Christ,
in the fullness of time,
to unite all things in Christ,
things in heaven and things on
earth. **Glory*...**

READING

God knows the best human instruments to use in the work of making us saints, which is the work of making us God-like; and they must necessarily be those who will cause us to put aside our own ways and desires and views to take on [God's own]. It is a matter of...following the Holy Spirit instead of our own spirit, of letting that mind be in us that was in Christ Jesus.

Mother Aloysius Rogers, OCD, *Fragrance from Alabaster*, p. 3, (6)

RESPONSORY

You create us in your image, O God, we are co-creators with you.
—**You create...**
We are nothing without you; —**we are...**
Glory to you, Source of all Being, Eternal Word and Holy Spirit.
—**You create...**

CANTICLE OF MARY

Ant. I rejoice in your greatness, O God.

INTERCESSIONS

O God, you invite us to: "Let light shine out of darkness";
  —give us the courage to embrace the darkness and walk with
  you toward the light.
You hear the prayers of those in need;
  —give us the grace to open our hearts, our homes, and our
  spaces of worship to those who are in distress.
You marveled at the faith of the Centurion;
  —help us to recognize that truth and wisdom are often found
  where we least expect it.
Spirit of God, guide us in our use of power;
  —let our methods be constructive and sensitive to the needs
  of all.
May we realize that life itself is a blessing;
  —comfort those who are preparing for the blessings of
  eternal life.

PRAYER: God of wisdom, God of our way, we have walked with
you from early morning. Renew our strength this night
that we may rise to serve you and one another with
clear vision and strong hope. We pray especially for all
who will awake this night to the vision of your glory.
This we ask through Jesus who is the light of the
world. Amen.

TUESDAY

MORNING PRAYER

**Ant. 1 O God, let us walk as
people of light, that we may
know what is pleasing to you.**

Psalm 43

Defend me, O God, and plead my
  cause against a godless nation.
From the deceitful and the unjust
rescue me, O God.

For in you I take refuge;
why have you cast me off?
Why do I go mourning
because of oppression?

O send out your light and your
  truth;
let these be my guide.
Let them bring me to your holy hill
and to your dwelling place.

Then I will go to the altar of God,
to God, my exceeding joy;
and I will praise you with the lyre,
O God, my God.

Why are you cast down, my soul,
why groan within me?
Hope in God;—

I shall again praise, my savior and my God. **Glory*...**

Ant. 2 Seek first the reign of God, and all things shall be yours as well.

Cant: Isaiah 38:10–14, 17b–20

Once I said,
"In the noontime of life, I must depart!
I am consigned to the gates of death for the rest of my years."

I said, "I shall not see God
in the land of the living.
No longer shall I see my companions
among the dwellers of this world."

My dwelling is plucked up and removed from me
like a shepherd's tent;
like a weaver I have rolled up my life;
being cut off from the loom.

Day and night you give me over to torment;
I cry for help until daybreak;
like a lion you break all my bones;
day and night you give me over to torment.

Like a swallow or crane, I clamor,
I moan like a dove.
My eyes grow weary gazing upward.
I am oppressed; be my security!

Restore me to health, make me live!
It was for my welfare that I had great bitterness;
you have held back my life from the pit of destruction,
you have cast all my sins behind your back.

For the nether world cannot thank you,
death cannot praise you;
those who go down to the pit cannot hope for your faithfulness.

The living, the living give you thanks, as I do this day;
Parents make known to their children,
O God, your faithfulness.

You, O God, will save us;
we will sing to stringed instruments
all the days of our lives,
in your holy dwelling.
Glory*...

Ant. 3 Consider the lilies of the field; they neither toil nor spin.

Psalm 65

Praise is due to you,
O God in Zion;
and to you shall vows be made,
to you who hear our prayer.

To you shall all flesh come because of its sins.
When our offenses bear us down,
you forgive them all.

Blessed are we whom you choose and draw near,
to dwell in your courts!
We are filled with the goodness of your house,
your holy temple!

With wonders you deliver us,
O God of our salvation.
You are the hope of all the earth
and of far distant seas.

By your strength, you established the mountains,
girded with might;—

you still the roaring of the seas,
the roaring of their waves,
and the tumult of the peoples.

Those who dwell at earth's farthest
  bounds
stand in awe at your wonders;
you make the sunrise and sunset
  shout for joy.

You care for the earth, give it water,
you fill it with riches.
Your river in heaven brims over
to provide its grain.

You visit the earth and water it,
greatly enriching it;—

you level it, soften it with showers,
blessing its growth.

You crown the year with your
  bounty;
Abundance flows in your path.
The pastures of the wilderness
  flow,
the hills gird themselves with joy,
the meadows clothe themselves
  with flocks,
the valleys deck themselves with
  grain,
they shout and sing together for
  joy. **Glory*...**

READING

It is so thoughtful and commendable to thank those who do us favors
that if we glance around, we will find this truth naturally inheres in all
creatures who, even though unable to speak, offer better thanks to their
benefactors through action than we humans do in word. We see that
when earth is regaled by heaven's waters and sunlight, it sends forth
grass and flowers in grateful payment for the gift. Very tenderly the
gardener cares for [the] trees so that, having grown quite tall, they bend
down their fruit...to pick, almost as if to say: "Take this fruit in return
for your kind care."

Francisco de Osuna, *The Third Spiritual Alphabet*, p. 68, (1)

RESPONSORY

You know our frailty, O God; give us strength. **—You know...**
You fill us with hope; **—give...**
Glory to you, Source of all Being, Eternal Word and Holy Spirit.
  —You know...

CANTICLE OF ZECHARIAH

Ant. You, O God, have raised up a horn of salvation for us.

INTERCESSIONS

Jesus, tax collectors and public sinners experienced your
goodness and changed their lives;
  —help us to enable others to grow and realize their worth.

You had compassion on the weak and sorrowful;
—open our eyes and hearts to the ways we can comfort others.
You were a gift to all who came to you in faith;
—fill us with love that is creative and fruitful for your people and the world.
No one is beyond the reach of your care;
—bless those in refugee camps and all who are uprooted from their homes and land.
Make us wise as serpents and simple as doves;
—make us a people after your own heart.

PRAYER: All loving God, let us know your presence as we begin this day. Guide us as we strive to choose what is good and just. Lift up our hearts to you when the demands of the day threaten to lead us astray. This we ask through Jesus who is our way, our truth and our life. Amen.

DAYTIME PRAYER

Ant. 1 Blessed are they who hear your word and keep it.

Psalm 119:49–56

Remember your word to your servant
by which you gave me hope.
This is my comfort in my affliction
that your promise gives me life.

Though the proud utterly deride me,
I do not turn from your law.
When I think of your precepts of old,
I take comfort, O God.

I am seized with indignation because of the wicked
who forsake your law.
Your statutes have been my songs
in the house of my pilgrimage.

I remember your name in the night,
and keep your law.—

This blessing has been given to me,
the keeping of your precepts.
Glory*...

Ant. 2 You free us from the bondage of sin and restore us to life.

Psalm 53

Fools say in their hearts:
"There is no God."
They are corrupt, doing wicked things;
there are none that do good.

God looks down from heaven
on the peoples of the earth,
to see if any are wise,
if any seek God.

They have all fallen away;
they are all alike depraved;
there are none that do good,
no, not even one.

Have the evildoers no
understanding,
who eat up my people just as they
eat bread,
and do not call upon God?

There they are, in great terror,
such terror as has not been!
For God will chastise the
oppressors;
they will be put to shame.

O that salvation might come from
Zion!
When you restore the fortunes of
your people,
Jacob will rejoice and Israel be
glad. **Glory*...**

**Ant. 3 O God, my eyes rejoice in
your salvation.**

Psalm 54:1–6, 8–9

Save me, O God, by your name;
deliver me by your might.
O God, hear my prayer;
give ear to the words of my mouth.

For the insolent have risen against
me,
the ruthless seek my life;
they set themselves before you.
But I have you for my helper;
You uphold my life.

With a willing heart I make
sacrifice;
and give thanks to your name.
You deliver me from all trouble,
my eyes rejoice in your salvation.
Glory*...

PRAYER: O God, you sent your son, Jesus, to call us to your
realm of mercy and love. Let our memories of his words
and deeds overflow into our lives, that following him,
we may lead others to salvation. We ask this through
the intercession of all those who lived as true disciples
and now live eternally with you. Amen.

EVENING PRAYER

**Ant. 1 Our riches lie in the glory
of God.**

Psalm 49

Hear this, all you peoples!
Give heed, all dwellers of the world,
you, both low and high,
rich and poor together!

My lips will speak words of wisdom;
my heart will ponder your ways.
I will incline my ear to a proverb;
I will solve my riddle on the lyre.

Why should I fear in times of
trouble,
when the malice of my foes
surrounds me,
those who trust in their wealth,
and boast of the vastness of their
riches?

For we cannot buy our own
ransom,
or give to God the price for our
lives.
The ransom of our lives is beyond
us.—

It can never be enough,
to avoid going to the grave.

Both the wise and the foolish must
perish
and leave their wealth to others.
Their graves are their homes
forever,
their dwelling places to all
generations,
though their names spread wide
through the land.
They are like the beasts that
perish. **Glory*...**

**Ant. 2 Be not afraid, I go before
you.**

II

This is the fate of those with foolish
confidence,
the end of those who are pleased
with their portion.
Like sheep they are driven to the
grave;
death shall be their shepherd;
straight to the grave they descend,
and their form shall waste away;
the grave shall be their home.

But you will ransom my soul from
the power of the grave,
for you will receive me.

Be not afraid when people grow
rich,
when the glory of their houses
increases.
They carry nothing with them when
they die,
their glory will not go down with
them.

Though while they lived, they
thought themselves happy,
and thought themselves praised for
their success,
they will go to join their ancestors,
who will never more see the light.

People cannot abide in insolence;
they are like the beasts that perish.
Glory*...

**Ant. 3 Worthy is the Lamb who
was slain.**

Cant: Rev 4:11, 5:9, 10, 12

Worthy are you, O God, our God,
to receive glory and honor and
power.

For you have created all things;
by your will they came to be and
were made.

Worthy are you to take the scroll
and to open its seals,
For you were slain, and by your
blood,
you purchased for God
saints of every race and tongue,
of every people and nation.

You have made of them a kindom,
and priests to serve our God,
and they shall reign on the earth.

Worthy is the Lamb who was slain
to receive power and riches,
wisdom and strength,
honor and glory and praise.
Glory*...

READING

We are truly on the way with Christ, our Hope and our Promise, if we
live a life of thanksgiving for all that God has already revealed and done,

and of vigilance for what [God] wants us to do in the present moment, even if [God] wants to surprise us and lead us where we did not want to go. For those who put their trust in Christ, everything, even the most insignificant or the most unpleasant event, becomes a sign of grace and hope, a school of vigilance for the coming of our Lord.

Bernard Häring, *Prayer: The Integration of Faith and Life*, p. 29, (8)

RESPONSORY

Your compassion, O God, calls us to repentance.—**Your...**
Your love heals us, and —**call us...**
Glory to you, Source of all Being, Eternal Word and Holy Spirit.
  —Your...

CANTICLE OF MARY

Ant. My spirit rejoices in God, my Savior.

INTERCESSIONS

Eternal God, you create us and call us to realize our union with you;
  —help us to rise above all that undermines our calling.
Jesus, you were called a fool for our sake;
  —let us bear the inevitable humiliations of life with
   equanimity.
You brought joy and a new beginning to those who received you;
  —give us a hunger for your presence and your truth.
Spirit of God, your realm of love encompasses all of creation;
  —in times of temptation and doubt, draw us ever closer to you.
Your love is eternal;
  —bless and heal those who are burdened with hatred or
   unforgiveness.

PRAYER: Spirit of God, promise of Jesus, come to our help at the close of this day. Come with forgiveness and healing love. Come with light and hope. Come with all that we need to continue in the way of your truth. So may we praise you in the Trinity forever. Amen.

WEDNESDAY

MORNING PRAYER

Ant 1 You, O God, are faithful; all your ways are holy.

Psalm 77

I cry aloud to you, my God,
cry aloud that you may hear me.

In the day of my trouble I seek
you,
in the night I stretch out my hand
without tiring;
my soul refuses to be consoled.

I remember you and I moan;
I ponder, and my spirit faints.
You hold my eyelids from closing;
I am so troubled, I cannot speak.

I consider the days of old,
I remember the years long past.
I converse with my heart in the
night;
I ponder and search my spirit:

"God, will you spurn us forever,
and never again show us favor?
Has your love vanished forever?
Are your promises at an end for
all time?
Have you forgotten to be
gracious?
Has your anger withheld your
compassion?"

I say: "This is the cause of my
grief;
that the way of the Most High has
changed."
I will call to mind your deeds;
I will remember your wonders of
old,
I will meditate on all your works,
and ponder your mighty deeds.

Your ways, O God, are holy.
What god is great as our God?
You are the God who works
wonders,
who shows your power among the
peoples.
Your strong arm redeemed your
people,
the descendants of Jacob and
Rachel.

When the waters saw you, O God,
when the waters saw you, they
were afraid,
the depths were moved with
terror.
The clouds poured out water;
the skies gave forth thunder;
your arrows flashed to and fro.

Your thunder crashed in the
whirlwind;
your flashes lighted up the world;
the earth trembled and shook.
Your way was through the sea,
your path through the great
waters;
yet your footprints were not seen.

You led your people like a flock
by the hands of Moses and
Miriam. **Glory*...**

Ant. 2 My heart exults in God, the joy of my salvation.

Cant: 1 Samuel 2:1-10

My heart exults in the Most High,
my strength is exalted in my God.
My lips renounce all that is evil,
because I rejoice in your
salvation.

There is no Holy One like You;
there is no Rock like our God.
Speak no longer so boastfully,
nor let arrogance come from your
  mouth.
For God is a God of knowledge,
a God who weighs our deeds.

The bows of the mighty are
  broken,
but the feeble are circled with
  strength.
The full hire themselves out for
  bread,
while the hungry cease to
  hunger.
The barren have borne seven
  children,
but those who have many are
  forlorn.

O God, you put to death and give
  life;
you cast down to the grave and
  raise up.
You make poor and make rich;
you bring low, you also exalt.

You raise up the poor from the
  dust;
you lift the needy from the ash
  heap,
to seat them with those of renown
and inherit a seat of honor.

For the pillars of the earth are
  yours,
on them you set the world.
You will guard the steps of your
  faithful ones,
but wickedness shall perish in
  darkness.
For not by strength shall we
  prevail.

Against evil you will thunder on
  high.
You will judge the ends of the
  earth;
you will give strength to just
  leaders
and exalt the power of your
  anointed ones! **Glory*...**

**Ant. 3 Rejoice, our God comes
to save us.**

Psalm 97

You reign over all; let the earth
  rejoice;
let the many coastlands be glad!
Clouds and thick darkness are
  round about you;
righteousness and justice the
  foundation of your throne.

Fire goes before you,
burning up all that is evil.
Your lightnings lighten the world,
the earth sees and trembles.

Mountains melt like wax before
  you,
before you, Creator of all the
  earth.
The heavens proclaim your
  justice;
all peoples behold your glory.

All who pay homage to idols,
who boast in worthless gods,
are put to shame.
All gods bow down before you.

Zion hears and is glad;
the people of Judah rejoice,
because of your judgments, O
  God.
For you are most high over all the
  earth;
exalted far above all gods.

You love those who hate evil;
you preserve the lives of your
    saints;
you deliver them from
    wickedness.

Light dawns for the just
and joy for the upright of heart.
Rejoice in God, you that are just,
and give thanks to God's holy
    name. **Glory*...**

READING

This path of self-knowledge must never be abandoned, nor is there on this journey a soul so much a giant that it has no need to return often to the stage of an infant and a suckling.... There is no stage of prayer so sublime that it isn't necessary to return often to the beginning. Along this path of prayer, self-knowledge and the thought of one's sins is the bread with which all palates must be fed no matter how delicate they may be; they cannot be sustained without this bread. It must be eaten within bounds, nonetheless.

Teresa of Avila, *Life*, 13.15, (3)

RESPONSORY

O God, you are One, you love the singlehearted. **—O God,...**
The pure of heart shall see you; **—you love...**
Glory to you, Source of all Being, Eternal Word and Holy Spirit.
    —O God,...

CANTICLE OF ZECHARIAH

Ant. Deliver us, O God, from all that is evil.

INTERCESSIONS

O God, you have made a covenant of love with us;
    —dispel from our minds and hearts the fear that belies your
      care for us.
You have hidden yourself in every blade of grass and every
towering mountain;
    —give us eyes to see your creative love at work in our world.
Jesus, you responded to women with affirmation and love;
    —show us how to encourage and support women when
      others would prevent them from serving you.
You allowed the words of Scripture to form you and to guide your
life;
    —let the word of your life be the foundation of all we do and the
      guide for our lives.

Spirit of God, you are the very life of the church;
— invade us all with the wisdom, fortitude, and generosity to be
the people of God in deed and truth.

PRAYER: O God, our Creator, each morning we praise the
wonder of your love. Your tender care measures our
strength and calls us to grow. You give us courage
before the challenge of the day. O Eternal God, make
us worthy of the time you have given us. This we ask
for ourselves and for all of creation through Jesus, our
brother and friend. Amen.

DAYTIME PRAYER

**Ant. 1 Be gracious to me
according to your promise.**

Psalm 119:57–64

You, O God, are my portion;
I promise to obey your words.
I entreat your favor with all my
heart;
be gracious to me according to
your promise.

When I think of your ways,
I turn my feet to your will;
I hasten and do not delay
to keep your commandments.

Though the cords of the wicked
ensnare me
I do not forget your law.
At midnight I rise to praise you,
because of your just decrees.

I am a friend of all who revere
you,
of those who obey your precepts.
The earth is full of your steadfast
love;
teach me your statutes.
   Glory*...

**Ant. 2 Shelter me in the shadow
of your wings.**

Psalm 55:1–19, 22–24

O God, give ear to my prayer;
hide not from my supplication!
attend to me and answer me;
I am overcome by my troubles.

I am distraught by the lure of
corruption,
at oppression caused by
wickedness.
The evil that brings trouble upon
me,
and whose anger weighs on my
soul.

My heart is in anguish within me,
the terrors of death fall upon me.
Fear and trembling come upon
me,
and horror overwhelms me.

O that I had wings like a dove!
I would fly away and be at rest;
indeed, I would wander afar,
I would take refuge in the
wilderness,
I would haste to find me a shelter
from the raging wind and
tempest.

Overthrow this oppression, O God,
confuse all who seek to destroy.
For I see violence and strife all around me.
Day and night it patrols our cities;
They are full of wickedness and evil,
ruin is in their midst;
oppression and fraud do not depart
from their market places.
Glory*...

Ant. 3 Let us walk together in the ways of our God.
II

It is not our enemies who cause this;
then I might bear it;
it is not our foes who oppress,
I might hide from them.

But it is ourselves, our companions,
our familiar and intimate friends.
We used to speak together of justice;
We walked together in companionship in the ways of our God.

I will call out to you, O God,
and you will save me.
Evening, morning and at noon
I utter complaint and lament;
you will hear my voice.

You will deliver my soul in safety
in the attack waged all around;
for many things can bring me down,
but you will hear my cry.

You will give ear, and chastise us,
you, who reign from of old;
because we have not kept your law,
and have not revered you.

Cast your burdens on our God,
and you will be supported.
Never will God permit
the just ones to falter.

But you, O God, will bring down
to the pit of the grave,
all that is wicked and evil;
that oppresses the poor and the needy.

O God, we will trust in you.
Glory*...

PRAYER: O God, our daily burdens weigh us down and fear for our future is no stranger to us. Help us to remember the life and death of Jesus, that strengthened by his hope, we too may become totally open to your will. Grant this is Jesus' name. Amen.

EVENING PRAYER

Ant. 1 In silence and stillness, my heart waits for you.

Psalm 62

For God alone my soul waits in
  silence;
From God comes my salvation.
God alone is my rock and my
  stronghold,
my fortress; I shall not be moved.

How long will you set upon me
to break me down,
as though I were a leaning wall,
or a tottering fence?

They only plan to destroy.
They take pleasure in falsehood.
They bless with their mouths,
but inwardly they curse.

For God alone my soul waits in
  silence,
for my hope comes from the Most
  High.
God alone is my rock and my
  stronghold,
my fortress; I shall not be moved.

In you alone is my deliverance,
my mighty rock, my refuge.
We trust in you at all times
and pour out our hearts before
  you;
for you are our refuge.

Common folk are but a breath,
great persons are a delusion.
Placed on the scales, they go up;
together they are lighter than a
  breath.

Put no confidence in extortion,
set no vain hopes on robbery;—
do not set your heart on riches,
even if they should increase.

Once God has spoken; twice have
  I heard this:
that power belongs to God;
and to you, O God, steadfast love.
For you repay us according to our
  deeds. **Glory*...**

Ant. 2 Your spirit, O God, moves upon the face of the earth.

Psalm 67

O God, be gracious to us and
  bless us
and make your face shine upon
  us.
That your ways be known upon
  earth,
your saving power among all
  nations.
Let the peoples praise you, O
  God;
let all the peoples praise you.

Let the nations be glad and sing
  for joy,
for you judge the peoples with
  equity
and guide the nations on earth.
Let the peoples praise you, O
  God;
let all the peoples praise you.

The earth has yielded its
  increase;
God, our God, has blessed us.
You, indeed, have blessed us;
let all the earth revere you!
  Glory*...

Ant. 3 You are God's temple; God's spirit dwells in you.

Cant: Colossians 1:12-20

Let us give thanks to God
for having made us worthy
to share the inheritance of the
saints in light.

God has delivered us
from the power of darkness
and transferred us
into the kindom of God's beloved
Son, Jesus,
in whom we have redemption,
the forgiveness of our sins.

Jesus is the image of the invisible
God,
the first-born of all creation;
in him all things were created,
in heaven and on earth,
things visible and invisible.

All things were created through
him;
all were created for him.
He is before all else that is.
In him all things hold together.

He is the head of the body, the
church!
He is the beginning,
the firstborn from the dead,
that in everything, he might be
above all others.

In him all the fullness of God was
pleased to dwell,
and through him, to reconcile all
things to himself,
whether on earth or in heaven,
making peace by the blood of his
cross. **Glory*...**

READING

My God, how can You leave me to myself, for You are responsible for me? And how could I be harmed while You are my Ally? Or how could I be disappointed in You, my Welcomer? Here I am seeking to gain access to You by means of my need of You. How could I seek to gain access to You by means of what cannot possibly reach You? Or how can I complain to You of my state, for it is not hidden from You? Or how can I express myself to You in *my* speech, since it comes from You and goes forth to You? Or how can by hopes be dashed, for they have already reached You? Or how can my states not be good, for they are based on You and go to You? My God how gentle You are with me in spite of my great ignorance, and how merciful You are with me in spite of my ugly deeds!

Ibn 'Ata' Illah, *The Book of Wisdom*, p.120, (1)

RESPONSORY

You love the poor, O God; you feed them with your word.
—You love...
They call to you for life; **—you feed...**
Glory to you, Source of all Being, Eternal Word and Holy Spirit.
—You love...

CANTICLE OF MARY

Ant. Most holy be your name.

INTERCESSIONS

O God, you long to draw us to yourself in a realm of peace;
  —bless all who struggle with relationships in the home and in
  the workplace.
Your gift of faith to us grows by use and for the asking;
  —make us aware of this treasure; let us taste and share its
  fruits.
Jesus, you knew the sins of your followers, but you forgave and
encouraged them in the way of love;
  —let our awareness of our faults lead us to encourage one
  another to turn to you.
You eased the burdens of so many by healing their sickness and
wounds;
  —give nurses and doctors the skill and compassion they need to
  do the same.
The alien and stranger are dear to your heart;
  —give us the humility and generosity to welcome those who are
  different from us.

PRAYER: O God, we live in constant need. To whom shall we go
  but to you? You are both father and mother to us,
  tending our days with delicate care. We thank you for
  your love and mercy this day, and we ask you to help
  us to forgive as we have been forgiven; to give as we
  have received. This we, your children, ask of you in
  your tender mercy. Amen.

THURSDAY

MORNING PRAYER

Ant. 1 I am the vine, you are the branches. The one who abides in me will bear much fruit.

Psalm 80

Give ear, O Shepherd of Israel,
you who lead Joseph like a flock!—
You who are enthroned upon the
  cherubim,
shine before Ephraim, Benjamin
  and Manasseh!
Stir up your might and come to
  save us!

Restore us, God of hosts;
let your face shine, that we may be
  saved.
God of hosts, how long will you be
  angry
with your people's prayers?
You fed them with the bread of
  tears,
and gave them tears to drink in full
  measure.
You made us the scorn of our
  neighbors,
our enemies laugh among
  themselves.

Restore us, God of hosts;
let your face shine, that we may be
  saved.

You brought a vine out of Egypt;
you drove out the nations to plant
  it.
You cleared the ground before it;
it took root and filled the land.

The mountains were covered with
  its shade,
the mighty cedars with its
  branches;
it sent out its branches to the sea,
and its roots to the Great River.

Then why have you broken down
  its walls?
so that all who pass by pluck its
  fruit?
It is ravaged by the boar of the
  forest,
devoured by the beasts of the field.

Turn again, O God of hosts!
Look down from heaven, and see;
have regard for this vine,
the vine you have planted.
It has been burnt with fire and cut
  down.

Let your hand be on those you
  have chosen,
those you make strong for yourself!
Then we will never forsake you;
give us life, and we will call on your
  name.

Restore us, God of hosts!
let your face shine, that we may be
  saved. **Glory*...**

**Ant. 2 God is the joy of my
salvation.**

Cant: Isaiah 12:1–6

I will give thanks to you, O God;
for though you were angry with me,
your anger turned away,
and you did comfort me.

Behold, you are my savior;
I will trust, and will not be afraid;
you are my strength and my song,
you have become my salvation.

With joy we will draw water from
  the wells of salvation.
We will say on that day:
"We give you thanks and call upon
  your name;
make known your deeds among the
  nations,
proclaim how exalted is your name.

"We sing our praise to you,
for all your glorious deeds;
let this be known in all the earth."
Shout, and sing for joy, O people of
  Zion,
for great in your midst
is the Holy One of Israel!
  Glory*...

Ant. 3 Today if you should hear God's voice, harden not your heart.

Psalm 81

Sing aloud to God our strength;
shout for joy to the God of our
  people.

Raise a song and sound the
  timbrel,
the sweet-sounding harp and the
  lyre.
Blow the trumpet at the new moon,
when the moon is full on our feast.

For this is a statute for Israel,
a command of our God.
Who made it a decree with Joseph,
when he went against the land of
  Egypt.

A voice I had not known said to me:
"I relieved your shoulder of the
  burden;
your hands were freed from the
  basket.
In distress you called, and I
  delivered you;
I answered you, concealed in the
  storm cloud,
I tested you at the waters of
  Meribah.

Hear, O my people, while I
  admonish you!
O Israel, if only you would listen to
  me!
There shall be no strange god
  among you;

You shall not worship an alien god.
I am the Most High, your God,
who brought you up out of the land
  of Egypt.
Open wide your mouth, and I will
  fill it.

But my people did not listen to my
  voice;
Israel would have none of me.
So I gave them over to their
  stubborn hearts,
to follow their own counsels.

O that my people would listen to
  me,
that Israel would walk in my ways!
I would soon subdue their
  enemies,
and turn my hand against their
  foes.

I would feed you with the finest
  wheat,
and with honey from the rock I
  would fill you." **Glory*...**

READING

Within the Christian story it is possible to see that divine self-emptying in the incarnation and passion of Christ is not an uncharacteristic divine action. Rather, this historical moment discloses the pattern of Sophia-God's love always and everywhere operative. Divine freely self-giving love did not begin with God's personal entering into human history but is so typical that it plays out at the dawn of creation itself.

Elizabeth Johnson, *She Who Is*, p. 234, (2)

RESPONSORY

O God, you promise life eternal, asking only that we love.—**O God...**

You are kind to the brokenhearted; **—asking...**
Glory to you, Source of all Being, Eternal Word and Holy Spirit.
—O God...

CANTICLE OF ZECHARIAH

Ant. Let us serve our God in holiness.

INTERCESSIONS

O God, only you know the whole truth about us and our deeds;
 —guide us with your wisdom and compassion in our
 relationships with one another.
Every person and thing that you have created is precious to you;
 —bless those who are handicapped and all who assist them.
Jesus, you crossed the sea and encountered its dangers;
 —bless sailors and all who travel the waters of our world.
We know the story of your life, O Christ, yet mystery abounds;
 —let our search for truth keep us open to the inspiration of the
 Holy Spirit.
Spirit of God, joy is among your many gifts to us;
 —bless artists of every kind—all who lift up our hearts and fill
 the world with beauty and light.

PRAYER: God of the universe, you speak to us in all of creation,
but you call to us most surely in the depths of our
hearts. Help us to listen for your voice today, gentling
our work, our recreation, and our relationships with
others in ways that let us hear you. Deepen in us our
faith in your presence to us. Grant this through the
intercession of all your prophets who listened in
sincerity and truth. Amen.

DAYTIME PRAYER

**Ant. 1 Teach me discernment
that I may know your ways.**

Psalm 119:65–72

You have been good to your
 servant,
according to your word, O God.—

Teach me discernment and
 knowledge,
for I trust in you commands.

Before I was afflicted I went astray;
but now I keep your word.
You are good and your deeds are
 good;
teach me your commandments.

The proud smear me with lies,
yet I keep your precepts.
Their hearts are closed to good
but I delight in your law.

It was good for me to be afflicted,
that I might learn your statutes.
The law of your mouth is better to
  me
than silver and gold.   **Glory*...**

**Ant. 2 Take heart, it is I; have no
  fear.**
Psalm 56:1-7b, 9-14

Be gracious to me, O God,
some there are who crush me;
they trample upon me all day long,
for many fight proudly against me.

When I am afraid,
I put my trust in you.
In you, whose word I praise,
In you I trust without fear.
What can mortal flesh do to me?

All day long they injure my cause,
all their thoughts are for evil.
They band together, they lurk,
they watch my steps.

You have kept count of my
  wanderings;
you have kept a record of my tears!
Are they not written in your book?
Then my foes will be turned back
in the day when I call to you.

This I know, that God is with me.
In God, whose word I praise,
in the Holy One, whose word I
  praise,
in God I trust without a fear.
What can mortal flesh do to me?

My vows to you I will make, O God.
I will render you thanks.—

For you delivered my soul from
  death,
my feet from falling,
that I may walk before you
in the light of life.   **Glory*...**

**Ant. 3 My heart is steadfast; I
  will praise you all my days.**
Psalm 57

Have mercy on me, have mercy,
for in you my soul takes refuge.
In the shadow of your wings I take
  refuge
till the storms of destruction pass
  by.

I cry to God the Most High,
to God who has always been my
  help.
May you send from heaven and
  save me
and shame those who trample
  upon me.
O God, send your truth and your
  love.

My soul lies down among lions,
who greedily devour the peoples of
  the earth.
Their teeth are spears and arrows,
their tongues sharpened swords.

Be exalted, O God, above the
  heavens;
let your glory be over all the earth!

They laid a snare for my steps,
my soul was bowed down.
They dug a pit in my path
but they fell in it themselves.

My heart is steadfast, O God,
my heart is steadfast.
I will sing and make melody!
Awake, my soul,
awake, lyre and harp!
I will awake the dawn!

I will give thanks to you among the peoples,
I will praise you among the nations
for your love reaches to the heavens
your faithfulness to the skies.

Be exalted, O God, above the heavens!
let your glory be over all the earth!
Glory*...

PRAYER: O God, you bless those who hunger and thirst for justice. We ask for the gift of this desire. Imprint on our minds and in our hearts the longings of your son, Jesus, that our labor this day may be done justly and that we too may bless those who labor for the sake of justice. This we ask in Jesus who is our Way, our Truth, and our Life. Amen.

EVENING PRAYER

Ant. 1 You are the salt of the earth; you are the light of the world.

Psalm 72

Give justice to your Anointed, O God,
and righteousness to those Chosen!
That your people may be judged in righteousness,
and your poor with justice.

Let the mountains bring forth peace for the people,
and the hills, justice!
May your Anointed
defend the cause of the poor,
give deliverance to the needy,
and punish the oppressor!

May your Anointed endure like the sun,
and as long as the moon, through all ages,
like rain that falls on the mown grass,
like showers that water the earth.

In that day justice shall flourish
and peace till the moon be no more!
Your Anointed shall rule from sea to sea,
from the River to the ends of the earth!

May evil bow down before the Holy One,
and wickedness lick the dust!
The kings of Tarshish and of the isles shall render tribute.

May rulers of Sheba and Seba bring gifts.
All will fall down before the Anointed,
all nations serve and pay homage.
Glory*...

Ant. 2 God will save the poor from oppression and violence.
II

The Anointed delivers the needy when they call,
the poor and those who are helpless.—

Having pity on the weak and the
  needy,
saving the lives of the poor.

From oppression and violence they
  are redeemed;
and precious is their blood.
Long may your Chosen One live,
may gold of Sheba be given
to the one you have anointed,
and prayers be made without
  ceasing,
and blessings all the day!

May there be abundance of grain in
  the land,
waving on the tops of the
  mountains;
may its fruit be like Lebanon;
may people flourish in the cities
like the grass in the field!

May the name of your Anointed
  endure forever,
and continue as long as the sun!
Every tribe shall be blessed in the
  one you have chosen,
all nations bless your name.

Blessed be the God of Israel,
who alone does wondrous things.
Blessed be your name forever;
may your glory fill the earth.
Amen! Amen! **Glory*...**

**Ant. 3 Lamb of God, you take
away the sin of the world.
Cant: Rev 11:17–18;
12:10b–12a**

We praise you, God Almighty,
who is and who was.
You have assumed your great
  power,
you have begun your reign.

The nations have raged in anger,
but then came your day of wrath
and the moment to judge the dead;
the time to reward your servants
  the prophets
and the holy ones who revere you,
the great and the small alike.

Now have salvation and power
  come,
your reign, O God, and the
  authority of your Anointed One.
For the accusers of our loved ones
  have been cast out,
who night and day accused them.

By the blood of the Lamb have they
  been defeated,
and by the testimony of your
  servants;
love for life did not deter them from
  death.
So rejoice, you heavens,
and you that dwell therein!
      Glory*...

READING

In order to practice the virtues it is not necessary to be attentive to all of
them all of the time. In fact, this tends to turn one's thoughts and
affections back on oneself so that they become entangled. Humility and
charity are the dominant chords; all the other virtues are overtones of
these. It's only necessary that these two be carefully observed: one very
lowly, the other very lofty. The preservation of an entire structure
depends upon the foundation and the roof. If you continue the exercise
of these two with conviction, when you come up against the others, they

won't give you any difficulty. These are the mothers of the virtues; the others follow them as little chicks follow mother hens. (François de Sales)

Wendy Wright, *Bond of Perfection*, p. 81, (1)

RESPONSORY

You are bountiful, O God; all of your desires for us are good.
  —You...
Everything is a grace; **—all of...**
Glory to you, Source of all Being, Eternal Word and Holy Spirit.
  —You...

CANTICLE OF MARY

Ant. You have shown your power, O God; you have scattered the proud in their hearts' fantasy.

INTERCESSIONS

You hear our prayers and guide and protect us, O God;
  —be praised and thanked for all that we take for granted and for hidden gifts.
You offer us the grace to become a new person in Christ;
  —in times of boredom, awaken us to the world of the Spirit we so often ignore.
Jesus, you were content to hide your glory and to give in secret;
  —strengthen our inward self that we may find our true peace beyond the measure of others.
You challenged the status quo; you died for being different;
  —give courage and peace to all who live on the fringes of society.
You promised a peace that the world cannot give;
  —banish war from our world.

PRAYER: Jesus, our Savior and Guide, you gave yourself to us through a meal at the end of a day, at the end of your life. Be with us at the end of this day as we dedicate ourselves to all that you call us to be. Help us to say to God with you, "Thy will be done." Let us conclude this day strengthened by the remembrance of your total gift of self. We ask this through the power of your name. Amen.

FRIDAY

MORNING PRAYER

Ant 1 A contrite heart, O God, is pleasing in your sight.
Psalm 51

Have mercy on me, O God,
according to your steadfast love;
in your abundant mercy blot out
my sins.
Wash me thoroughly from my
offenses,
and cleanse me from my sin!

For I know my offenses,
and my sin is ever before me.
Against you, you alone, have I
sinned,
and done what is evil in your
sight,
so you are justified in your
sentence
and blameless in your judgment.
Behold, I was brought forth in a
sinful world.

For you desire truth in my
innermost being;
teach me wisdom in the depths of
my heart.
O purify me, and I shall be clean;
O wash me, I shall be whiter than
snow.
Fill me with joy and gladness;
let the bones you have broken
rejoice.
Hide your face from my guilt,
and blot out all my offenses.

Create in me a clean heart,
put a steadfast spirit within me.
Cast me not from your presence,
take not your spirit from me.
Give me again the joy of your
salvation,
with a willing spirit uphold me.

Then I will teach transgressors
your ways
and sinners will return to you.
Deliver me from death,
O God of my salvation,
and my tongue will sing out your
saving help.

Open my lips and my mouth will
sing your praises.
For you take no delight in
sacrifice;
were I to give a burnt offering,
you would not be pleased.
A broken spirit you accept;
a contrite heart, you will not
despise.

In your goodness, show favor to
Zion;
rebuild the walls of Jerusalem.
Then you will delight in just
sacrifices,
in gifts offered on your altar.
  Glory*...

Ant. 2 Your mercy reaches to the heavens; your mercy covers the earth.
Cant: Habakkuk 3:2–4, 13a, 15–19

O God, I have heard your renown,
and your work, O God, do I
revere.
In the course of the years renew
it;
in the course of the years make it
known;
in your wrath remember mercy!

God came from Teman,
and the Holy One from Mount
Paran.—

Your glory covered the heavens,
O God,
and the earth was full of your
praise.

Your brightness was like the
light,
rays flashed forth from your
hand;
there you veiled your power.
You went forth to save your
people,
for the salvation of your anointed.

You trampled the sea with your
horses,
the surging of mighty waters.
I hear, and my body trembles,
my lips quiver at the sound.

Decay enters my bones,
my legs totter beneath me.
I wait for the day of trouble
to come on those who oppress us.
Glory*...

**Ant. 3 Hear the word of God, O
people.**
Psalm 147:12–20

O praise the Most High,
Jerusalem!
Praise your God, O Zion!

For God strengthens the bars of
your gates,
blessing your children within
you,
establishing peace in your
borders,
feeding you with the finest of
wheat.

You send out your word to the
earth;
your command runs swiftly,
giving snow like wool,
scattering hoarfrost like ashes.

You cast forth your ice like
crumbs;
who can stand before your cold?
You send forth your word, and
melt them;
you make the wind blow, and the
waters flow.

You make your word known to
your people,
your statutes and decrees to
Israel.
You have not dealt thus with any
other nation;
you have not taught them your
decrees. **Glory*...**

READING

Sometimes, as we look at the night sky, a single bright star will appear.
In its brightness it transforms the night; every star in the sky is changed
in relation to this new appearance. It is as if this one star, in
unparalleled beauty, crowns the entire beauty of the night. Christ in
God is like that bright star, illumining the actuality of the primordial
nature through the beauty of his manifestation of that nature in our
history. Through Christ the depths of God are touched for the world;
new possibilities for reflecting divine harmony in human history shine
out for us. The church is born.

Marjorie Hewitt Suchocki, *God, Christ, Church*, p. 132, (2)

RESPONSORY

Who will deliver us, O God, from our weakness and sin?
—**Who will...**
Jesus Christ has saved us —**from our...**
Glory to you, Source of all Being, Eternal Word and Holy Spirit.
—**Who will...**

CANTICLE OF ZECHARIAH

Ant. You are compassionate, O God, and forever faithful to your promise.

INTERCESSIONS

O God, you have created us for what eye has not seen and ear has not heard;
—give us open minds and largeness of heart that we may see and serve beyond ourselves.
Jesus, you served and saved others—ridicule did not shrink your compassion;
—make us singlehearted in our care for others.
With religious authority against you and disciples slow to understand, you stayed your course to the end;
—give perseverance to the new and creative in our culture, that your message may live on in us.
Jesus, you knew the innocence and vulnerability of childhood;
—guide and protect the children of our disturbed and violent world.
Spirit of God, you promote progress—you make all things new;
—give us the vision we need to develop for the better without destroying our vital heritage.

PRAYER: O God, your son, Jesus, died giving the message of your love to us. Have mercy on us. Give us the courage to die rather than cause the death of another. Help us to allow his death to mean new life for us. Never let us stand in the way of your saving grace. Grant this through the intercession of Jesus and all who have given their lives for others. Amen.

DAYTIME PRAYER

Ant. 1 Blessed be God who comforts us in all our affliction.

Psalm 119:73–80

Your hands have made me and
  have fashioned me;
give me understanding that I may
  learn your commandments.
Those who revere you will see me
  and rejoice,
because I have hoped in your
  word.

I know that your judgments are
  right,
that in faithfulness you afflicted
  me.
Let your love be ready to comfort
  me
according to your promise.

Let your mercy come to me, that I
  may live;
for your law is my delight.
Let the godless be put to shame,
who have corrupted me with
  guile,
while I will ponder on your
  precepts.

Let those who revere you turn to
  me,
that they may know your will.
May my heart be blameless in
  your commandments,
that I may not be put to shame!
Glory*...

Ant. 2 We have a treasure in earthen vessels, to show the power of God.

Psalm 59:1–5, 10–11, 17–18

Deliver me from evil, O my God,—

protect me from those who
  oppress me,
deliver me from all that is wicked,
and save me from all cruelty.

Calamity lies in wait for my life;
misfortune bands together
  against me.
For no offense or sin of mine,
for no fault, they run and make
  ready.
Rouse yourself, come to my aid
  and see!

O my Strength, I will sing praises
  to you;
for you, O God, are my
  stronghold.
In your steadfast love you will
  meet me;
O God, come to my aid,
let me triumph over oppression.

As for me, I will sing of your
  might;
each morning sing of your love.
For you have been to me a
  stronghold
and a refuge in the day of
  distress.

O my Strength, I will sing praises
  to you,
for you, O God, are my
  stronghold,
the God who shows me love
without end. **Glory*...**

Ant. 3 Blessed are you, O God; you heal us while wounding us.

Psalm 60

O God, you have rejected us and
broken our defenses;—

You have turned your face;
  restore us.
You have made the land to quake,
  torn it open;
Repair its breaches for it totters.
You have made your people suffer
  hard things,
and have given us wine that
  made us reel.

You have set up a signal for those
  who fear you,
to rally to it from the bow.
That your faithful ones may be
  delivered,
help us by your hand and give
  answer!

You have spoken from your
  sanctuary:
"With exultation I will divide
  Shechem—

and portion out the Vale of
  Succoth.

Gilead is mine and Manasseh;
Ephraim is my helmet,
Judah is my scepter.

Moab is my washbasin;
upon Edom I cast my shoe.
Over Philistia I will shout in
  triumph."

Who will bring me to the fortified
  city?
Who will lead me to Edom?
Have you not rejected us, O God?
You did not go forth with our
  armies.

Give us help against the foe,
for human help is vain.
With you we shall do valiantly;
it is you who will tread down
  oppression. **Glory*...**

PRAYER: Lord Jesus Christ, the marvel of your love lives on and
challenges everyone who comes to know you. In you we
know the love of God; through you we know the will
and ways of God. Be with us now that we may live for
one another as you have lived and died for us. Grant
this through your Spirit of Love. Amen.

EVENING PRAYER

**Ant. 1 You are gracious, O God,
and full of compassion.**

Psalm 116:1–9

I love you, O God, for you have
  heard
my voice and my supplications.
You have inclined your ear to me,
I will call on you as long as I live.

The snares of death encompassed
  me;—

the pangs of the grave laid hold
  on me;
I suffered distress and anguish.
Then I called on your name, O
  God:
"O God, I pray you, save my life!"

Gracious are you and just;
merciful and full of compassion.
You preserve those with simple
  hearts;
when I was brought low, you
  saved me.

Return my soul, to your rest;
for God has dealt kindly with you,
delivering my soul from death,
my eyes from tears,
my feet from stumbling.

I will walk before you, O God,
in the land of the living.
   Glory*...

Ant. 2 God is my comforter and help in time of need.

Psalm 121

I lift up my eyes to the hills.
From whence comes my help?
My help comes from you, O God,
who made heaven and earth.

You will not let my foot stumble,
you, who preserve me, will not
   sleep.
Behold, you who keep Israel
will neither slumber nor sleep.

You, O God, are our keeper;
you are our shade.—

The sun shall not smite us by
   day,
nor the moon by night.

You will guard us from all evil;
you will preserve our lives.
You will protect our goings and
   comings
both now and forever.
   Glory*...

Ant. 3 Ruler of all the ages, just and true are your ways.

Cant: Rev 15:3–4

Great and wonderful are your
   works,
God the Almighty One!
Just and true are your ways,
Ruler of all the ages!

Who shall refuse you honor,
or the glory due your name?

For you alone are holy,
all nations shall come and
   worship in your presence.
Your judgments are clearly seen.
   Glory*...

READING

I would have you know that every virtue of yours and every vice is put into action by means of your neighbors. If you hate me, you harm your neighbors and yourself as well (for you are your chief neighbor), and the harm is both general and in particular. I say general because it is your duty to love your neighbors as your own self. In love you ought to help them spiritually with prayer and counsel, and assist them spiritually and materially in their need—at least with your good will if you have nothing else. If you do not love me you do not love your neighbors...but it is yourself you harm most, because you deprive yourself of grace.

Catherine of Siena, *The Dialogue*, p. 33, (1)

RESPONSORY

Lord Jesus Christ, your yoke is easy and your burden is light.
   —Lord Jesus...
In you we will find rest; **—for your yoke...**

Glory to you, Source of all Being, Eternal Word and Holy Spirit.
  —Lord Jesus...

CANTICLE OF MARY

Ant. You put down the mighty from their throne and lift up the lowly.

INTERCESSIONS

Jesus, you washed the feet of your followers;
  —teach all civic and religious leaders how to govern with humility and reverence.
You did not call your disciples servants but friends;
  —help us to establish your kindom by mutual collaboration and loving respect.
You shared a meal with one who had betrayed you;
  —give us the desire to set aside our mistrust of one another.
Jesus, you came into the world to testify to the truth;
  —make us credible witnesses to the truth of your gospel.
You suffered at the hands of those you served;
  —enable us to serve one another selflessly without regard for human success.

PRAYER: Holy Spirit, Living Love of God, you are in the world healing the wounds of sin and death. Warm the hearts of those embittered by sorrow and pain, encourage those crushed by failure, enlighten the minds of those dulled by pleasure or fatigue. Awaken in us all the remembrance of the overwhelming love of God made known to us in the life and death of Jesus. Help us to continue with renewed trust. This we ask of you, Life-giving Spirit, in the name of your Christ, God among us. Amen.

SATURDAY

MORNING PRAYER

Ant. 1 We acclaim your love in the morning and your faithfulness at night.

Psalm 92

It is good to give thanks to you,
to sing praises to your name, Most High,
to declare your love in the morning,
and your faithfulness by night,
to the music of the lute and the harp,
to the melody of the lyre.

For you make me glad by your deeds;
at the work of your hands I sing for joy.
How great are your works, O God!
Your thoughts are very deep!

The foolish ones cannot know;
the stupid cannot understand this:
though the wicked spring up like grass
and all evildoers flourish,
they are doomed to their own devices.
But you, O God, are on high forever.
All wickedness shall perish;
all oppression be wiped out.

You give me the strength of the wild ox;
you pour oil over my head.
My eyes have seen the downfall of evil,
my ears have heard the doom of corruption.
The just shall flourish like the palm tree
and grow like a cedar in Lebanon.

They are planted in your holy house,
they flourish in your courts.
They still bring forth fruit in old age,
they are ever full of sap and green,
to show that you, O God, are just;
you are my rock; in you there is no injustice. **Glory*...**

Ant. 2 We declare your greatness, O God.

Cant: Deut 32:1–12

Give ear, O heavens, while I speak;
let the earth hear the words of my mouth.
May my teaching soak in like the rain,
and my speech permeate like the dew,
like a gentle rain upon the tender grass,
like a shower upon the herbs.

For I will proclaim your name, O God.
Declare your holy greatness!
"My Rock, your work is faultless;
all your ways are justice.
A faithful God, without deceit,
how just and right you are!

Yet basely have you been dealt with by your sinful children,
a perverse and crooked generation.
Is God to be thus requited,
you foolish and senseless people?
Is God not your source, who created you,
who made you and established you?

Remember the days of old,
Consider the years of many
  generations;
Ask your parents and they will
  inform you,
ask your elders and they will tell
  you.

When the Most High gave the
  nations their inheritance,
separating the children of the
  earth,
the Most High fixed the boundaries
  of the peoples
according to the number of those in
  your court.
But your portion, O God, is your
  people,
Jacob, your allotted heritage.

You found them in a desert land,
in the howling waste of the
  wilderness;
encircling them and caring for
  them,
guarding them as the apple of your
  eye.

Like an eagle that stirs up its nest,
that flutters over its young,
so you spread your wings to catch
  them,
and bear them on your pinions.
You alone were their leader,
no strange god was with our God."
    Glory*...

Ant. 3 How great is your name in all the earth.

Psalm 8

How great is your name, O God,
in all the earth!

You whose glory above the heavens
is chanted on the lips of babes,
have founded a defense against
  your foes,
to silence the cries of the rebels.

When I look at the heavens,
the work of your hands,
the moon and the stars which you
  established;
who are we that you should keep
  us in mind,
mortal flesh that you care for us?

Yet you have made us little less
  than God,
and crowned us with glory and
  honor.
You entrust us with the works of
  your hands,
to care for all your creation.

All sheep and oxen,
and even the beasts of the field,
the birds of the air, and the fish of
  the sea,
whatever passes along the paths of
  the sea.

How great is your name, Creator
  God,
in all the earth!   **Glory*...**

READING

I feel the *vocation* of the WARRIOR, THE PRIEST, THE APOSTLE, THE DOCTOR, THE MARTYR. Finally, I feel the need and the desire of carrying out the most heroic deeds for *You, O Jesus....* I feel in me the *vocation* of the PRIEST. With what love, O Jesus, I would carry You in my hands when, at my voice, You would come down from heaven. And with what love would I give you to souls!... I would like to travel over the whole earth to preach your Name...one mission alone would not be enough for me. I would want to preach the Gospel on all the five continents simultaneously and even to the most remote isles. I would be a missionary, not for a few years only but from the beginning of creation until the consummation of the ages. But above all, O my Beloved Savior, I would shed my blood for You even to the last drop.

Thérèse of Lisieux, *Story of a Soul*, p. 192, (3)

RESPONSORY

Those who wait for you, O God, shall never be disappointed.
—Those who...
They shall see you face to face; **—and shall...**
Glory to you, Source of all Being, Eternal Word and Holy Spirit.
—Those who...

CANTICLE OF ZECHARIAH

Ant. Guide our feet into the way of peace.

INTERCESSIONS

O God, you know of what we are made, and you give us all that we need;
—let us mirror your compassion to one another.
Jesus, many dismissed your teaching because of your common origin;
—help us to look beyond surface impressions to the true value of each person.
Our attachments and addictions lay heavy burdens upon us;
—teach us how to listen to your freeing word written in our hearts.
You knew rejection and derision;
—give us the desire to serve all and the grace to be at peace when we cannot please everyone.
Our culture tends to reward the strong and powerful and to dismiss the weak;
—make all that we do reflect your gospel—your good news to the poor.

PRAYER: Merciful God, we often stray from your call and our own good intentions, but you meet us with forgiveness and creative love. Give us the gift of patience and understanding that we too may lure others to new life.

May all who die this day enjoy life with you as they see you face to face. Grant this through Mary, who brought new life to us in Jesus. Amen.

DAYTIME PRAYER

Ant. 1 In your love spare my life, that I may keep your decrees.

Psalm 119:81–88

My soul pines for your salvation;
I hope in your word.
My eyes fail with watching for your promise;
"When will you comfort me?"

Though parched and exhausted with waiting
I have not forgotten your commands.
How long must your servant endure?
When will you requite me?

Evil waits to entrap me
to sin against your law.
All your commandments are sure;
then help me when oppressed by falsehood!

Death lurks to make an end of me;
but I forsake not your precepts.
In your steadfast love spare my life,
that I may do your will. **Glory*...**

Ant. 2 O God, you are my refuge, my stronghold against evil.

Psalm 61

Hear my cry, O God,
listen to my prayer;
from the end of the earth I call,
when my heart is faint.

Set me on the rock that is higher than I;
for you are my refuge,
my stronghold against evil.

Let me dwell in your tent forever!
Hide me in the shelter of your wings!
For you, O God, have heard my vows,
you have given me the heritage of those who love your name.

May you lengthen the lives of just rulers:
may their years cover many generations!
May they ever be enthroned before you;
bid love and truth watch over them.

So will I ever sing your praises,
as I pay my vows day after day.
Glory*...

Ant. 3 O God, preserve my life from corruption.

Psalm 64

Hear my voice, O God, in my complaint;
preserve my life from all that is evil,
hide me from the tempter's snare,
from the scheming wiles of my heart.

Evil sharpens its tongue like a sword;—

aiming bitter words like arrows
shooting from ambush at the
  innocent,
shooting suddenly and without
  fear.

Holding fast to its evil purpose;
conspiring to lay secret snares
thinking: "Who can see us?
Who can search out our crimes?"

But you know well our inmost
  thoughts,
the depth of the heart and mind!
You will shoot your arrow at
  them;—

they will be wounded suddenly.
Our own tongues bring us to
  ruin.

Then let all people fear;
they will tell what you have
  wrought,
and ponder what you have done.
The just will rejoice in you, O
  God,
and fly to you for refuge.
Let the upright in heart exult.
  Glory*...

PRAYER: Another week has passed, O God, and we see all that
we have done and what we might have done differently.
We give all of our endeavors to you. Bless the good and
heal the faulty. Inspire us to do your will more
creatively an generously in the week to come. We ask
this through Jesus who shows us the way. Amen.

WEEK III

SUNDAY, EVENING PRAYER I

Ant 1 Your glory is above the heavens; we praise your name.

Psalm 113

We your servants, praise you!
Praise your holy name!
Blessed be your name, O God,
from now and forevermore!
From the rising of the sun to its
  setting
your name is to be praised!

You are high above all nations,
and your glory above the
  heavens!
Who is like unto you, O God,
who is seated upon the heights,
who looks far down upon us,
upon the heavens and the earth?

You raise the poor from the dust,
lift the needy from the ash heap,
to set them in the company of
  rulers,
with the rulers of your people.
To the barren you give a home,
and gladden their hearts with
  children. **Glory*...**

Ant 2 I will lift up the cup of salvation and call on your holy name.

Psalm 116:10–19

I kept faith, even when I said:
"I am greatly afflicted;"—

*Glory to you, Source of all Being, Eternal Word and Holy Spirit,

As it was in the beginning is now and will be forever. Amen.

I said in my dismay,
"No one can be trusted."

What shall I render to you,
for all your goodness to me?
I will lift up the cup of salvation
and call on your holy name.

I will make my vows to you
in the presence of all your people.
Precious in your sight
is the death of your faithful ones.

Indeed, I am your servant;
you have loosened my bonds.
I will offer sacrifice of
  thanksgiving
and call on your holy name.

I will make my vows to you
in the presence of all your people,
in the courts of your holy house,
in the midst of all your saints.
  Glory*...

Ant 3 Every tongue will proclaim: Jesus Christ is Lord!

Cant: Phil 2:6–11

Though he was in the form of
  God,
Jesus did not count equality with
  God
something to be grasped at.

But emptied himself
taking the form of a slave,
being born in human likeness.

Being found in human estate,
he humbled himself and became
  obedient,
obediently accepting death,
even death on a cross!

Therefore God has highly exalted him
and bestowed on him the name
above every other name.

So that at the name of Jesus
every knee should bow,—

in heaven, on the earth,
and under the earth,
and every tongue proclaim
to the glory of God:
Jesus Christ is Lord! **Glory*...**

READING

...What we believe we understand about our own soul is, after all, only a fleeting reflection of what will remain God's secret until the day all will be made manifest. My great joy consists in the hope of that future clarity. Faith in the secret history must always strengthen us when what we actually perceive (about ourselves or about others) might discourage us.

Edith Stein: Self-Portrait in Letters, p. 331, (3)

RESPONSORY

We sing to you, O God, and bless your name. —**We sing...**
Tell of your salvation day after day; —**and bless...**
Glory to you, Source of all Being, Eternal Word and Holy Spirit.
   —**We sing...**

CANTICLE OF MARY

Ant. You have helped your servant, Israel, remembering your mercy.

INTERCESSIONS

O God, you speak to us in many ways;
   —keep us open to your guidance from sources however
      great or humble.
We cherish our call to serve you, and we endeavor to be faithful;
   —deliver us from the plethora of idols that beckon to us
      daily.
Bless all who are united in marriage;
   —let the grace of the sacrament enable them to love and
      support one another.
Jesus, you knew the challenge of choosing your direction in life;
   —send your Spirit to guide those who struggle with
      vocational choices.
Spirit of God, grant wisdom, understanding, and fortitude to all
involved in the media;

—let the highest values and principles govern their decisions and programs.

PRAYER: All holy, ever present God, at the close of this day we offer to you the world's struggle toward wholeness. We are confident that our darkness and sin have been redeemed through the life and death of Jesus and that your mercy has no limit. Give us the gift of mercy for ourselves and for others. We ask this in Jesus' name. Amen.

MORNING PRAYER

Ant 1 Glory to God in the highest.

Psalm 93

O God, you are our Sovereign,
you are robed in majesty;
you are girded with strength.
The world is made firm;
it shall never be moved;
your throne is established from of old;
from all eternity, you are.

The waters have lifted up, O God,
the waters have lifted up their voice,
the waters have lifted up their thunder.
Mightier than the roaring of the waters,
mightier than the surgings of the sea,
You, O God, are glorious on high!

Your decrees are to be trusted.
Holiness befits your house,
O God, for evermore.
    Glory*...

Ant 2 Praise and exalt God above all, forever.

Cant: Daniel 3:57–88, 56

All you works of God, praise our God.
Praise and exalt God above all forever.
All you angels, sing God's praise,
you heavens and waters above.
Sun and moon, and stars of heaven,
sing praise with the heavenly hosts.

Every shower and dew, praise our God.
Give praise all you winds.
Praise our God, you fire and heat,
cold and chill–dew and rain.
Frost and chill, praise our God.
Praise God, ice and snow.
Nights and days, sing hymns of praise,
light and darkness,
lightnings and clouds.

Let all the earth bless our God.
Praise and exalt God above all forever.
Let all that grows from the earth give praise—

together with mountains and hills.
Give praise, you springs,
you seas and rivers,
dolphins and all water creatures.
Let birds of the air,
beasts, wild and tame,
together with all living peoples,
praise and exalt God above all
  forever.

O Israel, praise our God.
Praise and exalt God above all
  forever.
Give praise, you priests,
servants of the Most High,
spirits and souls of the just.
Holy ones of humble heart,
sing your hymns of praise.
Hannaniah, Azariah, Mishael,
  praise our God.
Praise and exalt God above all
  forever.

Let us bless our God, Holy
  Mystery,
Source of All Being, Word and
  Spirit.
Let us praise and exalt God above
all forever.
Blessed are you, O God, in the
  firmament of heaven.
Praiseworthy and glorious and
  exalted above all forever.

**Ant 3 Praise God from the
  heavens.**

Psalm 148

Praise God from the heavens,
Praise God in the heights!—

Praise God, all you angels,
Praise God, you heavenly hosts!

Praise God, sun and moon,
Praise God, shining stars.
Praise God, highest heavens,
and the waters above the heavens!

Let them praise the name of God,
who commanded and they were
  created.
God established them forever;
fixed their bounds which will not
  pass away.

Praise God, all you on earth,
sea monsters and all deeps,
fire and hail, snow and frost,
stormy winds that obey God's
  word!

Mountains and all hills,
fruit trees and all cedars!
Beasts, wild and tame,
reptiles and birds on the wing!

All earth's rulers and peoples,
leaders and those of renown!
Young men and women,
the old together with children!

Let us praise your name, O God,
for your name alone is exalted;
your glory above heaven and
  earth.

You exalt the strength of your
  people,
you are praise for all your saints,
for all the faithful near to you.
  Glory*...

READING

Thus says the [Most High God]: I am going to open your graves, and
bring you up from your graves, O my people; and I will bring you back
to the land of Israel. And you shall know that I am [your God], when I
open your graves, and bring you up from your graves, O my people. I

will put my spirit within you, and you shall live, and I will place you on your own soil; then you shall know that I, [your God], have spoken and will act," says the [Most High].

Ezek 37:12–14

RESPONSORY

Our hearts rejoice, O God, in your tender care. —**Our hearts...**
We live in peace; —**in your...**
Glory to you, Source of all Being, Eternal Word and Holy Spirit.
   —**Our hearts...**

CANTICLE OF ZECHARIAH

Ant. You have visited and redeemed your people, O God.

INTERCESSIONS

O God, we are one in you, and all that we do affects the whole;
   —make us aware of our power to seed the world with
      good or ill by every thought, word, and deed.
Our hearts are torn by the realization of the sufferings of others;
   —grant that we may never be a stumbling block to others
      or a culpable cause of their pain.
Jesus, you chose laborers, and tax collectors, to be your
companions;
   —preserve us from deciding what people are by what they
      do, and let us see the worth of every person and the
      value in every kind of work.
Bless those who have lost their life companion through death or
divorce;
   —let the people of God be a saving support and comfort to
      them.
Spirit of God, enlighten the minds and renew the hearts of the
hierarchy of the churches;
   —let their ministry be a healing service for all of your people.

PRAYER: God of the universe, you create the night as well as
   the day. You are with us in good fortune and bad
   times. You order all things for our well being and you
   lure us to truth and holiness. For these and all your
   gifts to us we sing your praise through Jesus Christ
   who is our way, our truth and our life. Amen.

DAYTIME PRAYER

Ant. 1 You are my companion, my helper on the way.

Psalm 118

I

We give thanks to you, for you are good,
and your steadfast love endures forever.
Let the descendants of Israel say:
"Your steadfast love endures forever."
Let the descendants of Aaron say:
"Your steadfast love endures forever."
Let those who fear you say:
"Your steadfast love endures forever."

In my distress, I called to you;
you answered me and set me free.
With you at my side I do not fear.
What can anyone do against me?
You are at my side to help me:
I shall withstand all evildoers.

It is better to take refuge in you,
than to trust in people:
it is better to take refuge in you
than to trust in our leaders.
Glory*...

Ant. 2 You are my saving God; you chastise and you bless.

II

All wickedness surrounded me;
in your name I crushed it.
It surrounded me, surrounded me
on every side;
in your name I cut it off.
It surrounded me like bees;
it blazed like a fire among thorns.
In your name I crushed it.

I was pushed hard, and was falling
but you came to help me.—

You are my strength and my song;
you are my salvation.

O God, you have triumphed;
your reign is exalted.
You have triumphed over all;
I shall not die, I shall live
and recount your wondrous deeds.
You have chastened me sorely,
but have not given me over to
death. **Glory*...**

Ant. 3 Blessed is the one who comes in the name of our God.

III

Open to me the gates of justice,
that I may enter and give thanks.
This is your gate, O God;
the just shall enter through it.
I thank you for you have answered me
you alone are my salvation.

The stone which the builders rejected
has become the cornerstone.
This is your doing, O God,
it is marvelous in our eyes.
This is the day which you have made;
let us rejoice and be glad in it.

Save us, we beseech you, O God!
O God, grant us success.
Blessed are those who enter
in your holy name.
For you O God, are our God,
and you have given us light.

Let us go forward in procession
with branches,
up to your holy altar.
You are my God, I thank you.
You are my God, I praise you.

We give thanks to you for you are good;— and your steadfast love endures forever. **Glory*...**

PRAYER: God of mercy, your goodness encompasses the great and the small. Help us to know your presence in the most hidden suffering, the most secret pain. Remind us again of your unfailing love and give us new hope. This we ask through the intercession of all who suffered in hope and now live with you. Amen.

EVENING PRAYER II

Ant. 1 God revealed to the Anointed One, "Sit at my side."

Psalm 110:1-5, 7

God's revelation to the Anointed One:
"Sit at my side:
till I put injustice beneath your feet."

God will send forth from Zion your scepter of power:
rule in the midst of your foes.

Your people will give themselves freely
on the day you lead your host upon the holy mountains.
From the womb of the morning your youth will come like dew.

God has sworn an oath that will not be changed.
"You are a priest forever,
after the order of Melchizedek."

The Anointed standing by your side,
will shatter rulers on the day of wrath.

Drinking from your streams by the wayside
shall the Chosen One be refreshed. **Glory*...**

Ant. 2 In your gracious mercy, you cause us to remember your wonderful works.

Psalm 111

I will give thanks to you with all my heart,
in the company of the great assembly.
Great are the works of the Most High;
pondered by all who delight in them.

Full of honor and majesty is your work,
your justice endures for ever.
You enable us to remember your wonders;
you are gracious and merciful.

You give food to those who fear you;
you are mindful of your covenant.
You have shown your people the power of your works,
by giving them the heritage of the nations.

Your works are faithful and just;
your precepts are all trustworthy,
they are established forever and ever,—

to be done in uprightness and truth.

You sent redemption to your people,
and commanded your covenant forever.
Holy and awesome is your name!

To fear you is the beginning of wisdom;
all who do so prove themselves wise.
Your praise endures forever!
Glory*...

Ant. 3 We rejoice and exult in you.

Cant: Rev 19:1, 5–7

Salvation, glory, and power belong to you,—

your judgments are honest and true.

All of us, your servants, sing praise to you,
we worship you reverently, both great and small.

You, our almighty God, are Creator of heaven and earth.
Let us rejoice and exult, and give you glory.

The wedding feast of the Lamb has begun,
And the bride has made herself ready. **Glory*...**

READING

Blessed be the God...of our Lord Jesus Christ! By [God's] great mercy God has given us a new birth into a living hope through the resurrection of Jesus Christ from the dead, and into an inheritance that is imperishable, undefiled, and unfading, kept in heaven for you, who are being protected by the power of God through faith for a salvation ready to be revealed in the last time. In this you rejoice, even if now for a little while you have had to suffer various trials, so that the genuineness of your faith—being more precious than gold that, though perishable, is tested by fire—may be found to result in praise and glory and honor when Jesus Christ is revealed.

1 Pet 1:3–7

RESPONSORY

You create and sustain us, O God, with your love. **—You...**
From generation to generation **—with your...**
Glory to you, Source of all Being, Eternal Word and Holy Spirit.
—You...

CANTICLE OF MARY

Ant. Blessed are you among women and blessed is the fruit of your womb.

INTERCESSIONS

Life after death is a mystery to us, O God;
—let the resurrection of Jesus and his Spirit among us
witness to your eternal love and care for us.
You ask us to give, to empty ourselves, and to follow you in faith;
—only to fill us with solid nourishment that enables us to
live the journey of the gospel.
We know well your law of love; your Spirit lives within us;
—let no other rule take precedence in our lives.
You came to us bringing peace and reconciliation;
—may your gospel be the bridge that reconciles us—families,
communities, and nations.
Bless all who have a great fear of death;
—grant them peace of heart and friends to support them.

PRAYER: God of wisdom, your steadfast love gives meaning to
our lives. Remembering your goodness from ages past,
we have hope. Our very desire for you is a gift of your
love. Holy Mystery, we do believe; help our unbelief.
This we ask for ourselves, but especially for those
without hope and those who know no love. Hear our
prayer in Jesus' name. Amen.

MONDAY

MORNING PRAYER

**Ant 1 My soul is longing for the
living God.**

Psalm 84

How lovely is your dwelling place,
O God of hosts!

My soul longs and yearns
for the courts of the Most High;
my heart and lips sing for joy
to you, the living God.

Even the sparrow finds a home,
and the swallow a nest for its
brood,
where it may lay its young,
at your altars, O God of hosts!

Blessed are those who dwell in
your house,
forever singing your praise!
Blessed are those whose strength
you are,
in whose hearts are the roads to
Zion.

As they go through the Bitter
Valley,
they make it a place of springs;
the early rain covers it with pools.
They go from strength to
strength;
the God of gods will be seen in
Zion.

O God of hosts, hear my prayer;
give ear, O God of Jacob!
Look upon our shield, O God;
look on the face of your Anointed!

For one day in your courts is
  better,
than a thousand anywhere else.
I would rather stand at your
  threshold,
than dwell in the tents of
  wickedness.

For you are a sun and a shield;
you bestow favor and honor.
No good do you withhold
from those who walk uprightly.

O God! God of hosts!
Blessed are those who trust in
  you! **Glory*...**

**Ant. 2 Let us walk in your light,
O God.**

Cant: Isaiah 2:2–5

It shall come to pass in days to
  come,
that the mountain of the house of
  God
shall be established as the
  highest mountain,
and be raised above the hills.

All nations shall flow to it;
many peoples shall come and say:
"Come, let us go up to the
  mountain of God,
to the house of the God of Jacob;
that we may be taught in God's
  ways,
and walk in God's paths."

For from Zion shall go forth the
  law,
and the word of the Most High
  from Jerusalem.—

God shall judge between the
  nations,
and shall decide for many
  peoples;
they shall beat their swords into
  plowshares,
and their spears into pruning
  hooks;
nation shall not lift up sword
  against nation,
nor shall they teach war any
  more.

O house of Jacob, come,
let us walk in the light of our
  God! **Glory*...**

**Ant. 3 Let all things exult in
  your presence for you come to
  judge the earth.**

Psalm 96

O sing to God a new song;
sing to God, all the earth!
Sing and bless God's name.

We proclaim your salvation day
  by day,
declare your glory among the
  nations,
your wonders among all the
  peoples.

You are great and worthy to be
  praised;
to be feared above all gods.
The gods of the nations are idols;
but you made the heavens.
Honor and majesty are before
  you;
strength and beauty, in your
  sanctuary.

Give to God, you families of
  peoples,
give to God glory and power!
Give glory to God's holy name;—

bring an offering, and enter God's
courts!
Worship in the temple of the Most
High.
O earth, tremble before the
Almighty.

We proclaim to all nations:
"You, O God, are sovereign.
The world you established:
it shall never be moved;
you will judge the peoples with
equity."

Let the heavens be glad and the
earth rejoice;—

let the sea thunder, and all that
fills it;
let the field exult, and everything
in it!
Then shall all the trees of the
wood sing for joy
at your presence, O God, for you
come,
you come to judge the earth.

You will judge the world with
justice,
and the peoples with your truth.
Glory*...

READING

The advice [of François de Sales] was simple—she [Jeanne de Chantal]
was to learn to love beyond her present capacity. She was eventually to
learn to love all that life presented to her. By doing this she would open
herself radically to the presence of God in all events. She, like the Savior
she adored, would stretch out her arms to embrace all her "crosses,"
knowing that in the act of authentic loving, resignation in its most
profound sense, she was being fashioned in the image she loved and
bringing that image into the world.

Wendy Wright, *The Bond of Perfection*, p. 70, (1)

RESPONSORY

There is no limit, O God, to your love for us. **—There is...**
All that you do attests **—to your...**
Glory to you, Source of all Being, Eternal Word and Holy Spirit.
   —There is...

CANTICLE OF ZECHARIAH

Ant. Blessed be the great God of Israel.

INTERCESSIONS

You are our Creator, O God, our lives are in your hands;
   —make us humble and reverent of heart as we unravel
      some small part of the mystery of creation.
Jesus, people were drawn to you for you spoke with authority.
   —bless our public officials with insight for our good, and
      protect them from all that is not just in your sight.

You often spoke to those who were closed to your teaching;
—give us a contemplative attitude and the grace to
hear and live your message.
Spirit of God, you hovered over chaos and called forth a world of
life;
—calm us in times of anxiety; teach us how to live one
moment at a time in your loving presence.
Our hearts are drawn to glorify you, O God, and you receive our
humble praise;
—bless composers, singers and all musicians who enable
us to express our love and gratitude to you.

PRAYER: O God, we long to follow in the footsteps of Jesus,
bringing about your reign of love. Our weakness and
sinfulness stop us over and over again. Help us to
cooperate with your personal design for each of us and
by your strength to embrace your will and to grow in
love. Grant this through the intercession of all your
saints who inspire, challenge, and call us to the praise
of your glory now and forever. Amen.

DAYTIME PRAYER

**Ant. 1 I will not forget your
precepts; by them you give me
life.**
Psalm 119:89–96

Forever, O God, your word
is firmly fixed in the heavens.
Your faithfulness endures to all
generations;
you established the earth,
it will not be moved.

By your decree it stands to this
day;
for all things are your servants.
If your law had not been my
delight,
I would have died in my affliction.

I will never forget your precepts;
by them you have given me life.
Save me, for I am yours;—

I have sought your precepts.

Wickedness waits to destroy me;
but I ponder your will.
I have seen a limit to all
perfection,
but your commandment is
exceedingly broad.
Glory*...

**Ant. 2 You are my hope; my
trust from the days of my
youth.**
Psalm 71

In you, O God, I take refuge;
let me never be put to shame!
In your justice deliver and rescue
me;
incline your ear to me and save
me.

Be to me a rock of refuge,
a stronghold to save me,
for you are my rock and my
  stronghold.
Rescue me from the throes of
  oppression,
from the grip of injustice and
  greed.

For you, O God, are my hope,
my trust, O God, from my youth.
Upon you I have leaned from my
  birth;
from my mother's womb you
  claimed me.
I praise you forever and ever.

I have been a portent to many;
but you are my strong refuge.
My lips are filled with your praise,
with your glory all the day.
Do not cast me off in old age;
forsake me not when my strength
  is spent.

O God, be not far from me;
O God, make haste to help me!
Let evil see its own destruction,
and injustice turn on itself.
  Glory*...

**Ant. 3 Even in old age, O God,
  do not forsake your servant.**
  II

But as for me, I will always hope
and praise you more and more.
My lips will tell of your justice,
of your salvation all the day,
for your goodness cannot be
  numbered.

I will declare your mighty deeds,
I will proclaim your justice.
You have taught me from my
  youth,
and I proclaim your wonders still.

Now that I am old and gray-
  headed,
O God, do not forsake me,
till I proclaim your power
to generations to come.
Your power and your justice, O
  God,
reach to the highest heavens.

You have done marvelous things,
O God, who is like you?
You who have made me see many
  sore troubles
will revive me once again;
from the depths of the earth you
  will raise me.
You will exalt and comfort me
  again.

So I will praise you with the harp
for your faithfulness, O God;
I will sing praises to you with the
  lyre,
O Holy One of Israel.

My lips will shout for joy,
when I sing praises to you;
my soul also, which you have
  redeemed.
My tongue will tell of your justice
  all the day long,
for evil is put to rout, and all that
  sought to harm me.
  Glory*...

PRAYER: Help us, O God, to reach out to those in need. The poor,
    the elderly, the imprisoned, those who are ill call out to
    us as they fill out what is wanting in the suffering of
    Jesus. Give us the wisdom and generosity to minister

to them and to manifest your love. Grant this for Jesus' sake who came to set us free. Amen.

EVENING PRAYER

Ant. 1 Our eyes look to you till you have mercy upon us.

Psalm 123

To you I lift up my eyes,
you who are enthroned in the
    heavens!
Behold like the eyes of servants
look to the hand of their master,

Like the eyes of a maid
look to the hand of her mistress,
so our eyes look to you, O God,
till you have mercy upon us.

Have mercy on us, O God, have
    mercy,
for we are filled with contempt.
Too long has our soul been sated
with the scorn of the arrogant,
the contempt of the proud.
    Glory*...

Ant. 2 You will wipe away every tear from our eyes and death shall be no more.

Psalm 124

If you had not been on our side,
let Israel now say:
if you had not been on our side,
when oppression overwhelmed
    us,
then would we be swallowed
    alive,
when injustice raged against us.

Then the flood would have swept
    us away,
the torrent would have gone over
    us;—

over us would have gone the
    raging waters.

Blessed be God who did not give
    us
a prey to its teeth!
We have escaped like a bird
from the snare of the fowler;
indeed the snare is broken,
and we have escaped.

Our help is in the name of the
    Most High,
who made heaven and earth.
    Glory*...

Ant. 3 O God, you chose us in Jesus to be your children.

Cant: Ephesians 1:3–10

Praised be the God
of our Lord Jesus Christ,
who has blessed us in Christ
with every spiritual blessing in
    the heavens.

God chose us in him
before the foundation of the
    world,
that we should be holy
and blameless in God's sight.

We have been predestined
to be God's children through
    Jesus Christ,
such was the purpose of God's
    will,
that all might praise the glorious
    favor
bestowed on us in Christ.

In Christ and through his blood,
we have redemption,—

the forgiveness of our sins,
according to the riches of God's
  grace lavished upon us.

For God has made known to us
in all wisdom and insight,—

the mystery of the plan set forth
  in Christ.

A plan to be carried out in Christ,
in the fullness of time,
to unite all things in Christ,
things in heaven and things on
  earth. **Glory*...**

READING

What is that sweetness that is accustomed to touch me from time to
time and affects me so strongly and deliciously that I begin in a way to
be completely taken out of myself, and to be carried away I know not
where? All at once I am renewed and entirely changed; I begin to feel
well in a way that lies beyond description. Consciousness is lifted on
high, and all the misery of past misfortunes is forgotten. The intellectual
soul rejoices; the understanding is strengthened, the heart is
enlightened, the desires satisfied. I already see myself in a different
place that I do not know. I hold something within love's embrace, but I
do not know what it is. (Hugh of St. Victor)

Meister Eckhart, p. 139, (1)

RESPONSORY

Your mercy, O God, calls us to mercy. **—Your mercy...**
It manifests your greatness; **—and calls...**
Glory to you, Source of all Being, Eternal Word and Holy Spirit.
  —Your mercy...

CANTICLE OF MARY

Ant. Your regard has blessed me, O God.

INTERCESSIONS

In you, O God, resides all creative energy, and we receive our lives
from you;
    —inspire us with great desires, and let our hope be larger
      than our doubt.
We are a wounded people, afflicted by sin and ignorance;
    —guide and protect our police and all who are missioned
      to protect us; arm them with wisdom and compassion.
Jesus, for you and your people, hospitality was a sacred duty;
    —help us to transform our world into a place that is safe
      for mutual aid and neighborliness.

You were content to let weeds grow among wheat until harvest time;
—give us the patience to live with our own shortcomings and those of others.
Our days are often filled with interruptions;
—teach us how to reap the good fruit of patience from these times.

PRAYER: God our Creator, you have called us by name; we belong to you. Help us to believe in your truth, hope in your mercy, and love all people as you call us to love. Let our lives give joy to you and encouragement to one another. May our efforts to live in love give you praise this night and every day of our lives through all eternity. Amen.

TUESDAY
MORNING PRAYER

Ant. 1 O God, forgive the sins of your people.
Psalm 85

O God, once you favored your land,
restoring the fortunes of Rachel and Jacob.
You forgave the guilt of your people;
you pardoned all their sins.
You withdrew your wrath;
you calmed the heat of your anger.

Restore us again,
O God our salvation,
put away your grievance against us!
Will you be angry with us forever,
Will you prolong it to all generations?

Will you not restore us again,
that your people may rejoice in you?—

Show us your steadfast love,
and grant us your salvation.

Let me hear what you have to say,
for you will speak peace to your people,
to those who are near you,
and who turn to you in their hearts.
Your salvation is near for those who fear you,
that glory may dwell in our land.

Mercy and truth have embraced;
justice and peace will kiss.
Truth shall spring out of the earth,
and justice will look down from heaven.

You will give what is good,
our land will yield its increase.
Justice shall go before you
and make a path for your steps.
Glory*...

Ant. 2 O God, grant peace to all peoples.

Cant: Isaiah 26:1b–4, 7–9, 12

A strong city have we, O God;
you set up salvation
like walls and ramparts.
Open the gates
that the nation which keeps faith
may enter in.

You keep those in perfect peace,
whose minds are fixed on you,
because they trust in you,
trust in you forever.
For you are our God,
an everlasting Rock.

The way of the just is level;
you make smooth the path of the
    just.
In the path of your judgments,
we wait for you;
your name remembered from of
    old,
is the desire of our souls.

My soul yearns for you in the
    night,
my spirit within me keeps vigil;
when your judgments abide in the
    earth,
the inhabitants of the world learn
    justice.

O God, you ordain peace for all
    people,
you accomplish all our works.
    Glory*...

Ant. 3 In the light of your face there is life, O God.

Psalm 67

O God, be gracious to us and bless
    us
and make your face shine upon
    us.
That your ways be known upon
    earth,
your saving power among all
    nations.
Let the peoples praise you, O God;
let all the peoples praise you.

Let the nations be glad and sing
    for joy,
for you judge the peoples with
    equity
and guide the nations on earth.
Let the peoples praise you, O God;
let all the peoples praise you.

The earth has yielded its increase;
God, our God, has blessed us.
You, indeed, have blessed us;
let all the earth revere you!
    Glory*...

READING

Considering the mystical body of the Church, I had not recognized
myself in any of the members...or rather I desired to see myself in
them *all*. *Charity* gave me the key to my *vocation*. I understood that if
the Church had a body composed of different members, the most
necessary and most noble of all could not be lacking to it, and so I
understood that the Church *had a Heart and that this Heart was
BURNING WITH LOVE. I understood it was Love alone* that made the
Church's members act, that if *Love* ever became extinct, apostles
would not preach the Gospel and martyrs would not shed their blood. I

understood that LOVE COMPRISED ALL VOCATIONS, THAT LOVE
WAS EVERYTHING, THAT IT EMBRACED ALL TIMES AND
PLACES....IN A WORD, THAT IT WAS ETERNAL! Then, in the excess of
my delirious joy, I cried out: O Jesus, my Love...my *vocation*, at last I
have found it...MY VOCATION IS LOVE!

Thérèse of Lisieux, *Story of a Soul*, p. 194, (3)

RESPONSORY

It is good to give thanks to you and sing praise to your name.
—It is good...
At the works of your hands I shout for joy, **—and sing...**
Glory to you, Source of all Being, Eternal Word and Holy Spirit.
—It is good...

CANTICLE OF ZECHARIAH

**Ant. I will praise you from the rising of the sun to its going
down.**

INTERCESSIONS

O God, you have blessed humankind with understanding,
imagination and memory;
>—show us how to learn from the past and to plan for the
>future.

The gifts of the earth are distributed unevenly, and we long to lift
up those in need;
>—soften the hearts of those who place personal or national
>gain above the good of the whole.

Jesus, you have gifted us with the revelation of God's love;
>—let your love bear abundant fruit in our lives.

You preached to the crowds, inviting them to sit on grassy
hillsides;
>—open our eyes to the beauty of our world, and make us
>understand the need to protect our environment.

Spirit of God, life-giving presence to every person;
>—make your compassion and love known to those who
>suffer abuse, torture, and sub-human conditions.

PRAYER: Giver of hope, we begin a new day confident that you
come to us in all circumstances and make all things
work for the fulfillment of your purposes. We praise

you for your wonderful works through Christ who has shown us the way. Amen.

DAYTIME PRAYER

Ant. 1 I will ponder your law within my heart.

Psalm 119:97–104

How I love your law, O God!
It is my meditation all the day.
Your commandment makes me
  wiser than the learned,
for it is ever with me.

I have more understanding than
  all my teachers,
for your will is my meditation.
I have more understanding than
  the aged,
for I keep your precepts.

I turn my feet from evil ways,
to obey your word.
I turn not aside from your decrees,
for you, yourself, have taught me.

How sweet are your words to my
  taste,
sweeter than honey to my mouth!
Through your precepts I gain
  understanding;
therefore I hate every false way.
  Glory*...

Ant. 2 Restore your dwelling place within us.

Psalm 74

Why have you cast us off forever?
Why blaze with anger against the
  sheep of your pasture?
Remember your people whom you
  chose from of old,—

which you redeemed as your
  heritage!
Remember Mount Zion where you
  made your dwelling.

Direct your steps to the eternal
  ruins,
everything destroyed in your
  sanctuary!
Evil has roared in your house of
  prayer,
setting up its signs for symbols.

At the upper entrance they hacked
the wooden trellis with axes.
With hatchets and hammers,
broke down its carved wood.
The sanctuary they set on fire,
desecrating the place where you
  dwell.

They said to themselves, "We will
  utterly crush them;"
and burned all the shrines in the
  land.
We do not see our signs any more;
there is no longer a prophet,
no one knows how long it will last.

How long, O God, is evil to
  conquer?
Is your name to be scoffed forever?
Why do you hold back your hand,
Why do you keep your hand
  concealed?

Yet you are our ruler from of old,
working salvation in the midst of
  the earth. **Glory*...**

Ant. 3 Yours is the day, yours is the night; all things are in your hands.

II

It was you who divided the sea by your might,
who shattered the heads of the monsters in the sea.

You crushed the heads of Leviathan,
and gave them as food to the creatures of the wilderness.
You split open springs and brooks;
dried up the ever-flowing streams.

Yours is the day and yours is the night;
you fixed the stars and the sun.
You established all the bounds of earth;
you made both summer and winter.

Remember then, how evil scoffs,
and how your name is reviled.
Do not deliver your dove to the hawk:
do not forget the lives of your poor.

Remember your covenant of old;
for violence dwells in every corner of the land.
Let not the downtrodden be put to shame;
let the poor and the needy bless your name.

Arise, O God, defend your cause!
Remember how you are reviled all the day.
Quiet those who clamor against you,
who clamor against you day after day. **Glory*...**

PRAYER: God of love, you gave us this universe filled with your gifts. Help us to reverence all of your creation, respecting the rights of all species, and the integrity of the elements. Teach us to realize in our hearts as well as in our minds that we praise you when we use your gifts as you meant them to be used. May we unite with all suffering creation in the struggle for liberation from all that seeks to destroy. Grant this that all creation may live with you for all eternity. Amen.

EVENING PRAYER

Ant. 1 You are round about your people, both now and forever.

Psalm 125

Those who put their trust in you are like Mount Zion;
it cannot be moved, but stands forever.

As the mountains are round about Jerusalem,
so are you round about your people,
both now and forever.

For the scepter of wickedness shall not rest
over the land of the just,—

lest the just put forth their hands
to turn to evil ways.

Do good, O God, to those who are
  good,
to those who are upright of heart!
But those who turn to evil ways,
will be chastised and punished!

On Israel, peace! **Glory*...**

**Ant. 2 Blessed are those who are
  pure of heart.**

Psalm 131

O God, my heart is not lifted up,
my eyes are not raised too high;
I have not occupied myself
with marvels beyond me.

I have calmed and quieted my
  soul,
like a child at its mother's breast;
like a child in its father's arms,
even so my soul.

O Israel, hope in your God
both now and forever.
  Glory*....

**Ant. 3 Let all creation serve you,
  for you created all things.**

Cant: Rev 4:11, 5:9, 10, 12

Worthy are you, O God, our God,
to receive glory and honor and
  power.

For you have created all things;
by your will they came to be and
  were made.

Worthy are you to take the scroll
  and to open its seals,

For you were slain, and by your
  blood,
you purchased for God
saints of every race and tongue,
of every people and nation.

You have made of them a kindom,
and priests to serve our God,
and they shall reign on the earth.

Worthy is the Lamb who was slain
to receive power and riches,
wisdom and strength,
honor and glory and praise.
  Glory*...

READING

Happy, indeed, is [the one] to whom it is given to share this sacred
banquet, to cling with all her heart to [God] whose beauty all the
heavenly hosts admire unceasingly, whose love inflames our love, whose
contemplation is our refreshment, whose graciousness is our joy, whose
gentleness fills us to overflowing, whose remembrance brings a gentle
light, whose fragrance will revive the dead, whose glorious vision will be
the happiness of all the citizens of the heavenly Jerusalem.

Clare of Assisi, *Francis and Clare*, p. 204, (1)

RESPONSORY

Teach us to number our days that we may gain wisdom
  of heart.—**Teach us...**
Let your works be manifest to your servants; —**that we...**

Glory to you, Source of all Being, Eternal Word and Holy Spirit.
—**Teach us...**

CANTICLE OF MARY

Ant. You who are mighty have done great things for me.

INTERCESSIONS

O God, the wonders of communication have made our world smaller but more complex;
>   —bless the United Nations with wise and magnanimous
>   leaders.

Jesus, you teach us of the realm of God with wonderful and effective images;
>   —inspire teachers and writers with the creativity they need
>   to expand our minds and hearts.

Ask, knock, seek is your invitation to us to take our needs to God;
>   —make us quick to respond to the needs of those who ask;
>   make us aware of those so needy they cannot ask.

Spirit of God, you take flesh in us and for us;
>   —keep us open to all who inspire us to grow; prophets,
>   athletes, philosophers, artists, and all who serve us in
>   your name.

Time is your gift to us, O God; let us not take it for granted;
>   —show us efficient ways to use and share it.

PRAYER: O God, you are both mother and father to us. Help us to reverence all people with whom we share such great love, and show us the way to peace in our world. We ask this as your children through Jesus, our brother. Amen.

WEDNESDAY

MORNING PRAYER

Ant 1 Gladden my soul, O God; for to you I lift up my heart.

Psalm 86

Incline your ear and give answer,
for I am poor and needy.
Preserve my life, for I am
   faithful:—

save the servant who trusts in
   you.

You are my God, have mercy on
   me,
for to you I cry all the day.
Gladden the soul of your servant,
for to you I lift up my soul.

O God, you are good and
　forgiving,
abounding in love to all who call.
Give ear to my prayer;
hearken to my supplication.
In the day of my trouble I call on
　you,
for you will answer me.

There is none like you among the
　gods,
nor works to compare with yours.
All the nations you made
shall come and bow down,
shall glorify your name.
For you are great and do
　wondrous things,
you alone are God.

Teach me your way, O God,
that I may walk in your truth;
cause my heart to fear your
　name.
I give thanks to you with all my
　heart,
and glorify your name forever.
For great toward me is your love;
you deliver my soul from the
　grave.

Pride has risen against me;
corruption pursues my life,
evil pays you no heed.
But you are merciful and
　gracious,
slow to anger, abounding in love.

Turn to me and take pity;
give strength to your servant,
and save your handmaid's child.
Show me a sign of your favor;
let injustice be put to shame,
help me and give me your
　comfort. **Glory*...**

**Ant. 2 Blessed are the just, who
speak the truth.**

Cant: Isaiah 33:13–16

Hear, you who are far off,
what I have done;
you who are near,
acknowledge my might.

The sinners in Zion are afraid;
trembling grips the impious;
"Who of us can live with the
　devouring fire?
Who of us can live with the
　everlasting flames?"

Those who walk justly and speak
　honestly,
who spurn what is gained by
　oppression,
who shake their hands,
free of contact with a bribe;
who stop their ears,
lest they hear of bloodshed,
who close their eyes,
lest they look on evil.

They shall dwell on the heights;
their place of refuge
shall be the rocky fortress;
their food will be given,
their water will be sure.
　Glory*...

**Ant. 3 Let us sing a joyful song
in the presence of our God.**

Psalm 98

We sing to you a new song,
for you have done wonderful
　things!
Your saving hand and your holy
　arm
have given the victory.

You have made known your salvation;
have revealed your justice to the nations.
You have remembered your love and your faithfulness
for the house of Israel.
All the ends of the earth have seen
the salvation of our God.

Make a joyful noise, all the earth;
break forth into joyous song!
Sing praise to God with the harp,
with the lyre and the sound of music!—

With trumpets and the sound of the horn
make a joyful noise to our God.

Let the sea roar and all that fills it;
the world and those who dwell in it!
Let the rivers clap their hands;
and the hills ring out their joy.

All creation sings before God
who comes to judge the earth.
God will judge the world with justice
and the peoples with equity.
Glory.

READING

Rahner asserts that to speak of the human is to speak of the divine and vice versa. He describes God as the mystery in human experience. For him, then, God is the depth dimension in experiences such as solitude, friendship, community, death, hope and, as such, is the orientation toward the future. Rahner goes so far as to say that loneliness, disappointments and the ingratitude of others can be graced moments because they open us to the transcendent. The silence of God, the toughness of life and the darkness of death can be graced events. This mystery of grace discloses itself as a forgiving nearness, a hidden closeness, our real home, a love which shares itself, something familiar which we can turn to from the alienation of our own empty and perilous lives. When we are in touch with ourselves authentically, we experience God.

Annice Callahan, RSCJ, *Traditions of Spiritual Guidance,* p. 341, (32)

RESPONSORY

Satisfy us in the morning with your steadfast love, that we may rejoice and be glad all our days. —**Satisfy us...**
Let the favor of God be upon us; —**that we...**
Glory to you, Source of all Being, Eternal Word and Holy Spirit. —**Satisfy us...**

CANTICLE OF ZECHARIAH

Ant. Remember the mercy you promised long ago.

INTERCESSIONS

Jesus, you preached a kindom not of this world, but you were ever mindful to provide food for your followers;
> —grant success to those who draw food from our waters and fields; keep them safe and their methods environmentally sound.

You blessed little children and warned us against misleading them;
> —give wisdom to those who become parents while they are still children themselves.

O God, you call us all to unity through Jesus;
> —show yourself to those who are estranged from one another, and bridge their differences with the fire of your love.

Jesus, you frowned upon the ambitions of your apostles;
> —let our ambition and goal be to offer you a life of love and dedicated service as we care for one another.

Bless the ministers of your church;
> —guide them to serve as you have served.

PRAYER: God of unity and peace, may the gift of your life within us show itself in concrete ways so that we may make clear with our lives the good news of Jesus Christ. Especially today we pray for all the children of this world, that they may know your love and the hope of peace on earth. Grant this prayer that all may know the gift you gave in Jesus. Amen.

DAYTIME PRAYER

Ant. 1 Your Word is the true light that enlightens all who come into the world.

Psalm 119:105–112

O God, your word is a lamp to my feet
and a light for my path.
I have sworn an oath and confirmed it
to observe your commandments.

I am sorely afflicted:
give me life according to your word!
Accept my offerings of praise,
and teach me your decrees.

Though I hold my life in my hands,
I do not forget your law.
Though the wicked try to ensnare me,
I do not stray from your precepts.

Your will is my heritage forever,
the joy of my heart.
I incline my heart to carry out
 your will forever, to endless
 ages. **Glory*...**

**Ant. 2 Hear my prayer and
 hasten to help me.**
Psalm 70

Be pleased, O God, to save me!
O God, make haste to help me!
Fill me with shame and confusion
if I turn away from life!

O let me turn back in confusion,
when I delight in wrongdoing!
Let me retreat in my shame,
when I trifle with evil.

May all who seek you
rejoice and be glad!
May those who love your
 salvation
proclaim, "Our God is great!"

But I am poor and needy;
hasten to me, O God!
You are my help, my deliverer;
O God, do not delay. **Glory*...**

**Ant. 3 You know the hearts of
 all; your judgment is right and
 true.**
Psalm 75

We give thanks to you, O God;—

we give you thanks;
we call on your name
and recount your wondrous
 deeds.

"At the time which I appoint
I will judge with equity.
When the earth totters,
and all its inhabitants,
it is I who steady its pillars.

To the boastful I say: 'Do not
 boast,'
to the wicked, 'Do not flaunt your
 strength,
do not flaunt your strength on
 high,
or speak with insolent pride.'"

For not from the east or from the
 west,
or from the wilderness comes
 judgment,
but you, O God, are the judge,
putting down one, lifting up
 another.

But I will rejoice forever,
I will sing praises to you on high.
You shall break the power of
 wickedness,
while the strength of the just
 shall be exalted. **Glory*...**

PRAYER: O God, you both comfort us and disturb our
complacency through your Spirit. May we recognize
the blind, the lame and the prisoner in the
circumstances of our lives, and understand our
call to proclaim the good news to the poor. We
ask this through Jesus who is our way, our truth,
and our life. Amen.

EVENING PRAYER

Ant. 1 You will not reject me; you will fill my mouth with laughter.

Psalm 126

When God restored the fortunes
   of Zion,
it seemed like a dream.
Then our mouth was filled with
   laughter,
and our tongue with shouts of
   joy;

Then they said among the
   nations,
"God has done great things for
   them."
You have done great things for
   us!
Indeed we are glad.

Restore our fortunes, O God,
like the streams in the desert!
May those who sow in tears
reap with shouts of joy!

They that go forth weeping,
bearing seed for the sowing,
shall come home with shouts of
   joy,
bringing their sheaves with them.
   Glory*...

Ant. 2 Wisdom has built herself a house!

Psalm 127

If God does not build the house,
its builders labor in vain.
If God does not watch over the
   city,
in vain is the vigil kept.

It is vain to rise up early
and go late to rest,
eating the bread of anxious toil:—

for you, O God, give sleep to your
   beloved.

Truly children are a gift from the
   Most High,
the fruit of the womb, a blessing.
Like arrows in the hand of a
   warrior
are the children of one's youth.

Happy the couple who have their
   quiver full of them!
They shall not be put to shame
when they encounter distress.
   Glory*...

Ant. 3 Jesus is the image of the invisible God.

Cant: Colossians 1:12–20

Let us give thanks to God
for having made us worthy
to share the inheritance of the
   saints in light.

God has delivered us
from the power of darkness
and transferred us
into the kindom of God's beloved
   Son, Jesus,
in whom we have redemption,
the forgiveness of our sins.

Jesus is the image of the invisible
   God,
the first-born of all creation;
in him all things were created,
in heaven and on earth,
things visible and invisible.

All things were created through
   him;
all were created for him.
He is before all else that is.
In him all things hold together.

He is the head of the body, the church!
He is the beginning,
the firstborn from the dead,
that in everything, he might be above all others.

In him all the fullness of God was pleased to dwell,
and, through him, to reconcile all things to himself,
whether on earth or in heaven,
making peace by the blood of his cross. **Glory*...**

READING

...These things that come home to us and hurt our self-love and humble us in the dust, these are some of God's best graces, full of promise, and never think that you are at the end of them. There will come more revelations ever more humbling, ever more intimate and ever more true. But never let them cast you down. Remember that they are birthdays, the putting away of the things of a child. And your vocation beaten by storms, will come out all the truer. (Janet Erskine Stuart, RSCJ)

Maud Monahan, *Life and Letters of Janet Erskine Stuart*, p. 499, (15)

RESPONSORY

You will cover us with your pinions, and under your wings we will find refuge. **—You will...**
We will not fear the terror of the night; **—and under...**
Glory to you, Source of all Being, Eternal Word and Holy Spirit. **—You will...**

CANTICLE OF MARY

Ant. Holy is the name of our God.

INTERCESSIONS

Jesus, you knew a laborer's day;
—bless those who live by the work of their hands; help all to find the employment they need.
The world still longs for the peace that only you can give;
—guard and protect those whose work is to keep the peace in lands torn by war and revolution.
In your kindom the last shall be first and the first last;
—encourage and liberate minorities, those whose lot is mostly last.
Enlighten and encourage those committed to you in religious vocations;
—let their lives reflect their calling.

Have mercy on all who are touched by the drug epidemic in our world;
> —lead them to freedom through the good news enfleshed in those who reach out to them.

PRAYER: Jesus, light of the world, for the many who have followed you today through the darkness of temptation, doubt, or pain, you are the promise of an eternal dawn. We give thanks for all that has been given to us through you, and we ask for the grace to be your faithful disciples. May we praise you all the days of our lives. Amen.

THURSDAY

MORNING PRAYER

Ant. 1 Blessed are those who delight in your law, O God.

Psalm 1

Blessed are those who walk not in
 the counsel of the wicked,
nor stand in the way of sinners,
nor sit with those who scoff;
but delight in your law, O God,
pondering it day and night.

They are like a tree
planted by streams of water,
that yields its fruit in due season,
and whose leaves never fade.
May they prosper in all they do.

It is not so with wickedness.
Like chaff the wind drives it away.
Evil cannot stand before you,
nor injustice before your face.

For you guide the path of the
 faithful,
but renounce the way of
 oppression. **Glory*...**

Ant. 2 God will come with justice for all the people.

Cant: Isaiah 40:10–17

Behold, you come with power,
O God, the Almighty,
ruling with your strong arm;
behold, your reward is with you,
and your recompense before you.

You will feed your flock like a
 shepherd,
you will gather the lambs in your
 arms,
carrying them in your bosom,
gently leading the ewes with
 young.

Who else had measured the waters
in the hollows of their hands,
and marked off the heavens with a
 span,
enclosed the dust of the earth in a
 measure
weighed the mountains in scales
and the hills in a balance?

Who has directed your spirit,
or who has been your
 counselor?—

Whom did you consult for
enlightenment,
who taught you the path of justice,
or showed you the way of
understanding?

Behold, the nations are like a drop
from a bucket,
accounted as dust on the scales;
you take up the isles like powder.

Lebanon would not suffice for fuel,
nor its beasts be enough for burnt
offering.
All the nations are as nothing
before you,
as nothing and void are they
accounted. **Glory*...**

**Ant. 3 We worship and give
praise to you, Most High.**

Psalm 99

O God, you reign on high;
let all the peoples tremble!
You are throned on the cherubim;
let the earth quake!
You are great in Zion.

You are exalted over all peoples.
Let them praise your name,—

awesome and great!
Holy are you over all!

Mighty Sovereign, lover of justice,
you have established equity;
you have ruled with justice.
We extol you, Most High God;
worshipping at your footstool!
You alone are holy.

Moses and Aaron were among
your priests,
among your petitioners, Judith
and Esther.
They invoked you, and you
answered.
You spoke to them in the pillar of
cloud;
they kept your will,
and the precepts that you gave
them.

O God, our God, you answered
them;
you were a forgiving God to them,
yet you punished their offenses.

We extol you, Most High God,
and worship on your holy
mountain;
for you alone are holy.
     Glory*...

READING

Let us look at our own shortcomings and leave other people's alone;
for those who live carefully ordered lives are apt to be shocked at
everything and we might well learn very important lessons from the
persons who shock us. Our outward comportment and behavior may
be better than theirs, but this, though good, is not the most important
thing; there is no reason why we should expect everyone else to travel
by our own road, and we should not attempt to point them to the
spiritual path when perhaps we do not know what it is.... It is better to
attempt to...live in silence and in hope, and [God] will take care of
[God's] own.

Teresa of Avila, *Interior Castle*, p. 229, (3)

RESPONSORY

No one who practices deceit shall dwell in your house.
   —No one...
They who walk in the way that is blameless **—shall dwell...**
Glory to you, Source of all Being, Eternal Word and Holy Spirit.
   —No one...

CANTICLE OF ZECHARIAH

Ant. Guide our feet, O God, into the way of peace.

INTERCESSIONS

O God, we praise you for the gift of faith and for all that our
baptism means to us;
   —help us to keep our commitment to you alive and active
      and to cherish and remember special moments of insight.
You answer our prayers and fulfill our needs;
   —make us aware of the needs of others and generous in
      ministering to them.
Jesus, you were called the carpenter's son, an attempt to
discredit you;
   —give us the grace we need to see one another in truth, to
      hold each other's heritage with reverence, and to realize
      that we are one in you.
Your disciples left all to follow you;
   —be praised in the missionaries who leave all that is
      familiar to them to give your message to the world.
You are resurrection and life to all who hope in you;
   —give courage and peace to those who await your coming.

PRAYER: O God, we are the work of your hands, and you have
               made us for communion with you and one another. As
               we begin the business of this day, we recall that you
               alone can fill our hearts. We ask to remain by love in
               your holy presence with Jesus who incarnated your
               presence among us. Amen.

DAYTIME PRAYER

Ant. 1 Sustain me, O God, according to your promise.

Psalm 119:113–120

I have no love for the half-hearted,
but I love your law.
You are my shelter, my shield;
I hope in your word.

Rid me of all that is evil,
that I may keep your
　commandments.
Uphold me according to your
　promise,
that I may live in your way,
let my hopes not be in vain!

Sustain me and I shall be safe
and ever observe your statutes.
Help me spurn all that is evil;
let its cunning be in vain!

You overthrow all that is wicked;
therefore I love your will.
I tremble before you in awe,
I am afraid of your judgments.
　Glory*...

Ant. 2 Rescue us, O God, for the sake of your name.

Psalm 79:1–5, 8–11, 13

O God, the nations have invaded
　our land,
they have defiled your holy temple;
Jerusalem is in ruins.
They have given the bodies of your
　servants
as food to the birds of the air,
and the flesh of your faithful
　to the beasts of the earth.

They have poured out blood like
　water round about Jerusalem,
no one is left to bury the dead.—

We have become the taunt of our
　neighbors,
mocked and derided by those
　round about us.

How long, O God? Will you be
　angry forever,
how long will your anger burn like
　fire?
Do not hold against us the guilt of
　our ancestors;
Let your compassion hasten to
　meet us;
for we are brought very low.

Help us, O God, our savior,
for the glory of your name;
deliver us, and forgive us our sins,
rescue us for the sake of your
　name.

Why should the nations say,
"Where is their God?"
Let us see oppression overthrown,
may justice come to Jerusalem!
Let the groans of the prisoners
　come before you;
let your strong arm preserve those
　condemned to die!

Then we your people, the flock of
　your pasture,
will give you thanks for ever;
from generation to generation
we will recount your praise.
　Glory*...

Ant. 3 O God, you are the vinedresser; prune the vine that it may bear fruit.

Psalm 80

Give ear, O Shepherd of Israel,
you who lead Joseph like a flock!
You who are enthroned upon the
　cherubim,—

shine forth before Ephraim,
Benjamin and Manasseh!
Stir up your might and come to
save us!

Restore us, God of hosts;
let your face shine, that we may be
saved.
God of hosts, how long will you be
angry
with your people's prayers?
You fed them with the bread of
tears,
and gave them tears to drink in
full measure.
You made us the scorn of our
neighbors,
our enemies laugh among
themselves.

Restore us, God of hosts;
let your face shine, that we may be
saved.

You brought a vine out of Egypt;
you drove out the nations to plant
it.
You cleared the ground before it;
it took root and filled the land.

The mountains were covered with
its shade,—

the mighty cedars with its
branches;
it sent out its branches to the sea,
and its roots to the Great River.

Then why have you broken down
its walls?
so that all who pass by pluck its
fruit?
It is ravaged by the boar of the
forest,
devoured by the beasts of the field.

Turn again, O God of hosts!
Look down from heaven, and see;
have regard for this vine,
the vine your own hand has
planted.
It has been burnt with fire and cut
down.

Let your hand be on those you
have chosen,
those you make strong for
yourself!
Then we will never forsake you;
give us life, and we will call on
your name.

Restore us, God of hosts!
let your face shine, that we may be
saved. **Glory*...**

PRAYER: Renew in our hearts, O God, the gift of your Holy
Spirit, so that we may love you fully in all that we do
and love one another as Christ loves us. May all that
we do proclaim the good news that you are God with
us. Amen.

EVENING PRAYER

**Ant. 1 Let us enter your courts
with shouts of praise.**

Psalm 132

O God, remember David,—

all the many hardships he
endured;
the oath he swore to you,
his vow to the Strong One of
Jacob.

"I will not enter my house or get
  into my bed;
I will give no sleep to my eyes,
or slumber to my eyelids,
till I find a place for my God,
a dwelling for the Strong One of
  Jacob."

We heard of it in Ephratah,
we found the ark in the fields of
  Jaar.
"Let us go to the place of God's
  dwelling;
let us worship at God's footstool."

Go up, O God, to the place of your
  rest,
you and the ark of your might.
Let your priests be clothed with
  justice,
and your faithful shout for joy.
For the sake of David your servant
do not reject your anointed.
    Glory*...

Ant. 2 You, O God, have chosen Zion as your dwelling place.
II

You swore an oath to David;
from which you will not turn back:
"A son, the fruit of your body,
I will set upon your throne.

If your offspring keep my covenant
  in truth,
and my laws which I shall teach
  them,
their descendants also forever
shall sit upon your throne."

For you have chosen Zion;
you desired it for your dwelling:
"This is my resting place forever;
here I have desired to dwell.

I will abundantly bless its
  provisions;—

I will satisfy its poor with bread.
I will clothe its priests with
  salvation
and its faithful will shout for joy.

There David's stock will flower:
I will prepare a lamp for my
  anointed.
Treacherous plots will be put to
  shame,
but on him my crown shall shine."
    Glory*...

Ant. 3 The glory of God is the light of the city and its lamp is the Lamb.
Cant: Rev 11:17–18; 12:10b–12a

We praise you, God Almighty,
who is and who was.
You have assumed your great
  power,
you have begun your reign.

The nations have raged in anger,
but then came your day of wrath
and the moment to judge the
  dead;
the time to reward your servants
  the prophets
and the holy ones who revere you,
the great and the small alike.

Now have salvation and power
  come,
your reign, O God, and the
  authority of your Anointed One.
For the accusers of our loved ones
  have been cast out,
who night and day accused them.

By the blood of the Lamb have
  they been defeated,
and by the testimony of your
  servants;
love for life did not deter them
  from death.—

So rejoice, you heavens,
and you that dwell therein!
   Glory*...

READING

As long as persons are constrained to wait for a time when the creative
spirit will inspire them, and then they will create, meditate, sing—this is
an indication that their souls have not yet been illuminated. Surely the
soul sings always. It is robed in might and joy, it is surrounded by a
noble delight, and persons must raise themselves to the height of
confronting the soul, of recognizing its spiritual imprints, the rushing of
its wings that abound in the majesty of the holy of holies, and...always
be ready to listen to the secret of its holy discourse. Then they will know
that it is not at one time rather than another, on one occasion rather
than another, that the soul engenders in us new thrusts of wisdom and
thought, song and holy meditation. At all times, in every hour, it
releases streams of precious gifts. And the streams that flow from it are
holy treasures, fountains of understanding, stored with good sense.
God's compassions are new each morning, great is God's faithfulness.

Abraham Isaac Kook, *Lights of Holiness*, p. 214, (1)

RESPONSORY

How great are your works, O God. Your thoughts are very deep.
   —How great...
The dull of heart will never know. **—Your thoughts**
Glory to you, Source of all Being, Eternal Word and Holy Spirit.
   —How great...

CANTICLE OF MARY

Ant. Your mercy endures through all generations.

INTERCESSIONS

Jesus, you invited Peter to follow you in ways beyond his courage;
   —increase our faith, that we may be ready and willing
      instruments of your love.
You caution us over and over again to stay awake, to be on guard;
   —give us the gift of discernment; help us to live consciously,
      learning from the past as we plan for the future.
O God, bless those whom you call to the single life;
   —let their commitment to the gospel be a joy to you,
      enrichment for them, and a service to others that mirrors
      your Christ.

O God, give us a desire for true and lasting values;
  —let our faith in you inform all that we are and do.
Spirit of God, you bring both peace and fire to our hearts;
  —teach us how to challenge and affirm one another in a
    spirit of harmony.

PRAYER: Most gentle God, you have fed us this day with your
holy Word and life-giving Bread. May we continue to
discern your calls in life, family, community and in the
movements of our hearts. May we always be among
those who worship you in spirit and in truth. We ask
this through the intercession of all those who gave their
lives that others may have bread and a better quality of
life. Amen.

FRIDAY

MORNING PRAYER

**Ant 1 A humble, contrite heart,
O God, you will not despise.**

Psalm 51

Have mercy on me, O God,
according to your steadfast love;
in your abundant mercy blot out
  my sins.
Wash me thoroughly from my
  offenses,
and cleanse me from my sin!

For I know my offenses,
and my sin is ever before me.
Against you, you alone, have I
  sinned,
and done what is evil in your
  sight,
so you are justified in your
  sentence
and blameless in your judgment.
Behold, I was brought forth in a
  sinful world.

For you desire truth in my
  innermost being;—

teach me wisdom in the depths of
  my heart.
O purify me, and I shall be clean;
O wash me, I shall be whiter than
  snow.
Fill me with joy and gladness;
let the bones you have broken
  rejoice.
Hide your face from my guilt,
and blot out all my offenses.

Create in me a clean heart,
put a steadfast spirit within me.
Cast me not from your presence,
take not your spirit from me.
Give me again the joy of your
  salvation,
with a willing spirit uphold me.

Then I will teach transgressors
  your ways
and sinners will return to you.
Deliver me from death,
O God of my salvation,
and my tongue will sing out your
  saving help.

Open my lips and my mouth will
  sing your praises.
For you take no delight in
  sacrifice;
were I to give a burnt offering,
you would not be pleased.
A broken spirit you accept;
a contrite heart, you will not
  despise.

In your goodness, show favor to
  Zion;
rebuild the walls of Jerusalem.
Then you will delight in just
  sacrifices,
in gifts offered on your altar.
    Glory*...

**Ant. 2 You bring us to springs
  of water; you will wipe away
  every tear from our eyes.**

Cant: Jeremiah 14:17–21

Let my eyes stream with tears
night and day, without rest,
for the virgin daughter of my
  people
is smitten with a great wound,
with a very grievous blow.

If I walk out into the field,
behold those slain by the sword!
If I enter the city,
behold the diseases of famine!
Both the prophet and the priest
ply their trade throughout the
  land,
ignorant of their doings.

Have you utterly rejected Judah?
Is Zion loathsome to you?
Why have you smitten us—
so that there is no healing?

We looked for peace to no avail;
for a time of healing,
but terror comes instead.
We acknowledge our wickedness,
and the guilt of our ancestors,
for we have sinned against you.

Spurn us not for your name's
  sake;
do not dishonor your glorious
  throne;
remember your covenant with us,
and break it not.   **Glory*...**

**Ant. 3 We are your people, the
  sheep of your pasture.**

Psalm 100

All the earth cries out to you with
  shouts of joy, O God,
Serving you with gladness;
coming before you, singing for
  joy.

You, Creator of all, are God.
You made us, we belong to you,
we are your people, the sheep of
  your pasture.

We enter your gates with
  thanksgiving,
and your courts with songs of
  praise!
We give you thanks and bless
  your name.

Indeed, how good you are,
enduring, your steadfast love.
You are faithful to all generations.
    Glory*...

READING

I went into the garden before Prime, and, sitting down beside the pool, I
began to consider what a pleasant place it was. I was charmed by the
clear water and flowing streams, the fresh green of the surrounding

trees, the birds flying about, especially the doves. But most of all, I loved the quiet, hidden peace of this secluded retreat. I asked myself what more was needed to complete my happiness in a place that seemed to me so perfect, and I reflected that it was the presence of a friend, intimate, affectionate, wise, and companionable to share my solitude. And then you, my God, source of ineffable delights, who, as I believe, did but inspire the beginning of this meditation to lead it back to yourself, made me understand that, if I were to pour back like water the stream of graces received from you in that continual gratitude I owe you; if, like a tree, growing in the exercise of virtue, I were to cover myself with the leaves and blossoms of good works; if, like the doves I were to spurn earth and soar heavenward; and if, with my senses set free from passions and worldly distractions, I were to occupy myself with you alone; then my heart would afford you a dwelling most suitably appointed from which no joy would be lacking.

Gertrude of Helfta, The Herald of Divine Love, p. 97, (1)

RESPONSORY

Return, O God! How long? Have pity on your servants. —**Return...**
Satisfy us in the morning with your steadfast love. —**Have...**
Glory to you, Source of all Being, Eternal Word and Holy Spirit.
    —**Return...**

CANTICLE OF ZECHARIAH

Ant. Give light to those in darkness and the shadow of death.

INTERCESSIONS

O God, a humble heart is more pleasing to you than sacrifice;
    —lift up all who are humiliated and despised because of
        their own faults or those of others.
Faith is your free gift to us, O God;
    —enlighten us with ways of sharing it with others.
O God, your love is eternal, and we fail you "seven times a day";
    —preserve us from measuring you by our own pettiness;
        never let fear keep us from turning to you.
Jesus, you have made yourself as available to us as bread;
    —help us to realize our need to live in your presence and to
        listen to the voice of your spirit in our hearts.
Spirit of God, love is your gift to us and the gift you desire from us;
    —receive our desire and poor efforts to offer you our lives
        this day.

PRAYER: Direct our activity this day, O merciful God, that we may reflect your goodness and love to our companions. Help us to be mindful of the many people who are oppressed, and may we be aware of the ways that we oppress others. We ask this in the name of Jesus who died to set us free. Amen.

DAYTIME PRAYER

Ant. 1 The servant of God was stricken; smitten by God, and afflicted.

Psalm 22

O God, my God, why have you forsaken me?
Why are you so far from helping me,
from the sound of my groaning?
I cry out by day, but you do not answer;
by night, but find no rest.

Yet you alone are holy,
enthroned on the praises of Israel.
In you our ancestors trusted;
they trusted and you delivered them.
To you they cried, and were saved;
In you they trusted,
and were not disappointed.

But I am a worm and not human,
scorned and despised by the people.
All who see me mock at me,
they curl their lips, they wag their heads;
"You trusted in God, let God save you;
let God rescue you
for God delights in you!"

Yet it was you who took me from the womb;
you kept me safe upon my mother's breasts.
Upon you was I cast from my birth,
since my mother's womb you have been my God.
Be not far from me in my distress;
there is no one else to help.
     Glory*...

Ant. 2 By oppression and judgment, the just one was cut off from the land of the living.

II

Many bulls encompass me,
strong bulls of Bashan surround me;
they open wide their mouths,
like a ravening and roaring lion.

I am poured out like water,
disjointed are all my bones;
my heart has become like wax,
melted within my breast;
my strength is dried up like burnt clay,
my tongue cleaves to my jaws;
you lay me in the dust of death.

Many dogs are round about me;
a band of evildoers encircles me;
they pierce my hands and my feet;—

I can count every one of my
   bones.
They stare and gloat over me;
they divide my garments among
   them,
for my raiment they cast lots.

But you, O God, be not far off!
O my help, hasten to my aid!
Deliver my soul from the sword,
my life from the grip of the dog!
Save me from the jaws of the lion,
my poor soul from the horns of
   the wild ox!

I will tell of your name to my
   kinsfolk
and praise you in the assembly.
   Glory*...

**Ant. 3 For a moment I hid my
   face, but I will have
   compassion on you.**
            III

You who fear God, give praise!
You descendants of Jacob, give
   glory!
Stand in awe, children of Israel!

For you, O God, have not
   despised
nor scorned the affliction of the
   poor;—

you have not hid your face from
   them,
but heard them when they cried
   to you.

To you comes praise from the
   great assembly;
my vows I will pay before those
   who fear you.
The poor shall eat and be
   satisfied;
those who seek you shall sing
   your praise!
May their hearts live forever and
   ever!

All the earth shall remember
and turn to you, O God;
all families of the nations
shall worship before you.
For sovereignty belongs to you;
you rule over the nations.

All the mighty of the earth
bow down before you;
before you shall bow
all who go down to the dust.

Posterity shall serve you;
They shall tell of you
to generations yet to come,
and proclaim your deliverance
to a people yet unborn:
"These things our God has done."
            Glory*...

PRAYER: Look upon us, most gracious God, as we gather at
   midday. Bless the work of our hands and hearts. May
   all peoples be blessed with the dignity of work, with an
   understanding of their gifts, and with generous spirits
   so that together we may further your reign among us.
   Help all who are unemployed and those who are
   disabled. May all know their worth and dignity. Grant
   this is Jesus' name. Amen.

EVENING PRAYER

Ant. 1 Our God is high above all other gods.

Psalm 135

We praise your name, O God,
all your servants give praise,
those who stand in your holy
house,
in the courts of your house, O
God!

We praise you, for you are good.
Sing to your name for you are
gracious!
For you have chosen Jacob for
yourself,
Israel as your own possession.

For I know that you are great,
that you are high above all gods.
You do whatever you please,
in heaven and on earth,
in the seas and all the deeps.

You summon clouds from the end
of the earth,
make lightning for the rain,
and bring forth wind from your
storehouse.

You smote the firstborn of Egypt,
both of human and beast alike.
Signs and wonders you worked
in the midst of the land of Egypt,
against Pharaoh and all his
servants.

You smote many nations
and slew mighty rulers,
Sihon, king of the Amorites,
Og, the king of Bashan,
and all the kingdoms of Canaan.
You gave their land as a heritage,
a heritage to your people.
     Glory*...

Ant. 2 You are the living God come down from heaven.
     II

O God, your name endures
forever,
your renown throughout all ages.
You will work justice for your
people,
and have compassion on your
servants.

The idols of the nations are silver
and gold,
the work of human hands.
They have eyes, but they cannot
see;
they have ears, but they cannot
hear;
nor is there any breath on their
lips.
Like them be those who make
them!
And everyone who trusts in them!

Descendants of Israel, bless our
God!
Descendants of Aaron, bless our
God!
Descendants of Levi, bless our
God!
You who fear, bless the Most
High!

Blessed are you from Zion, O
God,
you who dwell in Jerusalem!
     Glory*...

Ant. 3 Behold I make all things new!
     Cant: Rev 15:3–4

Great and wonderful are your
works,
God the Almighty One!—

Just and true are your ways,
Ruler of all the ages!

Who shall refuse you honor,
or the glory due your name?

For you alone are holy,
all nations shall come and
  worship in your presence.
Your judgments are clearly seen.
Glory*...

READING

On the one hand, Jeanne de Chantal's life appears as one of unfolding
potential, a life of a woman whose circumstance allowed her to gain the
fullness of her personal vision. While this is true, it is also true that the
backdrop behind this vocational scenario was the experience of great
personal loss. It should be remembered that this was a woman with
deep affection for those closest to her. Life did not spare her grief on
that account. The death of her adored husband was only one in a long
series of losses that were to cut cruelly through the fabric of her life....
To this sad history of loss must be added the experience of loss in the
interior life.... For most of her adult life she suffered from what she
called 'temptations', doubts of faith that merged into an intense
experience of inner pain and turbulence. But this constant interior
suffering was not reflected in her daily life. Her letters, the advice she
gave others, the reports of those nearest her suggest that this was a
hidden experience.

Wendy Wright, "Two Faces of Christ: Jeanne de Chantal," pp. 355–56, (7)

RESPONSORY

When the cares of my heart are many, your consolations cheer
  my soul. **—When the...**
You have become my stronghold; **—your...**
Glory to you, Source of all Being, Eternal Word and Holy Spirit.
  —When the...

CANTICLE OF MARY

Ant. Fill the hungry with bread of earth and bread of heaven.

INTERCESSIONS

You are our Creator, O God, and you know of what we are made;
  —have mercy on those who are forced to work beyond their
    strength or to bear their limit of suffering.
We thank and praise you for the talents you have given to those
who make our lives less burdensome by invention and more
delightful through art;
  —give them the grace to live balanced and holy lives.

The future is always a mystery to us; our lives are in your hands;
—grant us a childlike peace as we place our trust in you
   and do our best to serve you.
Jesus, you prayed for unity on the night before you died for us;
—heal us of our prejudices, and grant success to our efforts
   toward ecumenism.
You radiated the joy that is the sign of the Spirit;
—let our joy and good humor reveal your presence in our
   lives.

PRAYER: Most loving God, at evening's end we pray for all who
near the evening of their lives. Grant them your peace
and reconciliation with all who love them. May they
know the hope and joy that awaits them when they see
you face to face. This we ask through the intercession
of Joseph and of all who died in your embrace. Amen.

SATURDAY

MORNING PRAYER

Ant. 1 You are near at hand, O God, and all your ways are true.

Psalm 119: 145–152

With all my heart, I cry to you;
answer me, O God.
I cry to you; save me,
that I may observe your will.

I rise before dawn and cry for help;
I hope in your words.
My eyes watch throughout the
  night
meditating on your promises.

Hear my voice in your steadfast
  love;
in your justice preserve my life.
Those who persecute me draw
  near;
they are far from your law.

But you, O God, are near at hand,
all your commands are true.—

Long have I known that your will
endures forever.
Glory*...

Ant. 2 Give us your Spirit of Wisdom in all our affairs.

Cant: Wisdom 9:1–6, 9–11

God of our ancestors, God of
  mercy,
you who have made all things by
  your word
and in your wisdom have
  established us
to care for the creatures produced
  by you,
to govern the world in holiness
  and justice,
and to render judgment in
  integrity of heart.

Give us Wisdom, the attendant at
  your throne,—

and reject us not from among your children;
for we are your servants; weak and short-lived
and lacking in comprehension of judgment and of laws.
Indeed, though some be perfect among all the peoples of this earth,
if Wisdom, who comes from you, be not with them,
they shall be held in no esteem.

Now with you is Wisdom, who knows your works
and was present when you made the world;
who understands what is pleasing in your eyes
and what is conformable with your commands.

Send her forth from your holy heavens—
and from your glorious throne dispatch her
that she may be with us and work with us,
that we may know what is your pleasure.

For she knows and understands all things,
and will guide us discreetly in our affairs
and safeguard us by her glory.
Glory*....

Ant. 3 O God, your faithfulness endures forever.

Psalm 117

Praise our God, all you nations!
Acclaim the Most High, all you peoples!

For great is your love for us;
and your faithfulness endures forever. **Glory*...**

READING

Simplicity means that we live close enough to the limits of our resources so that we can rely on God's providence and appreciate the beauty of life. Simplicity fosters spontaneity, truthfulness, and clear speech. Simplicity also is required of anyone who seeks justice, peace, and equitable stewardship of resources. Simplicity is not a simple way to live. It requires serious reflection to sort out what is necessary and what is luxury. With all the pressures to buy this and have that, it is difficult to be satisfied with having just enough to be generous and caring. It is not simple to speak plainly and truthfully. We are tempted to equivocate, massage the truth, and manipulate our speech. Only conscious and consistent meditation, prayer, and examination can help us live the simplicity of Jesus.

     Audrey Gibson and Kieran Kneaves, *Praying with Louise de Marillac*, p. 84, (42)

RESPONSORY

I will give heed to the way that is blameless. When will you come to me? —**I will...**
I will walk with integrity of heart within my house. —**When...**

Glory to you, Source of all Being, Eternal Word and Holy Spirit.
    —I will...

CANTICLE OF ZECHARIAH

Ant. May we serve you in holiness all the days of our lives.

INTERCESSIONS

Jesus, you taught your followers the deepest lessons of life;
    —show us how to teach our children your ways of forgiveness,
        reverence for one another, and mutual support.
To all who would listen, you revealed God as a tender mother
and an understanding father;
    —teach us how to develop and balance the feminine and
        masculine aspects of our lives.
O God, our desires are boundless, but we are limited on every
side;
    —let the discipline of reality be a spur to our creativity.
Bless all children; let their school years be maturing and fruitful
ones for them;
    —inspire our teachers with ways to draw out the best in all.
You left your mother to follow the call of the Spirit;
    —be with those who must leave their families to find work
        in other countries.

PRAYER: You are a God of Wonder, Most Holy One, as you call
        us into being and set us free in your loving plan. Help
        us to grow in understanding the meaning of our
        freedom, so that we may discern wisely and respect
        the gift of freedom in all our sisters and brothers.
        Grant this through the intercession of all who have
        died that others may be free. Amen.

DAYTIME PRAYER

**Ant. 1 Deal with us according to
the greatness of your love.**

Psalm 119:121–128

I have done what is right and
    just:
let me not be oppressed.—

Guarantee the goodness of your
    servant
let not the proud oppress me.

My eyes grow weak watching for
    salvation,
and the fulfillment of your
    promise.—

Treat your servant according to
  the greatness of your love,
and teach me your statutes.

I am your servant; give me
  knowledge,
that I may know your will!
It is time for you to act, O God,
for your law has been broken.

Therefore I love your
  commandments
more than finest gold.
I guide my steps by your
  precepts:
I hate the ways of falsehood.
  Glory*...

**Ant. 2 Happy are those who
take refuge in you.**

Psalm 34

I will bless you, O God, at all
  times,
your praise always on my lips.
My soul makes its boast in you;
the afflicted shall hear and be
  glad.
Glorify our God with me.
Together let us praise God's
  name.

I sought you, and you answered
  me;
and delivered me from all my
  fears.
Look towards the Most High, and
  be radiant;
let your faces not be ashamed.
These poor ones cried; you heard
  them,
and saved them from all their
  troubles.

Your angel, O God, is encamped
  around those who revere you, to
  deliver them.—

Taste and see that God is good!
Happy are they who take refuge
  in you.

Revere the Most High, all you
  saints.
Those who revere you, have no
  want!
Young lions suffer want and
  hunger;
but those who seek you lack no
  blessing. **Glory*...**

**Ant. 3 Deliver the
brokenhearted from all their
troubles.**

II

Come children, listen to me,
I will teach you to reverence the
  Most High.
Who among you longs for life
and many days to enjoy
  prosperity?

Keep your tongue from evil,
your lips from speaking deceit.
Turn aside from evil and do good;
seek peace and pursue it.

God's eyes are turned to the
  righteous,
God's ears toward their cry.
God's face turns away from evil,
that it not be remembered on
  earth.

When the just cry, the Most High
  hears,
and delivers them from their
  troubles.
God is close to the
  brokenhearted;
saving those whose spirits are
  crushed.

Many are the afflictions of the
  just;—

they will be delivered from them all.
God will keep guard over all their bones,
not one of them shall be broken.

Evil shall be its own destruction;
oppression shall be condemned.
You redeem the lives of your servants;
those who take refuge in you shall not be condemned.
Glory*...

PRAYER: You gather us together in faith, O God, as a loving mother and a gentle father. Help us to remember that your dwelling place is built upon love and peace, and that to bring about your reign on earth we must follow your way of peace. We pray for all governments and legislatures that they may be mindful of the rights of all peoples of this world to live in peace and dignity. Grant this is the name of Jesus. Amen.

WEEK IV

SUNDAY, EVENING PRAYER I

Ant 1 Peace be within you!

Psalm 122

I was glad when they said to me:
"let us go to the house of God!"
And now our feet are standing
within your gates, O Jerusalem!

Jerusalem, built as a city
bound firmly together,
to which the tribes go up,
the tribes of our God,
as was decreed for Israel,
to give thanks to your holy name.
There thrones for judgment were
  set,
the thrones of the house of David.

Pray for the peace of Jerusalem!
"Peace be to your homes!
Peace be within your walls,
and security within your borders!

For love of my family and friends
I will say: "Peace be within you!"
For the sake of the house of our
  God,
I seek your good. **Glory*...**

**Ant 2 From sunrise to sunset,
my soul waits for you.**

Psalm 130

Out of the depths I cry to you,
O God, hear my voice!
Let your ears be attentive
to the voice of my supplication.

***Glory to you, Source of all
Being, Eternal Word and Holy
Spirit,**

**As it was in the beginning is
now and will be forever. Amen.**

If you should mark our iniquities,
O God, who could stand?
But with you is found
  forgiveness:
for this we revere you.

My soul waits for you,
in your word I hope;
my soul waits for you
more than those who watch for
  daybreak.

Let Israel hope in you!
For with you there is love,
and fullness of redemption.
And you will redeem Israel
from all its iniquities.
      Glory*...

**Ant 3 Let every knee bow at
the name of Jesus.**

Cant: Phil 2:6–11

Though he was in the form of
  God,
Jesus did not count equality with
  God
something to be grasped at.

But emptied himself
taking the form of a slave,
being born in human likeness.

Being found in human estate,
he humbled himself and became
  obedient,
obediently accepting death,
even death on a cross!

Therefore God has highly exalted
  him
and bestowed on him the name
above every other name.

So that at the name of Jesus
every knee should bow,
in heaven, on the earth,
and under the earth,—

and every tongue proclaim
to the glory of God:
Jesus Christ is Lord! **Glory*...**

READING

"Christ is risen!" does not mean that Jesus lives on in history as Lenin
lives on in his revolution.... Jesus does not live on because people
have faith in him and proclaim his teaching. The reverse is true.
People have faith in him and proclaim his teaching because he lives....
When the ointment bearing women went to the tomb on that first
Easter morning they only expected to see the dead body of Jesus.
When they heard the words, "...He is not here, He is risen!", all life
radically changed for them forever—and so it must be for us.
Everything in our lives that is not based on a Resurrection faith in
Jesus and his message must be rejected. Once one has found the
"pearl of great price" he or she automatically sells everything of lesser
value to procure it.

Emmanuel Charles McCarthy, "Stations of the Cross of Non-Violent Love," p. 22, (36)

RESPONSORY

From daybreak to sunset, we praise your name, O God.
   —From daybreak...
Your glory fills the heavens; **—we praise...**
Glory to you, Source of all Being, Eternal Word and Holy Spirit.
   —From daybreak...

CANTICLE OF MARY

Ant. Blessed are the pure of heart, for they shall see God.

INTERCESSIONS

O God, your invitation to grow is ever before us;
   —free us from the need to control; deepen our trust in your
      desire for our good.
Nothing is impossible for you;
   —let our desires be your own, then grant our requests.
Jesus, you promise to raise up those who have died with you;
   —help us to remember that the suffering of life is not
      meaningless.
Bless those who break under the stress of life;
   —give them understanding and compassionate mentors.
Help the agencies of the world that help others;
   —enable them to find homes and sustenance for all refugees.

PRAYER: All-loving God, you restored your people to eternal life by raising Jesus from the dead. Make our faith strong and our hope sure. May we never doubt that you will fulfill the promises you have made to us and to all the peoples of this world. Grant this through the prayers of all who without seeing have believed and now enjoy the gift of eternal life. Amen.

MORNING PRAYER

Ant. 1 We praise you for your steadfast love.
Psalm 118
I

We give thanks to you, for you are good,
and your steadfast love endures forever.

Let the descendants of Israel say:
"Your steadfast love endures forever."
Let the descendants of Aaron say:
"Your steadfast love endures forever."
Let those who fear you say:
"Your steadfast love endures forever."

In my distress, I called to you;
you answered me and set me free.
With you at my side I do not fear.
What can anyone do against me?
You are at my side to help me:
I shall withstand all evildoers.

It is better to take refuge in you,
than to trust in people:
it is better to take refuge in you
than to trust in our leaders.

All wickedness surrounded me;
in your name I crushed it.
It surrounded me, surrounded me
on every side;
in your name I cut it off.—

It surrounded me like bees;
it blazed like a fire among thorns.
In your name I crushed it.

I was pushed hard, and was falling
but you came to help me.
You are my strength and my song;
you are my salvation.

O God, you have triumphed;
your reign is exalted.
You have triumphed over all;
I shall not die, I shall live
and recount your wondrous deeds.
You have chastened me sorely,
but have not given me over to
death.

Open to me the gates of justice,
that I may enter and give thanks.
This is your gate, O God;
the just shall enter through it.
I thank you for you have answered
me
you alone are my salvation.

The stone which the builders
rejected
has become the cornerstone.
This is your doing, O God,
it is marvelous in our eyes.
This is the day which you have
made;
let us rejoice and be glad in it.

Save us, we beseech you, O God!
O God, grant us success.—

Blessed are those who enter
in your holy name.
For you O God, are our God,
and you have given us light.

Let us go forward in procession
  with branches,
up to your holy altar.
You are my God, I thank you.
You are my God, I praise you.
We give thanks to you for you are
  good;
and your steadfast love endures
  forever. **Glory*...**

**Ant. 2 May all your works bless
  you, (alleluia).**
  Cant: Daniel 3:52–57

Blessed are you, God of our
  ancestors,
praiseworthy and exalted above all
  forever.

Blessed be your holy and glorious
  name,
praiseworthy and exalted above all
  for all ages.

Blessed are you in the temple of
  your glory,
praiseworthy and exalted above all
  forever.

Blessed are you on the throne of
  your kindom,
praiseworthy and exalted above all
  forever.

Blessed are you who look into the
  depths
from your throne upon the
  cherubim,
praiseworthy and exalted above all
  forever.

Blessed are you in the firmament
  of heaven,
praiseworthy and glorious forever.

Blessed are you by all your works.
We praise and exalt you above all
  forever. **Glory*...**

**Ant. 3 You are wonderful in all
  your works, O God.**
  Psalm 150

We praise you, O God, in your holy
  sanctuary;
we praise you in your mighty
  heavens.
We praise you for your powerful
  deeds;
we praise you according to your
  greatness.

We praise you with trumpet
  sound;
We praise you with lute and harp!
We praise you with strings and
  pipe!

We praise you with sounding
  cymbals,
We praise you with clashing
  cymbals!
Let everything that breathes,
give praise to you, O God.
  Glory*...

READING

Remember Jesus Christ, raised from the dead, a descendant of David.
The saying is sure: If we have died with him, we will also live with him; if
we endure, we will also reign with him; if we deny him, he will also deny
us; if we are faithless, he remains faithful—for he cannot deny himself.

                                                    2 Tim 2:8a, 11–13

RESPONSORY

We praise your goodness, O God, with songs of thanksgiving.
   —We praise...
We rejoice in your presence; **—with songs...**
Glory to you, Source of all Being, Eternal Word and Holy Spirit.
   —We praise...

CANTICLE OF ZECHARIAH

Ant. Give us this day our daily bread.

INTERCESSIONS

O God, the whole world was changed and raised up by the coming
of your son;
   —let us never take his life or gospel for granted.
You give us the power to be light or darkness for one another on
the way to salvation;
   —show us how to transform the stumbling blocks in our lives
      to ladders of grace for ourselves and for others.
There are many who do not know you or your Christ;
   —send laborers into your harvest.
Jesus, you ate with sinners and stayed with them;
   —let the Eucharist that we share remind us of your forgiveness
      and constant presence in our lives.
Spirit of God, lead us to wholesome recreations that delight and
nourish us;
   —keep us safe as we play, and let us do so with moderation
      and gratitude.

PRAYER: O God of the morning, you call us to a new day and to a
life of resurrection and union with you. Help us to live
this day as a people of hope in a world of chaos. May
all who face oppression, terror, abuse, or suffering in
any way know that you call us to life and happiness in
this world as well as the world to come. We ask this
through the intercession of all who lived as people of
hope in the midst of despair and now live with you in
everlasting peace. Amen.

DAYTIME PRAYER

Ant. 1 You are the bread of life, (alleluia).

Psalm 23

O God, you are my shepherd;
I shall not want.
You make me to lie in green
  pastures.
You lead me to restful waters,
to restore my soul.

You guide me in paths of
  righteousness
for the sake of your name.
Even though I walk through the
  valley of the shadow of death,
I fear no evil;
for you are with me;
your crook and your staff
give me comfort.

You prepare a table before me
in the presence of my foes;
you anoint my head with oil,
my cup overflows.

Surely goodness and mercy shall
  follow me
all the days of my life;
and I shall dwell in your holy
  house forever and ever.
  Glory*...

**Ant. 2 More glorious are you
than the everlasting
mountains, (alleluia).**

Psalm 76

O God, you are known in Judah;
Your abode you established in
  Jerusalem,
your dwelling place in Zion.—

There you broke the flashing
  arrows,
the sword, and the weapons of
  war.

Glorious are you, more majestic
than the everlasting mountains.
Warriors were stripped of their
  spoil,
sinking into death;
those engaged in war, made
  powerless at your word.
At your rebuke, O God,
the makers of war lay stunned.
  Glory*...

**Ant. 3 God arose in judgment to
save the oppressed on earth,
(alleluia).**

II

You, alone, O God, strike terror!
Who can stand before you
when your anger is aroused?
From the heavens you utter
  judgment;
the earth feared and was still,
when you rose to establish
  judgment
to save the oppressed of the
  earth.

Human anger will serve to praise
  you;
its residue gird you round.
We make vows to you, and fulfill
  them.
Let your faithful bring you gifts;
you, who are worthy of awe,
who cut short the lives of leaders
who strike terror in the rulers of
  the earth. **Glory*...**

PRAYER: Creator of all, by the paschal mystery you touch our
  lives with the healing power of your love. You have

given us the freedom of the children of God. May all people know this freedom in their hearts and in their lives, so that they may celebrate your gift and find joy in it now and forever. Amen.

EVENING PRAYER II

Ant. 1 We are a priestly people; let us give thanks, (alleluia).

Psalm 110:1-5, 7

God's revelation to the Anointed One:
"Sit at my side:
till I put injustice beneath your feet."

God will send forth from Zion your scepter of power:
rule in the midst of your foes.

Your people will give themselves freely
on the day you lead your host
upon the holy mountains.
From the womb of the morning your youth will come like dew.

God has sworn an oath that will not be changed.
"You are a priest forever,
after the order of Melchizedek."

The Anointed standing by your side,
will shatter rulers on the day of wrath.

Drinking from your streams by the wayside
shall the Chosen One be refreshed. **Glory*...**

Ant. 2 Those who give to the poor will have treasure in heaven.

Psalm 112

Happy are they who fear the Most High,
who greatly delight in God's commands.
Their children will be mighty in the land;
the offspring of the upright will be blessed.

Wealth and riches are in their homes;
their justice endures forever.
Light rises in the darkness for the upright:
God is gracious, merciful and just.

It is well for those who are generous and lend,
who conduct their affairs with justice.
The upright will never be moved;
they will be remembered forever.

They have no fear of evil tidings;
their hearts are firm, trusting in God.
With steadfast hearts, they will not fear;
they will withstand all deception.

Open-handed, they give to the poor;
their justice endures forever.
Their power is exalted in glory.

The wicked see and are angry,
gnash their teeth and melt away;
the desire of the wicked comes to
nought. **Glory*...**

**Ant. 3 May all who serve you,
give you praise, (alleluia).**

Cant: Rev 19:1, 5-7

Salvation, glory, and power
belong to you,
your judgments are honest and
true.

All of us, your servants, sing
praise to you,
we worship you reverently, both
great and small.

You, our almighty God, are
Creator of heaven and earth.
Let us rejoice and exult, and give
you glory.

The wedding feast of the Lamb
has begun,
And the bride has made herself
ready. **Glory*...**

READING

Those who are seized by the peace of Christ and who preserve peace in
their hearts, radiate peace, give witness to peace and cooperate as much
as possible in making peace attainable, are assured of great beatitude.
"They shall be called sons and daughters of God" (Mt 59). They reveal
themselves as genuine brothers and sisters of Jesus Christ, Prince of
Peace. They find security and joy in God. For them it is happiness to
lead people to God's peace, and to peace among themselves. "The
[kindom] of heaven is theirs", for the [kindom] of God is justice, peace,
and joy, inspired by the Holy Spirit" (Rom 14:17).

Bernard Häring, *The Healing Power of Peace and Nonviolence*, p. 23, (1)

RESPONSORY

Glorious are your works, God of the universe. —**Glorious...**
Nothing can surpass your greatness; —**God...**
Glory to you, Source of all Being, Eternal Word and Holy Spirit.
     —**Glorious...**

CANTICLE OF MARY

Ant. Blessed are the meek, for they shall inherit the earth.

INTERCESSIONS

O God, you are present to us, yet our minds cannot contain the
mystery of your being;
     —let what we know of you in the life and love of Jesus draw
          us to you in ever deepening faith.
It is difficult to wait with hope for what we think is good and just;

—increase our faith, and help us to hold fast to our
  dedication to you.
Let the harvest of our land yield enough for all;
  —banish famine from our world; teach us to share.
Eye has not seen, nor ear heard, what you have prepared for
those who love you;
  —let the hundredfold that we seek be only to love you totally
    with grateful hearts.
Jesus, you prayed that we all might be one;
  —help us to recognize those who differ from us as our sisters
    and brothers sharing this one earth that you came to save.

PRAYER: O holy God, as evening falls remain with us. Remember
our good deeds and forgive our failings. Help us to
reflect upon and live according to your covenant of
love. Be with our lonely and elderly sisters and
brothers in the evening of their lives. May all who long
to see you face to face know the comfort of your
presence. This we ask in union with Simeon and Anna
and all who have gone before us blessing and
proclaiming you by the fidelity of their lives. Amen.

MONDAY

MORNING PRAYER

**Ant 1 Give success to the work
  of our hands, O God.**

Psalm 90

O God, you have been our shelter
from one generation to the next.
Before the mountains were
  formed,
or the earth or the world brought
  forth,
from everlasting to everlasting
you are God.

You turn us back to dust, and
  say:
"Go back, peoples of the earth!"
For a thousand years in your
  sight—

are like yesterday, when it is
  past,
no more than a watch in the
  night.

You sweep us away like a dream,
like grass which is renewed in the
  morning:
in the morning it flowers and is
  renewed;
in the evening it fades and
  withers.

So we are consumed by your
  anger;
by your wrath we are
  overwhelmed.—

You set our iniquities before you,
our secret sins in the light of your
  face.
All our days pass away in your
  anger.
Our years are over like a sigh.
The years of our life are seventy,
or eighty for those who are
  strong;
yet their span is but toil and
  trouble;
they pass swiftly and we are gone.

Who understands the power of
  your anger
and fears the strength of your
  wrath?
Teach us to number our days
that we may gain wisdom of
  heart.

Relent, O God! How long?
Have pity on your servants!
In the morning, fill us with your
  love,
that we may rejoice and be glad
  all our days.
Balance with joy our days of
  affliction,
and the years when we knew
  misfortune.

Let your word be manifest to your
  servants,
your glorious power to their
  children.
Let your favor, O God, be upon
  us:
give success to the work of our
  hands,
give success to the work of our
  hands. **Glory*...**

**Ant. 2 You turn darkness into
light and make the rough ways
smooth!**

Cant: Isaiah 42:10–16

Sing to our God a new song,
Sing praise from the ends of the
  earth!

Let the sea and what fills it
  resound,
the coastlands and their
  inhabitants.
Let the desert and its cities cry
  out,
the villages where Kedar dwells.

Let the inhabitants of Sela exult,
let them shout from the top of the
  mountains.
Let them give glory to the Most
  High,
and declare God's praise in the
  coastlands.

You go forth, O God, like a hero,
like a warrior you stir up your
  fury;
crying out and shouting aloud,
against the oppression of your
  poor.

For a long time I held my peace,
I kept still and restrained myself;
now, I will cry like a woman in
  labor, gasping and panting.

I will lay waste mountains and
  hills,
and dry up all their herbage;
I will turn the rivers into islands,
and dry up all the streams.

I will lead the blind on their
  journey,
in a way that they know not,
in unknown paths I will guide
  them.—

I will turn darkness before them
  into light,
and rough places into level
  ground. **Glory*...**

**Ant. 3 You are gracious, O God;
you call us to be your people.**

Psalm 135

We praise your name, O God,
all your servants give praise,
those who stand in your holy
  house,
in the courts of your house, O
  God!

We praise you, for you are good.
Sing to your name for you are
  gracious!
For you have chosen Jacob for
  yourself,
Israel as your own possession.

For I know that you are great,
that you are high above all gods.–

You do whatever you please,
 ⌐ in heaven and on earth,
in the seas and all the deeps.

You summon clouds from the
  ends of the earth,
make lightning for the rain,
and bring forth wind from your
  storehouse.

You smote the firstborn of Egypt,
both of human and beast alike.
Signs and wonders you worked
in the midst of the land of Egypt,
against Pharaoh and all his
  servants.

You smote many nations
and slew mighty rulers,
Sihon, king of the Amorites,
Og, the king of Bashan,
and all the kingdoms of Canaan.
You gave their land as a heritage,
a heritage to your people.
  Glory*...

READING

We live in a culture of achievement and production which believes that
people should and do get what they deserve. As Christians we know
that this is not so. The infinite bounty of God begins with the gift of life
itself and continues with everything that sustains it. Our activity is not
so much an earning our way as a cooperating with the Creator God in
transforming history into God's reign of justice and love. Building this
attitude of grateful response into our lives requires a constant
cultivation of faith against the seeming self-evident "way things are"
around us.

Sandra M. Schneiders, IHM, *New Wineskins*, p. 186, (1)

RESPONSORY

All nations rejoice and praise God our creator. **—All...**
Sing with joy to the Most High; **—and praise...**
Glory to you, Source of all Being, Eternal Word and Holy Spirit.
  —All...

CANTICLE OF ZECHARIAH

Ant. Come to us this day and set your people free.

INTERCESSIONS

Jesus, you preached a gospel of love and forgiveness;
—may those who hear your word be freed from unfounded guilt and a misguided conscience.

You healed those who could not hear or speak;
—may we close our ears to falsehood and endeavor to speak the truth in love.

We know well how to plan for the things we want;
—help us to plan as surely for ways to open ourselves to your Spirit within us.

O God, mobility is a sign of our times; the whole world is within our reach;
—protect us all, and guide those who are responsible for our trips on land, sea, and in the air.

You desire our good, and you have compassion on all who suffer;
—be merciful to those who are in constant pain; comfort and sustain them.

PRAYER: O God of life, you bring us to this day and we are grateful for your gift. Enable us to be and to work for one another in order that justice may reign, that the needs of the poor be met, and that the oppressed may be liberated. We pray this in the name of Jesus who came that we may be free. Amen.

DAYTIME PRAYER

Ant. 1 Teach me to follow in your steps, that I may be your disciple.

Psalm 119:129–136

Your will is wonderful indeed;
therefore will I obey it.
The unfolding of your words gives light;
it imparts wisdom to the simple.

I open my mouth and I sigh
as I yearn for your commandments.
Turn to me and be gracious,
treat me as one who loves your name.

Keep my steps steady in your way,
according to your promise;
let no iniquity rule over me.—

Redeem me from human
  oppression,
that I may keep your precepts.

Let your face shine on your
  servant
and teach me your statutes.
My eyes shed streams of tears,
because your law is disobeyed.
  Glory*...

**Ant. 2 Blessed are the merciful,
mercy shall be theirs.**

Psalm 82

God stands in the divine
  assembly;
holding judgment in the midst of
  the gods:

"How long will you judge unjustly
and favor the cause of the
  wicked?
Give justice to the weak and the
  orphan;
defend the afflicted and the
  needy.
Rescue the weak and the
  destitute;
deliver them from the hand of the
  wicked."

They have neither knowledge nor
  understanding,
they walk about in darkness;—

the foundations of the world are
  shaken.

God says, "You are gods,
children of the Most High, all of
  you;
yet, you shall die like human
  beings,
and fall like any of their leaders."

Arise, O God, judge the earth;
for to you belong all the nations.
  Glory*...

**Ant. 3 Guide us in your way of
peace.**

Psalm 120

In my distress, I cry to you,
that you may answer me:
"Deliver my soul from lying lips,
and from a deceitful tongue."
What shall be given you in
  return,
you deceitful tongue?
The warrior's arrows sharpened
and coals, red-hot blazing.

Alas, that I sojourn in Meshech,
dwell among the tents of Kedar!
Too long have I had my dwelling
among those who hate peace.
I am for peace; but when I speak,
  they are for war! **Glory*...**

PRAYER: O God, in your love you have given each of us gifts and
talents to serve the common good. Help us to use them
generously and lovingly, for we are your children. Free
us from the desire to serve only our own interests, and
help us to grow in the spirit of love that makes us
sisters and brothers. This we ask for the sake of all
who are in bondage through our selfishness and that of
our governments. Grant us our prayer that your love
and peace may reign now and forever. Amen.

EVENING PRAYER

Ant. 1 Your love, O God, endures forever.

Psalm 136

We give thanks to you, for you are good,
for your love endures forever.
We thank you, O God of gods,
for your love endures forever.
We thank you, Creator of the universe,
for your love endures forever.

You alone have done great wonders,
for your love endures forever.
Your wisdom made the heavens,
for your love endures forever.
You spread out the earth upon the waters,
for your love endures forever.

It was you who made the great lights,
for your love endures forever.
the sun to rule over the day,
for your love endures forever.
the moon and the stars to rule over the night,
for your love endures forever.
   Glory*...

Ant. 2 With outstretched arm you lead us out of darkness.
II

The first born of the Egyptians you smote,
for your love endures forever;
and brought Israel out from their midst,
for your love endures forever;—

with arm outstretched and power in your hand,
for your love endures forever.

You divided the Red Sea in two,
for your love endures forever;
you made Israel pass through the midst,
for your love endures forever;
you flung Pharaoh and his host in the sea,
for your love endures forever.

You led your people through the desert,
for your love endures forever.
Nations in their greatness you struck,
for your love endures forever.
Rulers in their splendor you slew,
for your love endures forever.

Sihon, king of the Amorites,
for your love endures forever;
and Og, the king of Bashan,
for your love endures forever.

Their land you gave as a heritage,
for your love endures forever;
a heritage to your faithful people,
for your love endures forever.

You remembered us in our distress,
for your love endures forever;
and you rescued us from oppression,
for your love endures forever.
You give food to all living things,
for your love endures forever.

We give thanks to you, God of heaven,
for your love endures forever.
   Glory*...

Ant. 3 In Christ, God's grace is revealed.

Cant: Ephesians 1:3-10

Praised be the God
of our Lord Jesus Christ,
who has blessed us in Christ
with every spiritual blessing in
  the heavens.

God chose us in him
before the foundation of the
  world,
that we should be holy
and blameless in God's sight.

We have been predestined
to be God's children through
  Jesus Christ,
such was the purpose of God's
  will,—

that all might praise the glorious
  favor
bestowed on us in Christ.

In Christ and through his blood,
we have redemption,
the forgiveness of our sins,
according to the riches of God's
  grace lavished upon us.

For God has made known to us
in all wisdom and insight,
the mystery of the plan set forth
  in Christ.

A plan to be carried out in Christ,
in the fullness of time,
to unite all things in Christ,
things in heaven and things on
  earth. **Glory*...**

READING

Meister Eckhart wrote, "As thou art in church or cell, that same frame of mind carry out into the world, into its turmoil and its fitfulness." Deep within us all there is an amazing inner sanctuary of the soul, a holy place, a Divine Center, a speaking Voice, to which we may continuously return. Eternity is at our hearts, pressing upon our time-torn lives, warming us with intimations of an astounding destiny, calling us home unto Itself.

Thomas R. Kelly, Quaker Spirituality, p. 290, (1)

RESPONSORY

O God, receive our prayer which is lifted up to you. **—O God,...**
Like the fragrance of incense, **—which is...**
Glory to you, Source of all Being, Eternal Word and Holy Spirit.
  —O God,...

CANTICLE OF MARY

Ant. Blessed are the merciful, for they shall obtain mercy.

INTERCESSIONS

O God, slavery is a reality in our world in many forms;
    —grant us a new consciousness of the equality of all people.

You created a new covenant of peace through your Son, Jesus, yet
we live in fear of one another;
   —show us how to re-seed the world with trust; help us to
      put love where there is no love.
You delight in those who receive your gifts with gratitude;
   —bless all who endeavor to develop their talents; encourage
      and enlighten all students, and keep them in your care.
Jesus, you revealed yourself to a woman of Samaria, an
unwelcoming land;
   —enable world leaders to overcome national rivalries and
      centuries of mutual retaliation.
You gave us the power to bind and to loose;
   —free us from our need to control, and give us the grace to
      free others from our expectations.

PRAYER: O God, as darkness falls, remain with us as our light.
         Help us to meet you in the scriptures that we read, in
         the bread that we break, and in the neighbor that we
         welcome into our hearts. Grant this prayer that your
         reign will come, that your will be done in us as it was
         in Jesus, now and forever. Amen.

TUESDAY

MORNING PRAYER

**Ant. 1 Look with favor upon us
that we may dwell with you
forever.**

Psalm 101

I sing of fidelity and justice;
to you, O God, I will sing.
I will pay heed to the way that is
   blameless.
Oh when will you come to me?

I will walk with integrity of heart
   within my house;
I will not set before my eyes
   anything that is base.

I renounce the ways of
   wrongdoers;—

they shall not adhere to me.
Perverseness of heart shall be far
   from me;
I will know nothing of evil.

Those who slander their neighbor
   secretly
I will ignore.
Those of haughty looks and proud
   hearts
I will not endure.

I will look with favor on all who
   are faithful,
that they may dwell with me;
they who walk in the way that is
   blameless
shall minister to me.

No one who practices deceit shall
dwell in my house;
no one who utters lies shall
remain in my presence.

Morning by morning I will
renounce
all the oppression in the land,
uprooting from the city of God all
that is evil. **Glory*...**

**Ant. 2 Look upon us with
compassion, O God, and heal
us.**
  **Cant: Daniel 3:26, 27,
    29, 34–41**

Blessed are you, and
praiseworthy,
O God of our ancestors,
and glorious forever is your
name.

For you are just in all you have
done;
all your deeds are faultless, all
your ways right,
and all your judgments proper.

For we have sinned and
transgressed
by departing from you,
and we have done every kind of
evil.

For your name's sake, do not
deliver us up forever,
or make void your covenant.

Do not take away your mercy
from us,
for the sake of those beloved by
you:
Sara and Abraham, Rebecca and
Isaac, Rachel and Jacob, your
holy ones,

To whom you promised to
multiply their offspring
like the stars of heaven,
or the sands on the shore of the
sea.

For we are reduced beyond any
other nation,
brought low everywhere in the
world this day because of our
sins.

We have in our day no ruler,
prophet, or leader,
no holocaust, sacrifice, oblation,
or incense,
no place to offer first fruits, to
find favor with you.

But with contrite heart and
humble spirit let us be received;
as though it were holocausts of
rams and bullocks, or
thousands of fat lambs,
so let our sacrifice be in your
presence today as we follow you
unreservedly;
for those who trust in you cannot
be put to shame.

And now we follow you with our
whole heart,
we fear you and we pray to you.
  Glory*...

**Ant. 3 O God, you are my
shield. In you I take refuge.**

Psalm 144:1–10

Blessed are you, O God, my rock,
who trains my hands for war,
and my fingers for battle.

You are my rock and my fortress,
my stronghold and my deliverer,
my shield in whom I take refuge,
You bring peoples under your
rule.

Who are we that you care for us,
mortal flesh, that you keep us in
  mind?
We, who are merely a breath,
whose days are like a passing
  shadow.

Lower your heavens and come
  down!
Touch the mountains that they
  smoke!
Flash your lightnings and scatter
  them,
shoot your arrows and put them
  to flight.

Stretch forth your hand from on
  high,
rescue me from the mighty
  waters,
from the hands of alien foes,
whose mouths are filled with lies,
and whose hands are raised in
  perjury.

To you will I sing a new song.
On a ten-stringed harp I will play
to you, who give rulers their
  victory,
who rescue David, your servant.
        Glory*...

READING

For Mary MacKillop God's will was her guiding principle.... "To me the
Will of God is a dear book which I am never tired of reading, which has
always some new charm for me.... I cannot tell you what a beautiful
thing the Will of God seems to me."

When overcome by sadness she clung to the Will of God as her only
support: "...[I] was so weary of the struggle, and felt so utterly alone,
could not pray or say my ordinary Rosaries, only offered my weary
heart's trials to my God...."

                                    Bl. Mary MacKillop, RSJ, (10)

RESPONSORY

Answer my plea, O God; I trust in your word. **—Answer...**
Before the first rays of dawn, I come to you. **—I trust...**
Glory to you, Source of all Being, Eternal Word and Holy Spirit.
    —Answer...

CANTICLE OF ZECHARIAH

**Ant. Protect us from the grasp of evil, and lead us not into
    temptation.**

INTERCESSIONS

O God, your love is greater than our guilt;
    —have mercy on those who are sentenced to death.
Too often our faith exists only in our minds and words;
    —awaken us to new and practical ways to enflesh our
        commitment to your will.

Our lives are fragile, and you surround us with men and women in life-preserving professions;
  —guard and guide our police, fire fighters, rescue workers,
    and all who labor and risk their lives for our safety.
Open our minds to the ways that we are destroying the gifts of the earth;
  —bless again the land and water and all of the life that
    sustains us.
Jesus, you knew the sweetness of friendship, and you gave new life to those who received you;
  —keep us faithful to you and to one another.

PRAYER: O God, you call us to begin this day in dedication to you. May all who need your help today experience your love and compassion through us and through all who have come to know you. Bless all the children of this world; protect them from abuse. May they come to know their worth and dignity as your children, rightful citizens of this earth. This we ask in union with all the innocent and pure of heart who stand in your presence now and forever. Amen.

DAYTIME PRAYER

Ant. 1 You are true to your promise in which I delight.

Psalm 119:137–144

Just are you, O God,
and right are your judgments.
You have decreed your will in
  justice
and in all faithfulness.

I am consumed with zeal
because your words are forgotten.
Your promise is tried in the fire,
the delight of your servant.

Though I am weak and despised
I do not forget your precepts.
Your justice is righteous forever,
and your law is true.

Trouble and anguish come upon
  me,
but your commands are my
  delight.
The justice of your will is eternal;
give me understanding that I may
  live. **Glory*...**

Ant. 2 Listen to the sound of my call, O God, I cry for your help.

Psalm 88

My God, I call for help by day;
I cry out in the night before you.
Let my prayer come into your
  presence,
incline your ear to my cry!
For my soul is full of troubles,—

and my life draws near to the
grave.

I am reckoned as one in the
tomb;
I have reached the end of my
strength,
like one forsaken among the
dead,
like the slain that lie in the grave,
like those you no longer
remember,
for they are cut off from your
hand.

You have laid me in the depths of
the tomb,
in the regions dark and deep.
Your anger lies heavy upon me,
you overwhelm me with all your
waves. **Glory*...**

**Ant. 3 Hide not your face from
me, O God, in time of distress.**
II

All my companions now shun me;
to them I am a thing of horror.
I am shut in so that I cannot
escape;
my eye grows dim through
sorrow.

Every day I call upon you;
to you I stretch out my hands.
Do you work wonders for the
dead?
Do phantoms rise up to praise
you?

Is your love declared in the grave,
or your faithfulness in the
bottomless pit?
Are your wonders known in the
darkness,
or your salvation in the land of
forgetfulness?

But I, O God, cry out to you:
in the morning my prayer comes
before you.
Why do you cast me off, O God?
Why hide your face from me?

Afflicted and close to death from
the days of my youth,
I suffer your trials; I am helpless.
Your chastisements swept over
me;
your dread assaults destroy me.

They surround me like a flood all
day long;
they close in upon me together.
Friend and neighbor shun me;
my companions are in darkness.
Glory*...

PRAYER: Loving God, you sent the Holy Spirit to the early
Christians as their source of courage and fidelity. Send
your Spirit to us that we, too, may be witnesses of your
love to all peoples on this earth. We pray especially for
the homeless, the displaced, the nameless, the ignored.
May all come to know your love and care, for you are
both mother and father to us all. Help us to recognize
all as our sisters and brothers. We ask this in union
with Jesus, our friend and brother. Amen.

EVENING PRAYER

Ant. 1 May we remember your covenant in this land of exile.

Psalm 137:1–6

By the waters of Babylon,
we sat down and wept,
when we remembered Zion.
On the willows there we hung up
our harps.

For there our captors required of
us songs,
and our tormentors, mirth,
saying,
"Sing us one of the songs of
Zion!"

How shall we sing God's song in a
foreign land?
If I forget you, Jerusalem,
let my hand wither!

Let my tongue cleave to the roof
of my mouth,
if I do not remember you,
if I do not set Jerusalem above all
my joys! **Glory*...**

Ant. 2 Your name and your word are above all forever.

Psalm 138

I give you thanks with all my
heart;
before the gods I sing your praise;
I bow down before your holy
temple
and give thanks to your name
for your steadfast love and your
faithfulness;
for exalted above all are your
name and your word.

On the day I called, you answered
me;
you increased the strength of my
soul.

All of earth's rulers shall praise
you
for they have heard the words of
your mouth;
they shall sing of your ways for
great is your glory, O God.
Though you are high, you look on
the lowly
and the haughty you know from
afar.

Though I walk in the midst of
trouble,
you preserve my life;
you stretch out your hand and
save me.
You will fulfill your purpose for
me;
your steadfast love endures
forever.
Do not forsake the work of your
hands. **Glory*...**

Ant. 3 Salvation and glory belong to our God, (alleluia)!

Cant: Rev 4:11, 5:9, 10, 12

Worthy are you, O God, our God,
to receive glory and honor and
power.

For you have created all things;
by your will they came to be and
were made.

Worthy are you to take the scroll
and to open its seals,—

For you were slain, and by your
  blood,
you purchased for God
saints of every race and tongue,
of every people and nation.

You have made of them a kindom,
and priests to serve our God,—

and they shall reign on the earth.

Worthy is the Lamb who was
  slain
to receive power and riches,
wisdom and strength,
honor and glory and praise.
  Glory*...

READING

Saint Teresa says prayer is not thinking much but loving much.
Everything becomes simple when we realize that here we are dealing
with what is, first of all, a matter of the heart. It is not then a case of
straining the mind, but simply of uniting our hearts to God.... It seems
to be often [God's] way, however, not to let us see results, and even to
let us be aware of our lack of success; but this can keep us humble. All
the while [God] continues to work within our souls, though in darkness
and in silence.

Mother Aloysius Rogers, OCD, *Fragrance from Alabaster*, p. 7, (6)

RESPONSORY

In your presence, O God, I will find all my joy.—**In your...**
When I see you face to face; —**I will...**
Glory to you, Source of all Being, Eternal Word and Holy Spirit.
  —**In your...**

CANTICLE OF MARY

Ant. Blessed are the poor in spirit, the reign of God is theirs.

INTERCESSIONS

O God, you have created us free, but our prisons are full;
    —help us to cultivate an environment that inspires life-
      giving choices.
You have created us to choose the good;
    —bless our children that they may know the good and
      pursue it.
You have created us in your image;
    —give us the joy of radiating your goodness, truth, and
      beauty.
Jesus, you experienced the worst of human weakness;
    —grant heroic courage and strength to those who are
      tortured; erase this horror from our world.

You promised to be with us to the end of the world;
—let us never lose hope in you, and help us to trust one
another.

PRAYER: O gracious God, open our hearts and our eyes to the
wonders of your presence among us. May we see the
signs of your beauty within and about us and ever be
in awe of the simple gifts of life. Help us to reach
beyond ourselves and to give thanks for all of your
creation that shares this universe with us: peoples of
every nation, animals of every species, all forms of
vegetation, the planets, stars, and all the elements. We
pray this in union with the incarnate Word of God in
whose image all was created. May you be blessed
throughout the ages and for all eternity. Amen.

WEDNESDAY

MORNING PRAYER

**Ant 1 I will give thanks to you
among the peoples.**

Psalm 108

My heart is steadfast, O God, my
heart is steadfast!
I will sing and make melody!
Awake, my soul!
Awake, lyre and harp!
I will awake the dawn!

I will give thanks to you among
the peoples,
I will sing praises to you among
the nations.
For your steadfast love is great
above the heavens,
your faithfulness reaches to the
clouds.

Be exalted, O God, above the
heavens!
Let your glory be over all the
earth!—

That your beloved may be
delivered,
give help with your hand, and
answer me!

You have promised in your
sanctuary:
"With exultation I will divide up
Shechem,
and portion out the Vale of
Succoth.
Gilead is mine, and Manasseh;
Ephraim is my helmet;
Judah my scepter.
Moab is my washbasin;
upon Edom I cast my shoe;
over Philistia I shout in triumph."

Who will bring me to the fortified
city?
Who will lead me to Edom?
Have you not rejected us, O God?
You no longer go forth with our
armies.—

Give us help against this
  oppression,
for human help is vain!
With you, we shall do valiantly;
it is you who will conquer
  injustice. **Glory*...**

**Ant. 2 Justice and peace will
  spring forth before all nations.**

Cant: Isaiah 61:10–62:5

I will greatly rejoice in you, O
  God,
in you my soul shall exult;
for you clothe me with garments
  of salvation,
you cover me with the robe of
  justice,
like a bridegroom bedecked with
  a garland,
like a bride adorned with her
  jewels.

As the earth brings forth its
  shoots,
and a garden makes its seeds
  spring up,
so will you make justice and
  praise
to spring forth before all the
  nations.

For Zion's sake I will not be
  silent,
for Jerusalem's sake I will not
  rest,
until its vindication shines forth
  like the dawn
and its salvation like a burning
  torch.

Nations shall behold its
  vindication,
and all rulers see its glory;
it shall be called by a new name—

which your own mouth will give.
It shall be a crown of beauty,
a royal diadem held in your hand,
  O God.

No more shall they call it
  "Forsaken,"
or its land be termed "Desolate;"
but it shall be called "My delight,"
  and its land "Espoused;"
for you, O God, delight in it,
and take it as a spouse.

For as young lovers are espoused,
so shall its children espouse
  Zion,
and as newlyweds rejoice in each
  other,
so shall you rejoice over Zion.
  Glory*...

**Ant. 3 You set us free, O God,
  from the chains that bind us.**

Psalm 146

My soul, give praise to my God!
I will praise the Most High as long
  as I live;
I will sing praises to my God
  while I have being.

Put no trust in sovereigns,
in mortal flesh in whom there is
  no help.
When their breath departs they
  return to the earth;
on that day their plans perish.

Happy are they whose help is the
  Most High,
whose hope is in the Creator of
  all,
who alone made heaven and
  earth,
the seas, and all that is in them;
who keeps faith forever;—

who executes justice for the
oppressed;
who gives food to the hungry.

For you, O God, set prisoners
free;
you open the eyes of the blind.
You lift up those who are bowed
down;—

you love the upright of heart.
You watch over the sojourners;
uphold the bereaved and the
orphaned.

O God, you will reign forever and
ever,
through all generations.
Glory*...

READING

This prayer is called "recollection," because the soul collects its faculties
together and enters within itself to be with its God.... Those who by
such a method can enclose themselves within this little heaven of our
soul, where the Maker of heaven and earth is present, and grow
accustomed to refusing to be where the exterior senses in their
distraction have gone or look in that direction should believe they are
following an excellent path and that they will not fail to drink water from
the fount; for they will journey far in a short time.

Teresa of Avila, *Way of Perfection*, 28, 4–5, (3)

RESPONSORY

I will sing your praise, O God, every day of my life. **—I will...**
From sunrise to sunset, **—every day...**
Glory to you, Source of all Being, Eternal Word and Holy Spirit.
—I will...

CANTICLE OF ZECHARIAH

Ant. In joy and holiness let us serve God our Savior.

INTERCESSIONS

You invite us to be co-creators with you, O God; work is our
privilege;
   —bless employers with all they need to provide safe and
      satisfying work for people in their service.
You have given us stewardship over the earth;
   —make us all responsible workers in time's "vineyard."
Jesus, you teach us to serve one another and to shun ambitious
pride;
   —help us to realize that our nobility lies in our relationship
      to God, whom you have revealed to us.
You knew loneliness and misunderstanding;

—comfort and sustain those who have been betrayed or abandoned.

You came to serve and not to be served;

—let all who are elected to leadership rise to the responsibility of their office and serve with justice and integrity.

PRAYER: See in us, O God, the face of your Christ, and forgive us our sins. Help all who must live with the strain of broken and tense relationships. Give us the courage to love in spite of loss and the mercy to forgive all who have injured us in any way. May our work this day bring us and all the world nearer to the quality of life to which you call us. Grant this through the intercession of the Holy Family and of all the families like them that image your life in the trinity of love. Amen.

DAYTIME PRAYER

Ant. 1 Day and night I hope in your words.

Psalm 119:145–152

With all my heart, I cry to you;
answer me, O God.
I cry to you; save me,
that I may observe your will.

I rise before dawn and cry for
  help;
I hope in your words.
My eyes watch throughout the
  night
meditating on your promises.

Hear my voice in your steadfast
  love;
in your justice preserve my life.
Those who persecute me draw
  near;
they are far from your law.

But you, O God, are near at hand,
all your commands are true.—

Long have I known that your will
  endures forever.
  Glory*...

Ant. 2 Do good to those who hate you, bless those who curse you, pray for those who abuse you.

Psalm 94

O God, avenging God,
avenging God, appear!
Judge of the earth, arise,
render injustice its deserts!
How long, O God, shall
  oppression,
how long shall oppression exult?

They bluster with arrogant
  speech,
they boast, all the evildoers.
They crush your people, O God,
they afflict the ones you have
  chosen.—

They kill the helpless and the
  poor,
and murder the parentless child.
They say: "God does not see;
their God pays no heed!"

Understand, O dullest of people!
Fools, when will you be wise?
Can God who made the ear, not
  hear?
The one who formed the eye, not
  see?
Will God who chastens nations,
  not punish?
God who imparts knowledge
  knows our thoughts,
knows they are no more than a
  breath. **Glory*...**

**Ant. 3 Judge not, and you will
not be judged; condemn not
and you will not be
condemned.**

II

Happy are those whom you
  chasten,
whom you teach by means of
  your law
to give them respite from days of
  trouble,
until oppression is no more.
You will not abandon your
  people;—

you will not forsake your
  heritage;
for justice will return to the
  righteous,
and the upright in heart will
  follow it.

Who will rise against oppression?
Who will stand against injustice?
If you had not been my help,
I would soon dwell in the land of
  silence.

When I think: "My foot is
  slipping,"
your steadfast love upholds me.
When the cares of my heart are
  many,
your consolations cheer my soul.

Can unjust rulers be your
  friends,
who do injustice under cover of
  law?
They attack the life of the
  helpless,
and condemn the innocent to
  death.

But you have become my
  stronghold,
my God, the rock of my refuge.
Injustice will turn on itself,
and evil will destroy evil.
  Glory*...

PRAYER: Compassionate God, we pause to rest in your
  presence. May the work we have begun this day find
  fulfillment in you for our good and the good of all
  people on this earth. We ask this is in the name of
  Jesus who is our way, our truth, and our life. Amen.

EVENING PRAYER

Ant. 1 Behold, I am with you always.

Psalm 139:1–18, 23–24

O God, you have searched me
and you know me,
you know when I sit and when I
stand;
you discern my thoughts from
afar.
You mark when I walk or lie
down,
with all my ways you are
acquainted.

Before a word is on my tongue,
behold, O God, you know the
whole of it.
Behind and before you besiege
me,
You lay your hand upon me.
Such knowledge is too wonderful
for me:
too high, beyond my reach.

O where can I go from your spirit,
or where can I flee from your
presence?
If I climb to heaven, you are
there!
If I lie in the grave, you are there!

If I take the wings of the morning
and dwell in the depths of the
sea,
even there your hand shall lead
me,
your hand shall hold me fast.

If I say: "Let darkness cover me,
and the light around me be
night,"
even darkness is not dark to
you—

and the night is as bright as the
day;
for darkness is as light to you.
Glory*...

Ant. 2 O God, I praise you for the wonder of my being.
II

For it was you who formed my
inmost parts,
knit me together in my mother's
womb.
I praise you for the wonder of my
being,
for the wonder of all your works.

Already you knew me well;
my body was not hidden from
you,
when I was being made in secret
and molded in the depths of the
earth.

Your eyes beheld my unformed
substance;
in your book they all were
written,
the days that you had formed for
me
when none of them yet were.

How precious to me are your
thoughts!
How vast the sum of them!
If I count them, they are more
than the sand.
When I awake, I am still with you.

Search me, O God, and know my
heart!
O test me and know my thoughts!
See that I follow not the wrong
way
and lead me in the way of life
eternal. **Glory*...**

Ant. 3 Christ is the firstborn of all creation.

Cant: Colossians 1:12–20

Let us give thanks to God
for having made us worthy
to share the inheritance of the
saints in light.

God has delivered us
from the power of darkness
and transferred us
into the kindom of God's beloved
Son, Jesus,
in whom we have redemption,
the forgiveness of our sins.

Jesus is the image of the invisible
God,
the first-born of all creation;
in him all things were created,—
in heaven and on earth,
things visible and invisible.

All things were created through
him;
all were created for him.
He is before all else that is.
In him all things hold together.

He is the head of the body, the
church!
He is the beginning,
the firstborn from the dead,
that in everything, he might be
above all others.

In him all the fullness of God was
pleased to dwell,
and, through him, to reconcile all
things to himself,
whether on earth or in heaven,
making peace by the blood of his
cross. **Glory*...**

READING

Over and over again, [Rahner] urges simple fidelity to duty and daily humdrum love.... [His] contemplative approach to the mystery of God in human experiences can enable us who are convinced that we live in a world of grace to speak of God in secular terms. His understanding of the Christian life as a mysticism of everyday faith can free us to seek and find God not only in times of formal prayer, but also in times of suffering, celebrations, service, and self-emptying, which we can view as opportunities for faith. His experience of prayer as surrender of the heart can help us to concentrate on its fruits, the ways we let go of all that can keep us from being open to the mystery of God in our lives....

Annice Callahan, RSCJ, *Traditions of Spiritual Guidance*, p. 347 (32)

RESPONSORY

Keep us, O God, on the path to life. —**Keep us...**
May your hand ever guide us —**on the path...**
Glory to you, Source of all Being, Eternal Word and Holy Spirit.
—**Keep us...**

CANTICLE OF MARY

Ant. Blessed are they who mourn for they shall be comforted.

INTERCESSIONS

Your justice is governed by mercy, O God;
  —strengthen those whose work exposes them to temptations
    of greed or unjust dealings.
Inspire those who can to give aid to worthy endeavors;
  —let their hundredfold be a deepened awareness of your
    presence in their lives.
Have mercy on abused spouses and children and on those who
abuse them;
  —help us to enable them to begin life anew.
Spirit of God, joy and peace are your gifts to us;
  —bless all who lighten our burden by their thoughtfulness,
    humor, and creativity.
Jesus, you remind us that we cannot serve two masters;
  —give us a single heart that seeks what is good, receiving all
    from God with trust.

PRAYER: O God, look upon the poverty of our hearts with
compassion and love. Enable us to give lovingly and
freely of our possessions and gifts. May those who work
with the poor and needy receive joy in this life and
fullness of life forever. This we ask through the
intercession of all the saints, especially of those whose
legacy of service we carry on today. Grant that we may
be faithful as they were faithful so that we too may live
with you forever. Amen.

THURSDAY

MORNING PRAYER

Ant. 1 In the early morning, O God, I remember your steadfast love.

Psalm 143:1–11

Hear my prayer, O God;
give ear to my supplication!
In your justice and faithfulness
  answer me!—

Do not call your servant to
  judgment
for no one is righteous before
  you.

For evil pursues my soul,
crushing my life to the ground,
making me dwell in darkness
like the dead, long forgotten.—

Therefore my spirit faints within
  me;
my heart within me is appalled.

I remember the days gone before,
I ponder on all you have done;
I muse on what you have
  wrought.
To you I stretch out my hands;
my soul thirsts for you like
  parched land.

O God, make haste to answer me!
My spirit fails within me!
Hide not your face from me,
lest I be like those who go down
  to the grave.

Let me hear in the morning of
  your steadfast love,
for in you I put my trust.
Teach me the way I should go,
for to you I lift up my soul.

Deliver me, O God, from all evil!
I have fled to you for refuge!
Teach me to do your will,
for you are my God!
Let your good spirit lead me
in ways that are level and
  smooth!

For your name's sake, save my
  life!
In your justice bring me out of
  trouble. **Glory*...**

**Ant. 2 I have sheltered you as a
hen shelters her brood!**

Cant.: Isaiah 66:10–14a

"Rejoice with Jerusalem, and be
  glad for her, all you who love
  her;
rejoice with her in joy,
all you who mourn over her;—

that you may suck and be
  satisfied with her consoling
  breasts;
that you may drink deeply with
  delight from the abundance of
  her glory."

For thus says God Most High:
"Behold, I will extend prosperity
  to her like a river,
and the wealth of the nations like
  an overflowing stream.

As nurslings, you shall be carried
  upon her hip,
and fondled on her lap.

As a parent comforts a child,
  so will I comfort you;
you shall be comforted in
  Jerusalem.

You shall see, and your hearts
  shall rejoice;
your beings flourish like the
  grass. **Glory*...**

**Ant. 3 Through you, the blind
see, the lame walk, and the
poor hear your good news.**

Psalm 147:1–11

It is good to sing praise to you;
for you are gracious and merciful;
to you our praise is due.

You, O God, build up Jerusalem;
you gather the outcasts of Israel.
You heal the broken-hearted,
and bind up their wounds.
You fix the number of the stars,
and give to each its name.

You are great and almighty,
your wisdom beyond all measure.
For you lift up the poor and
  downtrodden,
you put oppression to rout.

We sing to you with thanksgiving;
make melody upon the lyre!

You cover the heavens with
   clouds,
you prepare rain for the earth,
make mountains sprout with
   grass.
You provide beasts with their
   food,—

and the young ravens that cry.
You delight not in the strength of
   the horse,
nor take pleasure in human
   indulgence;
but you delight in those who
   revere you,
in those who hope in your love.
   Glory*...

READING

Transformation through immersion and consciousness depends on our
capacity to be penetrated by the Mystery of Christ. Our being, our
substance, must be porous in order for the Mystery to enter, to
penetrate. That is the crux of the matter. It is not enough simply to be
immersed in...life. We must let ourselves be plowed so that the furrows
of our person become deeper and deeper, so that our earth becomes
softer and softer. This is something our being craves, but this plowing is
kenosis [emptying, the death which must precede new life, rebirth] and
kenosis is not easy. In the measure that our being becomes porous,
open, grace can penetrate us. Depth is possible. Transformation is
possible. Thus an ever deepening penetration by the Mystery can fill us
with spiritual being.

Jean-Marie Howe, "Cistercian Monastic Life/Vows: A Vision," p. 367, (7)

RESPONSORY

O God, you have made of us a priesthood, baptized in the blood of
   Christ. —**O God...**
You send us to all nations; —**baptized...**
Glory to you, Source of all Being, Eternal Word and Holy Spirit.
   —**O God...**

CANTICLE OF ZECHARIAH

**Ant. Send your light and your truth to those who dwell in
   darkness.**

INTERCESSIONS

O God, no one is beyond the reach of your love;
   —help us to appreciate one another as we are, not expecting
      more than we can do or give.

Our culture is heavy with the lure of material gain;
  —deliver us from the temptation to use others for our own
    profit.
Jesus, your Spirit dwells in our hearts;
  —keep us open to the wisdom and gifts of everyone.
Wealthy men and women were among your followers, and they
supported your mission;
  —show us how to use whatever we have in keeping with your
    gospel.
We have walked on the moon, and technology reaches deeper and
deeper into the galaxies;
  —may scientific research deepen our thirst for the wisdom and
    knowledge of God.

PRAYER: O God, you call us to be your people and to minister to
one another. Look with pity on all who are held captive
by the bonds of addiction. Free us from our own
destructive impulses that we may choose life and
enable others to find what is life-giving for them. Give
discernment and wisdom to all who minister to those
seeking liberation from any forms of addiction, that we
may all know the joy of the freedom that is ours as
your children. This we ask of you, who are our Mother,
our Father, our Guardian, our God, Creator and
Preserver of us all, both now and in eternity. Amen.

DAYTIME PRAYER

**Ant. 1 Give me life according to
  your justice.**

Psalm 119:153–160

Look on my affliction and deliver
  me,
for I remember your law.
Plead my cause and redeem me;
give me life according to your
  promise!

Salvation is far from the wicked,
for they do not seek your
  statutes.—

Great is your mercy, O God;
give me life according to your
  justice.

Though my foes and oppressors
  are many,
I have not swerved from your will.
I look at evil with disgust,
because it seeks to snare me.

See how I love your precepts!
Preserve my life in your love.
The whole of your word is truth;
your decrees are eternal.
  Glory*...

Ant. 2 Bless the work of our hands, O God.

Psalm 128

Blessed are they who fear you, O God,
and walk in your ways!

By the labor of their hands they shall eat.
A husband will be happy and prosper;
a wife like a fruitful vine
  in the heart of her house;
their children like olive shoots
  around their table.

Indeed thus shall be blessed
those who fear you, O God.

May you bless them from Zion
all the days of their lives!
May they see their children's
  children in a happy Jerusalem!
  Glory*...

Ant. 3 Deliver me for the sake of your love.
Psalm 6

O God, rebuke me not for my
  frailties,—
nor chastise me in my weakness.
Be gracious to me for I am
  languishing;
heal me, for my bones are
  troubled.
My soul is sorely troubled.
But you, O God—how long?

Turn, O God, save my life;
deliver me for the sake of your
  love.
For in death there is no
  remembrance of you;
in the grave who can give you
  praise?

I am weary with my moaning;
every night I flood my bed with
  tears;
I drench my couch with my
  weeping.
My eyes waste away because of
  my grief,
they grow weak because of my
  misfortune.

Let this darkness depart from me;
hear the sound of my weeping.
You will hear my supplication;
you will accept my prayer.
  Glory*...

PRAYER: Bountiful God, you nourish us daily with the bread of life and the bread that is the work of our hands. May all the peoples and creatures of this earth have the nourishment they need to live their lives fully. Help us to solve the problems of food distribution, drought, expanding deserts, malnutrition, famine, and disease, that all may share in the banquet and none will be in want. We ask this through Jesus, our Bread of Life. Amen.

EVENING PRAYER

Ant. 1 I will sing a new song to you, for you are my refuge.

Psalm 144:1–10

Blessed are you, O God, my rock,
who train my hands for war,
and my fingers for battle.

You are my rock and my fortress,
my stronghold and my deliverer,
my shield in whom I take refuge,
You bring peoples under your
rule.

Who are we that you care for us,
mortal flesh, that you keep us in
mind?
We, who are merely a breath,
whose days are like a passing
shadow.

Lower your heavens and come
down!
Touch the mountains that they
smoke!
Flash your lightnings and scatter
them,
shoot your arrows and put them
to flight.

Stretch forth your hand from on
high,
rescue me from the mighty
waters,
from the hands of alien foes,
whose mouths are filled with lies,
and whose hands are raised in
perjury.

To you will I sing a new song.
On a ten-stringed harp I will play
to you, who give rulers their
victory,
who rescue David, your servant.
    Glory*...

Ant. 2 Happy are the people whose God is our God.

II

To you I will sing a new song;
I will play on the ten-stringed
harp,
to you who give rulers their
victory,
who set David your servant free.

You set him free from the evil
sword,
and delivered him from alien foes,
whose mouths were filled with
lies,
whose hands were raised in
perjury.

Let our sons in their youth be like
plants full grown,
our daughters like graceful
columns
adorned as though for a palace.

Let our granaries be full, with
crops of every kind;
may our sheep bring forth
thousands
and ten thousands in our fields;
may our cattle be heavy with
young,
suffering no mischance in
bearing.

May there be no ruined wall, no
exile,
no cry of distress in our streets.
Happy the people with such
blessings!
Happy the people whose God is
our God.   **Glory*...**

Ant. 3 Now is the time of salvation for those who revere your name.

Cant: Rev 11: 17–18; 12:10b–12a

We give thanks to you, God Almighty,
who is and who was.
You have assumed your great power,
you have begun your reign.

The nations raged, but your wrath came,
and the time for the dead to be judged,
for rewarding your servants, the prophets and saints,—

and those who revere your name,
the great and small alike.

Now the salvation, the power and the reign have come,
of God and of the Christ,
for the accusers of our loved ones have been thrown down,
who accuse them day and night.

They have been conquered by the blood of the Lamb,
and by the word of their testimony,
for love of life did not deter them from death.
Rejoice then, O heavens,
and you that dwell therein!
Glory*...

READING

If you will it,...observe the light of the divine presence that pervades all existence. Observe the harmony of the heavenly realm, how it pervades every aspect of life, the spiritual and the material, which are before your eyes of flesh and your eyes of the spirit. Contemplate the wonders of creation, the divine dimension of their being, not as a dim configuration that is presented to you from the distance but as the reality in which you live. Know yourself, and your world; know the meditations of your heart, and of every thinker; find the source of your own life, and of the life beyond you, around you, the glorious splendor of the life in which you have your being.

Abraham Isaac Kook, Lights of Holiness, p. 207, (1)

RESPONSORY

You bless the peacemakers, and call them your children.
 —You bless...
You give them your spirit, **—and call...**
Glory to you, Source of all Being, Eternal Word and Holy Spirit.
 —You bless...

CANTICLE OF MARY

Ant. Blessed are the peacemakers, for they shall be called children of God.

INTERCESSIONS

O God, creator of all that is;
  —bless the work of our hands.
Jesus, revelation of God to us;
  —teach us to speak and live the truth.
Holy Spirit, dwelling in our hearts;
  —deepen our love for God and for one another.
Triune God, Eternal Love;
  —bless our families, communities, and the nations of the
    world.
Holy God, Holy Available One;
  —never let us be separated from you.

PRAYER: God of the nations, look upon the lands devastated by
war and show us the way to peace. Turn our guns into
plows and our bombs into bread. Remove hatred from
our hearts and vengeance from our memories. Give us
the wisdom and the will to end terrorism and war
whether in lands far or near, or in the confines of our
families and communities. Help us to remember that
we are one world and one family. Grant this through
the intercession of all the peacemakers of all times and
all places, especially those who suffered persecution
and death for the sake of justice and peace. Amen.

FRIDAY

MORNING PRAYER

**Ant 1 Remember me, O God,
make yourself known in time
of affliction.**

Psalm 51

Have mercy on me, O God,
according to your steadfast love;
in your abundant mercy blot out
  my sins.
Wash me thoroughly from my
  offenses,
and cleanse me from my sin!

For I know my offenses,
and my sin is ever before me.
Against you, you alone, have I
  sinned,
and done what is evil in your
  sight,
so you are justified in your
  sentence
and blameless in your judgment.
Behold, I was brought forth in a
  sinful world.

For you desire truth in my
 innermost being;
teach me wisdom in the depths of
 my heart.
O purify me, and I shall be clean;
O wash me, I shall be whiter than
 snow.
Fill me with joy and gladness;
let the bones you have broken
 rejoice.
Hide your face from my guilt,
and blot out all my offenses.

Create in me a clean heart,
put a steadfast spirit within me.
Cast me not from your presence,
take not your spirit from me.
Give me again the joy of your
 salvation,
with a willing spirit uphold me.

Then I will teach transgressors
 your ways
and sinners will return to you.
Deliver me from death,
O God of my salvation,
and my tongue will sing out your
 saving help.

Open my lips and my mouth will
 sing your praises.
For you take no delight in
 sacrifice;
were I to give a burnt offering,
you would not be pleased.
A broken spirit you accept;
a contrite heart, you will not
 despise.

In your goodness, show favor to
 Zion;
rebuild the walls of Jerusalem.
Then you will delight in just
 sacrifices,
in gifts offered on your altar.
 Glory*...

**Ant. 2 Your love and your
kindness extend to all the
nations of the earth.**

Cant: Tobit 13:8–11, 13–15

Let all speak of your majesty, O
 God,
and sing your praises in
 Jerusalem.

O Jerusalem, holy city,
God scourged you for the works
 of your hands,
but will again pity the children of
 the righteous.

Praise the goodness of God,
and bless the Sovereign of the
 ages,
so that the holy tent may be
 rebuilt in you with joy.

May God gladden within you all
 who were captives;
cherishing within you all who
 were ravaged
for all generations to come.

A bright light will shine to all
 parts of the earth;
many nations shall come to you
 from afar,
and the inhabitants of all the
 limits of the earth,
drawn to you by the name of the
 Most High God,
bearing in their hands their gifts
 for the Almighty.

Every generation shall give joyful
 praise to you,
and shall call you the chosen
 one,
through all ages forever.

Go, then, rejoice over the children
 of the righteous,—

who shall all be gathered together
and shall bless the God of the
ages.

Happy are those who love you,
and happy those who rejoice in
your prosperity.
Happy are they who shall grieve
over you,
over all your chastisements,
for they shall rejoice in you
as they behold your joy forever.

My spirit blesses you, my God.
Glory*...

**Ant. 3 You feed us with the
finest wheat.**

Psalm 147:12–20

O praise the Most High,
Jerusalem!
Praise your God, O Zion!

For God strengthens the bars of
your gates,
blessing your children within
you,—

establishing peace in your
borders,
feeding you with the finest of
wheat.

You send out your word to the
earth;
your command runs swiftly,
giving snow like wool,
scattering hoarfrost like ashes.

You cast forth your ice like
crumbs;
who can stand before your cold?
You send forth your words, and
melt them;
you make the wind blow, and the
waters flow.

You make your word known to
your people,
your statutes and decrees to
Israel.
You have not dealt thus with any
other nation;
you have not taught them your
decrees. **Glory*...**

READING

She [Teresa of Avila] is a guide for the heights, those moments on the
mount of unitive embrace; for the lowlands, when we wonder if we can
ever climb up again; for the plateaus, when we would just as soon set
up a tent and stop moving. In every situation, positive or negative,
Teresa is with us, urging us to see where we are as simply another
starting point for further journeying inward to God. "And if [a] person
should do no more than take one step, the step will contain in itself so
much power that [they] will not have to fear losing it, nor will [they] fail
to be very well paid." (Teresa of Avila, *Way of Perfection*)

Margaret Dorgan, "St. Teresa of Avila: A Guide for Travel Inward," pp. 351–52, (7)

RESPONSORY

O God, freedom is your gift to all, whether rich or poor.
—O God...
You care for all peoples of the earth, **—whether...**

Glory to you, Source of all Being, Eternal Word and Holy Spirit.
   —O God...

CANTICLE OF ZECHARIAH

Ant. Heal the wounds of our sins and grant us new life.

INTERCESSIONS

O God, you have planted the seed of your word in our lives;
   —let its nourishment be the deciding factor in what we choose
      to see and hear.
Faith as small as a mustard seed is enough for us;
   —give us an appreciation of what we have, living in your
      presence day by day.
We long to be instruments of unity and peace in the world;
   —teach us how to support husbands and wives in their efforts
      to be faithful; show us ways to make our culture supportive.
Jesus, again and again you assured your followers with a
calming, "Fear not!"
   —Grant your peace to those who live in fear for their lives or
      dignity, those for whom fear is an abiding reality.
Bless the aging who live alone, with family, or in nursing homes;
   —reveal your love for them through those who care for them.

PRAYER: O God, look with mercy on those who are in prison.
         Fill their hearts with courage and peace, and let those
         who minister to them do so with justice built on
         compassion. Free political prisoners, prisoners of
         conscience, and all those who are imprisoned unjustly.
         Grant this through Jesus who was unjustly condemned
         but now lives and reigns with you forever and ever.
         Amen.

DAYTIME PRAYER

**Ant. 1 Your word is my
   treasure, O God.**

Psalm 119:161–168

Rulers oppress me without cause
but my heart stands in awe of
   your words.—

I rejoice in your word
like one who finds great treasure.

I hate and abhor falsehood, but I
   love your law.
Seven times a day I praise you for
   your just decrees.

Great peace have those who love
your law;
nothing can make them stumble.
I hope for your salvation, O God,
I fulfill your commandments.

My soul obeys your will and loves
it exceedingly.
I obey your precepts and your
will,
for all my ways are before you.
Glory*...

**Ant. 2 Let us love one another
for love is of God.**

Psalm 133

How good and how pleasant it is,
when we live together in unity!

It is like precious oil upon the
head,
running down upon the beard of
Aaron,
running down the collar of his
robes!

It is like the dew of Hermon
which falls on the mountains of
Zion!
For there God gives us the
blessing,
life for evermore. **Glory*...**

**Ant. 3 Guard me, O God, from
the snares of darkness.**

Psalm 140:1-9, 13-14

Rescue me from evil;
preserve me from violence.
Deliver me from an unclean
heart,
from the chaos of a troubled
mind.
Preserve me from a malicious
tongue,
from sharp and poisonous words.

Guard me, O God, from my
darkness,
and from those who lure me to
evil,
who darken my light with gloom.
Pride and arrogance lay a snare;
greed and covetousness spread a
net;
by my pathway they lie in wait.

I say to you: "You are my God."
Give ear to my supplication!
O God, my strong deliverer,
you shield my head in battle.
Grant not the desires of
darkness;
protect me against its snares.

I know you uphold the afflicted,
you effect justice for the needy.
Surely the just shall give thanks
to your name;
the upright shall dwell in your
presence. **Glory*...**

PRAYER: O God, we remember the agonizing death of Jesus. In
your compassion deliver those who suffer from the
cruelty of others, and heal the minds and hearts of
those who inflict pain. Give us a sensitivity to others
that is worthy of your children. This we ask through
the intercession of all who suffered persecution and
death for the sake of others. Amen.

EVENING PRAYER

Ant. 1 Every day I will bless you and praise your name forever.

Psalm 145

I will extol you, O God my God,
and bless your name forever and
ever.

Every day I will bless you,
and praise your name forever.
For you are great and highly to be
praised,
your greatness is unsearchable.

Age to age shall proclaim your
works,
and declare your mighty deeds.
I will ponder your glorious
splendor,
and the wonder of all your works.

Your people will proclaim the
might of your deeds,
and I will declare your greatness.
They will pour forth the fame of
your goodness,
and sing with joy of your justice.

You are gracious and merciful,
slow to anger, abounding in love.
Your compassion extends to all
you have made;
how good you are to all!

All your works shall give you
thanks;
all your friends shall bless you!
They shall speak of the glory of
your creation,
and declare your marvelous
might,
to make known to the children of
earth the glory of your deeds,
and the glorious splendor of all
you have made.

Yours is an everlasting realm,
and your dominion endures
through all generations.
Glory*...

Ant. 2 You are near to all who call to you with sincere and upright hearts.
II

O God, you are faithful in all your
words,
and gracious in all your deeds.
You uphold all who are falling,
and raise up all who are bowed
down.

The eyes of all creatures look to
you,
to give them their food in due
season.
You open wide your hand,
and satisfy the desires of every
living thing.

You are just in all your ways,
and loving in all your deeds.
You are near to all who call on
you,
who call on you from their hearts.

You fulfill the desires of those
who revere you,
you hear their cries and save
them.
You protect all who love you, O
God;
but evil you will utterly destroy.

Let me speak your praises, O
God,
let all humankind bless your
name forever,
for ages unending. **Glory*...**

Ant. 3 Your works, O God, are great and wonderful.

Cant: Rev 15:3–4

Great and wonderful are your works,
God the Almighty One!
Just and true are your ways,
Ruler of all the ages!

Who shall refuse you honor,
or the glory due your name?

For you alone are holy,
all nations shall come and
worship in your presence.
Your judgments are clearly seen.
Glory*...

READING

Nowadays I always feel transported into Napoleonic times, and I can imagine in what tension people lived then everywhere in Europe. I wonder: will we live to see the events of our days become "history"? I have a great desire to see all this sometime in the light of eternity. For one realizes ever more clearly how blind we are toward everything. One marvels at how mistakenly one viewed a lot of things before, and yet the very next moment one commits the blunder again of forming an opinion without having the necessary basis for it.

Edith Stein: Self-Portrait in Letters, p. 315, (3)

RESPONSORY

Your ways are mysterious, O God, but your love is our light.
   —Your ways...
Your Word became flesh; **—your love...**
Glory to you, Source of all Being, Eternal Word and Holy Spirit.
   —Your ways...

CANTICLE OF MARY

Ant. Guide us in your truth lest we go astray.

INTERCESSIONS

O God, you adorn the earth with the beauty of each season;
   —awaken us to your loving care as you lift up our hearts
      with color and surprise.
You share your life with us through the talents you give us;
   —make us worthy stewards, eager to grow, mindful of our
      use of time.
Your Spirit dwells in our hearts, the very power of your love;
   —let us remember that you are at work in us, never asking
      what is beyond our power.

Lord Jesus, teach us to pray as you taught your apostles;
  —show us how to live quietly and to know how to
    distinguish want from need.
Heart of Jesus, once in agony,
  —have pity on the dying.

PRAYER: God, source of all life, have pity on the dying and on
those who mourn. Help them to experience this
transition as a birth to new life; this loss in time as a
realization of eternity. Ease their pain and grant them
your peace which Jesus proclaimed after that first
Good Friday. We ask this in his name. Amen.

SATURDAY

MORNING PRAYER

**Ant. 1 We proclaim your love in
the morning and your
faithfulness at night.**

Psalm 92

It is good to give thanks to you, O
  God,
to sing praise to your name, O
  Most High,
to proclaim your love in the
  morning,
and your faithfulness by night,
to the music of the lute and the
  harp,
to the melody of the lyre.

For you make me glad by your
  deeds;
at the work of your hands I sing
  for joy.
O God, how great are your works!
Your thoughts are very deep!

The foolish ones cannot know
  this,
and the dull cannot understand:
though wickedness sprouts like
  grass—

and evil seems to flourish,
they are doomed to destruction
  forever.
But you are forever on high.

You exalt my strength like that of
  the ox;
you pour over me fresh oil.
My eyes looked in triumph over
  evil,
my ears heard the doom of
  oppression.

The just will flourish like the
  palm tree
and grow like a cedar of Lebanon.
They are planted in your holy
  house,
they flourish in your courts, O
  God.
They still bring forth fruit in old
  age,
they are ever full of sap and
  green,
to show that you are just;
you are my rock, in you is no
  injustice. **Glory*...**

Ant. 2 Give us hearts of flesh, O God, that we may serve you.

Cant: Ezekiel 36:24–28

I will take you from the nations,
and gather you from foreign
  countries,
and bring you back to your own
  land.

I will sprinkle clean water upon
  you
to cleanse you from all your
  impurities,
and from all your idols I will
  cleanse you.

A new heart I will give you,
and a new spirit I will put within
  you;
and I will take out of your body
  the heart of stone
and give you a heart of flesh.

I will put my spirit within you,
and make you live by my
  statutes,
careful to observe my decrees.

You shall dwell in the land which
  I gave to your ancestors;
you shall be my people,
and I will be your God.
  Glory*...

Ant. 3 Your name is great in all the earth.

Psalm 8

How great is your name, O God,
  in all the earth!

You, whose glory above the
  heavens
is chanted on the lips of babes,
have found a defense against
  your foes,
to silence the cries of the rebels.

When I look at the heavens,
the work of your hands,
the moon and the stars which
  you established;
who are we that you should keep
  us in mind,
mortal flesh that you care for us?

Yet you have made us little less
  than God,
and crowned us with glory and
  honor.
You entrust us with the works of
  your hands;
to care for all your creation.

All sheep and oxen,
and even the beasts of the field,
the birds of the air, and the fish
  of the sea,
whatever passes along the paths
  of the sea.

How great is your name, Creator
  God, in all the earth! **Glory*...**

READING

In order for thanksgiving and the voice of praise, which are one and the same, to be found in your soul, you must rejoice and be glad in the [One] who created it, and then from joy and gladness proceed to the thanksgiving of which we speak and which is so perfect that for good reason Our Lady is said to have invented the manner of speech used by all religious when they say *Deo gratias,* which means "let us give thanks to God."

Francisco de Osuna, *The Third Spiritual Alphabet,* p. 72, (1)

RESPONSORY

O God, you are father and mother to us; your love never ceases.
   —O God,...
We have sinned against you; **—your love...**
Glory to you, Source of all Being, Eternal Word and Holy Spirit.
   —O God,...

CANTICLE OF ZECHARIAH

Ant. Fill our days with peace that we may sing your praise.

INTERCESSIONS

O God, time often leaves us longing for more, for we are created
for eternity;
    —help us to find you within, where time and eternity are more
       clearly one.
Your commandments are guides for our way to fullness of life;
    —remind us that law follows life.
Our short lives are a history of your gifts to us;
    —may all that we do give you thanks and praise.
You are ever present to us in our need;
    —let us never be indifferent to the suffering of others.
Spirit of God, our advocate and guide;
    —teach us how to be an effective voice for the powerless.

PRAYER: O God, your love is truth, yet we so often fear you.
You regard us with mercy, yet we see you as judge.
Open our eyes to your goodness and let us realize the
life to which we are called. We ask this through the
intercession of Mary, mother of Jesus, who knew and
proclaimed your goodness to all generations. Amen.

DAYTIME PRAYER

**Ant. 1 I delight in your law;
teach me discernment
according to your will.**

Psalm 119:169–176

Let my cry come before you, O
   God;—

give me discernment according to
   your word.
Let my supplication come before
   you;
deliver me as you have promised.

My lips will pour forth praise
because you teach me your
   commands.—

My tongue will sing of your
   promise,
for all your commands are just.

Let your hand be ready to help
   me,
for I have chosen your precepts.
I long for your saving help
and your law is my delight.

Let me live, that I may praise you,
and let your precepts help me.
I have gone astray like a lost
   sheep;
seek your servant, for I do not
   forget your commands.
   Glory*...

**Ant. 2 Listen to my prayer, O
God.**

Psalm 61

Hear my cry, O God,
listen to my prayer;
from the end of the earth I call,
when my heart is faint.

Set me on the rock that is higher
   than I;
for you are my refuge,
my stronghold against evil.

Let me dwell in your tent forever!
Hide me in the shelter of your
   wings!
For you, O God, have heard my
   vows,
you have given me the heritage
of those who love your name.

May you lengthen the lives of just
   rulers:
may their years cover many
   generations!
May they ever be enthroned
   before you;
bid love and truth watch over
   them.

So will I ever sing your praises,
as I pay my vows day after day.
   Glory*...

**Ant. 3 The needy fly to you for
refuge.**

Psalm 64

Hear my voice, O God, in my
   complaint;
preserve my life from all that is
   evil,
hide me from the tempter's snare,
from the scheming wiles of my
   heart.

Evil sharpens its tongue like a
   sword;
aiming bitter words like arrows
shooting from ambush at the
   innocent,
shooting suddenly and without
   fear.

Holding fast to its evil purpose;
conspiring to lay secret snares
thinking: "Who can see us?
Who can search out our crimes?"

But you know well our inmost
   thoughts,
the depth of the heart and mind!
You will shoot your arrow at
   them;
they will be wounded suddenly.
Our own tongues bring us to
   ruin.

Then let all people fear;
they will tell what you have
   wrought,
and ponder what you have done.
The just will rejoice in you, O
   God,
and fly to you for refuge.
Let the upright in heart exult.
   Glory*...

PRAYER: Deliver us, O God, from those who would hurt us and from our own selfishness. Guard us from all that would prevent our growth, and let us not be stumbling blocks to others. We ask this in the name of Jesus who is our way, our truth and our life. Amen.

INVITATORY

Psalm 95

O come, let us sing to our God;
let us make a joyful noise to the rock
  of our salvation!

We come into your presence with thanksgiving,
rejoicing with songs of praise!
For you, O God, are our God,
a great Ruler over all other gods.
In your hands are the depths of the earth;
the heights of the mountains as well.
The sea is yours, for you made it;
and your hands formed the dry land.

We bow down before you and worship,
kneeling before you, our Maker!
For you are our God, and we are your people,
the flock that you shepherd.

Today let us hearken to your voice:
"Harden not your hearts, as at Meribah,
as on the day at Massah in the desert,
when your ancestors tested me,
and put me to the test,
though they had seen my works."
    Glory...

EASTER SUNDAY
(Psalms from Sunday, Week I, p. 3)

MORNING PRAYER

Ant 1 I am risen and still with you, alleluia!

Ant 2 And behold, there was a great earthquake; for an angel came down from heaven, rolled back the stone and sat upon it, alleluia!

Ant 3 The angel spoke and said to the women, "Do not be afraid; for I know that you seek Jesus," alleluia!

READING

The Sun arising in the East,
Though he give light, and th' East perfume;
If they should offer to contest
With thy arising, they presume.

Can there be any day but this,
Though many suns to shine endeavor?
We count three hundred, but we miss:
There is but one, and this one ever.

George Herbert, Easter (II), p. 156, (1)

(In place of the responsory the following is said:)

Ant This is the day our God has made; let us give praise in song, alleluia!

CANTICLE OF ZECHARIAH

Ant Early on the first day of the week, at sunrise, the women went to the tomb, alleluia.

INTERCESSIONS

God has raised up for us a mighty savior who chose to lay down his life for us. With renewed confidence, let us pray:
Raise us up with you, Christ Jesus!

Lamb of God, you returned from death to bring peace;
—may we learn to return blessing for injury.
Servant of God, you showed us the way to reveal your God and ours;
—live in us your spirit of service to all without discrimination.

Passionate Lover of humanity, you emptied yourself to become like us;
  —may the fire of your Spirit transform us to your likeness.
Rising Dawn of our universe, First-born of all creation,
  —draw us with you into eternal light.
Giver of life, bring to new birth in water and Spirit all our catechumens;
  —may they find unending joy as your people.

PRAYER: Most merciful, loving God, you have been revealed in Christ Jesus as he rises to bring us the message of forgiveness and all-embracing love. May we who have passed with him from death to life in the mysteries we have celebrated, be signs of your life among us. We ask this through Jesus, our risen Savior. Amen.

DAYTIME PRAYER

Ant 1 Christ having risen from the dead, will die no more; death shall no longer have dominion over him, alleluia. (Ps. 8, p. 92)

Ant 2 Put to death indeed in the flesh, Jesus was brought to life in the spirit, alleluia. (Ps. 19a, p. 57)

Ant 3 The cross has become our victory; let us live in the holiness of Christ, alleluia. (Ps. 19:7–14, p. 12)

(Prayer as in Morning Prayer)

EVENING PRAYER
(Psalms from Sunday, Week I, p. 7)

Ant 1 After the Sabbath, toward the dawn of the first day of the week, Mary Magdalen and the other Mary went to see the tomb, alleluia.

Ant 2 The angel said to the women, "Go quickly, tell his disciples that he has risen from the dead," alleluia.

Ant 3 Jesus said to them: "Do not be afraid; see, I was dead, but now I live and am among you," alleluia.

READING

When we begin a life journey with Jesus we must go all the way with him if we would find ourselves. We need not only Christmas but the cross in order to understand Christmas and in order to be given Easter. We are the companions of this child and the crucified savior. If we feel unworthy, we must remember that Jesus, in his birth and in his burial, in the virgin's womb and Calvary's tomb, reverses all expectations. Easter is a return of Christ to those who felt unworthy but who did not stop loving. We come as wise men and women to the manger, as disciples to the cross, as an Easter people to the empty tomb.

Anthony T. Padavano, Christmas to Calvary, p. 15, (1)

(In place of the responsory the following is said:)

Ant This is the day our God has made; let us give praise in song, alleluia!

CANTICLE OF MARY

Ant On the evening of that day, the first day of the week, the doors being shut where the disciples were, Jesus came and stood among them and said to them: "Peace be with you," alleluia!

INTERCESSIONS

You broke the reign of death, O Christ and we are free! With joyful voice we proclaim:

Glory and praise to you!

Redeemer of all, enlighten us who still walk in the shadow of death;
— that with your new life we may conquer our addictions and prejudices.

Risen Savior, you appeared first to women, and sent them with the glad tidings;
— free all women bound by traditions and cultures that inhibit their human development.

Hallowed Stranger, you appeared this evening to the disillusioned disciples on the road to Emmaus;
— enkindle our hearts to recognize you in the unlikely circumstances of our lives.

Savior of the world, your message is peace in a world racked with violence;
— teach us the way of non-violence toward all creation.

PRAYER: Most merciful, loving God, you have been revealed in Christ Jesus as he rises to bring us the message of forgiveness and all-embracing love. May we who have passed with him from death to life in the mysteries we have celebrated, be signs of your life among us. We ask this through Jesus, our risen Savior. Amen.

EASTER MONDAY
(Psalms from Sunday, Week I, p. 3)
MORNING PRAYER

Ant 1 I am risen and still with you, alleluia!

Ant 2 Jesus said to the women, "Do not be afraid; go and tell my brothers to go to Galilee; there they will see me," alleluia!

Ant 3 God raised him up, having freed him from death, for it was not possible for Jesus to be held by its power, alleluia.

READING

As for Mary Magdalene, so for the two disciples (on the way to Emmaus), faith is a joyous and grateful acceptance of Christ's coming, of his gracious presence, and therefore of the mission of bringing the good news to others by word and life. This is, and will always be, the very heart of evangelization. Those who have found the risen Lord and who hear him with a sincere heart will be witnesses of his saving presence.

Bernard Häring, Prayer: The Integration of Faith and Life, p. 63, (8)

(In place of the responsory the following is said:)

Ant This is the day our God has made; let us give praise in song, alleluia!

CANTICLE OF ZECHARIAH

Ant. Go and tell his disciples that Christ is alive again, alleluia.

INTERCESSIONS

Christ Jesus appears among us today as the Morning Star rising in our hearts. In gratitude we cry out:
Light of Christ, we praise you!

You are among us as light for our world; awaken us to new consciousness;

—that your Spirit may have full sway in our lives.
You are among us as truth; open the ears of our hearts;
 —that we may listen untiringly for the good, the true, and
 the beautiful which emanates from you.
You are among us as the Way; lure us into your ways;
 —that all our paths may be peaceful and all our ways, love.
You are among us as Life; may we surrender to that life;
 —that all peoples may be irresistibly drawn toward
 unending life in you.

PRAYER: O God, through this paschal mystery you have saved
the world. Uphold your people with your grace that
they may walk in perfect freedom on their way to life
eternal. This we ask through Jesus, our risen Savior.
Amen.

DAYTIME PRAYER

Ant 1 Christ having risen from the dead, will die no more; death
shall no longer have dominion over him, alleluia.
(Ps. 8, p. 92)

Ant 2 Put to death indeed in the flesh, Jesus was brought to life
in the spirit, alleluia. (Ps. 19a, p. 57)

Ant 3 The cross has become our victory; let us live in the
holiness of Christ, alleluia. (Ps. 19:7–14, p. 12)

(Prayer as in Morning Prayer)

EVENING PRAYER
(Psalms from Sunday, Week I, p. 7)

Ant 1 After the Sabbath, toward the dawn of the first day of the
week, Mary Magdalen and the other Mary went to see the
tomb, alleluia.

Ant 2 The angel said to the women, "Go quickly, tell his disciples
that he has risen from the dead," alleluia.

Ant 3 Jesus said to them: "Do not be afraid; see, I was dead, but
now I live and am among you," alleluia.

READING

So in our true Mother Jesus our life is founded in his own prescient
wisdom from without beginning, with the great power of the Father and
the supreme goodness of the Holy Spirit. And in accepting our nature
he gave us life, and in his blessed dying on the Cross he bore us to
endless life. And since that time, now and ever until the day of
judgment, he feeds us, and fosters us, just as the great supreme
lovingness of motherhood wishes, and as the natural need of childhood
asks. Fair and sweet is our heavenly Mother in the sight of our soul,
precious and lovely are the children of grace in the sight of our heavenly
Mother, with gentleness and meekness and all the lovely virtues which
belong to children by nature.

Julian of Norwich, Showings, p. 304, (1)

(In place of the responsory the following is said:)

Ant This is the day our God has made; let us give praise in song,
     alleluia!

CANTICLE OF MARY

Ant The angel said: Why do you seek the living among the dead?
     He is not here but has risen, alleluia!

INTERCESSIONS

Jesus is the Evening Star which lights our path to heaven; in joy
let us cry out:
     Stay with us, for the day is now far spent.

O Christ, your resurrection sounds the death knell of sin;
  —may we live out courageously our struggle for true freedom
     and wholeness.
The tomb could not contain you, O Jesus, who had freely
submitted to death;
  —lead us out of our sterile selfishness to genuine surrender.
You won paradise for the thief; grant eternal joy to all who have
died;
  —that they may praise your mercy forever.
In taking flesh among us you raised all creation to a new dignity;
  —teach us to have an ever-growing reverence for the work of
     your hands and a sense of responsibility for its
     preservation.

PRAYER: O God, through this paschal mystery you have saved
          the world. Uphold your people with your grace that

they may walk in perfect freedom on their way to life eternal. This we ask through Jesus, our risen Savior. Amen.

EASTER TUESDAY

(Psalms from Sunday, Week I, p. 3)

MORNING PRAYER

Ant 1 Jesus said to her, "Woman, why are you weeping? Whom do you seek?" Alleluia.

Ant 2 Mary Magdalene went and announced to the disciples, "I have seen the Lord!" alleluia.

Ant 3 We know with certainty that God has made him both Lord and Christ, this Jesus who was crucified, alleluia!

READING

Easter is a day of joy for us because through his resurrection Jesus took the past of the apostles—as he does ours—and forgave the worst of it and saved the best of it. He conquered the future by making death a door to be opened instead of a dead end. Most happily of all, he gave each of us his Presence, his Spirit, to be the Way through which we live toward that future which "eye hath not seen nor ear heard."

Elizabeth Meluch, OCD, (11)

(In place of the responsory the following is said:)

Ant This is the day our God has made; let us give praise in song, alleluia!

CANTICLE OF ZECHARIAH

Ant. Woman, why are you weeping, whom do you seek? Sir, if you have carried him away, tell me where you have laid him and I will take him away!

INTERCESSIONS

God raised up the temple of your body, as you prophesied, O Christ. By that power won for us, we joyfully cry out:
May the whole world come to fullness of life.

Christ Jesus, your victory has changed our sorrow into joy;
help us to share that joy with all we meet today.

You have overcome death by your total acceptance of death;
—let your courage live in us as we strive for a non-violent
    way of life.
It was love that overcame your fear and dread;
—strengthen in that love all who face mortal anguish.
You breathed peace into your disciples and sent them to share the
good news;
—fill us with that peace that brands us as your own.
Your death has swallowed up death;
—may all who have died awake to life with you.

PRAYER: O God, we praise you in the victory of life over death in
         Jesus, our Savior. Help us to comprehend the awesome
         mystery of its effects in our lives and make us tireless
         witnesses of this good news. We ask this in his name.
         Amen.

DAYTIME PRAYER

Ant 1   Christ having risen from the dead, will die no more; death
shall no longer have dominion over him, alleluia.
(Ps. 8, p. 92)

Ant 2   Put to death indeed in the flesh, Jesus was brought to life
in the spirit, alleluia. (Ps. 19a, p. 57)

Ant 3   The cross has become our victory; let us live in the
holiness of Christ, alleluia. (Ps. 19:7–14, p. 12)

(Prayer as in Morning Prayer)

EVENING PRAYER
(Psalms from Sunday, Week I, p. 7)

Ant 1   After the Sabbath, toward the dawn of the first day of the
week, Mary Magdalen and the other Mary went to see the
tomb, alleluia.

Ant 2   The angel said to the women, "Go quickly, tell his disciples
that he has risen from the dead," alleluia.

Ant 3   Jesus said to them: "Do not be afraid; see, I was dead, but
now I live and am among you," alleluia.

READING

When you have loved [Jesus], you shall be chaste, when you have touched [Jesus], you shall become pure; when you have accepted [Jesus], you shall be a virgin. Whose power is stronger, whose generosity is more abundant, whose appearance more beautiful, whose love more tender, whose courtesy more gracious. In whose embrace you are already caught up; who has adorned your breast with precious stones and has placed priceless pearls in your ears and has surrounded you with sparkling gems as though blossoms of springtime and placed on your head *a golden crown as a sign [to all] of your holiness.*

Clare of Assisi, Francis and Clare, p. 191, (1)

(In place of the responsory the following is said:)

Ant This is the day our God has made; let us give praise in song, alleluia!

CANTICLE OF MARY

Ant. Jesus said to Mary: do not cling to me, for I have not yet ascended, but go to my sisters and brothers and say to them, I am ascending to my God and your God.

INTERCESSIONS

As we recall your return to those you loved, our hearts cry out in joy as we say:

Return with us, Jesus, for the day is now far spent!

You sent your holy women, Christ Jesus, to be apostles to the apostles;

—show your special regard for all women who are still shackled by the slavery of our culture, and free them to be good news for the world.

You rewarded the undaunted search of Mary Magdalen with your glorified presence;

—grant that we may be persevering in our efforts to find you in the ordinary events of our lives.

You have opened a new way of hope for our world;

—may our lives incarnate that hope to the despairing, the indifferent, and the lonely.

Your resurrection, O Christ, has transformed our universe;

—sensitize us to a new, all-embracing concern for our environment, and a humble regard for all creatures who share a common source, a loving Creator.

PRAYER: O God, we praise you in the victory of life over death in Jesus, our Savior. Help us to comprehend the awesome mystery of its effects in our lives and make us tireless witnesses of this good news. We ask this in his name. Amen.

EASTER WEDNESDAY
(Psalms from Sunday, Week I, p. 3)

MORNING PRAYER

Ant 1 As they were walking to Emmaus, Jesus himself came near and went with them, alleluia.

Ant 2 "Oh how foolish you are and slow of heart to believe...was it not necessary that the Messiah should suffer these things and then enter into his glory?" Alleluia.

Ant 3 Jesus took bread, blessed, and broke it, and their eyes were opened, and they recognized him, alleluia.

READING

Luke tells a long and beautiful story about two disciples at Emmaus who spend Easter afternoon and evening with Jesus. They recognize him the way we recognize him, in hearing what the Scriptures proclaim and in the breaking of the bread. We are an Emmaus community this morning watching the sun rise, sensing Christ at our side as the Scriptures are opened and the bread is blessed.

Anthony T. Padavano, Christmas to Calvary, p. 83, (1)

(In place of the responsory the following is said:)

Ant This is the day our God has made; let us give praise in song, alleluia!

CANTICLE OF ZECHARIAH

Ant. They said to each other, "Were not our hearts burning within us while he was talking to us on the road, while he was opening the scriptures to us?" Alleluia.

INTERCESSIONS

Behold the lion of the tribe of Juda, the root of David, has overcome death to open the scroll and its seven seals. In grateful praise we cry out saying:

**Thanksgiving, power, honor, and glory to you,
Christ Jesus!**

You have shown your power, O Jesus, in taking on our weakness;
—help us to share in your victory by standing with the
oppressed whenever the opportunity presents itself.
You have freed us by shedding your blood;
—help us to accept that freedom and to use it responsibly
for the building up of our world, and for lifting up the
down-trodden.
You have called us to be liberators of our inner resources;
—give us the humility to cultivate those lesser talents
which we often overlook.
You called blessed those who visit prisoners;
—may our prayers this day touch all those imprisoned for
any reason, that healing may come to their suffering,
and opportunities for rehabilitation be given to all in need.

PRAYER: O God, through the self-emptying of the Word made
flesh you have raised up our fallen world and shown us
the way of true glory. Help us to abide in this love that
we, too, may radiate Christ's humble, self-giving love to
all. We ask this Jesus' name. Amen.

DAYTIME PRAYER

Ant 1 Christ having risen from the dead, will die no more; death
shall no longer have dominion over him, alleluia.
(Ps. 8, p. 92)

Ant 2 Put to death indeed in the flesh, Jesus was brought to life
in the spirit, alleluia. (Ps. 19a, p. 57)

Ant 3 The cross has become our victory; let us live in the
holiness of Christ, alleluia. (Ps. 19:7–14, p. 12)

(Prayer as in Morning Prayer)

EVENING PRAYER
(Psalms from Sunday, Week I, p. 7)

Ant 1 After the Sabbath, toward the dawn of the first day of the
week, Mary Magdalen and the other Mary went to see the
tomb, alleluia.

Ant 2 The angel said to the women, "Go quickly, tell his disciples
that he has risen from the dead," alleluia.

Ant 3 Jesus said to them: "Do not be afraid; see, I was dead, but now I live and am among you," alleluia.

READING

Life from the Center is a life of unhurried peace and power. It is simple. It is serene. It is amazing. It is triumphant. It is radiant. It takes no time, but it occupies all our time. And it makes our life programs new and overcoming. We need not get frantic. [God] is at the helm. And when our little day is done we lie down quietly in peace, all is well.

Thomas R. Kelly, Quaker Spirituality, p. 305, (1)

(In place of the responsory the following is said:)

Ant This is the day our God has made; let us give praise in song, alleluia!

CANTICLE OF MARY

Ant. They drew near to the village to which they were going. He appeared to be going further, but they constrained him, saying, "Stay with us, for it is towards evening and the day is now far spent." Alleluia.

INTERCESSIONS

Christ Jesus is risen as he promised, yet disguised in many ways. In faith, let us pray:
Let us see your glory, O Christ!

You come to us in our deprived sisters and brothers; show us how to lighten their burdens;
  —that they may retain their dignity and hope.
You come to us in the helplessness of little children seeking affirmation, touch our hearts;
  —that we may encourage them, and meet their needs.
You come to us in the weariness and powerlessness of the elderly. Give us your wisdom;
  —that we may recognize you in them by showing them tender, reverent love, heartfelt gratitude, and service.
You come to us in the breaking of the bread;
  —that we may celebrate our oneness with all humankind and give our lives in service.

PRAYER: O God, through the self-emptying of the Word made flesh you have raised up our fallen world and shown us the way of true glory. Help us to abide in this love that we, too, may radiate Christ's humble, self-giving love to all. We ask this in Jesus' name. Amen.

EASTER THURSDAY
(Psalms from Sunday, Week I, p. 3)
MORNING PRAYER

Ant 1 Jesus stood among them and said to them, "Peace be with you," alleluia!

Ant 2 "Look at my hands and feet; see that it is I myself," alleluia!

Ant 3 "You are my witnesses to proclaim repentance and forgiveness to all the nations," alleluia!

READING

Let us establish ourselves in the divine *milieu*. There, we shall be within the inmost depths of souls and the greatest consistency of matter. There, at the confluence of all the forms of beauty, we shall discover the ultra-vital, ultra-perceptible, ultra-active point of the universe; and, at the same time, we shall experience in the depths of our own being the effortless deployment of the *plenitude* of all our powers of action and our adoration.

Teilhard de Chardin, Hymn of the Universe, p. 140, (14)

(In place of the responsory the following is said:)

Ant This is the day our God has made; let us give praise in song, alleluia!

CANTICLE OF ZECHARIAH

Ant. Jesus stood in the midst of his disciples and said to them: "Peace be to you! It is I, do not be afraid," alleluia.

INTERCESSIONS

Jesus has gone down into the valley of death for our sake and has come back in triumph. Let us cry out with confidence:
  Good Shepherd, bring us to wholeness.

You have known the depths of suffering, grant solace to the sick and the dying;
  —that they may experience the joy of your saving help.

You have known the anguish of betrayal, loss, and desolation, draw near to all who suffer;
    —that they may know the power of your resurrection in
      their lives.
You have befriended the lonely and the orphan, now you have entrusted them to our care;
    —guide us that we may have the wisdom to aid them
      according to their needs.
You looked upon the young and loved them. Help us to live lives that inspire, encourage, and befriend them especially in difficult times;
    —that their discouragement may be transformed into
      enthusiasm.

PRAYER: O God, in the paschal mystery you have saved the world. Support the weakness of your people by your grace that they may attain to true freedom and walk in the way of eternal life, following the steps of Jesus, our shepherd. We ask this in his name. Amen.

DAYTIME PRAYER

Ant 1 Christ having risen from the dead, will die no more; death shall no longer have dominion over him, alleluia. (Ps. 8, p. 92)

Ant 2 Put to death indeed in the flesh, Jesus was brought to life in the spirit, alleluia. (Ps. 19a, p. 57)

Ant 3 The cross has become our victory; let us live in the holiness of Christ, alleluia. (Ps. 19:7–14, p. 12)

(Prayer as in Morning Prayer)

EVENING PRAYER
(Psalms from Sunday, Week I, p. 7)

Ant 1 After the Sabbath, toward the dawn of the first day of the week, Mary Magdalen and the other Mary went to see the tomb, alleluia.

Ant 2 The angel said to the women, "Go quickly, tell his disciples that he has risen from the dead," alleluia.

Ant 3 Jesus said to them: "Do not be afraid; see, I was dead, but now I live and am among you," alleluia.

READING

After about the third day...when the numbness of the shock had worn away...the life-transforming creativity previously known only in fellowship with Jesus began again to work in the fellowship of the disciples. It was risen from the dead. Since they had never experienced it except in association with Jesus, it seemed to them that the man Jesus himself was actually present, walking and talking with them. Some thought they saw him and touched him in physical presence. But what rose from the dead was not the man Jesus; it was creative power. It was the living God that works in time. It was the Second Person of the Trinity. It was Christ the God, not Jesus the man.

Henry Nelson Wieman, The Source of Human Good, p. 44, (52)

(In place of the responsory the following is said:)

Ant This is the day our God has made; let us give praise in song, alleluia!

CANTICLE OF MARY

Ant. While they still disbelieved in joy and wonder, he said to them: Have you anything to eat? They gave him a piece of broiled fish, and he took it and ate before them. Alleluia.

INTERCESSIONS

Christ, our Pasch, is sacrificed. In joy let us cry out:
> **Worthy are you, O Christ, to receive honor, glory and praise!**

You laid down your life that we might live;
—give us courage to die to all selfishness that we may live for others.
You were the joy of the disciples;
—be our joy and perennial hope.
You call us out of disbelief by your care for our daily needs;
—may we rejoice in such love and pass it on.
You are the firstborn from the dead;
—may all who have died experience the joy of your presence.

PRAYER: O God, in the paschal mystery you have saved the world. Support the weakness of your people by your grace that they may attain to true freedom and walk in the way of eternal life, following the steps of Jesus, our shepherd. We ask this in his name. Amen.

EASTER FRIDAY
(Psalms as in Sunday, Week I, p. 3)
MORNING PRAYER

Ant 1 Just after daybreak, Jesus stood on the beach, but they did not know him, alleluia!

Ant 2 Jesus said to them, "Cast your net to the other side," alleluia!

Ant 3 None of the disciples dared to ask him, "Who are you?" because they knew it was the Lord, alleluia!

READING

"Risen from the dead" means that [Jesus] *was* dead and then ceased to be dead. But could not the initial resurrection experience be the change *of the disciples* from experiencing him as dead to experiencing him as not among the dead? This would mean that the resurrection experience was their changing from the condition of sinners into the new condition of the redeemed. And this is what the resurrection experience has been in the Church and its liturgy ever since. It is the total experience of release from sin.

Sebastian Moore, *The Crucified Jesus Is No Stranger*, p. 65, (1)

(In place of the responsory the following is said:)

Ant This is the day our God has made; let us give praise in song, alleluia!

CANTICLE OF ZECHARIAH

Ant. Just as the day was breaking, Jesus stood on the shore; yet the disciples did not know that it was Jesus. Alleluia.

INTERCESSIONS

Christ, risen from the dead, is the crown of all creation. Let us give praise, saying:

**Glory, honor, praise, and thanksgiving
be to you, Christ Jesus!**

In your rising, Jesus, you gave us your Spirit;
—that we may live out the vocation to which we are called.
You broke the reign of death, O Christ;
—that divisions may be healed and new life spring up again.
You rescued us from the power of darkness;
—that you might bring us to the fullness of light.
You, Christ Jesus, are the fullness of God among us;
—through you may we be reconciled and be people of peace.

PRAYER: All powerful, ever-living God, you have reconciled humanity through the paschal mystery. Grant that what we celebrate today in faith we may actualize in our lives. We ask this through Jesus, our savior. Amen.

DAYTIME PRAYER

Ant 1 Christ having risen from the dead, will die no more; death shall no longer have dominion over him, alleluia. (Ps. 8, p. 92)

Ant 2 Put to death indeed in the flesh, Jesus was brought to life in the spirit, alleluia. (Ps. 19a, p. 57)

Ant 3 The cross has become our victory; let us live in the holiness of Christ, alleluia. (Ps. 19:7–14, p. 12)

(Prayer as in Morning Prayer)

EVENING PRAYER
(Psalms from Sunday, Week I, p. 7)

Ant 1 After the Sabbath, toward the dawn of the first day of the week, Mary Magdalen and the other Mary went to see the tomb, alleluia.

Ant 2 The angel said to the women, "Go quickly, tell his disciples that he has risen from the dead," alleluia.

Ant 3 Jesus said to them: "Do not be afraid; see, I was dead, but now I live and am among you," alleluia.

READING

Mary Magdalen, who had eyes for Jesus alone, saw him and mistook him for the gardener. Two disciples walked miles with him between Jerusalem and Emmaus, talked hours with him, and thought him a stranger. To recognize the risen Jesus, you would have needed a special grace—as when Jesus murmured to Magdalene "Mary", or broke bread with Cleopas and his friend at Emmaus. And still, for all the mystery of this new Jesus, at once seated with [God] in glory and moving magically through the barriers of our earth, he is the same Jesus who was fashioned from a teen-agers's flesh, the same Jesus who walked our dust and waked our dead, the same Jesus who hung three hours between two robbers, the same Jesus who, Scripture proclaims, "always lives to make intercession for [us]" (Heb. 7:25). Without *so* risen a Christ, without *so* living a Lord, Christianity is a sham and a scam.

Walter J. Burghardt, sj, Lovely in Eyes Not His, pp. 43–44, (1)

(In place of the responsory the following is said:)

Ant This is the day our God has made; let us give praise in song, alleluia!

CANTICLE OF MARY

Ant. None of the disciples dared to ask him, "Who are you?" They knew it was the Christ, alleluia.

INTERCESSIONS

Let us praise the wonderful works of God as we say:
> **Your mighty works are clearly seen!**

When Christ arose, you filled the earth with glory, O God;
> —may we radiate that glory to all we meet today.

Through the mystery of Christ's rising may we begin anew;
> —to direct all our desires to the coming of the fullness of life.

Light of the world, help us to recognize your presence;
> —that we may cultivate discernment as a way of life.

May the redemption which Jesus won for us make us joyful;
> —that we may be alleluia people both in thought and deed.

PRAYER: All powerful, ever-living God, you have reconciled humanity through the paschal mystery. Grant that what we celebrate today in faith we may actualize in our lives. We ask this through Jesus, our savior. Amen.

EASTER SATURDAY
(Psalms from Sunday, Week I, p. 3)

MORNING PRAYER

Ant 1 Jesus appeard first to Mary Magdalene, alleluia!

Ant 2 When those who had been with them heard that he was alive and had been seen by her, they would not believe it, alleluia!

Ant 3 Jesus upbraided them because they had not believed those who saw him after he had risen, alleluia!

READING

Jesus calls us to a new way of being in the world. What this means for the spiritual journey of marginal persons such as women is that God's redeeming action is taking place right now as they seek their own liberation and that of others. Far from supporting the oppression of women, Jesus' vision calls for the elimination of structures of domination and submission. All who call themselves his disciples share this prophetic mission. The stories of women in the New Testament portray the liberating power of Jesus' presence and message.

Kathleen Fischer, *Women at the Well*, p. 83, (1)

(In place of the responsory the following is said:)

Ant This is the day our God has made; let us give praise in song, alleluia!

CANTICLE OF ZECHARIAH

Ant. Now when Jesus was risen early on the first day of the week, he appeared first to Mary Magdalen, alleluia.

INTERCESSIONS

O splendor of eternal light and sun of justice, to you risen from the dead, we pray:
Illumine our pathway to heaven!

You appeared to Mary Magdalen and the other women and sent them as your first witnesses;
—break down the barriers that inhibit women from following your call.
You died reviled, and returned to us breathing peace;
—that we may be schooled to non-violence.
You died with passionate love for all;
—teach us an all-embracing love of every race, creed, nation, and of those rejected or despised.
You were risen from death as promise of our future life;
—grant to all who have died a share in your glory.

PRAYER: O most loving God, grant that we who have celebrated these paschal mysteries with great joy may come to share in the joy that is eternal. We ask this through Jesus, our risen savior. Amen.

DAYTIME PRAYER

Ant 1 Christ having risen from the dead, will die no more; death shall no longer have dominion over him, alleluia. (Ps. 8, p. 92)

Ant 2 Put to death indeed in the flesh, Jesus was brought to life in the spirit, alleluia. (Ps. 19a, p. 57)

Ant 3 The cross has become our victory; let us live in the holiness of Christ, alleluia. (Ps. 19:7–14, p. 12)

(Prayer as in Morning Prayer)

SECOND SUNDAY OF EASTER

EVENING PRAYER I
(Psalms from Sunday, Week I, p. 7)

Ant 1 After the Sabbath, toward the dawn of the first day of the week, Mary Magdalen and the other Mary went to see the tomb, alleluia.

Ant 2 The angel said to the women, "Go quickly, tell his disciples that he has risen from the dead," alleluia.

Ant 3 Jesus said to them: "Do not be afraid; see, I was dead, but now I live and am among you," alleluia.

READING

Rise heart; thy Lord is risen. Sing his praise
    Without delays,
Who takes thee by the hand, that thou likewise
    With him mayst rise:
That, as his death calcined thee to dust,
His life may make thee gold, and much more just.

George Herbert, Easter (I), p. 155, (1)

(In place of the responsory the following is said:)

Ant This is the day our God has made; let us give praise in song, alleluia!

CANTICLE OF MARY

Ant After that Jesus appeared to his followers as they sat at table.

INTERCESSIONS

Handed over to death, Christ Jesus was raised to life for our justification. In living hope we pray:
Free us, Christ Jesus, from what still binds us!

You, who have shared our human condition, look on the oppressed and the deprived;
—that they may be aided in their struggle for self determination.
You, who have revealed in your being the compassion of God;
—grant relief to the sick and the dying through our own compassion.
You, who call us to use our God-given talents;
—give courage to us to further our own human development.
You, who call us each to wholeness, unsettle our complacencies;
—that we recognize our blindness and surrender to the guidance of your Spirit.

PRAYER: Most loving God, we have just celebrated the gift of the paschal mysteries. Grant that we may preserve their spirit in our way of life by the support of your abiding grace. We ask this through Jesus, our risen Savior. Amen.

MORNING PRAYER
(Psalms from Sunday, Week II, p. 49)

Ant 1 Jesus said to Thomas, "Put your finger here and see my hands; and put out your hand and place it in my side; do not be faithless, but believing."

Ant 2 Thomas answered him, "My Lord and my God."

Ant 3 Everyone who believes that Jesus is the Christ is a child of God.

READING

Whatever is born of God conquers the world. And this is the victory that conquers the world, our faith. Who is it that conquers the world but the one who believes that Jesus is the Son of God? This is the one who came by water and blood, Jesus Christ, not with the water only but with the water and the blood. And the Spirit is the one that testifies, for the Spirit is the truth.

1 Jn 5:4–6

(In place of the responsory the following is said:)

Ant This is the day our God has made; let us give praise in song, alleluia.

CANTICLE OF ZECHARIAH

Ant Peace be with you! As God has sent me, so do I send you, alleluia.

INTERCESSIONS:

The tomb of Christ has become death's burial place. In joy we cry out:
> **You have risen, O Christ, let heaven and earth rejoice!**

You taught the ways of peace and forgiveness in your return to us, Christ Jesus;
   —transform our own longing into deeds of mercy.
You appeared to many in their varied needs;
   —help us to respect the differences we see in one another
      and learn to appreciate them.
You died for us and have risen to help us come to wholeness and holiness;
   —may we, with renewed courage, uphold the human rights
      of all peoples.
Lamb of God, in your brokenness you sought to mend;
   —through your passion and death may we become healers
      of relationships and true lovers of humanity.

PRAYER: Most loving God, with joy we celebrate the gift of the paschal mysteries. Grant that we may preserve their spirit in our way of life by the support of your abiding grace. We ask this through Jesus, our risen savior. Amen.

DAYTIME PRAYER

Ant 1 Christ having risen from the dead, will die no more; death shall no longer have dominion over him, alleluia. (Ps. 8, p. 92)

Ant 2 Put to death indeed in the flesh, Jesus was brought to life in the spirit, alleluia. (Ps 19a, p. 57)

Ant 3 The cross has become our victory; let us live in the holiness of Christ, alleluia. (Ps. 19:7–14, p. 12)

(Prayer as in Morning Prayer)

EVENING PRAYER II
(Psalms from Sunday, Week I, p. 7)

Ant 1 Jesus said to Thomas, "You believed because you saw me, blessed are those who have not seen and yet believe."

Ant 2 Jesus breathed on them, and said, "Receive the Holy Spirit. If you forgive sins, they are forgiven; if you hold them bound, they are held bound."

Ant 3 These (signs) are written that you may believe that Jesus is the Christ, the Anointed One of God.

READING

Blessed be the God...of our Lord Jesus Christ! By [God's] great mercy God has given us a new birth into a living hope through the resurrection of Jesus Christ from the dead, and into an inheritance that is imperishable, undefiled, and unfading, kept in heaven for you, who are being protected by the power of God through faith for a salvation ready to be revealed in the last time. In this you rejoice, even if now for a little while you have had to suffer various trials, so that the genuineness of your faith—being more precious than gold that, though perishable is tested by fire—may be found to result in praise and glory and honor when Jesus Christ is revealed.

1 Pet 1:3–7

(In place of the responsory the following is said:)

Ant This is the day our God has made; let us give praise in song, alleluia.

CANTICLE OF MARY

Ant   On the evening of that day, the first day of the week, Jesus came and stood among them and said: "Peace!" Alleluia.

INTERCESSIONS

Now triumphant, Christ displays the spoils of victory, peace. In grateful praise we cry out:
Glory to you, Christ Jesus!

Jesus, your death has freed all creation from endless death;
   —make us liberators of earth's ecosystems.
Your free acceptance of death has overcome death;
   —free all prisoners of conscience from every bondage.
You showed us the way of true leadership;
   —inspire all church leaders in the ways of loving service.
Your disciples abandoned you, yet you loved them to the end;
   —help us to mend broken relationships and to be faithful to
   one another.

PRAYER: Most loving God, with joy we celebrate the gift of the paschal mysteries. Grant that we may preserve their spirit in our way of life by the support of your abiding grace. We ask this through Jesus, our risen savior. Amen.

SECOND MONDAY OF EASTER
(Psalms and Antiphons from Week II, p. 55)
MORNING PRAYER

READING

Christian faith speaks about the paschal mystery, about Jesus Christ's death and resurrection as the first fruit of an inclusive harvest, about new unimaginable life breaking out through death itself and as a corrective to death. Although for a time there was no glimmer of hope, God was near at hand, nevertheless, and Jesus was not ultimately abandoned. The victory arrives through the living communion of love, overcoming evil from within.

Elizabeth Johnson, *She Who Is*, p. 268, (2)

RESPONSORY

Christ rose from the grave, alleluia, alleluia. **—Christ...**
Conquering sin an death, **—alleluia...**

Glory to you, Source of all Being, Eternal Word, and Holy Spirit.
—**Christ...**

CANTICLE OF ZECHARIAH

Ant. I say to you, unless you are truly born anew, you cannot see the reign of God, alleluia.

INTERCESSIONS

Christ Jesus, you rose from the dead and showed yourself to the women; with joyful hearts we proclaim:
Wonderful are your works, O Christ.

Jesus, through your resurrection you call us to be born again;
—help us to recognize and to be open to your Spirit in our lives

You are the Good Shepherd and you guide us with tender care;
—enlighten our civic and religious leaders; give them your mind and heart.

You promise to send the Comforter to witness on your behalf;
—empowered with your Spirit, may we bear witness to you in word and deed.

O God, you have created all things, and all that you have created is good;
—help us to see others and all things as you see them.

PRAYER: O God, you granted to Nicodemus the consolation of the words of your beloved Christ, and the challenge to transform his life. Bless all who seek you, and encourage those who are too fearful to listen to your word. Let your creative love call us once again that we, too, may be living witness of your goodness. We ask this through Christ Jesus, risen from the dead. Amen.

DAYTIME PRAYER

Ant 1 Alleluia, Christ is risen, alleluia, alleluia.

Ant 2 The women and men who believed in Jesus rejoiced, alleluia, alleluia.

Ant 3 Stay with us, for it is toward evening and the day is far spent, alleluia, alleluia.

(Prayer as in Morning Prayer)

EVENING PRAYER

READING

Consolation has that special spiritual meaning of being drawn towards God in a love that knows and loves all beings in the ambit of this love. "Did not our hearts burn within us as he opened up the scriptures to us" (Lk 24:32). When I have appropriated my unique history in terms of my Christian faith, I receive a new experience of spiritual consolation that serves me in my decision-making and action. Briefly, it is God-given awareness that my history is meaningful and an expression of God's loving presence with me.

John English, SJ, Choosing Life, pp. 10–11, (1)

RESPONSORY

The followers of Jesus were filled with joy, alleluia, alleluia.
   —The followers...
When they saw him risen from the dead, **—alleluia...**
Glory to you, Source of all Being, Eternal Word, and Holy Spirit.
   —The followers...

CANTICLE OF MARY

Ant   That which is born of the flesh is flesh; and that which is born of the Spirit is spirit, alleluia.

INTERCESSIONS

Jesus, you rose from the dead and your disciples recognized you in the breaking of the bread. We proclaim in faith:
              Jesus is risen indeed.

Christ Jesus, through your Spirit you transformed your frightened apostles into fearless proclaimers of your word;
   —bless all missionaries with fortitude and perseverance.
By your life, death, and resurrection you invite all the nations of the world to be the people of God;
   —help us to live as true daughters and sons of our loving
     Creator.
Through your resurrection you give hope to all who believe in you;
   —through our daily deaths, transform our lives evermore
     into your likeness.
Following your example, Peter prayed for guidance in time of decision;
   —help us to realize the necessity of prayer in our lives.

By your death and resurrection you conquered death;
—have pity on the dying, be their light and peace.

PRAYER: O God, you granted to Nicodemus the consolation of the words of your beloved Christ, and the challenge to transform his life. Bless all who seek you, and encourage those who are too fearful to listen to your word. Let your creative love call us once again that we, too, may be living witness of your goodness. We ask this through Christ Jesus, risen from the dead. Amen.

SECOND TUESDAY OF EASTER
(Psalms and Antiphons from Week II, p. 62)
MORNING PRAYER

READING

If we pray and act in the name of Jesus the Good Shepherd, then we are already coming to a deeper understanding of all our brothers and sisters, and to more compassion and generosity towards them, and especially towards those who are like lost sheep, those with whom nobody falls in love, and who first need great love, encouragement, and respect before we can expect from them a satisfying response.

Bernard Häring, *Prayer: The Integration of Faith and Life*, p. 36, (8)

RESPONSORY

Christ rose from the grave, alleluia, alleluia. —**Christ...**
Conquering sin an death, —**alleluia...**
Glory to you, Source of all Being, Eternal Word, and Holy Spirit.
   —**Christ...**

CANTICLE OF ZECHARIAH

Ant. I am the Alpha and the Omega, the first and the last, the beginning and the end.

INTERCESSIONS

Jesus, risen from the dead, you dined with the women and men who followed you, served them, and strengthened their faith in you, and so we pray:
   How can we repay for your goodness to us.

Jesus, you came to do the will of God, and in death you were
raised up in glory;
   —have mercy on those who despair of meaning in life.
Your resurrection gave new hope to your small community of
followers;
   —let the celebration of that same resurrection bring new life
      to your church today.
You asked those who followed you to sell all and give to the poor;
   —teach us effective ways to feed the hungry and to house
      the homeless of our world.
You never cease to call us to greater intimacy with you;
   —transform the mustard seed of our faith into total
      dedication.

PRAYER: Jesus, by your death you taught us how to stop the
flow of revenge and evil that wounds our world. By your
resurrection, you show us the fruit of self-giving love.
We remember your love day by day. Help us to be your
true disciples, never counting the cost, faithful to the
end as you were faithful. Grant this in your name.
Amen.

DAYTIME PRAYER

Ant 1 Alleluia, Christ is risen, alleluia, alleluia.

Ant 2 The women and men who believed in Jesus rejoiced,
alleluia, alleluia.

Ant 3 Stay with us, for it is toward evening and the day is far
spent, alleluia, alleluia.

(Prayer as in Morning Prayer)

EVENING PRAYER

READING

Christ is essential to our spiritual life.... It is he who brings about the
inhabitation of God in us, and of us in God.... Christ lived in history. He
was the model and friend of a small group of people who are at the
origin of a tradition on which we depend. At his death a Church grew up
that gave body to his doctrine. Christ remains forever, living and active,

and in each epoch he continues to make himself known in the here and now of history and concrete human existence. Both passing and eternal, this mystery belongs to us. Along the obscurity of our path our spiritual life should make us ever attentive to this mystery, and in so doing should prepare the vision to come.

Yves Raguin, *Attention to the Mystery*, p. 119, (1)

RESPONSORY

The followers of Jesus were filled with joy, alleluia, alleluia.
—**The followers...**
When they saw him risen from the dead, —**alleluia...**
Glory to you, Source of all Being, Eternal Word, and Holy Spirit.
—**The followers...**

CANTICLE OF MARY

Ant. Did not our hearts burn within us while Jesus opened to us the scriptures? Alleluia.

INTERCESSIONS

Jesus, risen from the dead, you have filled the world with light and hope. With joy we sing:
This is the day that our God has made.

Jesus, your resurrection frees us from the bondage of death;
—free those who are enslaved or oppressed.
Your resurrection is a promise of new life;
—give hope and new opportunity for wholesome labor to migrant workers and to all who receive an inadequate wage.
By your resurrection you were freed from suffering and death;
—have mercy on all those who suffer from illness or abuse.
You rose from the dead and appeared to your mother and to your friends;
—bless our families, friends, and all who show us your love and mercy.

PRAYER: Jesus, by your death you taught us how to stop the flow of revenge and evil that wounds our world. By your resurrection, you show us the fruit of self-giving love. We remember your love day by day. Help us to be your true disciples, never counting the cost, faithful to the

end as you were faithful. Grant this in your name.
Amen.

SECOND WEDNESDAY OF EASTER
(Psalms and Antiphons from Week II, p. 69)

MORNING PRAYER

READING

The impression made on our minds by forty days of meditation on
Christ's humiliations, meekness, and unwearied perseverance will help
us on every difficult occasion, and we will endeavor to make Him the
only return He demands of us, by giving Him our whole heart, fashioned
on His own model—pure, meek, merciful and humble. All will then be
easy and sweet, no agitation, no particular desire except to please and
glorify God.

The Correspondence of Catherine McAuley 1827–1841, No. 206, p. 224, (63)

RESPONSORY

Christ rose from the grave, alleluia, alleluia. **—Christ...**
Conquering sin an death, **—alleluia...**
Glory to you, Source of all Being, Eternal Word, and Holy Spirit.
    —Christ...

CANTICLE OF ZECHARIAH

Ant. O God, you so loved the world that you gave your eternal
    Word, that all who have faith should not perish but have
    eternal life, alleluia.

INTERCESSIONS

Jesus is risen from the dead, a mystery revealed to little ones.
With sincere hearts we pray:
    Christ Jesus, make us humble of heart.

By your resurrection, you bring light to our darkness, hope to
despair;
    —give us a hunger for your words of life.
You will not leave us orphans;
    —help us to be aware of your presence throughout the day.
You have chosen us to follow your disciples in bringing our world
to fullness of life;
    —make us responsible Christians; let our lives proclaim our
    faith in you.

You promised the Spirit who would pray within us;
—quiet our minds and hearts; teach us to pray.

PRAYER: O God, you sent Christ Jesus to be our light and our salvation. Give us the grace to live with integrity and let our faith be manifested in all that we do. Heal the wound of falsehood in the world, and help us to love the light of truth. This we ask through Jesus, who is our way, our truth, and our life. Amen.

DAYTIME PRAYER

Ant 1 Alleluia, Christ is risen, alleluia, alleluia.

Ant 2 The women and men who believed in Jesus rejoiced, alleluia, alleluia.

Ant 3 Stay with us, for it is toward evening and the day is far spent, alleluia, alleluia.

(Prayer as in Morning Prayer)

EVENING PRAYER

READING

Humankind stands as a bridge between two worlds. Our greatest moments are when we have met, nakedly and face to face, the reality that saves and transforms, and then express this as part of our assimilating the experience. Our records of such experiences give us a further step on the road. They also give others light to find the path they must follow. Everyone's encounter and record brings more light and consciousness into this world and allows the forces of darkness to be beaten back.

Morton Kelsey, *The Other Side of Silence*, p. 28, (1)

RESPONSORY

The followers of Jesus were filled with joy, alleluia, alleluia.
  —The followers...
When they saw him risen from the dead, **—alleluia...**
Glory to you, Source of all Being, Eternal Word, and Holy Spirit.
  —The followers...

CANTICLE OF MARY

Ant. Christ came to save the world, not to condemn it, alleluia.

INTERCESSIONS

Jesus is risen from the dead. We, too, shall rise and so we lift our voices as we say:
Wonderful are your ways, O God.

Jesus, by your resurrection, you have overcome tyranny and injustice.
  —strengthen and encourage those who are victims of greed and misplaced power.
You appeared to your followers to free them from fear;
  —let us never allow our sins to keep us from turning to you.
Risen from the dead, you are the Good Shepherd seeking those who are lost;
  —teach us how to proclaim the good news to those who do not know you.
You revealed the secrets of God's designs to your followers;
  —help us to live the graces of our baptism.
You spoke to Peter about how he would die;
  —prepare us for death by a life of dedication to you.

PRAYER: O God, you sent Christ Jesus to be our light and our salvation. Give us the grace to live with integrity, and let our faith be manifested in all that we do. Heal the wound of falsehood in the world, and help us to love the light of truth. This we ask through Jesus, who is our way, our truth, and our life. Amen.

SECOND THURSDAY OF EASTER
(Psalms and Antiphons from Week II, p. 76)
MORNING PRAYER

READING

Julian of Norwich was not the first person to present Christ or the triune God as mother, but no Christian writer before Julian elaborated the image so powerfully and comprehensively.... Contemplating God as both mother and father leads to an appreciation of the fullness of divine reality in the inexhaustible fecundity and energy of [God's] mystery. Seeing God as both mother and father is a way of hinting at possibilities and realizations beyond all ordinary limits, a way of describing the indescribable perfection of God. God is always more than everything we can say about the divine totality, yet God never ceases to be utter simplicity.

Charles Cummings, "The Motherhood of God According to Julian of Norwich," p. 309, p. 313, (7)

RESPONSORY

Christ rose from the grave, alleluia, alleluia. —**Christ...**
Conquering sin an death, —**alleluia...**
Glory to you, Source of all Being, Eternal Word, and Holy Spirit.
   —**Christ...**

CANTICLE OF ZECHARIAH

Ant. The Christ whom God has sent speaks the words of God, alleluia.

INTERCESSIONS

O Christ, by your resurrection from the dead, the sorrow of the world is turned into joy. We cry out:
   Alleluia, alleluia, alleluia!

Christ Jesus, whoever believes in you has life eternal;
   —bless all those who do not know your name or gospel.
Through the love you bear for us;
   —help us to love and care for one another.
By your resurrection you transcend the needs of the flesh;
   —have mercy on those who live in deprivation of any kind.
In our daily dyings and risings;
   —be with us as we strive to enrich our quality of life and deepen our love for you.

PRAYER: O God, your Word Incarnate, Jesus Christ, was obedient even to death on a cross. As we celebrate his resurrection from the dead, grant us the grace so to love you that we, too, will spend our lives in your service. We ask this with Jesus who lives with you in the unity of the Holy Spirit, now and forever. Amen.

DAYTIME PRAYER

Ant 1 Alleluia, Christ is risen, alleluia, alleluia.

Ant 2 The women and men who believed in Jesus rejoiced, alleluia, alleluia.

Ant 3 Stay with us, for it is toward evening and the day is far spent, alleluia, alleluia.

(Prayer as in Morning Prayer)

EVENING PRAYER

READING

Each of us is still in the making, but as responsible for our lives as we are, we do not have to do it all alone. God is creating the world through us, but we are part of the world that God is helping us to create. If at times we can just be, just quietly sit in the sun of God's love for us, if we can believe that the One who formed us in the first place is waiting to transform us in the embrace of love, then in what we are doing with our lives, God will increase and we will decrease in the best sense of the word.

Elizabeth Meluch, OCD, (11)

RESPONSORY

The followers of Jesus were filled with joy, alleluia, alleluia.
   —The followers...
When they saw him risen from the dead, **—alleluia...**
Glory to you, Source of all Being, Eternal Word, and Holy Spirit.
   —The followers...

CANTICLE OF MARY

Ant. The one who believes in the Christ of God has eternal life, alleluia.

INTERCESSIONS

The risen Christ appeared to Mary Magdalen and called her by name, and so we pray:
   O Christ, call us again and again.

Jesus Christ, risen in glory, death could not contain you;
   —call to new life all that is dead or barren within us.
O Christ, on the cross you prayed for deliverance;
   —you were heard for your reverence and raised in glory.
Through your love for the earth and all of its fruits;
   —help us to redeem the harm we have done to this planet.
Rising from the dead, you returned to those with whom you had shared life;
   —be with all who are lonely or handicapped in society.

PRAYER: O God, your Word Incarnate, Jesus Christ, was obedient even to death on a cross. As we celebrate his resurrection from the dead, grant us the grace so to love you that we, too, will spend our lives in your service. We ask this with Jesus who lives with you in the unity of the Holy Spirit, now and forever. Amen.

SECOND FRIDAY OF EASTER
(Psalms and Antiphons from Week II, p. 84)

MORNING PRAYER

READING

When the little birds sing and chirp in greeting to the sun, who is to say that they do not sing thanks to the sun for coming with light and happiness to free them from the cold and peril of the night?... It would take too long to describe the gratitude of the animals. So great is the acknowledgment of thanks that we mortals find it difficult to believe what is written of them, and I believe it is our stinginess in giving that makes us reluctant to admit that gratitude in animals is deeper than our own. This is evident by the fact that we do not realize what is good until it is gone, and the loss we suffer is due to our insufficient thanks to the One who made the good things possible.

Francisco de Osuna, The Third Spiritual Alphabet, p. 68, (1)

RESPONSORY

Christ rose from the grave, alleluia, alleluia. **—Christ...**
Conquering sin an death, **—alleluia...**
Glory to you, Source of all Being, Eternal Word, and Holy Spirit.
   —Christ...

CANTICLE OF ZECHARIAH

Ant. Jesus took the bread and when he had given thanks, distributed it to those who were with him, alleluia.

INTERCESSIONS

Jesus risen from the dead has turned all our grief into joy, and so we pray:

Let all the earth sing praise!

Christ Jesus, you had compassion on the multitude in the desert and fed them;

—help us to do all in our power to feed the hungry and care
for all in need.

You fled from those who would make you king;
—give all in public office the courage to maintain their
integrity, and to labor for the public good.

You are our way to God, the Source of all that is;
—give us the grace to heed your works and to embrace your
gospel with our lives.

You taught and encouraged your disciples to the very end;
—make us tireless in sharing your gospel, patient and
compassionate with those who are slow to hear.

PRAYER: Christ Jesus, you fed your people in the desert and you
feed us with the bread of life. Let our celebration of
your life, death, and resurrection fill our minds and
hearts with zeal for the good of our earth. Help us to
bring it your peace. This we ask in your name. Amen.

DAYTIME PRAYER

Ant 1 Alleluia, Christ is risen, alleluia, alleluia.

Ant 2 The women and men who believed in Jesus rejoiced,
alleluia, alleluia.

Ant 3 Stay with us, for it is toward evening and the day is far
spent, alleluia, alleluia.

(Prayer as in Morning Prayer)

EVENING PRAYER

READING

...thou art Light and darkness both together:
If that be dark we cannot see:
The sun is darker than a Tree,
And thou more dark than either.

Yet thou art not so dark, since I know this,
But that my darkness may touch thine:
And hope, that may teach it to shine,
Since Light thy Darkness is.

Oh let my Soul, whose keys I must deliver
  Into the hands of senseless Dreams
  Which know not thee, suck in thy beams
    And wake with thee forever.

George Herbert, Evensong, p. 330, (1)

RESPONSORY

The followers of Jesus were filled with joy, alleluia, alleluia.
  —The followers...
When they saw him risen from the dead, **—alleluia...**
Glory to you, Source of all Being, Eternal Word, and Holy Spirit.
  —The followers...

CANTICLE OF MARY

Ant. When the people saw the signs Jesus worked they said:
    "This is indeed the prophet who has come into the world,"
    alleluia.

INTERCESSIONS

Christ Jesus, rising from the dead gives glory to God, and new
vision to all who believe. With hearts full of joy, we cry out:
    Glory and praise to you, O Christ!

You rose from the dead and proved that all your words are true;
  —in times of doubt let the light of your glory shine in our
    minds and hearts.
You rose from the dead and all your works are magnified;
  —give us the courage to face necessary deaths when new
    life beckons.
You rose from the dead having forgiven those who had crucified
you;
  —help us to return good for evil, and to pray for those who
    harm us.
You rose from the dead and call us to unity;
  —teach us to realize that all we think and do affects
    everyone and everything in the world.

PRAYER: Christ Jesus, you fed your people in the desert and you
    feed us with the bread of life. Let our celebration of
    your life, death, and resurrection fill our minds and
    hearts with zeal for the good of our earth. Help us to
    bring it your peace. This we ask in your name. Amen.

SECOND SATURDAY OF EASTER
(Psalms and Antiphons from Week II, p. 91)

MORNING PRAYER

READING

"I will love you, [God], my strength, my fortress, my refuge, my deliverer" (Ps 17:2–3), you who are everything I can desire and love. My God, my Helper, I shall love you in proportion to your gift and my capacity, less indeed than is just, but to do that is beyond me. Even though I cannot love you as much as I ought, still I cannot love you more than I am able. I shall be able to love you more only when you deign to give me more; and even then you can never find my love worthy.

Bernard of Clairvaux, *On Loving God*, p. 187, (1)

RESPONSORY

Christ rose from the grave, alleluia, alleluia. —**Christ...**
Conquering sin an death, —**alleluia...**
Glory to you, Source of all Being, Eternal Word, and Holy Spirit.
   —**Christ...**

CANTICLE OF ZECHARIAH

Ant. Peace to you, it is I; do not be afraid, alleluia.

INTERCESSIONS

Jesus, risen from the dead, lives on fulfilling the works of God, and so we pray:
   O Christ, live on in us.

Jesus, you call us to complete the work you have begun on earth;
   —teach us to put no limits on the power of your Spirit in
   our lives.
Jesus, Lord of heaven and earth, the winds and the seas obey you;
   —be merciful to us and guide our human freedom that we
   may serve you with upright hearts.
Your mother beheld your death and your resurrection;
   —bless all mothers with the strength and grace they need
   to bear and to guide their children.
Those who have seen you have seen God;
   —do not let the familiarity of your gospel blind us to seeing
   you as you are, son of Mary, son of God.

PRAYER: O God, your love abounds in our lives and you are our help in time of need. As we celebrate the resurrection of Jesus, bring new life to our church and to each of us. Give us a hunger to know you better and zeal to do your will. We ask this through Jesus, our way. Amen.

DAYTIME PRAYER

Ant 1 Alleluia, Christ is risen, alleluia, alleluia.

Ant 2 The women and men who believed in Jesus rejoiced, alleluia, alleluia.

Ant 3 Stay with us, for it is toward evening and the day is far spent, alleluia, alleluia.

(Prayer as in Morning Prayer)

THIRD SUNDAY OF EASTER

EVENING PRAYER I

(Psalms and antiphons from Week III, p. 96)

READING

If philosophy brings knowledge of death, Christian ascesis offers the art of going beyond it and thus anticipating the resurrection. Indeed, death is entirely in time. For those around a dying person,...death is dated, but for the one who has just died, it has no date, for [that one] already finds himself [or herself] in another dimension. Just as the end of the world will have no earthly tomorrow, death is not a day on the calendar for anyone, this is why the death of each one, like the end of the world, is *for today.* Likewise it is not tomorrow but the very day of the eucharistic repast when one enters into the [kindom].

Paul Evdokimov, The Struggle with God, p. 174, (1)

RESPONSORY

Christ our hope has risen, alleluia, alleluia. **—Christ our**...
Let us rejoice and give thanks, **—alleluia,**...
Glory to you, Source of all Being, Eternal Word and Holy Spirit.
   —Christ our...

CANTICLE OF MARY

Ant Beginning with Moses and the prophets, Jesus interpreted the scriptures in all things concerning his mission, alleluia.

INTERCESSIONS:

Christ Jesus has loved us and redeemed us by his death and rising. In joy let us proclaim:
Worthy is the Lamb to receive honor and glory, wisdom and peace!

Savior God, you have made us partakers of your priesthood;
—may we offer you continual thanks and praise.
You have conquered death; raise us to new life;
—that we may be your resurrection people.
You walked the way of Calvary's anguish;
—in your compassion succor all prisoners of conscience and those unjustly incarcerated.
By your resurrection, you promised life after death;
—may all who have died enjoy fullness of life with you.

PRAYER: O God, you call us to the banquet table of your Eucharist that we may realize our union with you. You overcome our lack of faith with everlasting fidelity. God of our life and our salvation, grant that we may always recognize you in the breaking of the bread and learn again the message of your Christ, that you are a God of love. We ask this in the name of Jesus, our risen Savior. Amen.

MORNING PRAYER
(Psalms from Sunday, Week III, p. 98)

Ant 1 Did not our hearts burn within us while he talked to us on the road, while he opened to us the scriptures.

Ant 2 He said to them, "Why are you troubled, see my hands and my feet, that it is I; touch me and see that a spirit has not flesh and bones as you see I have."

Ant 3 Peter said to Jesus, "Lord, you know everything, you know I love you." Jesus said to him, "Feed my sheep."

READING

You know that you were ransomed from the futile ways inherited from your ancestors, not with perishable things like silver and gold, but with the precious blood of Christ, like that of a lamb without defect or blemish. He was destined before the foundation of the world but was revealed at the end of the ages for your sake. Through him you have come to trust in God, who raised him from the dead and gave him glory, so that your faith and hope are in God.

1 Pet 1:18–21

RESPONSORY

The followers of Jesus were filled with joy, alleluia, alleluia.
—**The followers...**
When they saw him risen from the dead, —**alleluia...**
Glory to you, Source of all Being, Eternal Word and Holy Spirit.
—**The followers...**

CANTICLE OF ZECHARIAH

Ant Thus it is written, that the Christ should suffer and on the third day rise from the dead, and that repentance and forgiveness should be preached to all nations, alleluia.

INTERCESSIONS

Handed over to death, Christ Jesus was raised to life for our justification. In living hope we pray:
Free us, Christ Jesus, from what still binds us!

You, who have shared our human condition, look on the oppressed and the deprived;
—that they may be aided in their struggle for self-determination.
You, who have revealed in your being the compassion of God;
—grant relief to the sick and the dying through our own compassion.
You, who call us to use our God-given talents;
—give courage to further our own human development.
You, who call us each to wholeness, unsettle our complacencies;
—that we recognize our blindness and surrender to the guidance of your Spirit.

PRAYER: O God, you call us to the banquet table of your Eucharist that we may realize our union with you. You overcome our lack of faith with everlasting fidelity. God of our life and our salvation, grant that we may always recognize you in the breaking of the bread and learn again and again the message of your Christ, that you are a God of love. We ask this in the name of Jesus, our risen savior. Amen.

DAYTIME PRAYER

Ant 1 Alleluia, Christ is risen, alleluia, alleluia.

Ant 2 The women and men who believed in Jesus rejoiced, alleluia, alleluia.

Ant 3 Stay with us, for it is toward evening and the day is far spent, alleluia, alleluia.

(Prayer as in Morning Prayer)

EVENING PRAYER II

Ant 1 Jesus said to the apostles, "Come and have breakfast." None of them dared ask him, "Who are you?"

Ant 2 Jesus said to Peter, "When you were young, you walked where you would; but when you are old, another will carry you where you do not wish to go."

Ant 3 The apostles left the council, rejoicing that they were counted worthy to suffer dishonor for the name.

READING

[The two companions of Jesus] told what had happened on the road, and how he had been made known to them in the breaking of the bread. While they were talking about this, Jesus himself stood among them and said to them, "Peace be with you." They were startled and terrified, and thought they were seeing a ghost. He said to them, "Why are you frightened and why do doubts arise in your hearts? Look at my hands and feet; see that it is I myself. Touch me and see; for a ghost does not have flesh and bones as you see that I have." And when he had said this, he showed them his hands and his feet. While in their joy they were disbelieving and still wondering, he said to them, "Have you anything here to eat?" They gave him a piece of broiled fish, and he took it and ate in their presence.

Lk 24:35–43

RESPONSORY

You are our savior, O Christ, alleluia, alleluia. —**You**...
Your death brings us life, —**alleluia**...
Glory to you, Source of all Being, Eternal Word and Holy Spirit.
   —**You**...

CANTICLE OF MARY

Ant The disciple whom Jesus loved said to Peter, "It is the Lord,"
   alleluia.

INTERCESSIONS

Let us rejoice with Christ Jesus who manifests himself in the
breaking of the bread. In joy we pray:
                  You are risen indeed!

O Christ, you showed yourself to your disciples and assured them
with your touch;
   —give us the grace we need to embrace the mysteries of your
      life with our minds and hearts.
Your disciples recognized you in the miraculous catch of fish;
   —help us to see you in your care for us each day of our
      lives.
You challenged Peter's love and commissioned him to lead your
church;
   —fill our hearts with the love and zeal we need to fulfill our
      mission on earth.
Throughout your life and to the last, your message was a call to
love;
   —teach us how to hear and live your message in the
      complexity of our lives.

PRAYER: O God, you call us to the banquet table of your
         Eucharist that we may realize our union with you. You
         overcome our lack of faith with everlasting fidelity. God
         of our life and our salvation, grant that we may always
         recognize you in the breaking of the bread and learn
         again and again the message of your Christ, that you
         are a God of love. We ask this in the name of Jesus,
         our risen savior. Amen.

THIRD MONDAY OF EASTER
(Psalms and Antiphons from Week III, p. 104)
MORNING PRAYER

READING

John, the beloved disciple, is always the first to recognize the Lord, whether he comes during the dark night or in disguise, as at Lake Tiberius. The symbol of the fourth evangelist is the eagle: he has the eagle's eye. Because of his great love, he knows the Master even when he comes as a surprise. A humble and grateful faith, a profound love of the Master, does not try to impose one's own desires and plans on God, but adores...even when [God's] coming is unexpected and somehow painful.

Bernard Häring, *Prayer: The Integration of Faith and Life*, p. 102, (1)

RESPONSORY

Christ rose from the grave, alleluia, alleluia. —**Christ...**
Conquering sin an death, —**alleluia...**
Glory to you, Source of all Being, Eternal Word, and Holy Spirit.
    —**Christ...**

CANTICLE OF ZECHARIAH

Ant. Do not labor for the food which perishes, but for the food
    which endures to eternal life, alleluia.

INTERCESSIONS

Jesus, by your resurrection, you conquered sin and death, and revealed the power of God's love. We praise you and say:
    We will sing of your mercy forever.

Christ Jesus, your disciples hasten to give their lives for you;
    —let the sacrifice of all who serve you throughout the ages
    give life to your Church.
You fed your people bread in the wilderness;
    —nourish our hungry minds and hearts; teach us to seek
    the things that are to our peace.
You promised to send the Paraclete to teach us all things;
    —teach us to live your word of love that the fruits of your
    resurrection may encompass the whole world.
Risen Lord, you showed yourself to your disciples and their eyes
were opened;

—let us know your presence in our lives that we may love and serve you faithfully.

PRAYER: Jesus, our risen Savior, you offer us the bread of heaven, yet we cling to what will perish. We praise your long-suffering love and ask you, through the grace of your resurrection, to conquer our blindness and free us from our attachments that keep us from following you. We ask this in your holy name, for you are one with our Source and with the Spirit for all ages. Amen.

DAYTIME PRAYER

Ant 1 Alleluia, Christ is risen, alleluia, alleluia.

Ant 2 The women and men who believed in Jesus rejoiced, alleluia, alleluia.

Ant 3 Stay with us, for it is toward evening and the day is far spent, alleluia, alleluia.

(Prayer as in Morning Prayer)

EVENING PRAYER

READING

When we are praying the official prayers of the Church, uniting in praise, we are loving God. And because we are praying together, we are loving each other. Some may say this doesn't follow. But just the same, we know that when we are united together in the community room in this evening prayer, we are conscious of a Christian solidarity. As members of the Church we are united to the whole Church. We are united with Christ Himself who is head of the Mystical Body. We may not do it very well, our poor efforts may be feeble, our hearts may not be right, but the will is there, and united with [Christ] we partake of his merits. He is the only one who can pray right, and we are praying with him so our prayer is effective. Then, too, we are united with each other, and we benefit by all the merits and graces of our [sisters and brothers].

Dorothy Day, *Meditations*, p. 37–38, (1)

RESPONSORY

The followers of Jesus were filled with joy, alleluia, alleluia.
—The followers...
When they saw him risen from the dead, **—alleluia...**

Glory to you, Source of all Being, Eternal Word, and Holy Spirit.
—The followers...

CANTICLE OF MARY

Ant This is the work of God, that you believe in the Anointed One
sent by God, alleluia.

INTERCESSIONS

Jesus, risen from the dead, you promise to live in those who love
you. In homage we pray:
> **Keep us faithful to you all the days of our lives.**

Jesus, our salvation was your pearl of great price;
> —teach us to live and die for others and so rise with you.

You blessed little children and had time for them;
> —give us the wisdom, creativity, and generosity to provide
> for them and those who care for them.

Your apostles left all to follow you; at your death you seemed to
leave them;
> —help us to keep alive the hope of your resurrection both for
> ourselves and for those burdened with trials.

You knew the sorrow that death brings;
> —comfort those who mourn.

PRAYER: Jesus, our risen Savior, you offer us the bread of
heaven, yet we cling to what will perish. We praise your
long-suffering love and ask you, through the grace of
your resurrection, to conquer our blindness and free us
from our attachments that keep us from following you.
We ask this in your holy name, for you are one with
our Source and with the Spirit for all ages. Amen.

THIRD TUESDAY OF EASTER
(Psalms and Antiphons from Week III, p. 111)
MORNING PRAYER

READING

Love and sacrifice are the essentials for a life of union with God. How
many opportunities for both lie daily around us. Grace and great graces
are hidden in every one, if we are but generous enough to correspond
with the designs of Divine Providence in fashioning them. An ever

increasing faith sees God's design in even the most trivial things—a design to sanctify us. Whatever the future holds, [our] part is peaceful abandonment—there is no greater gift to God. It makes one a living Amen....

Mother Aloysius Rogers, OCD, Fragrance from Alabaster, p. 17, (6)

RESPONSORY

Christ rose from the grave, alleluia, alleluia. —**Christ...**
Conquering sin an death, —**alleluia...**
Glory to you, Source of all Being, Eternal Word, and Holy Spirit.
   —**Christ...**

CANTICLE OF ZECHARIAH

Ant. Truly I tell you: it was not Moses who gave you bread from heaven; God gives you the true bread from heaven, alleluia.

INTERCESSIONS

Jesus, risen from the dead, you forgave your disciples and gave them the power to forgive sins. We humbly pray:
   In your mercy, remember us.

O Christ, your wounds have become your sign of victory;
   —help us to transform our suffering and labor into means of growth.
You bless those who, without seeing you, believe in your word;
   —bless those who have not heard your word; send laborers into your harvest.
You promised to be with your church until the end of time;
   —make us willing instruments in building the unity of your church throughout the world.
You showed your wounds to your disciples and they believed in you;
   —enfold those who inflict torture on others; transform their lives and let them see your loving presence in themselves and in all people.
You lived and died a person of peace;
   —grant peace to all who have died in war and to all who live with its scars.

PRAYER: Jesus, risen from the dead, your gift of faithful love is the bread that nourishes us into eternal life, and the living water that quenches our thirst. Give us the wisdom to persevere in our love for you, that lured away from empty attachments, we may always choose life to the praise and glory of your name. Amen.

DAYTIME PRAYER

Ant 1   Alleluia, Christ is risen, alleluia, alleluia.

Ant 2   The women and men who believed in Jesus rejoiced, alleluia, alleluia.

Ant 3   Stay with us, for it is toward evening and the day is far spent, alleluia, alleluia.

(Prayer as in Morning Prayer)

EVENING PRAYER

READING

To choose the world is not...merely a pious admission that the world is acceptable because it comes from the hand of God. It is first of all an acceptance of a task and a vocation in the world, in history and in time. In my time, which is the present. To choose the world is to choose to do the work I am capable of doing, in collaboration with my [brothers and sisters], to make the world better, more free, more just, more livable, more human.

Thomas Merton, Contemplation in a World of Action, p. 149, (59)

RESPONSORY

The followers of Jesus were filled with joy, alleluia, alleluia.
   —The followers...
When they saw him risen from the dead, **—alleluia...**
Glory to you, Source of all Being, Eternal Word, and Holy Spirit.
   —The followers...

CANTICLE OF MARY

Ant.   The bread of God is that which comes down from heaven and gives life to the world, alleluia.

INTERCESSIONS

Jesus, you rose from the dead, the hope of all who believe in you. In faith we pray:
            Christ is our light and our salvation.

Jesus, by your resurrection you herald a new heaven and a new earth;
> —give us the grace to grow in love for you and in dedication to your gospel.

You are the vine and we are the branches;
> —help us to remember that whatever we say or do affects everyone and everything else.

You call us not servants, but friends, for you have revealed to us the will of God;
> —make us worthy of your gifts and your promises; help us to live the challenge of your gospel.

Jesus, to rise with you, we must take up our cross and follow you;
> —teach us to meet the challenge of each day as a gift and a call to serve you, accepting our limitations and sharing our strengths.

Jesus, our risen Savior, your forgiving heart reveals the mercy of God to us;
> —grant your peace to those who approach death with fear.

PRAYER: Jesus, risen from the dead, your gift of faithful love is the bread that nourishes us into eternal life, and the living water that quenches our thirst. Give us the wisdom to persevere in our love for you, that lured away from empty attachments, we may always choose life to the praise and glory of your name. Amen.

THIRD WEDNESDAY OF EASTER
(Psalms and Antiphons from Week III, p. 117)

MORNING PRAYER

READING

What you hold, may you [always] hold. What you do, may you [always] do and never abandon. But with swift pace, light step, [and] unswerving feet, so that even your steps stir up no dust, go forward securely, joyfully, and swiftly, on the path of prudent happiness, believing nothing, agreeing with nothing which would dissuade you from this resolution or which *would place a stumbling block* for you on the way, so that you may offer *your vows to the Most High* in the pursuit of that perfection to which the Spirit of [God] has called you.

Clare of Assisi, Francis and Clare, p. 196, (1)

RESPONSORY

Christ rose from the grave, alleluia, alleluia. —**Christ...**
Conquering sin an death, —**alleluia...**
Glory to you, Source of all Being, Eternal Word, and Holy Spirit.
   —**Christ...**

CANTICLE OF ZECHARIAH

Ant. This is the will of the Most High, that all who see and believe
    in the Anointed One should have eternal life, alleluia.

INTERCESSIONS

On the third day, the Sun of Justice arose, and darkness was
conquered forever. We joyfully sing your praises:
           Glory to you, O God!

O Christ, you receive all who come to you;
   —enlighten all who turn away from religion because of
     negative experiences.
Powerless in death, you rose in the power of God's love;
   —teach us the wisdom and necessity of nonviolence for the
     salvation of our planet.
You rose from the dead making known to all the power of God's
love for us;
   —help us to banish servile fear from our lives and to love as
     we are loved.
You appeared to your friends, each according to their need;
   —open our minds and hearts to your loving guidance in
     our lives.

PRAYER: Jesus, Bread of Life, Word of God, you nourish our
           minds and hearts and surround us with all that is
           good. As we celebrate your resurrection, help us to rise
           from our weaknesses and let the life of your Spirit
           renew us day by day. We ask this in the power of your
           name. Amen.

DAYTIME PRAYER

Ant 1 Alleluia, Christ is risen, alleluia, alleluia.

Ant 2 The women and men who believed in Jesus rejoiced,
       alleluia, alleluia.

Ant 3 Stay with us, for it is toward evening and the day is far spent, alleluia, alleluia.

(Prayer as in Morning Prayer)

EVENING PRAYER

READING

Oh, my Friend, there is an ingrafting into Christ, a being formed and new created in Christ, a living and abiding in him, and a growing and bringing forth fruit through him unto perfection. Oh, mayst thou experience all these things; and, that thou mayst so do, wait to know life, the springings of life, the separations of life inwardly from all that evil which hangs about it, and would be springing up and mixing with it, under an appearance of good; that life may come to live fully in thee, and nothing else.

Isaac Penington, Quaker Spirituality, p. 148, (1)

RESPONSORY

The followers of Jesus were filled with joy, alleluia, alleluia.
—**The followers...**
When they saw him risen from the dead, —**alleluia...**
Glory to you, Source of all Being, Eternal Word, and Holy Spirit.
—**The followers...**

CANTICLE OF MARY

Ant. I have come down from heaven to do the will of the One who sent me, alleluia.

INTERCESSIONS

Jesus rose from the dead and worked many signs and wonders in the presence of his disciples, and so we pray:
    O God, we long to see your face.

Jesus, you commission those who follow you to bear much fruit;
—give us the zeal to live disciplined lives, opening ourselves to your Spirit.
You promise that what we ask in your name will be granted;
—never let us be separated from you.
You kept the law of Moses and fulfilled it;
—give us the wisdom to discern those things that are for the glory of God.

You rose from the dead in the secret of night;
—keep us watchful and ready for the coming of your grace
   in our lives.
Your resurrection healed the hearts of your mother and your
disciples;
—be with those who mourn the death of their loved ones.

PRAYER: Jesus, Bread of Life, Word of God, you nourish our
minds and hearts and surround us with all that is
good. As we celebrate your resurrection, help us to rise
from our weaknesses and let the life of your Spirit
renew us day by day. We ask this in the power of your
name. Amen.

THIRD THURSDAY OF EASTER
(Psalms and Antiphons from Week III, p. 124)

MORNING PRAYER

READING

In his masterly study *Christian Conversion* Walter Conn gives this
definition: Christian religious conversion is a fundamental shift from the
instinctive but illusory assumption of absolute autonomy, the
spontaneously defensive posture of radical, self-sufficient egocentrism,
to the reflective openness and personal commitment of love in total
surrender of self to God. The realistic recognition that one's very being
is a gift of love prompts the loving gift of one's entire life (p. 258). Such a
conversion cannot be a once for all event, I believe. We do need to be
converted every day.

William A. Barry, SJ, Now Choose Life, p. 108, (1)

RESPONSORY

Christ rose from the grave, alleluia, alleluia. **—Christ...**
Conquering sin an death, **—alleluia...**
Glory to you, Source of all Being, Eternal Word, and Holy Spirit.
  —Christ...

CANTICLE OF ZECHARIAH

Ant.   Everyone who has heard and learned from the Most High
comes to me, alleluia.

INTERCESSIONS

Jesus, the lamb that was slain, is risen as he said, alleluia. Therefore, we proclaim:
> **By your wounds, O Christ, we are healed.**

Christ Jesus, you met violence with peace, lies with truth, and death with immortality;
> —be with those who defend the innocent in our courts, and bless all who labor to put an end to violence.

You commissioned women to proclaim the good news of your resurrection;
> —let the women you send today to proclaim a new word be heard.

Your resurrection consoled the pierced heart of your mother;
> —give comfort and courage to families of missing children; protect the children and return them to their homes.

You came to heal the sick;
> —give us insight into our brokenness, and draw us to your healing love.

PRAYER: Christ Jesus, you are the bread come down from heaven. Nourished on this manna, we shall never die. As we celebrate your glorious resurrection, revive in us a longing to be one with you, and give us grace to proclaim your gospel in word and deed. We ask this in your name. Amen.

DAYTIME PRAYER

Ant 1 Alleluia, Christ is risen, alleluia, alleluia.

Ant 2 The women and men who believed in Jesus rejoiced, alleluia, alleluia.

Ant 3 Stay with us, for it is toward evening and the day is far spent, alleluia, alleluia.

(Prayer as in Morning Prayer)

EVENING PRAYER

READING

Christ performed miracles reluctantly, and whenever possible, secretly. He exerted this kind of power only in desperate situations, in condescension to human weakness and human blindness. As he grew in grace and wisdom, and his followers grew with him and were more willing and able to live by the hidden power of his spirit, there were notably fewer miracles. After the Resurrection and the promulgation of it, culminating in Pentecost, there was hardly any need for miracles at all. The only miracle Jesus seemed to really care about was *metanoia*, a radical change of mind and heart. What good is bodily healing if there is no transformation of character, no integration of the personality?

William McNamara, OCD, Mystical Passion, p. 75, (1)

RESPONSORY

The followers of Jesus were filled with joy, alleluia, alleluia.
    —The followers...
When they saw him risen from the dead, **—alleluia...**
Glory to you, Source of all Being, Eternal Word, and Holy Spirit.
    —The followers...

CANTICLE OF MARY

Ant.   I am the living bread which came down from heaven; those who eat of this bread will live forever, alleluia.

INTERCESSIONS

Jesus has risen from the dead. The shroud of death is laid aside and in its place the robe of immortality! We sing and proclaim:
Your reign shall last forever!

O God, we are your creatures and our lives are in your hands;
    —make us worthy of the life, death, and resurrection of
        Christ.
Not a sparrow falls that you do not know it;
    —through the resurrection of Jesus, let all see the face
        of your love turned to every person of whatever race, sex,
        color, or creed.
You loved sinners and cared for them;
    —reassure those who suffer from the guilt or brokenness of
        their past lives; grant them your peace.

You ask us to forgive seventy times seven times;
—strengthen and encourage those who strive to overcome
addictions of any kind.
You wept for Lazarus, your friend, and raised him to life;
—befriend those who are ill; let them know your loving
presence.

PRAYER: Christ Jesus, you are the bread come down from
heaven. Nourished on this manna, we shall never die.
As we celebrate your glorious resurrection, revive in
us a longing to be one with you, and give us grace to
proclaim your gospel in word and deed. We ask this in
your name. Amen.

THIRD FRIDAY OF EASTER
(Psalms and Antiphons from Week III, p. 131)
MORNING PRAYER
READING

In [a] letter François [de Sales] also made the following statement [to
Jeanne de Chantal]: "You must no longer be a woman, you must have a
man's heart...." He meant this metaphorically in that he encouraged her
to remain virilely courageous and firm in her desire to serve God. It was
a meaningful statement for her. She would have to learn to do what she,
as a woman, had seldom been encouraged to do: to act in accordance
with her own deepest truth whether or not this was what others found
acceptable.

Wendy Wright, *Bond of Perfection*, p. 73, (1)

RESPONSORY

Christ rose from the grave, alleluia, alleluia. —**Christ...**
Conquering sin an death, —**alleluia...**
Glory to you, Source of all Being, Eternal Word, and Holy Spirit.
—**Christ...**

CANTICLE OF ZECHARIAH

Ant. The one who eats my flesh and drinks my blood has eternal
life, alleluia.

INTERCESSIONS

Christ Jesus, who fed the multitude in the desert, rises now as
the bread of eternal life. We humbly ask:
Give us this bread, today and always.

Jesus, you gave your life as food for eternal life;
—help us to see the needs of others and to give our time and
energies in their service.
You have called us to bear fruit for the healing of the world;
—during this Easter season remind us of the gift of our
baptism and renew our zeal in following you.
In you we are many parts, but one body living your gospel
throughout the ages;
—let us fulfill our mission through your Holy Spirit to the
glory and praise of your name.
You wept for a people who had not known you;
—through your resurrection, help us to recognize you in one
another, in all creation, and in all of the ways that you
come to us.

PRAYER: O God, you promise eternal life to all who believe
in you. As we celebrate the resurrection of Jesus
Christ, open our minds and hearts to his message of
love. Make of us the good earth that bears fruit a
hundredfold. Grant this through Jesus, who lives with
you in the unity of the Holy Spirit, now and always.
Amen.

DAYTIME PRAYER

Ant 1 Alleluia, Christ is risen, alleluia, alleluia.

Ant 2 The women and men who believed in Jesus rejoiced,
alleluia, alleluia.

Ant 3 Stay with us, for it is toward evening and the day is far
spent, alleluia, alleluia.

(Prayer as in Morning Prayer)

EVENING PRAYER

READING

Whoever believes in creation must encounter God in earthly tasks and assignments. In the eternal dream of progress and the flowering and fulfillment which impels [humankind] in...science, technology, and economic activity, the faith perceives the echo of the creative *fiat*: "In action I cleave to the creative power of God, I coincide with it; I become not only its instrument but its living promulgation."

Piet Smulders, *The Design of Teilhard de Chardin*, p. 217, (13)

RESPONSORY

The followers of Jesus were filled with joy, alleluia, alleluia.
   —The followers...
When they saw him risen from the dead, **—alleluia...**
Glory to you, Source of all Being, Eternal Word, and Holy Spirit.
   —The followers...

CANTICLE OF MARY

Ant. By his death and resurrection, our living Christ has redeemed all people, alleluia.

INTERCESSIONS

Christ, our Pasch, is sacrificed. In joy let us cry out:
   **Worthy are you, O Christ, to receive
   honor, glory and praise!**

You laid down your life that we might live;
   —give us courage to die to all selfishness that we may live
   for others.
You were the joy of the disciples;
   —be our joy and everlasting hope.
You call us out of disbelief by your care for our daily needs;
   —may we rejoice in such love and pass it on.
You are the firstborn from the dead;
   —may all who have died experience the joy of your presence.

PRAYER: O God, you promise eternal life to all who believe
   in you. As we celebrate the resurrection of Jesus
   Christ, open our minds and hearts to his message of
   love. Make of us the good earth that bears fruit a

hundredfold. Grant this through Jesus, who lives with you in the unity of the Holy Spirit, now and always. Amen.

THIRD SATURDAY OF EASTER

(Psalms and Antiphons from Week III, p. 138)

MORNING PRAYER

READING

Surrendering to violence and revenge leads to the death of the moral person that a victim once was. The desire to choose life is the catalyst that moves a victim to positive action. By deliberately choosing to pray for the offender, by reaching out to others in acts of goodness that engage and change one's thoughts to thoughts of love and peace—by such responses—one clears the air of violence and turns in the direction of healing and former well-being. Violence crucifies us all, but every time someone responds with love and forgiveness, that person and all humankind are raised up to a new vision and quality of life. This is salvation. This is mirroring the God who makes good come out of evil. This is the beginning of the end of violence.

Carmelites of Indianapolis, Hidden Friends, pp. 100–101, (5)

RESPONSORY

Christ rose from the grave, alleluia, alleluia. —**Christ...**
Conquering sin an death, —**alleluia...**
Glory to you, Source of all Being, Eternal Word, and Holy Spirit.
   —**Christ...**

CANTICLE OF ZECHARIAH

Ant. Simon Peter said: "Lord, to whom shall we go? You have the words of eternal life; we have believed and have come to know that you are the Holy One of God," alleluia.

INTERCESSIONS

Christ Jesus, dying you destroyed death; rising you restored life. In confidence let us pray:
   May we walk in the land of the living forever.

You were hated by many in your lifetime, but God raised you in glory;
   —help us to rise above the opinions and rejections of others as we strive to be faithful to you.

You chose your disciples because they did not adhere to this
world;
  —bless our world and our culture with values, directions,
    and leaders that derive their power from your gospel.
You told your disciples that they would suffer for your sake;
  —let the joy of your resurrection fill us with courage to live
    and to die for you.
You spent your life doing good;
  —may our celebration of this Easter season enable us to
    bring your word and work to life again.

PRAYER: Christ Jesus, your words are spirit and life; we long to
follow you unreservedly. Through your resurrection,
give us the grace to love and respect the gift of life each
day, and to be open to the depths and heights of the
new life to which you call us. Grant that someday we
may live with you for all eternity. Amen.

DAYTIME PRAYER

Ant 1 Alleluia, Christ is risen, alleluia, alleluia.

Ant 2 The women and men who believed in Jesus rejoiced,
alleluia, alleluia.

Ant 3 Stay with us, for it is toward evening and the day is far
spent, alleluia, alleluia.

(Prayer as in Morning Prayer)

FOURTH SUNDAY OF EASTER

EVENING PRAYER I
(Psalms and Antiphons from Sunday, Week IV, p. 143)

READING

...the "wounded healer" might be quite helpful for the very purpose of
fostering peace and nonviolence as well as for genuine human health.
We have first to seek in ourselves the deepest roots of peacelessness
and of temptations to aggressiveness. We will at the same time be able
to discover our own inner resources for healing. Then we shall be able
to help one another in the double effort of unmasking evil and
unhealthy tendencies and of discovering our inner strengths for peace

and health. All this will proceed much better if we are strongly motivated by earnest dedication to the gospel of peace. We learn to accept one another, appreciating the good without repressing the recognition of our shadows. Thus we shall join hands in the healing ministry of peace and nonviolence.

Bernard Häring, *The Healing Power of Peace and Nonviolence*, p. 13, (1)

RESPONSORY

Christ our hope has risen, alleluia, alleluia. **—Christ...**
Let us rejoice and give thanks, **—alleluia,...**
Glory to you, Source of all Being, Eternal Word, and Holy Spirit.
   —Christ...

CANTICLE OF MARY

Ant I came that you may have life and have it abundantly, alleluia.

INTERCESSIONS

You Christ Jesus, are the sign of our hope and joy. Gratefully we pray:
         Christ yesterday, today, and forever, alleluia!

You are the Good Shepherd; you know us and call us by name;
   —may we recognize the good shepherds in our midst and heed their prophetic calls.
You give us your gift of peace;
   —enable us to use our energies to create a world of peace and harmony.
You are the Lamb of God;
   —help us to see the signs of resurrection and new life around us.
You promise to make your home with us;
   —grant us the faith to believe that you truly desire to dwell within each of us.

PRAYER: O God, you sent Christ Jesus to be our shepherd and the lamb of sacrifice. Help us to embrace the mystery of salvation, the promise of life rising out of death. Help us to hear the call of Christ and give us the courage to follow it readily that we, too, may lead others to you. This we ask through Jesus, our shepherd and guide. Amen.

MORNING PRAYER
(Psalms from Sunday, Week IV, p. 145)

Ant 1 I am the Good Shepherd. I know my own and my own know me.

Ant 2 I am the door; anyone who enters by me will be saved.

Ant 3 I am the Good Shepherd; I lay down my life for my sheep, alleluia.

READING

I am the good shepherd. I know my own and my own know me, just as [God, who sent me], knows me and I know [God]. And I lay down my life for the sheep. I have other sheep that do not belong to this fold. I must bring them also, and they will listen to my voice. So there will be one flock, one shepherd. For this reason [God] loves me, because I lay down my life in order to take it up again. No one takes it from me, but I lay it down of my own accord. I have power to lay it down, and I have power to take it up again. I have received this command from the [One who has sent me].

Jn 10:14–18

RESPONSORY

You are our Savior, O Christ, alleluia, alleluia. **—You are...**
Your death brings us life, **—alleluia,...**
Glory to you, Source of all Being, Eternal Word and Holy Spirit.
   —You are...

CANTICLE OF ZECHARIAH

Ant I am the Good Shepherd, I lay down my life for my sheep, alleluia.

INTERCESSIONS

You, Christ Jesus, are the sign of our hope and joy. In gratitude we pray:
   Christ yesterday, today and forever, alleluia!

You are the Good Shepherd; you know us and call us by name;
   —may we recognize the good shepherds in our midst and
   heed their prophetic calls.
You give us your gift of peace;
   —enable us to use our energies to create a world of peace
   and harmony.

You are the Lamb of God;
 —help us to see the signs of resurrection and new life
  around us.
You promise to make your home with us;
 —grant us the faith to believe that you truly desire to dwell
  within each of us.

PRAYER: O God, you sent Christ Jesus to be our shepherd and
the lamb of sacrifice. Help us to embrace the mystery of
salvation, the promise of life rising out of death. Help
us to hear the call of Christ and give us the courage to
follow it readily that we, too, may lead others to you.
This we ask through Jesus, our shepherd and guide.
Amen.

DAYTIME PRAYER

Ant 1 Alleluia, Christ is risen, alleluia, alleluia.

Ant 2 The women and men who believed in Jesus rejoiced,
alleluia, alleluia.

Ant 3 Stay with us, for it is toward evening and the day is far
spent, alleluia, alleluia.

(Prayer as in Morning Prayer)

EVENING PRAYER II

Ant 1 I came that they may have life and have it abundantly.

Ant 2 I have other sheep, that are not of this fold; I must bring
them also, and they will heed my voice.

Ant 3 They shall never perish, and no one shall snatch them out
of my hand.

READING

Then [one of the elders] said to me, "These are they who have come out
of the great ordeal; they have washed their robes and made them white
in the blood of the Lamb. For this reason they are before the throne of
God, worshipping...day and night within [God's] temple; and the one
who is seated on the throne will shelter them. They will hunger no
more, and thirst no more; the sun will not strike them, nor any
scorching heat; for the Lamb at the center of the throne will be their

shepherd, and...guide them to springs of the water of life, and God will wipe away every tear from their eyes."

Rev 7:14–17

RESPONSORY

Christ is the sun that never sets, alleluia, alleluia. **—Christ**...
Giving light to our hearts, **—alleluia**...
Glory to you, Source of all Being, Eternal Word and Holy Spirit.
 —Christ...

CANTICLE OF MARY

Ant You were straying like sheep, but have now returned to the shepherd of your souls.

INTERCESSIONS

Those who have died with Christ will rise with him; God will wipe away every tear from their eyes, and so we rejoice:
 Worthy is the Lamb that was slain.

Jesus, you are the way, the truth, and the life; we go to God only through you;
 —let us always hear and follow your spirit of truth.
Your resurrection heralds a new heaven and a new earth;
 —help us to live daily with minds and hearts open to your Holy Spirit.
You tell us that people of faith will do works even greater than your own;
 —increase our faith that we, too, may bring healing and new life to the world.
We praise you for the bread of thanksgiving and the words of your gospel;
 —give us the grace to let these gifts of God bear fruit a hundredfold to God's glory.

PRAYER: O God, you sent Christ Jesus to be our shepherd and the lamb of sacrifice. Help us to embrace the mystery of salvation, the promise of life rising out of death. Help us to hear the call of Christ and give us the courage to follow it readily that we, too, may lead others to you. This we ask through Jesus, our shepherd and guide. Amen.

FOURTH MONDAY OF EASTER
(Psalms and Antiphons from Week IV, p. 151)

MORNING PRAYER

READING

If you suffer with Him, *you shall reign with Him*, [if you] weep [with Him], you shall rejoice with Him; [if you] die [with Him] on the cross of tribulation, you shall possess heavenly mansions *in the splendor of the saints* and, *in the Book of Life*, your *name* shall be called glorious among [all].

Clare of Assisi, Francis and Clare, p. 197, (1)

RESPONSORY

Christ rose from the grave, alleluia, alleluia. —**Christ...**
Conquering sin an death, —**alleluia...**
Glory to you, Source of all Being, Eternal Word, and Holy Spirit.
    —**Christ...**

CANTICLE OF ZECHARIAH

Ant. I am the Good Shepherd. I lay down my life for my sheep, alleluia.

INTERCESSIONS

Christ Jesus, you rose from the dead and showed yourself to the women; with joyful hearts we proclaim:
    Wonderful are your works, O Christ.

Jesus, through your resurrection you call us to be born again;
    —help us to recognize and to be open to your Spirit in our
      lives
You are the Good Shepherd and you guide us with tender care;
    —enlighten our civic and religious leaders; give them your
      mind and heart.
You promise to send the Comforter to witness on your behalf;
    —empowered with your Spirit, may we bear witness to you
      in word and deed.
O God, you have created all things, and all that you have created
is good;
    —help us to see others and all things as you see them.

PRAYER: O God, you gave Peter the wisdom and largeness of heart to open the sheepfold of your Church to the Gentiles and to all who would believe in your Word. Give us the vision and the generosity to remove the barriers that we place before those who seek to know and love you. Teach us how to share the fruits of the life, death, and resurrection of Jesus. Amen.

DAYTIME PRAYER

Ant 1 Alleluia, Christ is risen, alleluia, alleluia.

Ant 2 The women and men who believed in Jesus rejoiced, alleluia, alleluia.

Ant 3 Stay with us, for it is toward evening and the day is far spent, alleluia, alleluia.

(Prayer as in Morning Prayer)

EVENING PRAYER

READING

There were many who were antagonistic towards [Mary MacKillop] and who treated her unjustly. But her constant response was to find excuses for them, sympathize with them, and forgive them. During the period of excommunication she wrote to her mother: "It is far harder to have to think ill of others than to be the one thought ill of.... Remember that even good and holy servants of God have been used by the same good God as instruments, and I am sure that some at least of them must feel great pain at what they are doing." (22 November 1871) Her habitual response was to be generous, sympathetic, and forgiving as God is in Christ. (Eph. 4:32)

Bl. Mary MacKillop, RSJ, (10)

RESPONSORY

The followers of Jesus were filled with joy, alleluia, alleluia.
—**The followers...**
When they saw him risen from the dead, —**alleluia...**
Glory to you, Source of all Being, Eternal Word, and Holy Spirit.
—**The followers...**

CANTICLE OF MARY

Ant I have other sheep, not of this fold; they will heed my voice so there shall be one flock and one shepherd, alleluia.

INTERCESSIONS

Jesus, you rose from the dead and your disciples recognized you in the breaking of the bread. We proclaim in faith:
Jesus is risen indeed.

Christ Jesus, through your Spirit you transformed your frightened apostles into fearless proclaimers of your word;
—bless all missionaries with fortitude and perseverance.
By your life, death, and resurrection you invite all the nations of the world to be the people of God;
—help us to live as true daughters and sons of our loving Creator.
Through your resurrection you give hope to all who believe in you;
—through our daily deaths, transform our lives evermore into your likeness.
Following your example, Peter prayed for guidance in time of decision;
—help us to realize the necessity of prayer in our lives.
By your death and resurrection you conquered death;
—have pity on the dying, be their light and peace.

PRAYER: O God, you gave Peter the wisdom and largeness of heart to open the sheepfold of your Church to the Gentiles and to all who would believe in your Word. Give us the vision and the generosity to remove the barriers that we place before those who seek to know and love you. Teach us how to share the fruits of the life, death, and resurrection of Jesus. Amen.

FOURTH TUESDAY OF EASTER
(Psalms and Antiphons from Week IV, p. 158)
MORNING PRAYER

READING

These foundational teachings and their fruits are traceable to Catherine [of Siena] as a woman of prayer. *The Dialogue* itself is a lengthy prayer for self understanding, for the Church, for the whole world, for God's providential care. Time and again she returned to the absolute necessity of building in one's soul an interior cell into which one can return to be alone with God and attend to [God's] Word and will before venturing out into the world. One seeks in prayer the inspiration that will make one's actions effective and one's witness edifying.

Susan A. Muto, "Foundations of Christian Formation in the
Dialogue of St. Catherine of Siena," p. 283, (7)

RESPONSORY

Christ rose from the grave, alleluia, alleluia. —**Christ...**
Conquering sin an death, —**alleluia...**
Glory to you, Source of all Being, Eternal Word, and Holy Spirit.
   —**Christ...**

CANTICLE OF ZECHARIAH

Ant. The works that I do in God's name bear witness to me,
      alleluia.

INTERCESSIONS

Jesus, risen from the dead, you dined with the women and men who followed you, served them, and strengthened their faith in you, and so we pray:
      How can we repay you for your goodness to us.

Jesus, you came to do the will of God, and in death you were raised up in glory;
      —have mercy on those who despair of meaning in life.
Your resurrection gave new hope to your small community of followers;
      —let the celebration of that same resurrection bring new life
         to your church today.
You asked those who followed you to sell all and give to the poor;
      —teach us effective ways to feed the hungry and to house
         the homeless of our world.
You never cease to call us to greater intimacy with you;
      —transform the mustard seed of our faith into total
         dedication.

PRAYER: O God, you have sent Jesus to call us into the unity of
         one flock. Through his life, death, and resurrection, he
         has revealed your love for us and has freed us from the
         bondage of sin. Have mercy on us again and again.

Help us to hear his voice and to proclaim the message of the gospel with our lives. This we ask in the name of the Risen Savior. Amen.

DAYTIME PRAYER

Ant 1 Alleluia, Christ is risen, alleluia, alleluia.

Ant 2 The women and men who believed in Jesus rejoiced, alleluia, alleluia.

Ant 3 Stay with us, for it is toward evening and the day is far spent, alleluia, alleluia.

(Prayer as in Morning Prayer)

EVENING PRAYER

READING

The journey of prayer makes us conscious of our participation in God's life. God is already active in our life but our consent and energy is also required. Thus, prayer is about presence and relationship, specifically becoming consciously present to the Mystery we name God, a God whose self is further revealed to us in Jesus. As we grow more deeply into this relationship, new aspects of the God mystery encompass us.

Janet Ruffing, RSM, "As Refined by Fire," (4)

RESPONSORY

The followers of Jesus were filled with joy, alleluia, alleluia.
    —The followers...
When they saw him risen from the dead, **—alleluia...**
Glory to you, Source of all Being, Eternal Word, and Holy Spirit.
    —The followers...

CANTICLE OF MARY

Ant. My sheep hear my voice and they follow me, and I give them eternal life, alleluia.

INTERCESSIONS

Jesus, risen from the dead, you have filled the world with light and hope. With joy we sing:
    This is the day that our God has made.

Jesus, your resurrection frees us from the bondage of death;
  —free those who are enslaved or oppressed.
Your resurrection is a promise of new life;
  —give hope and new opportunity for wholesome labor to
    migrant workers and to all who receive an inadequate
    wage.
By your resurrection you were freed from suffering and death;
  —have mercy on all those who suffer from illness or abuse.
You rose from the dead and appeared to your mother and to your
friends;
  —bless our families, friends, and all who show us your love
    and mercy.

PRAYER: O God, you have sent Jesus to call us into the unity of
one flock. Through his life, death, and resurrection, he
has revealed your love for us and has freed us from the
bondage of sin. Have mercy on us again and again.
Help us to hear his voice and to proclaim the message
of the gospel with our lives. This we ask in the name of
the Risen Savior. Amen.

FOURTH WEDNESDAY OF EASTER
(Psalms and Antiphons from Week IV, p. 165)
MORNING PRAYER

READING

Our Lord [Jesus] showed himself to me, and he appeared to me more
glorified than I had seen him before, in which I was taught that our soul
will never have rest till it comes into him, acknowledging that he is full
of joy, familiar and courteous and blissful and true life. Again and again
our Lord said: I am he, I am he who is highest. I am he whom you love. I
am he in whom you delight. I am he whom you serve. I am he for whom
you long. I am he whom you desire. I am he whom you intend. I am he
who is all.

Julian of Norwich, Showings, p. 223, (1)

RESPONSORY

Christ rose from the grave, alleluia, alleluia. **—Christ...**
Conquering sin an death, **—alleluia...**
Glory to you, Source of all Being, Eternal Word, and Holy Spirit.
  —Christ...

CANTICLE OF ZECHARIAH

Ant. I have come as light into the world, that whoever believes in me may not remain in darkness, alleluia.

INTERCESSIONS

Jesus is risen from the dead, a mystery revealed to little ones. With sincere hearts we pray:
Christ Jesus, make us humble of heart.

By your resurrection, you bring light to our darkness, hope to despair;
　　—give us a hunger for your words of life.
You will not leave us orphans;
　　—help us to be aware of your presence throughout the day.
You have chosen us to follow your disciples in bringing our world to fullness of life;
　　—make us responsible Christians; let our lives proclaim our faith in you.
You promised the Spirit who would pray within us;
　　—quiet our minds and hearts; teach us to pray.

PRAYER: O God, you sent Christ Jesus into the world not to judge but to save it, to enable all people to live wholesome lives in the image of their Creator. Let this Easter Season renew our hope as we endeavor to do your will and to grow in love. We ask this in the name of Jesus. Amen.

DAYTIME PRAYER

Ant 1 Alleluia, Christ is risen, alleluia, alleluia.

Ant 2 The women and men who believed in Jesus rejoiced, alleluia, alleluia.

Ant 3 Stay with us, for it is toward evening and the day is far spent, alleluia, alleluia.

(Prayer as in Morning Prayer)

EVENING PRAYER

READING

Since we have a little postulant in the house again, I think often of our own young days in the Order and of the wonderful [providential] guidance that each one's way to Carmel signifies. Perhaps even more wonderful is the story of the souls *in* Carmel. They are hidden deep in the Divine Heart. And what we believe we understand about our own soul is, after all, only a fleeting reflection of what will remain God's secret until the day all will be made manifest. My great joy consists in the hope of that future clarity. Faith in the secret history must always strengthen us when what we actually perceive (about ourselves or others) might discourage us.

Edith Stein: Self-Portrait in Letters, p. 331, (3)

RESPONSORY

The followers of Jesus were filled with joy, alleluia, alleluia.
  —The followers...
When they saw him risen from the dead, **—alleluia...**
Glory to you, Source of all Being, Eternal Word, and Holy Spirit.
  —The followers...

CANTICLE OF MARY

Ant. Put your faith in me and in the One who sent me, alleluia.

INTERCESSIONS

Jesus is risen from the dead. We, too, shall rise and so we lift our voices as we say:
  Wonderful are your ways, O God.

Jesus, by your resurrection, you have overcome tyranny and injustice.
  —strengthen and encourage those who are victims of greed
    and misplaced power.
You appeared to your followers to free them from fear;
  —let us never allow our sins to keep us from turning to you.
Risen from the dead, you are the Good Shepherd seeking those who are lost;
  —teach us how to proclaim the good news to those who do
    not know you.

You revealed the secrets of God's designs to your followers;
  —help us to live the graces of our baptism.
You spoke to Peter about how he would die;
  —prepare us for death by a life of dedication to you.

PRAYER: O God, you sent Christ Jesus into the world not to judge but to save it, to enable all people to live wholesome lives in the image of their Creator. Let this Easter Season renew our hope as we endeavor to do your will and to grow in love. We ask this in the name of Jesus. Amen.

FOURTH THURSDAY OF EASTER
(Psalms and Antiphons from Week IV, p. 172)

MORNING PRAYER

READING

He who walked the streets of the material Jerusalem is no more, the Christ that reigns today in the spiritual Jerusalem, the Christ that is ever cognizant of the needs, the sins of the world that "God so loved" is an omnipresence. His spirit inclines as two or three meet touching anything we would ask. In our human thoughtlessness we, too, like James and John, may ask for an *end*, but Christ will teach us that the *means* only are for us; we may desire an *effect*, but it springs from its corresponding *cause*. The life which Jesus lived is a life of processes.

Jessie Evans, The Shakers, p. 142 (1)

RESPONSORY

Christ rose from the grave, alleluia, alleluia. —**Christ...**
Conquering sin an death, —**alleluia...**
Glory to you, Source of all Being, Eternal Word, and Holy Spirit.
  —**Christ...**

CANTICLE OF ZECHARIAH

Ant. I tell you all these things that you may know that I am the one sent from God, alleluia.

INTERCESSIONS

O Christ, by your resurrection from the dead, the sorrow of the world is turned into joy. We cry out:
Alleluia, alleluia, alleluia!

Christ Jesus, whoever believes in you has life eternal;
  —bless all those who do not know your name or gospel.
Through the love you bear for us;
  —help us to love and care for one another.
By your resurrection you transcend the needs of the flesh;
  —have mercy on those who live in deprivation of any kind.
In our daily dyings and risings;
  —be with us as we strive to enrich our quality of life and
    deepen our love for you.

PRAYER: O God, you know our hearts. Through the resurrection of Christ Jesus, call us to new growth; strengthen our weakness and direct our strength, that transformed in Christ, we may bring this healing and forgiving word to the world. Grant this through Jesus who lives with you and the Holy Spirit forever. Amen.

DAYTIME PRAYER

Ant 1 Alleluia, Christ is risen, alleluia, alleluia.

Ant 2 The women and men who believed in Jesus rejoiced, alleluia, alleluia.

Ant 3 Stay with us, for it is toward evening and the day is far spent, alleluia, alleluia.

(Prayer as in Morning Prayer)

EVENING PRAYER

READING

It is the prophetic task to announce that the world was created, not to be destroyed, but to be fulfilled; not to stand still, but to grow toward wholeness. It is part of the prophetic role to identify alternatives and encourage possible directions in that journey toward wholeness. In this regard there is a convergence between the prophetic presence in authentic religion and efforts within the world-order movement to identify the perilous course we are now traveling and explore alternative routes for the human community. It is part of the prophetic role to call us to task when we lose sight of that whole; to be, as Isaiah, a critic of the established order and institutions when they fail to advance or violate human growth.... It is the prophetic role to remind us that our "salvation" or "liberation" is worked out in history—in our time and space, here and now—not by a rejection of history or the world, but in the process of developing and actualizing its full potential.... The prophet reminds us that this is our time and place to Become who we can be.

Gerald and Patricia Mische, Toward a Human World Order, p. 337, (1)

RESPONSORY

The followers of Jesus were filled with joy, alleluia, alleluia.
   —The followers...
When they saw him risen from the dead, **—alleluia...**
Glory to you, Source of all Being, Eternal Word, and Holy Spirit.
   —The followers...

CANTICLE OF MARY

Ant. If you know the things of God, blessed are you if you do
     them, alleluia.

INTERCESSIONS

The risen Christ appeared to Mary Magdalen and called her by name, and so we pray:
O Christ, call us again and again.

Jesus Christ, risen in glory, death could not contain you;
   —call to new life all that is dead or barren within us.
O Christ, on the cross you prayed for deliverance;
   —you were heard for your reverence and raised in glory.
Through your love for the earth and all of its fruits;
   —help us to redeem the harm we have done to this planet.
Rising from the dead, you returned to those with whom you had shared life;
   —be with all who are lonely or handicapped in society.

PRAYER: O God, you know our hearts. Through the resurrection of Christ Jesus, call us to new growth; strengthen our weakness and direct our strength, that transformed in Christ, we may bring this healing and forgiving word to the world. Grant this through Jesus who lives with you and the Holy Spirit forever. Amen.

FOURTH FRIDAY OF EASTER

(Psalms and Antiphons from Week IV, p. 179)

MORNING PRAYER

READING

In moments of crushing solitude, humility alone can help us in recognizing the radical powerlessness of human nature. It inclines us to cast our whole being at the foot of the cross, and then our heavy burden is lifted by Christ in our place: "Learn of me.... For my yoke is easy, and by burden light" (Mt. 11:29–30). "Thy will be done," the fiat springs forth; I accept it as my own. I read in it what God has thought of me, and I recognize my destiny. We are no longer self-centered, but rendered joyful and lighthearted. "Behold the handmaid of the Lord" (Lk 1:38). "The friend of the bridegroom, who stands and hears him, rejoices exceedingly at the voice of the bridegroom. This my joy, therefore, is made full" (Jn 3:29).

Paul Evdokimov, *The Struggle with God*, pp. 59–60, (1)

RESPONSORY

Christ rose from the grave, alleluia, alleluia. —**Christ...**
Conquering sin an death, —**alleluia...**
Glory to you, Source of all Being, Eternal Word, and Holy Spirit.
   —**Christ...**

CANTICLE OF ZECHARIAH

Ant. Let not your hearts be troubled; believe in God, believe also in me, alleluia.

INTERCESSIONS

Jesus risen from the dead has turned all our grief into joy, and so we pray:

Let all the earth sing praise!

Christ Jesus, you had compassion on the multitude in the desert and fed them;
   —help us to do all in our power to feed the hungry and care for all in need.
You fled from those who would make you king;
   —give all in public office the courage to maintain their integrity, and to labor for the public good.

You are our way to God, the Source of all that is;
  —give us the grace to heed your works and to embrace your
    gospel with our lives.
You taught and encouraged your disciples to the very end;
  —make us tireless in sharing your gospel, patient and
    compassionate with those who are slow to hear.

PRAYER: O God, you have sent Christ Jesus to be our way,
our truth, and our life. Through his resurrection
remove from our lives all that prevents us from
following the gospel, all that would lead us into error,
and all that would keep us from embracing your call
wholeheartedly. We ask this in his name. Amen.

DAYTIME PRAYER

Ant 1 Alleluia, Christ is risen, alleluia, alleluia.

Ant 2 The women and men who believed in Jesus rejoiced,
alleluia, alleluia.

Ant 3 Stay with us, for it is toward evening and the day is far
spent, alleluia, alleluia.

(Prayer as in Morning Prayer)

EVENING PRAYER

READING

Loving *God* with the whole heart means for most of us, perhaps, the
need for a deep and lifelong conversion of being open to receive an
infinitely gratuitous love. The distinctive mark of Christian asceticism is
not the strenuous all-out effort at loving God, but rather the courageous
letting down of the barriers to receiving that love, barriers which
unbelief and lack of trust have erected. This is really the import of Paul's
teaching on justification by faith and not by works, by grace and not
according to merit.... To the degree that we accept the offer of this
undeserved love, a generous response will flow from the gratitude, joy,
and compunction generated by God's remembrance of that love. We will
love even as we are loved.
  W. Harold Grant, Magdala Thompson, Thomas E. Clarke, *From Image to Likeness*, pp. 190–91, (1)

RESPONSORY

The followers of Jesus were filled with joy, alleluia, alleluia.
  —The followers...
When they saw him risen from the dead, **—alleluia...**
Glory to you, Source of all Being, Eternal Word, and Holy Spirit.
  —The followers...

CANTICLE OF MARY

Ant. I go to prepare a place for you, that where I am you also
  may be, alleluia.

INTERCESSIONS

Christ Jesus, rising from the dead gives glory to God, and new
vision to all who believe. With hearts full of joy, we cry out:
  Glory and praise to you, O Christ!

You rose from the dead and proved that all your words are true;
  —in times of doubt let the light of your glory shine in our
  minds and hearts.
You rose from the dead and all your works are magnified;
  —give us the courage to face necessary deaths when new
  life beckons.
You rose from the dead having forgiven those who had crucified
you;
  —help us to return good for evil, and to pray for those who
  harm us.
You rose from the dead and call us to unity;
  —teach us to realize that all we think and do affects
  everyone and everything in the world.

PRAYER: O God, you have sent Christ Jesus to be our way,
  our truth, and our life. Through his resurrection
  remove from our lives all that prevents us from
  following the gospel, all that would lead us into error,
  and all that would keep us from embracing your call
  wholeheartedly. We ask this in his name. Amen.

FOURTH SATURDAY OF EASTER
(Psalms and Antiphons from Week IV, p. 186)

MORNING PRAYER

READING

On Easter morning when the apostles finally realized that Jesus was still with them and that he was not only offering them forgiveness but was inviting them to let his own Spirit of love live in them, the Easter morning became an alleluia morning. St. Paul tells us that if Jesus has not risen, we are all fools for believing. But if we do not accept Jesus' forgiveness, then again, his life, death, and rising are foolishness, for the reign of darkness is still upon us.

Elizabeth Meluch, OCD, (11)

RESPONSORY

Christ rose from the grave, alleluia, alleluia. —**Christ...**
Conquering sin an death, —**alleluia...**
Glory to you, Source of all Being, Eternal Word, and Holy Spirit.
   —**Christ...**

CANTICLE OF ZECHARIAH

Ant. The one who believes in me will also do the works I do, and greater works than these, alleluia.

INTERCESSIONS

Jesus, risen from the dead, lives on fulfilling the works of God, and so we pray:
   O Christ, live on in us.

Jesus, you call us to complete the work you have begun on earth;
   —teach us to put no limits on the power of your Spirit in our lives.
Jesus, Lord of heaven and earth, the winds and the seas obey you;
   —be merciful to us and guide our human freedom that we may serve you with upright hearts.
Your mother beheld your death and your resurrection;
   —bless all mothers with the strength and grace they need to bear and to guide their children.
Those who have seen you have seen God;
   —do not let the familiarity of your gospel blind us to seeing you as you are, son of Mary, son of God.

PRAYER: O God, giver of all that is good, we praise you in the life, death, and resurrection of Jesus Christ. During this Easter season, let his saving light live in us in abundance, bringing guidance, healing, and the peace that only you can give. We ask this in Jesus' name. Amen.

DAYTIME PRAYER

Ant 1 Alleluia, Christ is risen, alleluia, alleluia.

Ant 2 The women and men who believed in Jesus rejoiced, alleluia, alleluia.

Ant 3 Stay with us, for it is toward evening and the day is far spent, alleluia, alleluia.

(Prayer as in Morning Prayer)

FIFTH SUNDAY OF EASTER
EVENING PRAYER I
(Psalms and antiphons from Week I, p. 1)

READING

If the immediacy of the resurrection is hidden, the results are not. In fact, the resurrection might be considered through the metaphor of the sun. We cannot look directly at the sun, for the brightness would blind us—our eyes are not suited to that strength of light. Yet the sun, which we cannot see directly, illumines all else, and in its light we make our way in the world. We cannot look directly at the resurrection because it is not given for us to see. Nevertheless, it illumines the entire landscape of the New Testament: the resurrection is the confirmation of that which Jesus revealed in his life and death, and it is the catalyst that transforms the disciples, releasing the power that led to the foundation of the church.

Marjorie Hewitt Suchocki, *God Christ Church*, pp. 112–13, (2)

RESPONSORY

Christ our hope has risen, alleluia, alleluia. **—Christ our...**
Let us rejoice and give thanks, **—alleluia,...**
Glory to you, Source of all Being, Eternal Word and Holy Spirit.
   —Christ our...

CANTICLE OF MARY

Ant Let not your hearts be troubled. Believe in God; believe also in me, alleluia.

INTERCESSIONS

Christ Jesus has loved us and redeemed us by his death and rising. In joy let us proclaim:
> **Worthy is the Lamb to receive honor and glory, wisdom and peace!**

Savior God, you have made us partakers of your priesthood;
— may we offer you continual thanks and praise.
You have conquered death; raise us to new life;
— that we may be your resurrection people.
You walked the way of Calvary's anguish;
— in your compassion succor all prisoners of conscience and those unjustly incarcerated.
By your resurrection, you promised life after death;
— may all who have died enjoy fullness of life with you.

PRAYER: O God, you are One and all your works are holy. Who can fathom your wondrous love? Through Jesus, you call us all to life and count our love for each other as love for you. As we celebrate this Easter season, we ask you to increase our faith, to renew our hope, and to let our love abound to the praise of your glory, that we may live with you forever and ever. Amen.

MORNING PRAYER
(Psalms from Sunday, Week I, p. 3)

Ant 1 Let not your hearts be troubled; believe in God, believe also in me.

Ant 2 Those who abide in me and I in them will bear much fruit, for apart from me you can do nothing.

Ant 3 A new commandment I give to you, that you love one another even as I have loved you.

READING

Come to [the Lord Jesus], a living stone, though rejected by mortals yet chosen and precious in God's sight, and like living stones, let yourselves be built into a spiritual house, to be a holy priesthood, to offer spiritual sacrifices acceptable to God through Jesus Christ. But you are a chosen race, a royal priesthood, a holy nation, God's own people, in order that you may proclaim the mighty acts of [the One] who called you out of darkness into...marvelous light.

1 Pet 2:4–5, 9

RESPONSORY

Christ our hope has risen, alleluia, alleluia. —**Christ**...
Let us rejoice and give thanks, —**alleluia**...
Glory to you, Source of all Being, Eternal Word and Holy Spirit.
   —**Christ**...

CANTICLE OF ZECHARIAH

Ant I am the vine; you are the branches, alleluia.

INTERCESSIONS

Handed over to death, Christ Jesus was raised to life for our justification. In living hope we pray:
   Free us, Christ Jesus, from what still binds us!

Jesus, you have shared our human condition. Look on the oppressed and the deprived;
   —that they may be aided in their struggle for self-determination.
You have revealed in your being the compassion of God;
   —grant relief to the sick and the dying through our compassion.
You call us to use our talents;
   —give us courage to further our own human development.
You call us each to wholeness; unsettle our complacencies;
   —that we may recognize our blindness and surrender to the guidance of your Spirit.

PRAYER: O God, you are one and all your works are holy. Who can fathom your wondrous love? Through Jesus, you call us all to life and count our love for each other as love for you. As we celebrate this Easter season, we ask you to increase our faith, to renew our hope, and to let our love abound to the praise of your glory, that we may live with you forever and ever. Amen.

DAYTIME PRAYER

Ant 1   Alleluia, Christ is risen, alleluia, alleluia.

Ant 2   The women and men who believed in Jesus rejoiced, alleluia, alleluia.

Ant 3   Stay with us, for it is toward evening and the day is far spent, alleluia, alleluia.

(Prayer as in Morning Prayer)

EVENING PRAYER II

Ant 1   Jesus said, "I am the way, and the truth, and the life."

Ant 2   If you abide in me, and my words abide in you, ask whatever you will, and it shall be done for you.

Ant 3   Those who believe in me will also do the works that I do; and greater works than these will they do.

READING

Then I [John] saw a new heaven and a new earth; for the first heaven and the first earth had passed away, and the sea was no more. And I saw the holy city, the new Jerusalem, coming down out of heaven from God, prepared as a bride adorned for her husband. And I heard a loud voice from the throne saying, "See, [my home] is among mortals. [I] will dwell with them as their God; and they will be [my] people, and [I myself] will be with them; [I] will wipe every tear from their eyes. Death will be no more; mourning and crying and pain will be no more, for the first things have passed away." And the one who was seated on the throne said, "See, I am making all things new."

Rev 21:1–5

RESPONSORY

The stone which the builders rejected has become the
     corner stone. **—The stone**...
Christ risen from the dead, **—has become**...
Glory to you, Source of all Being, Eternal Word and Holy Spirit.
     —The stone...

CANTICLE OF MARY

Ant   By this will all know that you are my followers, if you have love for one another, alleluia.

INTERCESSIONS

Let us rejoice with Christ Jesus who manifests himself in the breaking of the bread. In joy we pray:
You are risen indeed!

O Christ, you showed yourself to your disciples and assured them with your touch;
—give us the grace we need to embrace the mysteries of your life with our minds and hearts.

Your disciples recognized you in the miraculous catch of fish;
—help us to see you in your care for us each day of our lives.

You challenged Peter's love and commissioned him to lead your church;
—fill our hearts with the love and zeal we need to fulfill our mission on earth.

Throughout your life and to the last, your message was a call to love;
—teach us how to hear and live your message in the complexity of our lives.

PRAYER: O God, you are one and all your works are holy. Who can fathom your wondrous love? Through Jesus, you call us all to life and count our love for each other as love for you. As we celebrate this Easter season, we ask you to increase our faith, to renew our hope, and to let our love abound to the praise of your glory, that we may live with you forever and ever. Amen.

FIFTH MONDAY OF EASTER
(Psalms and Antiphons from Week I, p. 10)
MORNING PRAYER

READING

Nothing is so deadly as the noblest and most righteous human purpose when it is made dominant over the creative event.... Creative interchange must dominate, whereby the needs and interests of others get across to me, transform my own mind, my own desires and felt needs, so as to include theirs and thereby vastly magnify the appreciable world for each and the depth of community among all. There is no other way to salvation; and the greater the power of [human beings], the more imperative becomes the demand of the living Christ to take sovereignty over human purpose.

Henry Nelson Wieman, *The Source of Human Good,* p. 46, (52)

RESPONSORY

Christ rose from the grave, alleluia, alleluia. —**Christ...**
Conquering sin an death, —**alleluia...**
Glory to you, Source of all Being, Eternal Word, and Holy Spirit.
   —**Christ...**

CANTICLE OF ZECHARIAH

Ant. Whatever you ask in my name I will do it, that God may be glorified, alleluia.

INTERCESSIONS

Jesus, by your resurrection, you conquered sin and death, and revealed the power of God's love. We praise you and say:
    We will sing of your mercy forever.

Christ Jesus, your disciples hasten to give their lives for you;
   —let the sacrifice of all who serve you throughout the ages
    give life to your Church.
You fed your people bread in the wilderness;
   —nourish our hungry minds and hearts; teach us to seek
    the things that are to our peace.
You promised to send the Paraclete to teach us all things;
   —teach us to live your word of love that the fruits of your
    resurrection may encompass the whole world.
Risen Lord, you showed yourself to your disciples and their eyes
were opened;
   —let us know your presence in our lives that we may love
    and serve you faithfully.

PRAYER: Christ Jesus, you promise to dwell in those who love you and are true to your word. We ask you to give us loving hearts. Make us faithful to you, that with you in us, we may labor for the reign of God. We ask this in your holy name. Amen.

DAYTIME PRAYER

Ant 1 Alleluia, Christ is risen, alleluia, alleluia.

Ant 2 The women and men who believed in Jesus rejoiced, alleluia, alleluia.

Ant 3 Stay with us, for it is toward evening and the day is far spent, alleluia, alleluia.

(Prayer as in Morning Prayer)

EVENING PRAYER

READING

The name "House of Providence" was applied to the Institute's homes for the destitute, because their maintenance depended, not on regular means of support but on God's Providence. In practice this meant that such houses were entirely supported by the Sisters begging from door to door. At the Process of Mary MacKillop's Cause for Canonization, her companions testified to their being trained in this virtue. She wrote in one of her letters: "You ever taught me to look up to and depend on Divine Providence in every trouble and when you saw me dull or unhappy you always had the same sweet reminder for me." (21 August 1867)

Bl. Mary MacKillop, RSJ, (10)

RESPONSORY

The followers of Jesus were filled with joy, alleluia, alleluia.
—**The followers...**
When they saw him risen from the dead, —**alleluia...**
Glory to you, Source of all Being, Eternal Word, and Holy Spirit.
—**The followers...**

CANTICLE OF MARY

Ant The Counselor will be with you and dwell in you forever, alleluia.

INTERCESSIONS

Jesus, risen from the dead, you promise to live in those who love you. In homage we pray:
Keep us faithful to you all the days of our lives.

Jesus, our salvation was your pearl of great price;
—teach us to live and die for others and so rise with you.
You blessed little children and had time for them;
—give us the wisdom, creativity, and generosity to provide for them and those who care for them.

Your apostles left all to follow you; at your death you seemed to leave them;

   —help us to keep alive the hope of your resurrection both for ourselves and for those burdened with trials.

You knew the sorrow that death brings;

   —comfort those who mourn.

PRAYER: Christ Jesus, you promise to dwell in those who love you and are true to your word. We ask you to give us loving hearts. Make us faithful to you, that with you in us, we may labor for the reign of God. We ask this in your holy name. Amen.

FIFTH TUESDAY OF EASTER
(Psalms and Antiphons from Week I, p. 16)

MORNING PRAYER

READING

There is a strange and important truth to living with Christ not only in his defeat but also in his resurrection. Life usually forces us to live out our sorrows and agony. In this way we are brought to search for some help outside ourselves, some way of finding a new beginning. But just as this search seldom starts until one can picture the nature of the need, so we usually stop short of finding new life until we are able imaginatively to experience the resurrection as a reality, a real possibility within ourselves. Those who have not imagined the events of the resurrection again and again in concrete images can hardly know the power of the Christian message, the ability of light to conquer darkness. Without some kind of experience of Christ's rising from the dead, we can scarcely know the meaning of the atonement, or accept the power of the Spirit to touch and heal the gaping wounds of the world.

Morton Kelsey, The Other Side of Silence, p. 213, (1)

RESPONSORY

Christ rose from the grave, alleluia, alleluia. **—Christ...**

Conquering sin an death, **—alleluia...**

Glory to you, Source of all Being, Eternal Word, and Holy Spirit. **—Christ...**

CANTICLE OF ZECHARIAH

Ant. Peace I leave with you, my peace I give to you, alleluia.

INTERCESSIONS

Jesus, risen from the dead, you forgave your disciples and gave them the power to forgive sins. We humbly pray:
In your mercy, remember us.

O Christ, your wounds have become your sign of victory;
—help us to transform our suffering and labor into means of growth.

You bless those who, without seeing you, believe in your word;
—bless those who have not heard your word; send laborers into your harvest.

You promised to be with your church until the end of time;
—make us willing instruments in building the unity of your church throughout the world.

You showed your wounds to your disciples and they believed in you;
—enfold those who inflict torture on others; transform their lives and let them see your loving presence in themselves and in all people.

You lived and died a person of peace;
—grant peace to all who have died in war and to all who live with its scars.

PRAYER: O God, our Risen Savior is the source of the peace the world cannot give. From that eternal well, let us inundate the world with the justice and mercy that flows from your very heart. This we ask through this same Christ who lives with you forever. Amen.

DAYTIME PRAYER

Ant 1 Alleluia, Christ is risen, alleluia, alleluia.

Ant 2 The women and men who believed in Jesus rejoiced, alleluia, alleluia.

Ant 3 Stay with us, for it is toward evening and the day is far spent, alleluia, alleluia.

(Prayer as in Morning Prayer)

EVENING PRAYER

READING

...spend the appointed time in prayer quietly and peacefully, doing nothing in God's presence save to content yourself with being there, and that without desiring devotion or making any act unless you can do so with facility, sitting there in inward and outward tranquility and reverence, with the conviction that this patience is a powerful prayer before God.... In a word, we must be content to be impotent, idle, insensible, before God, dried up and barren, when God permits it, as with facility and devotion...for our union with God consists wholly in loving the one way as much as the other.

The Spirit of Saint Jane Frances de Chantal as Shown by her Letters, p. 319–20, (15)

RESPONSORY

The followers of Jesus were filled with joy, alleluia, alleluia.
　—The followers...
When they saw him risen from the dead, **—alleluia...**
Glory to you, Source of all Being, Eternal Word, and Holy Spirit.
　—The followers...

CANTICLE OF MARY

Ant. If you love me, you would have rejoiced, because I go to the One who sent me, alleluia.

INTERCESSIONS

Jesus, you rose from the dead, the hope of all who believe in you. In faith we pray:
　　　　Christ is our light and our salvation.

Jesus, by your resurrection you herald a new heaven and a new earth;
　—give us the grace to grow in love for you and in dedication to your gospel.
You are the vine and we are the branches;
　—help us to remember that whatever we say or do affects everyone and everything else.
You call us not servants, but friends, for you have revealed to us the will of God;
　—make us worthy of your gifts and your promises; help us to live the challenge of your gospel.
Jesus, to rise with you, we must take up our cross and follow you;

—teach us to meet the challenge of each day as a gift and a call to serve you, accepting our limitations and sharing our strengths.

Jesus, our risen Savior, your forgiving heart reveals the mercy of God to us;

—grant your peace to those who approach death with fear of sadness.

PRAYER: O God, our Risen Savior is the source of the peace the world cannot give. From that eternal well, let us inundate the world with the justice and mercy that flows from your very heart. This we ask through this same Christ who lives with you forever. Amen.

FIFTH WEDNESDAY OF EASTER
(Psalms and Antiphons from Week I, p. 23)
MORNING PRAYER

READING

Love...means something much more than mere sentiment, much more than token favors and perfunctory alms deeds. Love means an interior and spiritual identification with one's [sisters or brothers], so that [they are] not regarded as an "object" to "which" one "does good." The fact is that good done to another as to an object is of little or no spiritual value. Love takes one's neighbor as one's other self, and loves [him or her] with all the immense humility and discretion and reserve and reverence without which no one can presume to enter into the sanctuary of another's subjectivity. From such love all authoritarian brutality, all exploitation, domineering and condescension must necessarily be absent.

Thomas Merton, *The Wisdom of the Desert*, pp. 17–18, (16)

RESPONSORY

Christ rose from the grave, alleluia, alleluia. —**Christ...**
Conquering sin an death, —**alleluia...**
Glory to you, Source of all Being, Eternal Word, and Holy Spirit.
    —**Christ...**

CANTICLE OF ZECHARIAH

Ant. I am the vine, you are the branches, alleluia.

INTERCESSIONS

On the third day, the Sun of Justice arose, and darkness was conquered forever. We joyfully sing your praises:
Glory to you, O God!

O Christ, you receive all who come to you;
—enlighten all who turn away from religion because of negative experiences.
Powerless in death, you rose in the power of God's love;
—teach us the wisdom and necessity of nonviolence for the salvation of our planet.
You rose from the dead making known to all the power of God's love for us;
—help us to banish servile fear from our lives and to love as we are loved.
You appeared to your friends, each according to their need;
—open our minds and hearts to your loving guidance in our lives.

PRAYER: Christ Jesus, by your resurrection you have made all things new. Give us the courage to pass beyond the familiar and to heed the voice of your Spirit in our lives. Let your healing and life-giving ways be a part of all that we do, and let us welcome all that magnifies your name. Amen.

DAYTIME PRAYER

Ant 1 Alleluia, Christ is risen, alleluia, alleluia.

Ant 2 The women and men who believed in Jesus rejoiced, alleluia, alleluia.

Ant 3 Stay with us, for it is toward evening and the day is far spent, alleluia, alleluia.

(Prayer as in Morning Prayer)

EVENING PRAYER

READING

To examine frequently our thoughts, words, and actions in the different situations in which we may find ourselves, and to do so in the light that radiates from our Lord, whom we are to imitate—in the light of the Holy

Spirit who guided him always—to weigh everything in relation to the divine glory, will show us clearly whether we are under the influence of the Holy Spirit, or our own. This little recommendation counseling a careful watch of our reactions is not intended to make us concentrate on our faults. Rather can it be a means of keeping the presence of God.

Mother Aloysius Rogers, ocd, *Fragrance from Alabaster*, p. 24, (6)

RESPONSORY

The followers of Jesus were filled with joy, alleluia, alleluia.
   —The followers...
When they saw him risen from the dead, **—alleluia...**
Glory to you, Source of all Being, Eternal Word, and Holy Spirit.
   —The followers...

CANTICLE OF MARY

Ant. If you live in me, and my words dwell in you, ask whatever you will, and it shall be done for you, alleluia.

INTERCESSIONS

Jesus rose from the dead and worked many signs and wonders in the presence of his disciples, and so we pray:
   O God, we long to see your face.

Jesus, you commission those who follow you to bear much fruit;
   —give us the zeal to live disciplined lives, opening ourselves
      to your Spirit.
You promise that what we ask in your name will be granted;
   —never let us be separated from you.
You kept the law of Moses and fulfilled it;
   —give us the wisdom to discern those things that are for the
      glory of God.
You rose from the dead in the secret of night;
   —keep us watchful and ready for the coming of your grace
      in our lives.
Your resurrection healed the hearts of your mother and your disciples;
   —be with those who mourn the death of their loved ones.

PRAYER: Christ Jesus, by your resurrection you have made all things new. Give us the courage to pass beyond the familiar and to heed the voice of your Spirit in our lives. Let your healing and life-giving ways be a part of all that we do, and let us welcome all that magnifies your name. Amen.

FIFTH THURSDAY OF EASTER
(Psalms and Antiphons from Week I, p. 29)
MORNING PRAYER
READING

The New Testament prohibits not only revenge but any form of vindictive justice, any grudge. Love of enemy is not just a divine commandment for all; it is the heart of God's own economy of salvation, fully manifest in Jesus Christ. Consequently, it is a central dimension of discipleship in the footsteps of Jesus and in the image and likeness of [God]. "Life in Jesus Christ" is unthinkable without an active and creative love of enemies, with the hope to rescue them and reconciliate them.

Bernard Häring, *The Healing Power of Peace and Nonviolence*, p. 59, (1)

RESPONSORY

Christ rose from the grave, alleluia, alleluia. **—Christ...**
Conquering sin an death, **—alleluia...**
Glory to you, Source of all Being, Eternal Word, and Holy Spirit.
　　—Christ...

CANTICLE OF ZECHARIAH

Ant. If you keep my commandments, you will abide in my love, alleluia.

INTERCESSIONS

Jesus, the lamb that was slain, is risen as he said, alleluia. Therefore, we proclaim:
　　By your wounds, O Christ, we are healed.

Christ Jesus, you met violence with peace, lies with truth, and death with immortality;
　　—be with those who defend the innocent in our courts, and bless all who labor to put an end to violence.
You commissioned women to proclaim the good news of your resurrection;
　　—let the women you send today to proclaim a new word be heard.

Your resurrection consoled the pierced heart of your mother;
  —give comfort and courage to families of missing children;
  protect the children and return them to their homes.
You came to heal the sick;
  —give us insight into our brokenness, and draw us to your
  healing love.

PRAYER: Jesus Christ, come to cast fire on the earth, you have
forgiven us, healed us, raised us from death, and died
for us. We give glory to God in this celebration of your
resurrection and ask you to live on in our lives,
forgiving, healing, raising up, and dying for others; that
we, too, may rise and live with you forever. Amen.

DAYTIME PRAYER

Ant 1 Alleluia, Christ is risen, alleluia, alleluia.

Ant 2 The women and men who believed in Jesus rejoiced,
alleluia, alleluia.

Ant 3 Stay with us, for it is toward evening and the day is far
spent, alleluia, alleluia.

(Prayer as in Morning Prayer)

EVENING PRAYER

READING

There is a holiness that builds and there is a holiness that destroys. The
benefits of the holiness that builds are visible, while the benefits of the
one that destroys are hidden, because it destroys in order to build what
is nobler than what has been already built. [Those] who understand the
secret of the holiness that destroys can mend many souls, and [their]
capacity for mending is in accordance with [their] understanding. From
the holiness that destroys there emerge the great warriors who bring
blessing to the world.... At times the vision ascends toward the heights,
enticing one with concerns of great universality and purity. Then the
lower concerns, the narrower ones, which are sustained by the
imagination, and the customary rules, together with such aspects of the
good and the holy that were linked to them, totter, and the person is
devastated. [One] remains so until a brighter light shines...to rebuild the
ruins of [one's own] spiritual edifice into a more noble structure....

Abraham Isaac Kook, *Lights of Holiness*, pp. 217–18, (1)

RESPONSORY

The followers of Jesus were filled with joy, alleluia, alleluia.
    —The followers...
When they saw him risen from the dead, **—alleluia...**
Glory to you, Source of all Being, Eternal Word, and Holy Spirit.
    —The followers...

CANTICLE OF MARY

Ant. These things I have spoken to you, that my joy may be in
     you, and that your joy may be full, alleluia.

INTERCESSIONS

Jesus has risen from the dead. The shroud of death is laid aside
and in its place the robe of immortality! We sing and proclaim:
          Your reign shall last forever!

O God, we are your creatures and our lives are in your hands;
    —make us worthy of the life, death, and resurrection of
      Christ.
Not a sparrow falls that you do not know it;
    —through the resurrection of Jesus, let all see the face
      of your love turned to every person of whatever race, sex,
      color, or creed.
You loved sinners and cared for them;
    —reassure those who suffer from the guilt or brokenness of
      their past lives; grant them your peace.
You ask us to forgive seventy times seven times;
    —strengthen and encourage those who strive to overcome
      addictions of any kind.
You wept for Lazarus, your friend, and raised him to life;
    —befriend those who are ill; let them know your loving
      presence.

PRAYER: Jesus Christ, come to cast fire on the earth, you have
          forgiven us, healed us, raised us from death, and died
          for us. We give glory to God in this celebration of your
          resurrection and ask you to live on in our lives,
          forgiving, healing, raising up, and dying for others; that
          we, too, may rise and live with you forever. Amen.

FIFTH FRIDAY OF EASTER
(Psalms and Antiphons from Week I, p. 36)

MORNING PRAYER

READING

Therefore be still a while from thy own thoughts, searching, seeking, desires, and imaginations, and be stayed in the principle of God in thee, to stay thy mind upon God, up to God; and thou wilt find strength from [God] and find [God] to be a present help in time of trouble, in need, and to be a God at hand.

George Fox, *Quaker Spirituality*, p. 99, (1)

RESPONSORY

Christ rose from the grave, alleluia, alleluia. —**Christ...**
Conquering sin an death, —**alleluia...**
Glory to you, Source of all Being, Eternal Word, and Holy Spirit.
  —**Christ...**

CANTICLE OF ZECHARIAH

Ant. This is my commandment, that you love one another as I
  have loved you, alleluia.

INTERCESSIONS

Christ Jesus, who fed the multitude in the desert, rises now as the bread of eternal life. We humbly ask:
  Give us this bread, today and always.

Jesus, you gave your life as food for eternal life;
  —help us to see the needs of others and to give our time and
    energies in their service.
You have called us to bear fruit for the healing of the world;
  —during this Easter season remind us of the gift of our
    baptism and renew our zeal in following you.
In you we are many parts, but one body living your gospel throughout the ages;
  —let us fulfill our mission through your Holy Spirit to the
    glory and praise of your name.
You wept for a people who had not known you;
  —through your resurrection, help us to recognize you in one
    another, in all creation, and in all of the ways that you
    come to us.

PRAYER: Christ Jesus, you call us friends and ask that we love one another. Help us to see the ways that selfishness rules our lives and to learn to live for others. Help us to give all and to be cheerful in giving. This we ask in your name. Amen.

DAYTIME PRAYER

Ant 1 Alleluia, Christ is risen, alleluia, alleluia.

Ant 2 The women and men who believed in Jesus rejoiced, alleluia, alleluia.

Ant 3 Stay with us, for it is toward evening and the day is far spent, alleluia, alleluia.

(Prayer as in Morning Prayer)

EVENING PRAYER

READING

Jesus lived God's love among us. It was joy to be in his company. He was a delight, sincerely sharing, obediently listening to the misery around him, and affectionately loving all those with whom he came in contact. After he left his disciples, they came together in communities Luke calls "churches." It is in one of those communities that Luke first meets the Spirit of Jesus. Immediately he recognizes it from within his own as yet unexpressed hopes and desires. He *remembers* the future!

Joseph G. Donders, Risen Life, p. 106, (22)

RESPONSORY

The followers of Jesus were filled with joy, alleluia, alleluia.
    —The followers...
When they saw him risen from the dead, **—alleluia...**
Glory to you, Source of all Being, Eternal Word, and Holy Spirit.
    —The followers...

CANTICLE OF MARY

Ant. I have called you friends, for I have told you all I have heard from the One who has sent me, alleluia.

INTERCESSIONS

Christ, our Pasch, is sacrificed. In joy let us cry out:
**Worthy are you, O Christ, to receive
honor, glory and praise!**

You laid down your life that we might live;
—give us courage to die to all selfishness that we may live
for others.
You were the joy of the disciples;
—be our joy and everlasting hope.
You call us out of disbelief by your care for our daily needs;
—may we rejoice in such love and pass it on.
You are the firstborn from the dead;
—may all who have died experience the joy of your presence.

PRAYER: Christ Jesus, you call us friends and ask that we love
one another. Help us to see the ways that selfishness
rules our lives and to learn to live for others. Help us to
give all and to be cheerful in giving. This we ask in your
name. Amen.

FIFTH SATURDAY OF EASTER
(Psalms and Antiphons from Week I, p. 43)

MORNING PRAYER

READING

Responsible prayer for the soul of a Christian consists in looking and
asking day and night for the love of Jesus Christ, so that the soul may
really love him, feeling comfort and delight in him, rejecting ideas of the
world and dishonest enterprises. And you may be certain that if you
long for his love faithfully and enduringly, so that no promptings of your
own body, nor vexations of the world, nor conversations, nor antipathy
of other people can pull you back and embroil you in a frenzy of activity
about material things, then you are bound to receive his love and find
and feel that one hour of it is more delightful than all the wealth which
we can behold here could supply from now to doomsday.

Richard Rolle, *The English Writings*, p. 146, (1)

RESPONSORY

Christ rose from the grave, alleluia, alleluia. **—Christ...**
Conquering sin an death, **—alleluia...**

Glory to you, Source of all Being, Eternal Word, and Holy Spirit.
—**Christ...**

CANTICLE OF ZECHARIAH

Ant. Christ Jesus died and rose from the grave. In death and in
life, Christ is our hope, alleluia.

INTERCESSIONS

Christ Jesus, dying you destroyed death; rising you restored life.
In confidence let us pray:
May we walk in the land of the living forever.

You were hated by many in your lifetime, but God raised you in
glory;
—help us to rise above the opinions and rejections of others
as we strive to be faithful to you.
You chose your disciples because they did not adhere to this
world;
—bless our world and our culture with values, directions,
and leaders that derive their power from your gospel.
You told your disciples that they would suffer for your sake;
—let the joy of your resurrection fill us with courage to live
and to die for you.
You spent your life doing good;
—may our celebration of this Easter season enable us to
bring your word and work to life again.

PRAYER: O God, you have sent your eternal Word, born of a
woman, to reveal your love, and to call us to new life.
Through his resurrection give us the grace to recognize
your love and to respond with open and loving hearts.
This we ask of you in the name of Jesus. Amen.

DAYTIME PRAYER

Ant 1 Alleluia, Christ is risen, alleluia, alleluia.

Ant 2 The women and men who believed in Jesus rejoiced,
alleluia, alleluia.

Ant 3 Stay with us, for it is toward evening and the day is far
spent, alleluia, alleluia.

(Prayer as in Morning Prayer)

SIXTH SUNDAY OF EASTER

EVENING PRAYER I

(Psalms and Antiphons from Sunday, Week II, p. 47)

READING

A simple reaching out directly toward God is sufficient, without any other cause except [God's self]. If you like, you can have this reaching out, wrapped up and enfolded in a single word. So as to have a better grasp of it, take just a little word, of one syllable rather than of two; for the shorter it is the better it is in agreement with this exercise of the spirit. Such a one is the word "God" or the word "love."... Fasten this word to your heart, so that whatever happens it will never go away. This word is to be your shield and your spear, whether you are riding in peace or in war. With this word you are to beat upon this cloud and this darkness above you....

The Cloud of Unknowing, pp. 133-34, (1)

RESPONSORY

Christ our hope has risen, alleluia, alleluia. —**Christ...**
Let us rejoice and give thanks, —**alleluia,...**
Glory to you, Source of all Being, Eternal Word, and Holy Spirit.
     —**Christ...**

CANTICLE OF MARY

Ant If you love me, you will keep my commandment. My commandment is that you love one another, alleluia.

INTERCESSIONS

You Christ Jesus, are the sign of our hope and joy. Gratefully we pray
     Christ yesterday, today, and forever, alleluia!

You are the Good Shepherd; you know us and call us by name;
     —may we recognize the good shepherds in our midst and heed their prophetic calls.
You give us your gift of peace;
     —enable us to use our energies to create a world of peace and harmony.
You are the Lamb of God;
     —help us to see the signs of resurrection and new life around us.

You promise to make your home with us;
   —grant us the faith to believe that you truly desire to dwell within each of us.

PRAYER: O God, we praise you in the resurrection of Jesus, sign of victory over death, the proclamation of your union with creation. As we endeavor to live the message and mystery of his life, grant us the grace to remain faithful to you. Let us rise from our daily deaths, and let our lives bear witness to our union with you. Grant this through Jesus who lives with you in the unity of the Holy Spirit for all eternity. Amen.

MORNING PRAYER
(Psalms from Sunday, Week II, p. 49)

Ant 1 Jesus said to his followers: "If you love me, you will keep my commandments."

Ant 2 These things I have spoken to you, that my joy may be in you, and that your joy may be full.

Ant 3 Yet a little while, and the world will see me no more, but you will see me; because I live, you will live also.

READING

If you love me, you will keep my commandments. And I will ask [the One who sent me], and [God] will give you another Advocate, to be with you forever. This is the Spirit of truth, whom the world cannot receive, because it can neither see...nor know [this Spirit]. You know [the Spirit] because [this Spirit of truth] abides with you, and...will be in you.

Jn 14:15–17

RESPONSORY

I will not leave you orphans; I will return. **—I will not...**
In a little while, **—I will...**
Glory to you, Source of all Being, Eternal Word and Holy Spirit.
   —I will not...

CANTICLE OF ZECHARIAH

Ant As God has loved me, so have I loved you; abide in my love, alleluia.

INTERCESSIONS

Lord Jesus, your love is eternal, and you promise us eternal life. We cry out in joy:

Alleluia, alleluia, alleluia!

O God, you send your Spirit to dwell with us always;
—make us conscious of your presence.

May all nations and peoples recognize the gifts of your Spirit;
—that our world might live in peace and harmony.

Through the gift of your Spirit, you enabled all to hear in their own tongue;
—give us a listening heart that we may hear the hearts of others and accept our differences.

Your Spirit, O God, comes in silence and thunder;
—open our hearts and the heart of the world that we may receive you in all your manifestations.

PRAYER: O God, we praise you in the resurrection of Jesus, sign of victory over death. As we endeavor to live the message and mystery of his life, grant us the grace to remain faithful to you. Let us rise from our daily deaths, and let our lives bear witness to our union with you. Grant this through Jesus who lives with you in the unity of the Holy Spirit for all eternity. Amen.

DAYTIME PRAYER

Ant 1 Alleluia, Christ is risen, alleluia, alleluia.

Ant 2 The women and men who believed in Jesus rejoiced, alleluia, alleluia.

Ant 3 Stay with us, for it is toward evening and the day is far spent, alleluia, alleluia.

(Prayer as in Morning Prayer)

EVENING PRAYER II

Ant 1 Greater love has no one than this, that one lay down one's life for one's friends.

Ant 2 Those who love me will be loved by God who sent me, and I will love them and manifest myself to them.

Ant 3 The Holy Spirit whom God will send in my name will teach you all things, and bring to your remembrance all that I have said to you.

READING

I saw no temple in the city, for its temple is the [Most High God] the Almighty and the Lamb. And the city has no need of sun or moon to shine on it, for the glory of God is its light, and its lamp is the Lamb.

Rev 21:22–23

RESPONSORY

The Spirit of truth will come, alleluia, alleluia. —**The Spirit**...
And guide you to all truth, —**alleluia**...
Glory to you, Source of all Being, Eternal Word and Holy Spirit.
   —**The Spirit**...

CANTICLE OF MARY

Ant Peace I leave with you, my peace I give you, alleluia.

INTERCESSIONS

Those who have died with Christ will rise with him; God will wipe away every tear from their eyes, and so we rejoice:
   Worthy is the Lamb that was slain.

Jesus, you are the way, the truth, and the life; we go to God only through you;
   —let us always hear and follow your spirit of truth.
Your resurrection heralds a new heaven and a new earth;
   —help us to live daily with minds and hearts open to your Holy Spirit.
You tell us that people of faith will do works even greater than your own;
   —increase our faith that we, too, may bring healing and new life to the world.
We praise you for the bread of thanksgiving and the words of your gospel;
   —give us the grace to let these gifts of God bear fruit a hundredfold to God's glory.

PRAYER: O God, we praise you in the resurrection of Jesus, sign of victory over death. As we endeavor to live the message and mystery of his life, grant us the grace to remain faithful to you. Let us rise from our daily deaths, and let our lives bear witness to our union with you. Grant this through Jesus who lives with you in the unity of the Holy Spirit for all eternity. Amen.

SIXTH MONDAY OF EASTER
(Psalms and Antiphons from Week II, p. 55)
MORNING PRAYER

READING

In eternity only will the dawn of understanding break in its radiant brightness, and we shall know why God willed it so. Do not be surprised or disheartened if nature finds a struggle, but calmly try to rise above all feeling, and as a genuine lover, rejoice at having a real gift for your Beloved—a gift having something of your heart in it. Peace, light, and strength will flow into your soul in consequence.

Mother Aloysius Rogers, OCD, Fragrance from Alabaster, p. 20, (6)

RESPONSORY

Christ rose from the grave, alleluia, alleluia. **—Christ...**
Conquering sin an death, **—alleluia...**
Glory to you, Source of all Being, Eternal Word, and Holy Spirit.
  —Christ...

CANTICLE OF ZECHARIAH

Ant. When the Counselor comes, the Spirit of truth whom I shall send you, you will bear witness to me, alleluia.

INTERCESSIONS

Christ Jesus, you rose from the dead and showed yourself to the women; with joyful hearts we proclaim:
    Wonderful are your works, O Christ.

Jesus, through your resurrection you call us to be born again;
  —help us to recognize and to be open to your Spirit in our lives.
You are the Good Shepherd and you guide us with tender care;
  —enlighten our civic and religious leaders; give them your mind and heart.

You promise to send the Comforter to witness on your behalf;
   —empowered with your Spirit, may we bear witness to you
      in word and deed.
O God, you have created all things, and all that you have created
is good;
   —help us to see others and all things as you see them.

PRAYER: Jesus, our risen Savior, you teach us to live in love and
to be prepared for persecution and death. You teach us
to live as you have lived. Help us to realize the presence
of your Spirit in us. In your goodness, teach, heal,
forgive sins, and give new life to others through us, to
the glory of your name. Amen.

DAYTIME PRAYER

Ant 1 Alleluia, Christ is risen, alleluia, alleluia.

Ant 2 The women and men who believed in Jesus rejoiced,
alleluia, alleluia.

Ant 3 Stay with us, for it is toward evening and the day is far
spent, alleluia, alleluia.

(Prayer as in Morning Prayer)

EVENING PRAYER

READING

If Jesus is risen and people are not finding him, then somebody is
hiding him—he is not hiding himself.... He came to cast fire on the
earth, and he walked Palestine as a Flame so alive with God's spirit of
love that when he was "blown out" on the cross, the Spirit did not die.
For that Fire had been caught by his disciples who have passed it down
to us through the centuries. It is the Fire of God's love for us that we
must uncover and give to others. That is the Presence, the meeting of
Jesus that makes us more blessed than a doubting Thomas. We are
relieved of the temptation to think that the presence of God's love was
limited to the few years Jesus walked the earth. We know he is risen
and lives forever, for *we* are where he is risen, *we* are where he lives. We
carry the flame of his life that must not be hidden under a bushel, that
cannot be destroyed in a tomb. We know that we will live forever in the
one who has lived for centuries through a love that cannot be
extinguished.

Miriam Elder, OCD, (11)

RESPONSORY

The followers of Jesus were filled with joy, alleluia, alleluia.
  —The followers...
When they saw him risen from the dead, **—alleluia...**
Glory to you, Source of all Being, Eternal Word, and Holy Spirit.
  —The followers...

CANTICLE OF MARY

Ant I have said all this that you may be faithful, alleluia.

INTERCESSIONS

Jesus, you rose from the dead and your disciples recognized you
in the breaking of the bread. We proclaim in faith:
  Jesus is risen indeed.

Christ Jesus, through your Spirit you transformed your frightened
apostles into fearless proclaimers of your word;
  —bless all missionaries with fortitude and perseverance.
By your life, death, and resurrection you invite all the nations of
the world to be the people of God;
  —help us to live as true daughters and sons of our loving
    Creator.
Through your resurrection you give hope to all who believe in you;
  —through our daily deaths, transform our lives evermore
    into your likeness.
Following your example, Peter prayed for guidance in time of
decision;
  —help us to realize the necessity of prayer in our lives.
By your death and resurrection you conquered death;
  —have pity on the dying, be their light and peace.

PRAYER: Jesus, our risen Savior, you teach us to live in love and
to be prepared for persecution and death. You teach us
to live as you have lived. Help us to realize the presence
of your Spirit in us. In your goodness, teach, heal,
forgive sins, and give new life to others through us, to
the glory of your name. Amen.

SIXTH TUESDAY OF EASTER
(Psalms and Antiphons from Week II, p. 62)

MORNING PRAYER

READING

So much growth and transformation are possible in one's relationship with God that those who are trying are like laborers in the vineyard. There is little difference between the one who has labored all day and the one who has been at work for only an hour. The first and the last are not far apart.... The practice of prayer and meditation is as complex and varied as human life itself. As we confront the reality of the Other, we bring every part of our being, our ideas and thoughts, our plans for the day, for the week, for our entire life to the Other. We disclose our fears, our hopes, our human love, our thirst for more than human love, our anger and vengeance, our depression, sorrow and lostness, the values that are imporant to us, our adoration and joy and thanksgiving. Leaving out any part of the spectrum of human life makes prayer and meditation incomplete....

Morton Kelsey, *The Other Side of Silence*, p. 18, (1)

RESPONSORY

Christ rose from the grave, alleluia, alleluia. —**Christ...**
Conquering sin an death, —**alleluia...**
Glory to you, Source of all Being, Eternal Word, and Holy Spirit.
　　—**Christ...**

CANTICLE OF ZECHARIAH

Ant. I will see you again and your hearts will rejoice, and no one will take your joy from you, alleluia.

INTERCESSIONS

Jesus, risen from the dead, you dined with the women and men who followed you, served them, and strengthened their faith in you, and so we pray:
　　How can we repay for your goodness to us.

Jesus, you came to do the will of God, and in death you were raised up in glory;
　　—have mercy on those who despair of meaning in life.
Your resurrection gave new hope to your small community of followers;
　　—let the celebration of that same resurrection bring new life to your church today.

You asked those who followed you to sell all and give to the poor;
—teach us effective ways to feed the hungry and to house
the homeless of our world.
You never cease to call us to greater intimacy with you;
—transform the mustard seed of our faith into total
dedication.

PRAYER: O God, we praise you in the life, death, and
resurrection of Jesus. You sent him into the world;
you send us into the world. Fill our minds with his
words of life, and our hearts with his unsurpassing
love. Let us live for one another as he did for us, to
the praise and glory of your name. Amen.

DAYTIME PRAYER

Ant 1 Alleluia, Christ is risen, alleluia, alleluia.

Ant 2 The women and men who believed in Jesus rejoiced,
alleluia, alleluia.

Ant 3 Stay with us, for it is toward evening and the day is far
spent, alleluia, alleluia.

(Prayer as in Morning Prayer)

EVENING PRAYER

READING

Late have I loved you, O Beauty, so ancient and so new, late have I
loved you! And behold, you were within me and I was outside, and there
I sought for you, and in my deformity I rushed headlong into the well-
formed things that you have made. You were with me, and I was not
with you. Those outer beauties held me far from you, yet if they had not
been in you, they would not have existed at all. You called, and cried
out to me and broke open my deafness; you shone forth upon me and
you scattered my blindness: You breathed fragrance and I drew in my
breath and I now pant for you: I tasted and I hunger and thirst; you
touched me, and I burned for your peace.

Augustine of Hippo, *The Confessions*, p. 144, (1)

RESPONSORY

The followers of Jesus were filled with joy, alleluia, alleluia.
—The followers...
When they saw him risen from the dead, **—alleluia...**

Glory to you, Source of all Being, Eternal Word, and Holy Spirit.
—The followers...

CANTICLE OF MARY

Ant. It is to your advantage that I go away, for if I do not go, the Counselor will not come to you, alleluia.

INTERCESSIONS

Jesus, risen from the dead, you have filled the world with light and hope. With joy we sing:
This is the day that our God has made.

Jesus, your resurrection frees us from the bondage of death;
—free those who are enslaved or oppressed.
Your resurrection is a promise of new life;
—give hope and new opportunity for wholesome labor to migrant workers and to all who receive an inadequate wage.
By your resurrection you were freed from suffering and death;
—have mercy on all those who suffer from illness or abuse.
You rose from the dead and appeared to your mother and to your friends;
—bless our families, friends, and all who show us your love and mercy.

PRAYER: O God, we praise you in the life, death, and resurrection of Jesus. You sent him into the world; you send us into the world. Fill our minds with his words of life, and our hearts with his unsurpassing love. Let us live for one another as he did for us, to the praise and glory of your name. Amen.

SIXTH WEDNESDAY OF EASTER
(Psalms and Antiphons from Week II, p. 69)
MORNING PRAYER

READING

...experience of the contemplative life in the modern world shows that the most crucial focus for contemplative and meditative discipline, and for the life of prayer, for many modern [men and women], is precisely this so-called sense of absence, desolation, and even apparent "inability to believe." I stress the word "apparent," because though this experience may to some be extremely painful and confusing, and raise all kinds of crucial "religious problems," it can very well be a sign of authentic Christian growth and a point of decisive development in faith, if they are able to cope with it. The way to cope with it is not to regress to an earlier and less mature stage of belief, to stubbornly reaffirm and to "enforce" feelings, aspirations, and images that were appropriate to one's childhood and first communion. One must, on a new level of meditation and prayer, live through this crisis of belief and grow to a more complete personal and Christian integration by experience.

Thomas Merton, *Contemplation in a World of Action*, p. 163, (59)

RESPONSORY

Christ rose from the grave, alleluia, alleluia. —**Christ...**
Conquering sin an death, —**alleluia...**
Glory to you, Source of all Being, Eternal Word, and Holy Spirit.
   —**Christ...**

CANTICLE OF ZECHARIAH

Ant.   I have yet many things to say to you, but you cannot bear
   them now. The Spirit of truth will come and guide you into
   all truth, alleluia.

INTERCESSIONS

Jesus is risen from the dead, a mystery revealed to little ones. With sincere hearts we pray:
   Christ Jesus, make us humble of heart.

By your resurrection, you bring light to our darkness, hope to despair;
   —give us a hunger for your words of life.
You will not leave us orphans;
   —help us to be aware of your presence throughout the day.
You have chosen us to follow your disciples in bringing our world to fullness of life;
   —make us responsible Christians; let our lives proclaim our
   faith in you.
You promised the Spirit who would pray within us;
   —quiet our minds and hearts; teach us to pray.

PRAYER: O God, you have created us and you sustain us daily
   with loving care. As we celebrate the resurrection of
   Jesus, confirm our faith in our own life after death.

Help us to live in your presence, to hear your voice and follow it, that we may live with you now and in eternity forever and ever. Amen.

DAYTIME PRAYER

Ant 1 Alleluia, Christ is risen, alleluia, alleluia.

Ant 2 The women and men who believed in Jesus rejoiced, alleluia, alleluia.

Ant 3 Stay with us, for it is toward evening and the day is far spent, alleluia, alleluia.

(Prayer as in Morning Prayer)

ASCENSION THURSDAY

EVENING PRAYER I

Ant 1 I go to prepare a place for you, so that you can be with me forever, alleluia. (Ps 113, p. 96)

Ant 2 As Jesus blessed his followers, he parted from them and was carried up into heaven, alleluia. (Ps 117, p. 44)

Ant 3 I will be with you until the end of time, alleluia.
(Rev 11: 17–18; 12:10b–12a, p. 34)

READING

[Jesus] replied, "It is not for you to know the times or periods that [God] has set by [God's] own authority. But you will receive power when the Holy Spirit has come upon you; and you will be my witnesses in Jerusalem, in all Judea and Samaria, and to the ends of the earth." When he had said this, as they were watching, he was lifted up, and a cloud took him out of their sight. While he was going and they were gazing up toward heaven, suddenly two [people] in white robes stood by them. They said, "[Galileans], why do you stand looking up toward heaven? This Jesus, who has been taken up from you into heaven, will come in the same way as you saw him go into heaven."

Acts 1:7–11

RESPONSORY

Christ ascends into splendor, alleluia, alleluia. — **Christ**...
The glory of God fills all creation, —**alleluia**,...
Glory to you, Source of all Being, Eternal Word and Holy Spirit.
   — **Christ**...

CANTICLE OF MARY

Ant You are my witnesses. Proclaim the good news to all the earth, alleluia, alleluia.

INTERCESSIONS

We give you thanks, Christ Jesus, for your appearances to your early followers and the many ways you appear to us. We cry out in joy:

Alleluia, alleluia, alleluia!

Christ Jesus, before your ascension you instructed the women and men who believed in you;
—continue to instruct all your faithful people, especially those responsible for the formation of the young, and those troubled in conscience.

You promised to send the Holy Spirit to empower us;
—help us to recognize and claim the gifts we have been given.

Christ Jesus, you cautioned your disciples to wait for the coming of the Spirit;
—protect us from impulsiveness and give us discerning hearts that we may act with prudence and wisdom.

After you ascended, your disciples hoped for your return;
—give us faith to believe that you have returned and are still with us as we carry on our daily activities.

PRAYER: O God, we believe that Jesus, your Incarnate Word, lives in you and in us. Strengthen our faith, hope, and love that your reign will be proclaimed in our lives and the presence of your Spirit be manifested in our thoughts, words, and actions. This we ask of you through Jesus and in the Holy Spirit. Amen.

MORNING PRAYER
(Psalms from Sunday, Week I, p. 3)

Ant 1 After his resurrection, Jesus appeared to his disciples, speaking often of the reign of God, alleluia.

Ant 2 When the Spirit comes, you shall remember all that I taught you, alleluia.

Ant 3 Jesus was taken from their sight and ascended into heaven, alleluia.

READING

The ascension is not an isolated episode. No scriptural text that presents the Lord being raised to heaven after his resurrection speaks of it thus. It is part of the mystery, it is a fact concerning the person and mission of the Son of God who came to dwell a little while among us, taking on human nature, and who, at a time established by [God], returned to [God]. As the mystery of God and...Christ, this fact concerns all people, pointing them to their salvation, collectively and individually. It cannot be envisioned except in this double dimension.

Days of the Lord, Vol. 3, p. 221, (9)

RESPONSORY

Jesus is glorified in heaven and we have seen his glory.
   —**Jesus**...
Shining through all creation, —**we have**...
Glory to you, Source of all Being, Eternal Word and Holy Spirit.
   —**Jesus**...

CANTICLE OF ZECHARIAH

Ant It is better for you that I go, that the Spirit of God may come to you, alleluia.

INTERCESSIONS

You mount your throne amid shouts of joy and so we sing your praise:

Praise to you, Christ Jesus!

O God, you invest some members of your church with authority;
   —grant them the wisdom and vision to govern with love and forbearance.
You distribute your gifts to all your people;
   —give them the vision to recognize their talents and the opportunity to use them in your service.
You empower us with your Spirit;
   —enable us to claim our power that the good news may continue to be proclaimed in us.
Your fullness is manifested in Christ, filling the universe in all its parts;

—give us reverence and respect for our universe, the temple
  of your glory.
Be with those who are terminally ill;
  —and grant them peace of mind as they await your coming.

PRAYER: O God, we believe that Jesus, your Incarnate Word,
lives in you and in us. Strengthen our faith, hope, and
love that your reign will be proclaimed in our lives and
the presence of your Spirit be manifested in our
thoughts, words, and actions. This we ask of you
through Jesus and in the Holy Spirit. Amen.

DAYTIME PRAYER

Ant 1 Glory to God in heaven and on earth, alleluia.

Ant 2 I am the Alpha and the Omega, the beginning and the end,
alleluia.

Ant 3 I am the bright Morning Star rising in the heavens,
alleluia.

(Prayer as in Morning Prayer)

EVENING PRAYER II

Ant 1 Shout to God with shouts of joy, alleluia.
(Ps 110:1–5, 7, p. 53)

Ant 2 The Christ of God reigns over all the earth, alleluia.
(Ps 47, p. 24)

Ant 3 Christ enlightens our innermost vision and calls us to
hope, alleluia. (Rev 11:17–18; 12:10b–12a, p. 34)

READING

Our Lord has ascended into heaven, but the work for which he came to
earth is to go on: the work of glorifying [God] and saving souls. His
external mission is ended, but he would continue it in each of us; and
he can do so only in so far as we are animated by the Spirit. Like the
apostles we have a work to perform. We are to conquer the world for
him, win souls to his love, but it is by the labors, trials, and sufferings
attendant upon the work of *our own sanctification.* Within our souls is
the place of our combat, and whatever may be our weakness, we know
the same Holy Spirit, who enlightened and strengthened the apostles to

accomplish such marvels...will give light and strength in the difficulties to be encountered in our great work...that of our own perfection.

Mother Aloysius Rogers, OCD, *Fragrance from Alabaster*, pp. 33–34, (6)

RESPONSORY

Christ ascends into splendor, alleluia, alleluia. — **Christ**...
The glory of God fills all creation, **—alleluia,**...
Glory to you, Source of all Being, Eternal Word and Holy Spirit.
   — **Christ**...

CANTICLE OF MARY

Ant We praise you, O Christ. You have ascended to your place
   with the Most High, yet you remain in our midst forever,
   alleluia.

INTERCESSIONS

Jesus promised to be with us till the end of time. With confidence we pray:
You are the Way, the Truth, and the Life.

Christ Jesus, you sent your followers to preach the good news to all creation;
   —may all people and all creatures experience your justice
   and love through those who profess faith in you.
You told us that signs and wonders would accompany our profession of faith;
   —safeguard us from literalism and give us the wisdom and
   insight to hear your words in the reality of our lives.
After leaving your disciples, you continued to work with them;
   —strengthen our faith in your presence in times of darkness
   and disillusionment.
Your disciples were to be found in the temple speaking the praises of God;
   —make us women and men of prayer that we may be your
   glory and your rest.

PRAYER: O God, we believe that Jesus, your Incarnate Word,
   lives in you and in us. Strengthen our faith, hope, and
   love that your reign will be proclaimed in our lives and
   the presence of your Spirit be manifested in our
   thoughts, words, and actions. This we ask of you
   through Jesus and in the Holy Spirit. Amen.

SIXTH FRIDAY OF EASTER

(Antiphons and Psalms from Friday, Week II, p. 84)

MORNING PRAYER

READING

When I came into the silent assemblies of God's people, I felt a secret power among them, which touched my heart; and as I gave way unto it, I found the evil weakening in me and the good raised up.

Robert Barclay, *Quaker Spirituality*, p. 15, (1)

RESPONSORY

Christ rose from the grave, alleluia, alleluia. — **Christ**...
Conquering sin and death, —**alleluia**...
Glory to you, Source of all Being, Eternal Word and Holy Spirit.
  — **Christ**...

CANTICLE OF ZECHARIAH

Ant I was dead but now I live; I hold the keys of life eternal, alleluia.

INTERCESSIONS

Christ Jesus, you ascended into heaven to prepare a place for us. In joyful help we pray:
  Be with us now and forever.

Christ Jesus, when we experience you as absent;
  —enhance our longing and desire for your presence.
When we experience you as present;
  —fill us with gratitude.
In the death of our loved ones;
  —may our grief be turned into joy.
Christ Jesus, you took leave of those you loved on earth;
  —ascend again in glory in those who will die this day.

PRAYER: O God, in times of darkness and in times of grief, give us the faith to believe that you will return again with your gift of peace. Grant this through Jesus in whom we place our trust. Amen.

DAYTIME PRAYER

(Prayer as in Morning Prayer)

EVENING PRAYER

READING

...it is necessary to pass through great interior and exterior trials which would frighten the soul if it were permitted to see them before actually experiencing them, and would even cause it to quit everything in order to avoid having to bear them, if a secret power did not sustain it. For it seems that the waters of tribulation through which a soul has passed, by means of so many spiritual circumcisions have extinguished the fire which consumed it so gently in the superior part of the soul when its powers were suspended and it enjoyed God in purity of spirit. If fact, the poor soul doesn't know where it is. It is enveloped in a spiritual cloud which has obscured its view and, so it seems to the soul, has taken away the portion which it possessed in its sovereign and unique Good, the adorable Word Incarnate. But finally the Word takes pity on the soul by causing the cloud to evaporate and making it experience rather belatedly the import of this passage, *Behold, my conduit has been made into a copious brook and has almost become a sea.*

The Autobiography of Venerable Marie of the Incarnation, OSU, p. 178, (19)

RESPONSORY

The Spirit of truth will come, alleluia, alleluia. —**The Spirit**...
And guide you into all truth, —**alleluia,**...
Glory to you, Source of all Being, Eternal Word and Holy Spirit.
    —**The Spirit**...

CANTICLE OF MARY

Ant If you have faith, God will grant whatever you ask in my
        name, alleluia.

INTERCESSIONS

You promised to send the Spirit, Christ Jesus, and so we pray:
        Come Holy Spirit, renew our hearts.

Send forth your Spirit over the earth;
    —bless our land and protect it from toxic waste.
Breathe forth your Spirit into our air;
    —encourage with success those who strive to keep it free
        from pollution and acid rain.
Rain down your Spirit upon our waters;
    —and upon those responsible for decisions concerning
        the purity of our seas and rivers.

Enkindle your Spirit in tongues of fire;
   —that fire may be used to replenish our forests and stores
     of energy rather than to destroy them.

PRAYER: O God, in times of darkness and in times of grief, give
us the faith to believe that you will return again with
your gift of peace. Grant this through Jesus in whom
we place our trust. Amen.

SIXTH SATURDAY OF EASTER
(Antiphons and Psalms from Saturday, Week II, p. 91)
MORNING PRAYER
READING

What, then shall I do, my true Life, my God? I shall pass even beyond
this power of mine, called memory, I shall pass beyond it that I may
draw near to you, sweet Light. What are you saying to me? I am now
ascending through my mind to you who dwell above me. I shall pass
beyond this power of mine called memory in the desire to touch you at
the point where you may be touched, to cleave to you where it is
possible to be in contact with you.... I shall pass beyond memory to find
you—oh, where, where shall I find you, my truly good and serene
delight?

Augustine of Hippo, The Confessions, p. 137, (1)

RESPONSORY

Christ rose from the grave, alleluia, alleluia. — **Christ**...
Conquering sin and death, —**alleluia**...
Glory to you, Source of all Being, Eternal Word and Holy Spirit.
  — **Christ**...

CANTICLE OF ZECHARIAH

Ant The Spirit, the Counselor, will teach you all things, alleluia.

INTERCESSIONS

Christ Jesus, you assured us that whatever we ask in your name
will be given to us, and so we pray:
Holy be your name.

Christ Jesus, by the power of your name;
   —may all people come to realize their individual dignity and
     respect the rights and dignity of others.

You assured us of God's love for us;
  —help us to respect our bodies and spiritual welfare by the moderate use of the goods of this world.
You came from God and returned to God;
  —make us ever aware that we, too, are God's children and in God is our true home.
You are the firstborn, the risen Savior;
  —may all who have died, live with you for all eternity.

PRAYER: Most loving God, you call us to make our home in you as you make yours in us. Graft us onto you that your life may flow through us in Jesus, who is our way, our truth, and our life. Fill us with your Spirit and help us to renew all creation. We ask this in Jesus' name. Amen.

DAYTIME PRAYER

(Prayer as in Morning Prayer)

SEVENTH SUNDAY OF EASTER
(Psalms from Sunday, Week III, p. 96)

EVENING PRAYER I

Ant 1 If you suffer in the name of Christ, you will share in the glory of Christ, alleluia.

Ant 2 Eternal life is this, to know the Most High God and Jesus Christ, the One sent by God, alleluia.

Ant 3 God gave glory to Christ, so that Christ in turn might give glory to God, alleluia.

READING

Christian service is a movement from a person to a person through a person. Through our Lord Jesus Christ, by his grace, I make it possible or easier for a man or woman to live a more human, a more Christian existence. It might be a word: a gracious greeting, a word of counsel, an expression of sympathy, a declaration of love.... It might be an action: food for the hungry, cold water for the thirsty, clothing for the naked, room for the stranger. Whatever the service, the Christian enables another in need to live more humanly, more Christianly. And the Christian does that in the power of Christ—for Christ's sake, literally.

Walter J. Burghardt, sj, *Still Proclaiming Your Wonders*, p. 125, (1)

RESPONSORY

The Holy Spirit will enlighten you, and teach you all things.
—The Holy Spirit...
The Spirit will breathe life into you, **—and teach**...
Glory to you, Source of all Being, Eternal Word and Holy Spirit.
—The Holy Spirit...

CANTICLE OF MARY

Ant I have made known your name to those you gave me, that
they may keep your word, alleluia.

INTERCESSIONS

You will not leave us orphans but will return and rejoice our
hearts. We cry out in joy:
Alleluia, alleluia, alleluia!

O God, you send your Spirit to dwell with us always;
—make us conscious of your presence in our innermost being.
May all nations and peoples recognize the gifts of your Spirit;
—that our world might live in peace and harmony.
Through the gift of your Spirit, you enabled all to hear in their
own tongue;
—give us a listening heart that we may hear the hearts of
others and accept our differences.
Your Spirit, O God, comes in silence and thunder;
—open our hearts and the heart of the world that we may
receive you in all your manifestations.

PRAYER: O God, you brood over our world and call us your sons
and daughters. Send your Spirit and renew us that we
may realize our eternal heritage with you. We ask this
in the name of Jesus, our brother. Amen.

MORNING PRAYER
(Psalms from Sunday, Week III, p. 98)

Ant 1 What was spoken in scripture by the Holy Spirit has come
to be, alleluia.

Ant 2 The heavens proclaim the glory of the Most High; God's
children rejoice in freedom, alleluia.

Ant 3 If we love one another, God lives within us, alleluia.

READING

While Peter was still speaking, the Holy Spirit fell upon all who heard the word. The circumcised believers who had come with Peter were astounded that the gift of the Holy Spirit had been poured out even on the Gentiles, for they heard them speaking in tongues and extolling God. Then Peter said, "Can anyone withhold the water for baptizing these people who have received the Holy Spirit just as we have?" So he ordered them to be baptized in the name of Jesus Christ.

Acts 10:44–48

RESPONSORY

You rose, O Christ, and are with us, that we might rise with you.
   —You...
Have mercy on us, your people, **—that we**...
Glory to you, Source of all Being, Eternal Word and Holy Spirit.
   —You...

CANTICLE OF ZECHARIAH

Ant For the sake of my followers, I consecrate myself, that they also may be consecrated in truth, alleluia.

INTERCESSIONS

Mindful that you call us not servants, but friends, we confidently pray:
Remain with us always.

Christ Jesus, you ascended and your spirit lives in us;
   —grant that all may experience your reign of justice and peace.
You prayed that all may be one;
   —unite us in a loving acceptance of diversity.
Christ Jesus, you asked God that we might see your glory;
   —open our eyes to see your wonders in our daily lives.
You are the Alpha and the Omega, the First and the Last, the Beginning and the End;
   —born in time but made in your image, may we breathe our last in your loving embrace.

PRAYER: O God, you brood over our world and call us your sons and daughters. Send your Spirit and renew us that we may realize our eternal heritage with you. We ask this in the name of Jesus, our brother. Amen.

DAYTIME PRAYER

Ant 1 If you suffer in the name of Christ, you will share in the glory of Christ, alleluia.

Ant 2 Eternal life is this, to know the Most High God and Jesus Christ, the One sent by God, alleluia.

Ant 3 God gave glory to Christ, so that Christ in turn might give glory to God, alleluia.

(Prayer as in Morning Prayer)

EVENING PRAYER II

Ant 1 You, O God, are our ruler, the Most High over all the earth, alleluia.

Ant 2 The heavens opened, and Jesus, the Christ appeared at the side of the throne of God, alleluia.

Ant 3 The Spirit and the Bride say: Come, Lord Jesus, alleluia!

READING

The Advocate, the Holy Spirit, whom [God] will send in my name, will teach you everything, and remind you of all that I have said to you. Peace I leave with you; my peace I give to you. I do not give to you as the world gives. Do not let your hearts be troubled, and do not let them be afraid.

Jn 14:26–27

RESPONSORY

The Holy Spirit will enlighten you, and teach you all things.
   —The Holy Spirit...
The Spirit will breathe life into you, **—and teach...**
Glory to you, Source of all Being, Eternal Word and Holy Spirit.
   —The Holy Spirit...

CANTICLE OF MARY

Ant Live in my love, that your unity may be complete, alleluia.

INTERCESSIONS

You bid us to drink of your life-giving water, and so we cry out:
   We thirst for you, Christ Jesus.

Send forth your Spirit, O God,
—for the healing of the nations and the renewing of the earth.
Send forth your Spirit, O God,
—upon the despondent, the despairing and the living dead.
Send forth your Spirit, O God,
—into the hearts of those who call you by another name.
Send forth your Spirit, O God,
—to accompany those you call to yourself this night.

PRAYER: O God, you brood over our world and call us your sons
and daughters. Send your Spirit and renew us that we
may realize our eternal heritage with you. We ask this
in the name of Jesus, our brother. Amen.

SEVENTH MONDAY OF EASTER
(Psalms and Antiphons from Week III, p. 104)
MORNING PRAYER

READING

It is with...delicate charity we should speak of one another if persons
happen to be the subject of our conversation either private or general,
and this is only possible when our own spirit is being guided by the
Holy Spirit whose light would cause us to see our neighbor "in the
Sacred Breast of the Savior," as St. Francis de Sales says. To be faithful
to this charity means the practice of much self-denial. It will be to give
place to that Spirit who is all charity, and whose fruits are peace, joy,
and holiness.

Mother Aloysius Rogers, OCD, *The Fragrance from Alabaster*, p. 19, (6)

RESPONSORY

Christ rose from the grave, alleluia, alleluia. —**Christ...**
Conquering sin an death, —**alleluia...**
Glory to you, Source of all Being, Eternal Word, and Holy Spirit.
—**Christ...**

CANTICLE OF ZECHARIAH

Ant. Paul laid his hands on the believers and the Holy Spirit
came upon them, alleluia.

INTERCESSIONS

O God, you send your Spirit that we may be confirmed in our faith. Let us pray:
O God, we believe; help our unbelief.

Christ Jesus, you spoke plainly to us that we might believe;
—help us to communicate simply and honestly with one another.
Only in you can we find our peace;
—be present to us when our hearts are in turmoil.
You remind us that we will suffer in this world;
—give us courage and belief in your final victory.
In the gift of the Spirit, you give us freedom;
—help us to claim that freedom, and to free ourselves from all that pulls us toward darkness.

PRAYER: Christ Jesus, send the Spirit of wisdom into our hearts that we may live our lives discerning your way for us. We ask this in your name. Amen.

DAYTIME PRAYER

(Prayer as in Morning Prayer)

EVENING PRAYER

READING

Place your mind before the mirror of eternity! Place your soul in *the brilliance of glory!* Place your heart in *the figure of the* divine *substance!* And *transform* your whole being *into the image* of the Godhead Itself through contemplation! So that you too may feel what [God's] friends feel as they taste *the hidden sweetness* which God...has reserved from the beginning for those who love [God].

Clare of Assisi, *Francis and Clare*, p. 200, (1)

RESPONSORY

The Spirit of truth will come, alleluia, alleluia. **—The Spirit...**
And guide you into all truth, **—alleluia,...**
Glory to you, Source of all Being, Eternal Word, and Holy Spirit.
—The Spirit...

CANTICLE OF MARY

Ant I have told you the truth that you may have peace. Rejoice, I have overcome the world, alleluia.

INTERCESSIONS

God of Wisdom, we pray to you as we say:
> **Send forth your Spirit upon us.**

O God, give us the eyes of faith to see the world as you see it;
> —and hearts to love as you love.

You speak to us in dreams and visions;
> —give us insight to see and to understand your revelations.

Your wisdom appears to many as foolishness;
> —grant us the courage to follow your ways in spite of ridicule or rejection.

You draw us to fullness of life;
> —free us from the superficial, and from dependence on the status quo.

PRAYER: Christ Jesus, send the Spirit of wisdom into our hearts that we may live our lives discerning your way for us. We ask this in your name. Amen.

SEVENTH TUESDAY OF EASTER
(Psalms and Antiphons from Week III, p. 111)
MORNING PRAYER

READING

Jesus reveals God as the power of resurrection. The future contains forms of death that frighten us, but the future is not obliterated by death. Rather, the future is resurrection as well. To know this through Jesus is to live into the future, looking for the forms of resurrection God gives us. God is stronger than all our deaths, and this strength is imparted to us so that we can live and die our many deaths. Through resurrection, Jesus is in our future and therefore opens us up to our futures.

Marjorie Hewitt Suchocki, *God Christ Church*, p. 120, (2)

RESPONSORY

Christ rose from the grave, alleluia, alleluia. **—Christ...**
Conquering sin an death, **—alleluia...**

Glory to you, Source of all Being, Eternal Word, and Holy Spirit.
    —Christ...

CANTICLE OF ZECHARIAH

Ant. I have given glory to God on earth by finishing the work I
    was given to do, alleluia.

INTERCESSIONS

You ascended on high, Christ Jesus, but did not leave us
orphans. With confident hope we pray:
    Be with us all our days.

O God, united with Jesus, we are your daughters and sons;
    —grant that we may some day receive our eternal
        inheritance.
Give us your Spirit of Understanding;
    —that we may care for our earth and help to renew it in
        Christ's image.
You are a God of mercy and forgiveness;
    —help us to live in harmony with our environment and all
        humankind.
You look upon our frailties with compassion;
    —ease the loneliness of the elderly and the alien, and comfort
        the dying.

PRAYER: O God, we stand before you with our weaknesses and
    limitations. Use them that your power may be
    manifested, and bring us all to the knowledge of our
    need for each other that we may grow in love and
    understanding. We ask this through Jesus who is our
    way. Amen.

DAYTIME PRAYER

(Prayer as in Morning Prayer)

EVENING PRAYER

READING

The total reality out of which each human occasion arises includes not
only the adjacent events in the brain and the past human experiences
but also God.... God entertains a purpose for the new occasion, differing

from that entertained by the previous human experience. [God] seeks to lure the new occasion beyond the mere repetition of past purposes and past feelings or new combinations among them. God is thus at once the source of novelty and the lure to finer and richer actualizations embodying that novelty. Thus God is the One Who Calls us beyond all that we have become to what we might be.... This way points to God's presence as coming to us from the open future rather than from the settled past.

John B. Cobb, Jr., *God and the World*, p. 82, (49)

RESPONSORY

The Spirit of truth will come, alleluia, alleluia. **—The Spirit...**
And guide you into all truth, **—alleluia,...**
Glory to you, Source of all Being, Eternal Word, and Holy Spirit.
    —The Spirit...

CANTICLE OF MARY

Ant. I entrust to you what God has entrusted to me, alleluia.

INTERCESSIONS

Christ Jesus, you were raised from the dead as you promised. We sing your praises and pray:
Send us the Spirit of Understanding.

O God, we live in countries populated by people of diverse cultures;
    —may it lead us to understanding and not to dissension.
We espouse a common faith expressed through our various nationalities;
    —may each expression lead us to freedom and away from
        bondage.
We live in families and communities with our individual personalities;
    —may our creeds lead us to love and not to violence.

PRAYER: O God, we stand before you with our weaknesses and limitations. Use them that your power may be manifested, and bring us all to the knowledge of our need for each other that we may grow in love and understanding. We ask this through Jesus who is our way. Amen.

SEVENTH WEDNESDAY OF EASTER
(Psalms and Antiphons from Week III, p. 117)

MORNING PRAYER

READING

When the patient man Job became impatient on his dung hill of suffering, God responded with something like, "Life, death, and resurrection is the way I operate, Job. Freedom is the field and love is the power. Can you think of a better way to do it, a better plan for creation?" Like a Divine Sun, God draws us to growth through the deaths of change and newness of life, but like the sun, God is not just "way out there." Every spark of insight, every touch of warm kindness that we enjoy flows from the burning furnace of wisdom and charity that we call God. The radiance of the fire of God's love, cast on the earth in Christ, is the atmosphere in which we live, move, grow, and have our being.

Elizabeth Meluch, OCD, (11)

RESPONSORY

Christ rose from the grave, alleluia, alleluia. —**Christ...**
Conquering sin an death, —**alleluia...**
Glory to you, Source of all Being, Eternal Word, and Holy Spirit.
   —**Christ...**

CANTICLE OF ZECHARIAH

Ant. The word of God enlarges our hearts and expands our vision, alleluia.

INTERCESSIONS

Christ Jesus, you prayed that we may share your joy completely and so we ask you;
   Make us one with you now and forever.

O God, you gift us with your Spirit;
   —help us to serve each other with the talents and gifts you give us.
You give us the gift of time;
   —may we cherish the moments we spend with you and with others.
In Jesus, you taught us that to love is to serve;
   —give us the willingness to put aside our plans, schedules, and activities when others call upon us.

You chose the weak of the world in preference to the strong;
  —comfort the sick, the suffering, and those who are mentally
    disturbed.

PRAYER: O God, be with us on our journey to fullness of life
            lived in you. Let us not be discouraged by our failures,
            but keep us resolute in our efforts to begin anew. This
            we ask in the name of Jesus. Amen.

DAYTIME PRAYER

(Prayer as in Morning Prayer)

EVENING PRAYER

READING

God and I, we are one. I accept God into me in knowing; I go into God in
loving. There are some who say that blessedness consists not in
knowing but in willing. They are wrong; for if it consisted only in the
will, it would not be one. Working and becoming are one. If a carpenter
does not work, nothing becomes of the house. If the axe is not doing
anything, nothing is becoming anything. In this working God and I are
one; [God] is working and I am becoming. The fire changes anything into
itself that is put into it and this takes on fire's own nature. The wood
does not change the fire into itself, but the fire changes the wood into
itself. So are we changed into God, that we shall know [God] as [God] is
(1 Jn 3:2).

Meister Eckhart, pp. 188–89, (1)

RESPONSORY

The Spirit of truth will come, alleluia, alleluia. **—The Spirit...**
And guide you into all truth, **—alleluia...**
Glory to you, Source of all Being, Eternal Word, and Holy Spirit.
   —The Spirit...

CANTICLE OF MARY

Ant. Loving God, keep those you have given me safe in your
      name, that they may be one, even as we are one, alleluia.

INTERCESSIONS

We pray to you, Holy Mystery, and ask with earnest hearts:
           Send us your gift of Knowledge.

O God, you created our universe and universes beyond our knowing;
—free us from ignorance and open our minds to your wonders.
You created diversity in vegetation, in animals, and in people;
—free us from narrow-mindedness that we may enjoy the variety and the differences.
You are the God that fills infinite space;
—help us to expand the frontiers of our universe, not for national gain, but for your glory.
Through scientists and scholars, new knowledge comes to light;
—may it further the quality of life for all people and all creatures on their journeys to wholeness.

PRAYER: O God, be with us on our journey to fullness of life lived in you. Let us not be discouraged by our failures, but keep us resolute in our efforts to begin anew. This we ask in the name of Jesus. Amen.

SEVENTH THURSDAY OF EASTER
(Psalms and Antiphons from Week III, p. 124)

MORNING PRAYER

READING

Without awareness of himself as human with all a human's limitations, could Jesus have been anything other than a puppet moved around by God? Would he have been a free human being, like us in all things except for sin, if he knew exactly what was to happen? Freedom of choice implies ignorance of what will happen.... Considerations such as these have led theologians to rethink the traditional assumption of the church that the knowledge of Jesus was unlimited and that as [human] he enjoyed the beatific vision. They acknowledge that Jesus' awareness of his union with [God] was unique but now think that this developed gradually in a special way, perhaps with the baptism in the Jordan and that he only fully knew who he was at the resurrection.... Jesus could be truly divine without clearly understanding who and what he was until the resurrection. For example, you were you and I was I when we were three-year-olds, but we didn't know much about who or what we were then. And how much do we know about ourselves now? We'll only know ourselves in our own resurrection.

Raymond T. Bosler, *New Wine Bursting Old Skins*, p. 103, (28)

RESPONSORY

Christ rose from the grave, alleluia, alleluia. **—Christ...**

Conquering sin an death, **—alleluia...**
Glory to you, Source of all Being, Eternal Word, and Holy Spirit.
    —Christ...

CANTICLE OF ZECHARIAH

Ant. May all those who were with me be one in us, that the world
    may believe you sent me, alleluia.

INTERCESSIONS

Strengthen us, O God, as we begin this day. We humbly ask you:
    Give us your Spirit.

Open our hearts to receive all things as gift with a deep sense of
gratitude;
    —knowing that your love works all things to our good.
Teach us to love and care for our world and our universe;
    —recognizing all as your gift to us to be cherished and
        protected.
Give us the unity Jesus prayed for;
    —that together we can enhance the quality of life for all
        living beings.
Reveal the glory manifested in Jesus;
    —to all who will die this day.

PRAYER: O God, we await your Spirit with eager hearts. Fill our
            longing with the fullness of your being that we may give
            witness to your love and concern for all that you made.
            We ask this through Jesus who lives with you and with
            the Holy Spirit for all ages. Amen.

DAYTIME PRAYER

(Prayer as in Morning Prayer)

EVENING PRAYER

READING

This Gospel is one of Peace...to all animated creation. It will conserve
the welfare of the body as well as of the soul; it will deal mercy in
preference to animal slaughter; will teach us to use all the blessings of
life for human comfort; it will teach equality of the sexes in the
administration of government; show us that every age and epoch must

have new revelations of truth to act upon, that these new truths are as essential as fresh air, or new machinery, or the thousand and one improvements which Progress has given us since Jesus lived.

Thomas Smith, *The Shakers*, p. 152, (1)

RESPONSORY

The Spirit of truth will come, alleluia, alleluia. —**The Spirit...**
And guide you into all truth, —**alleluia,...**
Glory to you, Source of all Being, Eternal Word, and Holy Spirit.
   —**The Spirit...**

CANTICLE OF MARY

Ant. I live in you, and you in me, that your joy may be complete, alleluia.

INTERCESSIONS

Filled with anticipation for your coming, we call out to you:
   Come, O Spirit of God, with your gift of Counsel.

You call us to relationship;
   —free us from the loneliness of personal decisions and enable us to see alternatives in difficult situations.
We continue our journey toward fullness of life in community and family;
   —bless all who help us through direction or personal guidance.
You speak to us in the people and circumstances of our everyday lives;
   —give us listening hearts and open minds that we may recognize your voice.
You promised to be with us all our days;
   —bless all those newborn today and those who will be born to eternal life.

PRAYER: O God, we await your Spirit with eager hearts. Fill our longing with the fullness of your being that we may give witness to your love and concern for all that you made. We ask this through Jesus who lives with you and with the Holy Spirit for all ages. Amen.

SEVENTH FRIDAY OF EASTER

(Psalms and Antiphons from Week III, p. 131)

MORNING PRAYER

READING

Peace is fostered by meekness and respect, and God abides where there is peace; works carried out in a spirit of meekness and peace are most pleasing to God, and [God] may be glorified by the good example they give our neighbor.

The Conferences of St. Vincent de Paul, Vol. I, p. 233, (13)

RESPONSORY

Christ rose from the grave, alleluia, alleluia. —**Christ...**
Conquering sin an death, —**alleluia...**
Glory to you, Source of all Being, Eternal Word, and Holy Spirit.
   —**Christ...**

CANTICLE OF ZECHARIAH

Ant.   "Simon, do you love me?" "Yes, Lord, you know that I love you."

INTERCESSIONS

You commissioned your Church, Christ Jesus, to feed your lambs and so we pray:
> **Good Shepherd, teach us your ways**
> **of gentleness and compassion.**

Give wisdom to all ecclesiastical and religious leaders;
   —that they may guide their people with love and patience.
Give wisdom to confessors, counselors, and directors;
   —that they may lift the burdens of those weighed down by
      legalism and fear.
May all who shepherd others be open to the Spirit;
   —who may lead them in ways they would not freely choose.
Call us back to you when we have strayed;
   —that we may again belong to your sheepfold.

PRAYER: O God, give us your Spirit that we may reverence you
            and all things that draw us to you. You know that we
            love you. Increase our desires that we may grow in this
            love and reverence, through Jesus Christ who lives and

reigns with you, Source of all life, and with the Holy Spirit. Amen.

DAYTIME PRAYER

(Prayer as in Morning Prayer)

EVENING PRAYER

READING

[The Spirit prays] in us when we do not know what to ask for. It is the mystery that enables us to pray always and everywhere.... We cannot always be conscious of the Divine Presence, but our hearts can be dedicated to God at work or play as well as at times especially given to prayer. In these latter times of solitary quiet prayer, we can make the conscious acceptance of all that we are in God and say yes to all that life has in store for us. This conscious commitment is the core that unites all that we are and do into one timeless gift of ourselves to God. Then whatever we are doing, we carry the assurance that we are in the Lord Jesus.

Carmelites of Indianapolis, Hidden Friends, p. 45, (5)

RESPONSORY

The Spirit of truth will come, alleluia, alleluia. **—The Spirit...**
And guide you into all truth, **—alleluia,...**
Glory to you, Source of all Being, Eternal Word, and Holy Spirit.
—The Spirit...

CANTICLE OF MARY

Ant. "You know all things; you know that I love you," alleluia.

INTERCESSIONS

We have received your Spirit in baptism and so we ask you:
Give us the gift of Fortitude.

Help us to be steadfast;
—in times of disappointment, discouragement, and trial.
Strengthen us as a community of believers;
—through the witness of those who choose life over death,
light over darkness, hope over despair.
Give us moral courage;

—when society or governments try to lead us toward
destruction of self or others.
Keep us patient, persevering, and open;
   —in committees, action groups, and other gatherings in
which we work with others to achieve a common good.

PRAYER: O God, give us your Spirit that we may reverence you
and all things that draw us to you. You know that we
love you. Increase our desires that we may grow in this
love and reverence, through Jesus Christ who lives and
reigns with you, Source of all life, and with the Holy
Spirit. Amen.

SEVENTH SATURDAY OF EASTER
(Psalms and Antiphons from Week III, p. 138)
MORNING PRAYER

READING

It is only through the Holy Spirit that Jesus is the Bread of life, available
for all, ready to be eaten by all who need him and it is only by the same
Holy Spirit that we ourselves, filled with gratitude for this greatest of
gifts, can be ready to abandon ourselves to Christ and to follow him as
servants of our [sisters and brothers].

Bernard Häring, Prayer: The Integration of Faith and Life, p. 69, (8)

RESPONSORY

Christ rose from the grave, alleluia, alleluia. **—Christ...**
Conquering sin an death, **—alleluia...**
Glory to you, Source of all Being, Eternal Word, and Holy Spirit.
   —Christ...

CANTICLE OF ZECHARIAH

Ant. I will pour out upon you my Spirit of Truth, alleluia.

INTERCESSIONS

O God, breathe within us the breath of your Spirit as we call out
to you:
Give us the gift of Piety.

Pray in us when we are unable;

—and free us from whatever inhibits us from taking the time to pray.
Open our eyes and our hearts;
—that we may be sensitive to the symbols that put us into contact with you.
Teach us to see all reality as holy;
—that we may meet you both in the unexpected and the ordinary.
Detach us from our spiritual possessions;
—that your grace may have sway in us.

PRAYER: Create in us a new heart and a new vision, O God, that the gifts of your Spirit may work in us and renew the face of the earth. May we be one with you so that our work is yours and your work is ours. We ask this in the name of Jesus, the Eternal Word, who lives with you and with the Holy Spirit, forever. Amen.

DAYTIME PRAYER

(Prayer as in Morning Prayer)

PENTECOST SUNDAY

EVENING PRAYER I

Ant 1 O my people, says our God, I will put my Spirit within you, and you shall live, alleluia. (Ps 113, p. 96)

Ant 2 The Spirit helps us in our weakness, for we do not know how to pray; it is the Spirit who prays in us, alleluia. (Ps 147:1–11, p. 173)

Ant 3 Receive the Holy Spirit. If you forgive the sins of any, they are forgiven, alleluia. (Rev 15:3–4, p. 185)

READING

Oh God, we are one with You. You have made us one with You. You have taught us that if we are open to one another, You dwell in us. Help us to preserve this openness and to fight for it with all our hearts. Help us to realize that there can be no understanding where there is mutual rejection. Oh God, in accepting one another wholeheartedly, fully, completely, we accept You, and we thank You, and we adore You, and we love You with our whole being, because our being is in Your being, our spirit is rooted in Your spirit. Fill us then with love, and let us be bound together with love as we go our diverse ways, united in this one spirit which makes You present in the world, and which makes You witness to the ultimate reality that is love. Love has overcome. Love is victorious. Amen.

The Asian Journal of Thomas Merton, pp. 318–19, (16)

RESPONSORY

I give you my Spirit, alleluia, alleluia. —**I give**...

You will be my witnesses, —**alleluia,**...

Glory to you, Source of all Being, Eternal Word and Holy Spirit.
    —**I give**...

CANTICLE OF MARY

Ant God declares: In the last days it shall be that I will pour out my Spirit upon all flesh, and your daughters and sons shall prophesy, alleluia.

INTERCESSIONS

On the day of Pentecost, the women and men gathered together were filled with the Holy Spirit and began to proclaim the works of God. Let us pray:

Come Holy Spirit, enkindle in us the fire of your love.

Holy Spirit, father and mother of the poor;
    —bring to birth in us the desire and means to deliver the poor from want.

Holy Spirit, strong and gentle comforter;
    —tend the grief of those who mourn those missing or dead.

Holy Spirit, free spirit;
    —liberate those bound by injustice or ignorance.

Holy Spirit, healing presence;
    —bind our broken relationships and teach us to forgive one another.

PRAYER: O God, you have sent your Holy Spirit to hover over the abyss of our broken world. Help us to be open to the grace of your coming that you may create us anew. Banish our darkness with your wisdom; set us on the firm ground of counsel and fortitude. Bless our coming and going with your sevenfold gifts, that your reign may come upon the earth, that we may live with you for all eternity. Amen.

MORNING PRAYER
(Psalms from Sunday, Week I, p. 3)

Ant 1 They were all filled with the Holy Spirit and began to speak in many tongues, alleluia.

Ant 2 Seas and rivers, bless the Most High; praise and exalt God forever, alleluia.

Ant 3 When they had prayed, they were all filled with the Holy Spirit and boldly spoke the word of God, alleluia.

READING

...the event of Pentecost is a mystery of universal importance. The miracle of tongues unhesitatingly entrusts the proclamation of the gospel to fragile human language, which is always changing. No longer is there a sacred language, determined once and for all or received from the past as the only one capable of authentically transmitting the good news.... The Spirit has been given to the Church so that it may assume every human language and all of the cultures expressed therein. In each one the good seed of the Word must be sown with both hands, because in each, the fruits of the Spirit may be borne a hundredfold. In its calling, the Church is confronted with the challenge of constantly translating the gospel into the native speech of "every nation under heaven."

Days of the Lord, Vol. 3, pp. 273–74, (9)

RESPONSORY

Flames as of fire rested over the disciples, alleluia, alleluia.
   —Flames...
They spoke as the Spirit gave utterance, **—alleluia...**
Glory to you, Source of all Being, Eternal Word and Holy Spirit.
   —Flames...

CANTICLE OF ZECHARIAH

Ant Peace be with you. Receive the Holy Spirit, alleluia.

INTERCESSIONS

The followers of Jesus began to speak in foreign tongues and all who heard them understood. Let us pray:
   **Holy Spirit, Light of God, shine on our minds
   and confirm us in truth.**

Jesus, you have sent your Holy Spirit to dwell in our hearts;
   —teach us to live quietly, ever attentive to your voice.

Through the power of the Holy Spirit, you guide your people to salvation;
—bless our church and all nations with enlightened and upright leaders.
You send your Spirit to remind us of all that you have taught us;
—endow scripture scholars with a love and understanding of your word, and with the means to enlighten us all.
Your Spirit of love can change our hearts;
—send that same Spirit to draw us to grow in our dedication and love for you.

PRAYER: Come, Holy Spirit, breathe new life into your people. Show us the true meaning of the gospel, and enkindle our hearts with a love that will transform our lives. Grant us the unity for which Jesus prayed—now and forever. Amen.

DAYTIME PRAYER

Ant 1 Jesus poured forth his Spirit into the hearts of his followers, alleluia. (Ps 120, p. 155)

Ant 2 Lord Jesus, send us your Spirit of wisdom and love, alleluia. (Ps 121, p. 89)

Ant 3 It is the Spirit who gives life and light, alleluia. (Ps 122, p. 143)

(Prayer as in Morning Prayer)

EVENING PRAYER II
(Psalms from Sunday, Week I, p. 7)

Ant 1 There are varieties of gifts, but the same Spirit who gives them, alleluia.

Ant 2 To each person is given the manifestation of the Spirit for the common good, alleluia.

Ant 3 By one Spirit we were all baptized into one body, and all were made to drink of the one Spirit, alleluia.

READING

When it was evening on that day, the first day of the week...Jesus came and stood among them and said, "Peace be with you." After he said this, he showed them his hands and his side. Then the disciples rejoiced when they saw the Lord. Jesus said to them again, "Peace be with you. As [God] has sent me, so I send you." When he had said this, he breathed on them, and said to them, "Receive the Holy Spirit. If you forgive the sins of any, they are forgiven them; if you retain the sins of any, they are retained."

Jn 20:10–23

RESPONSORY

Send forth your Spirit, O God, alleluia, alleluia. **—Send**...
Renew the face of the earth, **—alleluia**...
Glory to you, Source of all Being, Eternal Word and Holy Spirit.
 —Send...

CANTICLE OF MARY

Ant This day has God poured out the Spirit of Jesus on those gathered in Christ's name. The Holy Spirit inflamed the hearts of the believers who boldly went forth to proclaim God's word, alleluia alleluia.

INTERCESSIONS

The Holy Spirit descended with gifts of wisdom, fortitude, piety, and reverence for God. With longing hearts, we pray:
 Spirit of God, rain down your gifts on our parched spirits.

O God, you create and recreate with the power of love;
 —open our hearts to your indwelling Spirit that we may be one with you in all that we do.
You send your Spirit to banish fears and to bring us peace;
 —let our lives mirror your mercy and goodness and reveal your love.
Our ways are known to you; you are always with us;
 —bless all who are traveling, those who are lonely, and those who have no one to care for them.
You are faithful, O God and your mercy lasts forever;
 —send your Spirit to awaken in our hearts a readiness to praise you with loving confidence.

PRAYER: Come, Holy Spirit, breathe new life into your people. Show us the true meaning of the gospel, and enkindle our hearts with a love that will transform our lives. Grant us the unity for which Jesus prayed—now and forever. Amen.

TRINITY SUNDAY
SUNDAY AFTER PENTECOST
EVENING PRAYER I

Ant 1   We give glory to you: Creator, Redeemer, Spirit of Life, one God forever, alleluia. (Ps 113, p. 96)

Ant 2   I am your God, one and eternal; my presence will go with you and give you rest, alleluia. (Ps 147:12–20, p. 85)

Ant 3   We honor you, Holy Mystery: Source of all Being, Eternal Word, and Holy Spirit; we worship you forever, alleluia. (Eph 1:3–10, p. 61)

READING

Greatly ought we to rejoice that God dwells in our soul; and more greatly ought we to rejoice that our soul dwells in God.... And I saw no difference between God and our substance, but, as it were, all God; and still my understanding accepted that our substance is in God, that is to say that God is God, and our substance is a creature in God. For the almighty truth of the Trinity is our Father, for he made us and keeps us in him. And the deep wisdom of the Trinity is our Mother, in whom we are enclosed. And the high goodness of the Trinity is our Lord, and in him we are enclosed and he in us.

Julian of Norwich, *Showings*, p. 285, (1)

RESPONSORY

We give you glory, most Holy Trinity; Three in One. —**We give**...
We sing your praises; —**Three**...
Glory to you, Source of all Being, Eternal Word and Holy Spirit.
   —**We give**...

CANTICLE OF MARY

Ant   Honor and thanksgiving to you, O triune God, one and undivided, Source of life, grace, and love, alleluia.

INTERCESSIONS

To God, Source of all Being, Eternal Word, and Holy Spirit, be praise, honor, and glory forever. Let us pray:
Praise to you, most Blessed Trinity.

Creator God, saving Word, abiding Spirit, renew and enlighten your church and awaken the world to your presence;
—give all who believe in you the grace to proclaim your glory.
Holy Trinity, one in unity, guide to the truth all who profess your name,
—that the richness of your word may be magnified on the earth.
Blessed Trinity, eternal in unity, bless families and communities and all who bond together in your name;
—let our relationships be loving, mature, loyal and just.
Jesus, Word of God, you prayed that we all might be one with you;
—be for us the beginning and end of our life's journey.

PRAYER: Holy God, Holy Mighty One, you have created all things and you continue to call us to new life. Teach us to reverence in one another the gift of life that we share. Give us a hunger for your Word, and let us walk in union with your Spirit all the days of our lives. Glory to you, Source of all Being, Eternal Word, and Holy Spirit, forever and ever. Amen.

MORNING PRAYER
(Psalms from Sunday Week I, p. 3)

Ant 1 Alleluia! Glory and praise to our God for all ages; alleluia, alleluia!

Ant 2 All nations worship you, Holy Mystery, Blessed Trinity, alleluia.

Ant 3 All glory and honor is yours, Creator God, through Jesus Christ, by the power of the Spirit, alleluia.

READING

Trinity!! Higher than any being,
    any divinity, any goodness!
  Guide of Christians
  Higher in the wisdom of heaven!

Lead us up beyond unknowing and light,
   up to the farthest, highest peak
     of mystic scripture,
  where the mysteries of God's Word
    lie simple, absolute and unchangeable
    in the brilliant darkness of a hidden silence.
  Amid the wholly unsensed and unseen
    they completely fill our sightless minds
    with treasures beyond all beauty.

Pseudo-Dionysius, The Mystical Theology, p. 135, (1)

RESPONSORY

From God and through God and to God are all things.—**From**...
To God be glory forever; —**to God**...
Glory to you, Source of all Being, Eternal Word and Holy Spirit.
  —**From**...

CANTICLE OF ZECHARIAH

Ant You alone are the Holy One, triune God, yet undivided; we
    praise you with joy, alleluia.

INTERCESSIONS

What we believe of our Creator, we believe of the Word and of the
Holy Spirit. God, our God, is One. In adoration we pray:
All glory and praise to you!

O God, holy and undivided Trinity, all your judgments are just
and all your ways are true;
  —grant wisdom and integrity to all who lead our church and
    the nations of the world.
O God, Trinity whom we adore, you alone are holy;
  —bless our efforts to grow in the way of your
    commandments.
All the angels sing your praise, and you call us to union with you;
  —make us worthy of the promises of Christ.
Holy and Blessed Trinity, God of beauty, truth and goodness,
  —may we live and love in your image and likeness.

PRAYER: Holy God, Holy Mighty One, you have created all things
    and you continue to call us to new life. Teach us to
    reverence in one another the gift of life that we share.
    Give us a hunger for your Word, and let us walk in

union with your Spirit all the days of our lives. Glory to you, Source of all Being, Eternal Word, and Holy Spirit, forever and ever. Amen.

DAYTIME PRAYER

Ant 1 Glory to you, holy triune God, now and for all ages, alleluia.

Ant 2 All nations shall come and worship you, for you alone are holy, alleluia.

Ant 3 Blessed, triune God, in faith and hope we pray to you, alleluia.

(Prayer as in Morning Prayer)

EVENING PRAYER II
(Psalms from Sunday, Week I, p. 7)

Ant 1 Source of all Being, Eternal Word and Holy Spirit, you are one God and there is no other besides you, alleluia.

Ant 2 Holy Trinity, abiding in us, renew your people and all creation, alleluia.

Ant 3 Holy are you, Holy Mystery; the earth proclaims your glory, alleluia.

READING

When we are...constantly being loved into existence within the very divine trinitarian love and fashioned through graced knowledge and love into images of the Trinity, we are so constituted in our very being and powers, Thomas (Aquinas) teaches, that we have not only a natural capacity for such a divine-like (supernatural) existence and life but also a necessary drive implanted within us by God. Therefore, whether consciously or not, we are always seeking God as our only true beatitude, our only ultimate good or end. The gift of existence given us, within and by God's knowledge and love, implants in us an affective thirst to see and enjoy God perfectly, a thirst that can never be satisfied by any creaturely good. This inborn thirst, derived from knowledge, is the root source of human free choice, an essential component of any spirituality. Affectivity is at the center of all human striving for beatitude.

Walter Principe, csb, "Affectivity and the Heart in Thomas Aquinas' Spirituality" p. 52, (1)

RESPONSORY

We give you glory, most Holy Trinity; Three in One. **—We give**...
We sing your praises; **—Three**...
Glory to you, Source of all Being, Eternal Word and Holy Spirit.
—We give...

CANTICLE OF MARY

Ant Blessing and glory, wisdom and thanksgiving, honor an
power be to our God, forever and ever! Amen, alleluia!

INTERCESSIONS

To God, Source of all Being, Eternal Word, and Holy Spirit, be
praise, honor, and glory forever. Let us pray:
Praise to you, most Blessed Trinity.

Creator God, saving Word, abiding Spirit, renew and enlighten
your church and awaken the world to your presence;
   —give all who believe in you the grace to proclaim your glory.
Holy Trinity, one in unity, guide to the truth all who profess your
name,
   —that the richness of your word may be magnified on the earth.
Blessed Trinity, eternal in unity, bless families and communities
and all who bond together in your name;
   —let our relationships be loving, mature, loyal and just.
Jesus, Word of God, you prayed that we all might be one with
you;
   —be for us the beginning and end of our life's journey.

PRAYER: Holy God, Holy Mighty One, you have created all things
and you continue to call us to new life. Teach us to
reverence in one another the gift of life that we share.
Give us a hunger for your Word, and let us walk in
union with your Spirit all the days of our lives. Glory to
you, Source of all Being, Eternal Word, and Holy Spirit,
forever and ever. Amen.

SUNDAY AFTER TRINITY SUNDAY
THE FEAST OF THE BODY AND BLOOD OF CHRIST
EVENING PRAYER I

Ant 1 We thank you, O God, for you provide food for those who love you and are ever mindful of your covenant, alleluia. (Ps 111, p. 102)

Ant 2 In the sharing of the bread, we are made one people of God, alleluia. (Ps 147:12–20, p. 85)

Ant 3 The bread that comes from God gives life to the world, alleluia. (Rev 11:17–18; 12:10b–12a, p. 82)

READING

More than any other sacrament, the eucharist is at the heart of the life of the church. The "something about" the Jesus event that is offered in the eucharist is mediated and particularized not merely through bread and wine as things—but these and more: bread that is blessed, broken and shared by a people who are and who become the people of God by becoming the body of Jesus, the primordial symbol of God. The sacramental symbol is a realizing symbol. The cup of wine which is the cup of covenant in the blood of Jesus is blessed and shared by a people already responsible to and for each other before God and in Jesus, but now assimilating that covenant anew into the pattern of life which constitutes the becoming, and therefore the reality, of Christians.

Bernard Lee, *Religious Experience and Process Theology*, p. 295, (1)

RESPONSORY

You, O Christ, are the bread that we share; we live forever in you. **—You,...**

Yours is the cup of eternal salvation; **—we live...**

Glory to you, Source of all Being, Eternal Word and Holy Spirit. **—You,...**

CANTICLE OF MARY

Ant I will lift up the cup of salvation, O God; I will give thanks to you for all your goodness to us, alleluia.

INTERCESSIONS

We who eat your flesh and drink your blood will have eternal life, and you will raise us up on the last day. In faith, we proclaim:

This is the bread that came down from heaven.

Jesus, you longed to eat the paschal meal with your disciples
before you gave your life for us;
—teach us to walk your way of total self-giving.
On the night of your Last Supper, you washed the feet of your
disciples;
—help us to realize that the bread of life you give us is the
bread of service and reverence.
Jesus, the new Moses, you give a new law and a new manna;
—release us from all that is dead in our past and make us
eager to receive your word and bread of life.
Jesus, Good Shepherd and guardian of your church;
—open the way for all people to share and serve at your table.

PRAYER: Christ Jesus, through your life, death, and
resurrection, you have brought new life to the world.
Through the Holy Eucharist, the sacrament of unity,
you nourish that life and give us hope. Strengthened
by this bread, may we walk in your truth and learn to
love one another as you have loved us. We ask this in
your name. Amen.

MORNING PRAYER
(Psalms from Sunday, Week I, p. 3)

Ant 1 I will give you the food which endures to eternal life,
alleluia.

Ant 2 Your holy people offer you thanks with gifts of bread and
wine; alleluia.

Ant 3 I am the living bread which came down from heaven. They
who eat of this bread will live forever, alleluia.

READING

It becomes clear that the manna which nourishes the Christian on the
journey of faith and which enables hope to conquer cynicism and
despair is the commitment to loving service. This is the heart of the
teaching of Jesus and it is the deepest meaning of the Eucharistic
manna. For the body and blood of the Lord in the Eucharist are a body
broken for others and a blood poured out in sacrifice for others. To
receive this sacrificial body and blood is to commit oneself unalterably
to the loving service that they signify. Thus, a mysterious and wonderful

bonding occurs between Jesus and the Christian, not just from receiving the Eucharist, but also from living the love and unselfishness of Jesus.

Demetrius Dumm, OSB, *Flowers in the Desert*, p. 103, (1)

RESPONSORY

You sustain us with bread and wine unto life everlasting.
—You...
You, yourself, are life for us; **—unto...**
Glory to you, Source of all Being, Eternal Word and Holy Spirit.
—You...

CANTICLE OF ZECHARIAH

Ant The bread that I give you is my life for the salvation of the world; alleluia.

INTERCESSIONS

The bread that I shall give is my flesh for the life of the world. In gratitude, we exclaim:
You have prepared a banquet for your people.

Christ Jesus, priest of the new covenant, you invite all to your banquet table;
—let our lives lead others to know and love you.
Christ Jesus, Living Bread, you refresh those who are burdened and weary;
—help us to bear one another's burdens and so share the bread of your mercy.
You broke bread with those who would deny and betray you;
—may the sharing of the eucharistic meal bring a spirit of reconciliation to the world.
Every time we share the eucharistic meal, we proclaim your death until you come;
—may this same sharing make of our lives a proclamation of your goodness and love.

PRAYER: Christ Jesus, through your life, death, and resurrection, you have brought new life to the world. Through the Holy Eucharist, the sacrament of unity, you nourish that life and give us hope. Strengthened by this bread, may we walk in your truth and learn to

love one another as you have loved us. We ask this in
your name. Amen.

DAYTIME PRAYER
(Psalms from Sunday, Week I, p. 6)

Ant 1 When his hour had come, Jesus sat at table with his
disciples, alleluia.

Ant 2 Jesus took bread, gave thanks, broke the bread and gave
it to them; alleluia.

Ant 3 This is my body given for you. This is the cup of the new
covenant, my blood poured out for you; alleluia.

(Prayer as in Morning Prayer)

EVENING PRAYER II

Ant 1 Jesus, you are the bread of life, given up for us, alleluia.
(Ps 110:1–5, 7, p. 53)

Ant 2 The cup poured out for us is the cup of the covenant,
alleluia. (Ps 116:10–19, p. 96)

Ant 3 Jesus was revealed in the breaking of the bread, alleluia.
(Rev 19:1, 5–7, p. 54)

READING

Consider the congregation at liturgy on a given Sunday. Here is a
woman who comes early and enters by the side door that offers a ramp
for her invalid husband's wheelchair. There is the father of four whose
wife was recently diagnosed with cancer. The couple in back is
mourning the death of their newborn, and the mother on the aisle is
weeping for her son who was arrested in a drug raid.... It is well to
remember that while we attend the liturgy to praise God, we are there
also to support one another by our prayers, our presence, and our care.
Together we are the Body of Christ, a suffering body that can rise to the
challenges of life through the ministry of its members.

Carmelites of Indianapolis, *Hidden Friends*, p. 51, (5)

RESPONSORY

You, O Christ, are the bread that we share; we live forever
in you. **—You**...

Yours is the cup of eternal salvation; —**we live**...
Glory to you, Source of all Being, Eternal Word and Holy Spirit.
   —**You**...

CANTICLE OF MARY

Ant We praise you, O Christ, bread of heaven and pledge of
   eternal life; we proclaim you among us in the bread and wine
   of the new covenant, alleluia!

INTERCESSIONS

Those who eat your flesh and drink your blood will have eternal
life, and you will raise them up on the last day. In faith, we
proclaim:
   This is the bread that came down from heaven.

Jesus, you longed to eat the paschal meal with your disciples
before you gave your life for us;
   —teach us to walk your way of total self-giving.
On the night of your Last Supper, you washed the feet of your
disciples;
   —help us to realize that the bread of life you give us is the
   bread of service and reverence.
Jesus, the new Moses, you give a new law and a new manna;
   —release us from all that is dead in our past and make us
   eager to receive your word and bread of life.
Jesus, Good Shepherd and guardian of your church;
   —open the way for all people to share and serve at your table.

PRAYER: Christ Jesus, through your life, death, and
   resurrection, you have brought new life to the world.
   Through the Holy Eucharist, the sacrament of unity,
   you nourish that life and give us hope. Strengthened
   by this bread, may we walk in your truth and learn to
   love one another as you have loved us. We ask this in
   your name. Amen.

FRIDAY AFTER THE SECOND SUNDAY AFTER PENTECOST
FEAST OF THE SACRED HEART

EVENING PRAYER I

Ant 1 There is no greater love than to lay down one's life for a friend. (Ps 113, p. 96)

Ant 2 You shall love your God with all your heart, with all your soul, and with all your might. (Ps 146, p. 166)

Ant 3 You are faithful, O God, you keep your covenant with your people. (Rev 4:11, 5:9,10,12, p. 163)

READING

O my God, I desire to live as a victim offered in a spirit of penance and love. Then let me prepare all that is needed for a sacrifice of love whose perfume will rise even to the Heart of Jesus.... May my *love* be the consuming *fire*, and my yearning *desires* the *breeze* that fans it. Let me pour on it the *incense* and *perfume* of all virtues, and to this mystical sacrifice let me bring *all that I cling to*, that I may offer all, burn all, consume all, keeping back nothing for self. O Divine Love, my very God, accept this sacrifice which I desire to offer You at every instant of my life.

Louise Callan, RSCJ, Philippine Duchesne, p. 719, (13)

RESPONSORY

Your compassion, O God, is eternal, your love is everlasting.
   —Your...
Your faithfulness is renewed each day, **—your love...**
Glory to you, Source of all Being, Eternal Word and Holy Spirit.
   —Your...

CANTICLE OF MARY

Ant Let us love one another, for love is of God.

INTERCESSIONS

Jesus said to the disciples: I have come to cast fire on the earth and would that it were already enkindled! We pray with zealous hearts:

      **Send forth your Spirit, and enkindle in us
      the fire of your love.**

Jesus, you were moved to pity and you healed the widow's son;
  —teach us how to bring comfort and hope to those who
    mourn.
You wept over Jerusalem and longed to gather the people to your
heart;
  —increase our zeal for the development and safety of all people.
You cried out in pain at the death of your friend, Lazarus;
  —teach us and our children the value of loyal and faithful
    relationships.
You grieved for the women who wept as you carried your cross;
  —give us large hearts and teach us selfless love.

PRAYER: O God, you have revealed your love for us through the
compassionate heart of Jesus. Let his forgiving love call
us all to a change of heart. Strengthen in us the desire
to live for one another and for the glory of your name.
Amen.

MORNING PRAYER
(Psalms from Sunday, Week I, p. 3)

Ant 1 Out of love for us, God has made with us a covenant of
peace.

Ant 2 If God so loves us, we also must love one another.

Ant 3 I drew you to myself with bonds of compassion and love,
says our God.

READING

Towards the end of her life Mary MacKillop sent to the sisters a
reflection on her own spiritual experience in the form of "An Appeal of
the Sacred Heart to a Weary, Disappointed Soul". In it she reveals that it
was the tender, loving Heart of Jesus that spoke to her and brought her
to such peace and joy in his service. She concluded her reflection: "And
with this burning appeal came such a longing desire on my part to be
Its lover and own true child that, in a glance, the falseness of the world
appeared to me. The beauty, the pity, and the generosity of the Sacred
Heart in this loving appeal could not be resisted. And in It, I have never
known aught but true peace and contentment of heart. Its love makes
suffering sweet, Its love makes the world a desert. When storms rage,
when persecutions or dangers threaten, I quietly creep into Its abyss,

and securely sheltered there, my soul is in peace, though my body is tossed upon the stormy waves of a cold and selfish world." (21 June 1907)

Bl. Mary MacKillop, RSJ, (10)

RESPONSORY

Christ died for us, that we might live forever. —**Christ**...
Pouring forth the Spirit into our hearts, —**that we**...
Glory to you, Source of all Being, Eternal Word and Holy Spirit.
  —**Christ**...

CANTICLE OF ZECHARIAH

Ant Learn from me, for I am gentle and lowly in heart, and you
    will find rest.

INTERCESSIONS

Insults have broken my heart, I looked for comforters, but I found none. In loving response, we pray:
  By your wounds, we are healed.

Jesus, you forgave those who crucified you;
  —give us the grace to put no limits on our forgiveness of
    others.
You loved sinners and helped them to change their lives;
  —give us patience and understanding when we strive to
    help those who harm themselves and others.
Your love is everlasting; you never cease to call us to salvation;
  —give us the wisdom and generosity to follow you and to draw
    others to your heart.
A soldier pierced your heart with a lance;
  —open our hearts to the wonders of your love and to the
    challenge of your gospel.

PRAYER: Christ Jesus, you draw us to salvation with the loving
        heart of a friend. Teach us to find rest for our spirits in
        your way of humility and meekness. Set our hearts
        ablaze with zeal for the coming of your reign, fullness of
        life, both now and for all eternity. Amen.

DAYTIME PRAYER

Ant 1 May Christ dwell in our hearts by faith. (Ps 120, p. 155)

Ant 2 Let us know your love, O Christ, which surpasses all knowledge. (Ps 121, p. 89)

Ant 3 The heart of Christ was pierced, and blood and water flowed out. (Ps 122, p. 143)

(Prayer as in Morning Prayer)

EVENING PRAYER II

Ant 1 The love of God has been poured into our hearts by the Holy Spirit. (Ps. 110:1–5, 7, p. 53)

Ant 2 While we were yet sinners, Christ died for us. (Ps. 111, p. 102)

Ant 3 Rejoice with me, I have found the one who was lost. (Phil. 2:6–11, p. 48)

READING

In the real symbol of the heart of Christ, detachment and progress, prayer and action, love for God and love for the world are reconciled. The Sacred Heart no longer stands only for the love of Jesus for us, but also for the unifying meaning and force of that love as it unites and gives greater meaning to all our best hopes, aspirations and efforts. By the time of his 1939 retreat, Teilhard sees the heart of Jesus Christ risen as the heart of him who stands as the Omega point of Teilhard's Christology, the heart of him who draws all things to himself as the future focus of all evolution's convergence. In an essay of 1940, Teilhard explains how his concept of the Universal Christ is "born from an expansion of the heart of Jesus." And in the 1940s and 1950s Teilhard describes Jesus' heart as the heart of the Heart of the world, and the center of the Center of the universe.

Robert Faricy, SJ, "The Heart of Christ in the Writings of Teilhard de Chardin," pp. 182–83, (1)

RESPONSORY

Your compassion, O God, is eternal, your love is everlasting.
   —Your...
Your faithfulness is renewed each day, **—your love**...
Glory to you, Source of all Being, Eternal Word and Holy Spirit.
   —Your...

CANTICLE OF MARY

Ant All will know you are my followers if you have love for one another.

INTERCESSIONS

Jesus said to the disciples: I have come to cast fire on the earth and would that it were already enkindled! We pray with zealous hearts:

**Send forth your Spirit, and enkindle in us
the fire of your love.**

Jesus, you were moved to pity and you healed the widow's son;
—teach us how to bring comfort and hope to those who mourn.
You wept over Jerusalem and longed to gather the people to your heart;
—increase our zeal for the development and safety of all people.
You cried out in pain at the death of your friend, Lazarus;
—teach us and our children the value of loyal and faithful relationships.
You grieved for the women who wept as you carried your cross;
—give us large hearts and teach us selfless love.

PRAYER: O God, you have revealed your love for us through the compassionate heart of Jesus. Let his forgiving love call us all to a change of heart. Strengthen in us the desire to live for one another and for the glory of your name. Amen.

SIXTH SUNDAY IN ORDINARY TIME

EVENING PRAYER I

(Psalms and Antiphons from Sunday, Week II, p. 47)

READING

[Poverty] has none of that attachment which, like a band, binds the heart to earth and to earthly things and deprives us of that ease in rising and turning once more to God. It enables us to hear better in all things the voice—that is, the inspiration—of the Holy Spirit by removing the obstructions which hinder it. It gives greater efficacy to our prayers in the sight of God because "[God] hath heard the desire of the poor." It speeds us on our way along the path of virtue, like a traveler who has been relieved of all burdens. It frees us from that slavery common to so many of the world's great ones, in which everything obeys or serves money.

Letters of St. Ignatius of Loyola, pp. 148–49, (19)

RESPONSORY

From daybreak to sunset, we praise your name, O God.
　—From daybreak...
Your glory fills the heavens; **—we praise...**
Glory to you, Source of all Being, Eternal Word and Holy Spirit.
　—From daybreak...

CANTICLE OF MARY

Ant.　Blessed are the pure of heart, for they shall see God.

INTERCESSIONS and PRAYER: (from Sunday, Week II, p. 49)

MORNING PRAYER

(Psalms from Sunday, Week II, p. 49)

Ant 1　For great is the wisdom of God, who is mighty in power and sees everything.

Ant 2　Whether you eat or drink, or whatever you do, do all to the glory of God.

Ant 3　No eye has seen nor ear heard, nor human heart conceived, what has been prepared for those who love God.

READING

If you choose, you can keep the commandments, and to act faithfully is a matter of your own choice. God has placed before you fire and water; stretch out your hand for whichever you choose. Before each person are life and death, and whichever one chooses will be given. For great is the wisdom of God; who is mighty in power and sees everything; whose eyes are on those who fear the Most High, and who knows every human action. God has not commanded anyone to be wicked, and has not given anyone permission to sin.

Sir 15:15–20

RESPONSORY

Restore me to health, make me live! —**Restore**...
You are the hope of all the earth; —**make me**...
Glory to you, Source of all Being, Eternal Word and Holy Spirit.
   —**Restore**...

CANTICLE OF ZECHARIAH

Ant I say to you, everyone who is angry with a sister or brother shall be liable to judgment.

INTERCESSIONS (from Sunday, Week II, p. 51)

PRAYER: O God, you have given us the gift of freedom that we prize as much as life itself. Give us the grace to honor the gift by employing it with justice and mercy. Bless all who are enslaved in any way. Give comfort and strength to those who are ill, imprisoned, confused, or caught in some form of selfishness. Give us all freedom of heart. Enable us to live creatively. Let the mystery of the cross lead us to the hope of resurrection through Jesus Christ, who lives with you and the Holy Spirit forever. Amen.

DAYTIME PRAYER

Ant 1 Blessed are they who trust in God, whose hope is the Most High.

Ant 2 A leper came to Jesus beseeching him, and kneeling said to him, "If you will, you can make me clean."

Ant 3 Blessed are you poor, for yours is the reign of God.

(Prayer as in Morning Prayer)

EVENING PRAYER II
(Psalms from Sunday, Week II, p. 53)

Ant 1 Think not that I have come to abolish the law and the prophets; I have come not to abolish them but to fulfill them.

Ant 2 Christ has been raised from the dead, the first fruits of those who have fallen asleep.

Ant 3 Jesus was moved with pity and stretching out his hand he touched the man and said, "I will, be clean."

READING

So whether you eat or drink, or whatever you do, do everything for the glory of God. Give no offense to Jews or to Greeks or to the church of God, just as I try to please everyone in everything I do, not seeking my own advantage, but that of many, so that they may be saved. Be imitators of me, as I am of Christ.

1 Cor 10:31–11:1

RESPONSORY

May all who seek you, O God, rejoice and be glad.—**May all**...
May all who love your salvation —**rejoice**...
Glory to you, Source of all Being, Eternal Word and Holy Spirit.
　　—**May all**...

CANTICLE OF MARY

Ant Blessed are you that hunger now, for you shall be satisfied.

INTERCESSIONS (from Sunday, Week II, p. 55)

PRAYER: O God, you have given us the gift of freedom that we prize as much as life itself. Give us the grace to honor the gift by employing it with justice and mercy. Bless all who are enslaved in any way. Give comfort and strength to those who are ill, imprisoned, confused, or caught in some form of selfishness. Give us all freedom of heart. Enable us to live creatively. Let the mystery of the cross lead us to the hope of resurrection through Jesus Christ, who lives with you and the Holy Spirit forever. Amen.

SEVENTH SUNDAY IN ORDINARY TIME

EVENING PRAYER I

(Psalms and Antiphons from Sunday, Week III, p. 96)

READING

There are many ways to become open to our Divine Source so that we may be healed. There is life itself. Clearly the Divine Mystery can touch us in people, in nature, in music, in art.... Whatever spiritual disciplines we undertake, they are no band aid. The heavy and stubborn patterns which overlay our souls don't magically go away. Spiritual practice is essential, not for its own sake, but to link us up to God and to God's health which lives at the center of each of us. There is no way we can get out of God's love or away from the deep-seated health. We have resources available to us that are mightier than all the powers of the world, even that in us which is resistant to the light and the best interests of our own souls. What is needful is not perfect spiritual practice but our *willingness* to let God's gift of deep health come out of its hiding place and become the operative principle of our lives.

John P. Gorsuch, An Invitation to the Spiritual Journey, pp. 64–65, (1)

RESPONSORY

Shelter us, O God, in the safety of your dwelling place. **—Shelter...**
Your name is forever blessed; **—in the safety...**
Glory to you, Source of all Being, Eternal Word and Holy Spirit.
   —Shelter...

CANTICLE OF MARY

Ant. You are faithful to your word, forever.

INTERCESSIONS and PRAYER: (from Sunday, Week III, p. 97)

MORNING PRAYER

(Psalms from Sunday, Week III, p. 98)

Ant 1 You shall be holy, for I your God am holy.

Ant 2 Love your enemies that you may be children of God.

Ant 3 Judge not, and you will not be judged; condemn not, and you will not be condemned.

READING

Do you not know that you are God's temple and that God's Spirit dwells in you? If anyone destroys God's temple, God will destroy that person.

For God's temple is holy, and you are that temple. Do not deceive yourselves. If you think that you are wise in this age, you should become fools so that you may become wise. For the wisdom of this world is foolishness with God. So let no one boast about human leaders. For all things are yours, whether Paul or Apollos or Cephas or the world or life or death or the present or the future—all belong to you, and you belong to Christ, and Christ belongs to God.

1 Cor 3:16–19a, 21–23

RESPONSORY

God's temple is holy, and you are God's temple.—**God's temple**...
God's Spirit dwells in you; —**and you**...
Glory to you, Source of all Being, Eternal Word and Holy Spirit.
  —**God's temple**...

CANTICLE OF ZECHARIAH

Ant God makes the sun rise on those who do evil and on the good, and sends rain on the just and the unjust.

INTERCESSIONS (from Sunday, Week III, p. 100)

PRAYER: O God, our mother and father, we praise you in the wonder of your all-embracing love. Your compassion extends to all as you forgive us again and again. Give us the humility and love to forgive one another, living the prayer of your Divine Son—to forgive as we are forgiven. Make us sacraments of your healing love, bearers of the promise of Jesus, who lives with you and the Holy Spirit now and forever. Amen.

DAYTIME PRAYER

Ant 1 You shall love your neighbor as yourself: I am your God.

Ant 2 I am the One who blots out your transgressions for my own sake, and I will not remember your sins.

Ant 3 Just as we have borne the image of the creature of dust, we shall also bear the image of the One come down from heaven.

(Prayer as in Morning Prayer)

EVENING PRAYER II
(Psalms from Sunday, Week III, p. 102)

Ant 1 You, therefore must be perfect as your Creator in heaven is perfect.

Ant 2 God has put a seal upon us and has given us the Spirit in our hearts as a guarantee.

Ant 3 When Jesus saw their faith, he said to the paralytic, "My child, your sins are forgiven."

READING

Do not remember the former things, or consider the things of old. I am about to do a new thing; now it springs forth, do you not perceive it? I will make a way in the wilderness and rivers in the desert. The people whom I formed for myself so that they might declare my praise. Yet you did not call upon me, O Jacob; but you have been weary of me, O Israel! You have not brought me sweet cane with money, or satisfied me with the fat of your sacrifices. But you have burdened me with your iniquities. I, I am the One who blots out your transgressions for my own sake, and I will not remember your sins.

Is 43:18–19, 21–22, 24–25

RESPONSORY

Love your enemies; do good to those who hate you. —**Love your**...
Pray for those who persecute you —**do good**...
Glory to you, Source of all Being, Eternal Word and Holy Spirit.
    —**Love your**...

CANTICLE OF MARY

Ant The wisdom of this world is folly with God.

INTERCESSIONS (from Sunday, Week III, p. 104)

PRAYER: O God, our mother and father, we praise you in the wonder of your all-embracing love. Your compassion extends to all as you forgive us again and again. Give us the humility and love to forgive one another, living the prayer of your Divine Son—to forgive as we are forgiven. Make us sacraments of your healing love, bearers of the promise of Jesus, who lives with you and the Holy Spirit now and forever. Amen.

EIGHTH SUNDAY IN ORDINARY TIME
EVENING PRAYER I
(Psalms and Antiphons from Sunday, Week IV, p. 143)

READING

Let us consider, beloved, how [God] continually proves to us that there shall be a future resurrection, of which [God] has rendered the Lord Jesus Christ the first-fruits by raising him from the dead. Let us contemplate, beloved, the resurrection which is at all times taking place. Day and night declare to us a resurrection. The night sinks to sleep, and the day arises; the day again departs, and the night comes on. (St. Clement of Rome)

Mary E. Penrose, *Roots Deep and Strong*, p. 9, (1)

RESPONSORY

Living source of light and wisdom, be with us always. —**Living...**
In you we find new life; —**be with...**
Glory to you, Source of all Being, Eternal Word and Holy Spirit.
    —**Living...**

CANTICLE OF MARY

Ant. You are faithful to your promise, God of all the ages.

INTERCESSIONS and PRAYER: (from Sunday, Week IV, p. 144)

MORNING PRAYER
(Psalms from Sunday, Week IV, p. 145)

Ant 1 Seek first God's realm and way of holiness, and all else will be given you besides.

Ant 2 No one can serve two masters.

Ant 3 Christ will bring to light what is hidden in darkness and manifest the intentions of hearts.

READING

But Zion said, "The Most High has forsaken me, my God has forgotten me." Can a woman forget her nursling child, or show no compassion for the child of her womb? Even these may forget, yet I will not forget you.

Is 49:14–15

RESPONSORY

God is my stronghold, I shall not be disturbed; —**God is...**

My refuge and my salvation; —**I shall**...

Glory to you, Source of all Being, Eternal Word and Holy Spirit.
    —**God is**...

CANTICLE OF ZECHARIAH

Ant Our sole credit is from God, who has made us qualified
    ministers of a new covenant.

INTERCESSIONS (from Sunday, Week IV, p. 147)

PRAYER: Bountiful God, we are filled with wonder and gratitude
    as we strive to realize our calling to tell the message of
    the gospel with our lives. Let the promises of Christ give
    us the freedom to leave behind all that hinders the
    coming of your realm on earth. Give us the courage and
    peace of heart that comes from confidence in your care.
    Dispel the darkness of our lives with healing truth;
    make us ready for the new wine of the future. We ask
    this of you, God of time and eternity. Amen.

DAYTIME PRAYER

Ant 1 Can a woman forget her suckling child? Even these may
    forget, yet I will not forget you.

Ant 2 Our competence is from God who has made us competent
    to be ministers of a new covenant.

Ant 3 Out of the abundance of the heart the mouth speaks.

(Prayer as in Morning Prayer)

EVENING PRAYER II
(Psalms from Sunday, Week IV, p. 149)

Ant 1 I will betroth you to me in faithfulness; and you shall know
    your God.

Ant 2 Look at the birds of the air; they neither sow nor reap nor
    gather into barns, and yet your Father/Mother in heaven
    feeds them.

Ant 3 The fruit discloses the cultivation of a tree; so the
    expression of a thought discloses the cultivation of a
    person's mind.

READING

Therefore, I will now allure her, and bring her into the wilderness, and speak tenderly to her. There she shall respond as in the days of her youth, as at the time when she came out of the land of Egypt. And I will take you for my wife forever; I will take you for my wife in righteousness and in justice, in steadfast love, and in mercy. I will take you for my wife in faithfulness; and you shall know the Most High.

Hos 2:14–15, 19–20

RESPONSORY

Why look at the speck in another's eye, when you miss the
    plank in your own? —**Why look**...
How can you say to another, "Let me remove the speck from
your eye?" —**When you**...
Glory to you, Source of all Being, Eternal Word and Holy Spirit.
    —**Why look**...

CANTICLE OF MARY

Ant Each tree is known by its yield.

INTERCESSIONS (from Sunday, Week IV, p. 150)

PRAYER: Bountiful God, we are filled with wonder and gratitude as we strive to realize our calling to tell the message of the gospel with our lives. Let the promises of Christ give us the freedom to leave behind all that hinders the coming of your realm on earth. Give us the courage and peace of heart that comes from confidence in your care. Dispel the darkness of our lives with healing truth; make us ready for the new wine of the future. We ask this of you, God of time and eternity. Amen.

NINTH SUNDAY IN ORDINARY TIME

EVENING PRAYER I

(Psalms and Antiphons from Sunday, Week I, p. 1)

READING

The lives of the other ascetics he (Anthony the Great) knew became the training ground for his own practices:

He observed the graciousness of one, the earnestness at prayer in another; studied the even temper of one and the kindheartedness of another; fixed his attention on the vigils kept by one and on the studies pursued by another; admired one for his patient endurance, another for his fasting and sleeping on the ground; watched closely this person's meekness and the forbearance shown by another; and in one and all alike he marked especially devotion to Christ and the love they had for one another. (*Life of Anthony*)

Mary E. Penrose, *Roots Deep and Strong*, p. 68, (1)

RESPONSORY

You create us in your image, O God, we are co-creators with you.
   —You create...
We are nothing without you; **—we are...**
Glory to you, Source of all Being, Eternal Word and Holy Spirit.
   —You create...

CANTICLE OF MARY

Ant. I rejoice in your greatness, O God.

INTERCESSIONS and PRAYER: (from Sunday, Week I, p. 3)

MORNING PRAYER

(Psalms from Sunday, Week I, p. 3)

Ant 1 The centurion said to Jesus, "Lord, I am not worthy to have you come under my roof, but only say the word, and my servant will be healed."

Ant 2 While we live we are always being given up to death for Jesus' sake, so that the life of Jesus may be manifested in our mortal flesh.

Ant 3 You are my rock and my fortress; for your name's sake lead me and guide me.

READING

See, I am setting before you today a blessing and a curse: the blessing, if you obey the commandments of the Most High God that I am commanding you today; and the curse if you do not obey the commandments of the Most High God, but turn from the way that I am commanding you today to follow other gods that you have not known.

Deut 11:26–28

RESPONSORY

We praise your name, O God; all your servants give praise.
   —We praise...

Those who stand in your holy house; —**all your**...
Glory to you, Source of all Being, Eternal Word and Holy Spirit.
—**We praise**...

CANTICLE OF ZECHARIAH

Ant We have this treasure in earthen vessels, to show that the transcendent power belongs to God and not to us.

INTERCESSIONS (from Sunday, Week I, p. 5)

PRAYER: Eternal Wisdom, you have written your law of love in our hearts. Remove from our lives all that blinds us to your life-giving truth. Help us to transcend the fear and selfishness that would direct us away from you. Make us willing to pay the price of love that will bless the world with the mercy and healing it knew in the life of Jesus. May all that we do give praise to you now and forever. Amen.

DAYTIME PRAYER

Ant 1 For we hold that a person is justified by faith apart from works of law.

Ant 2 Observe the Sabbath day, to keep it holy, as your God, the Most High commanded you.

Ant 3 When Jesus heard this he marveled at him, saying "Not even in Israel have I found such faith."

(Prayer as in Morning Prayer)

EVENING PRAYER II
(Psalms from Sunday, Week I, p. 7)

Ant 1 Jesus said, "Not everyone who says to me, 'Lord, Lord,' shall enter the realm of heaven, but the one who does the will of God who is in heaven."

Ant 2 Am I now seeking the favor of people, or of God? If I were still pleasing people, I should not be a servant of Christ.

Ant 3 Jesus said, "Is it lawful on the sabbath to do good or to do harm, to save life or to kill?"

READING

It is the God who said, "Let light shine out of darkness," who has shone
in our hearts to give the light of the knowledge of the glory of God in the
face of Jesus Christ. But we have this treasure in clay jars, so that it
may be made clear that this extraordinary power belongs to God and
does not come from us. We are afflicted in every way, but not crushed;
perplexed, but not driven to despair; persecuted, but not forsaken;
struck down, but not destroyed; always carrying in the body the death
of Jesus, so that the life of Jesus may also be made visible in our
bodies. For while we live, we are always being given up to death for
Jesus' sake, so that the life of Jesus may be made visible in our mortal
flesh.

2 Cor 4:6–11

RESPONSORY

O God, your name endures forever; you will work justice for your people
   —O God...
You have compassion on your servants, **—you will...**
Glory to you, Source of all Being, Eternal Word and Holy Spirit.
   —O God...

CANTICLE OF MARY

Ant   The sabbath was made for the people, not the people for the
       sabbath; and so the Christ is head even of the sabbath.

INTERCESSIONS (from Sunday, Week I, p. 9)

PRAYER: Eternal Wisdom, you have written your law of love in
         our hearts. Remove from our lives all that blinds us to
         your life-giving truth. Help us to transcend the fear and
         selfishness that would direct us away from you. Make
         us willing to pay the price of love that will bless the
         world with the mercy and healing it knew in the life of
         Jesus. May all that we do give praise to you now and
         forever. Amen.

TENTH SUNDAY IN ORDINARY TIME

EVENING PRAYER I

(Psalms and Antiphons from Sunday, Week II, p. 47)

READING

In a word, SHE WHO IS discloses in an elusive female metaphor the
mystery of Sophia-God as sheer, exuberant, relational aliveness in the

midst of the history of suffering, inexhaustible source of new being in situations of death and destruction, ground of hope for the whole created universe, to practical and critical effect.

Elizabeth Johnson, She Who Is, p. 243, (2)

RESPONSORY

O God, you promise life eternal, asking only that we love. **—O God...**
You are kind to the brokenhearted; **—asking...**
Glory to you, Source of all Being, Eternal Word and Holy Spirit.
   —O God...

CANTICLE OF MARY

Ant. Most holy be your name.

INTERCESSIONS and PRAYER: (from Sunday, Week II, p. 49)

MORNING PRAYER
(Psalms from Sunday, Week II, p. 49)

Ant 1 The things that are seen are transient, but the things that are unseen are eternal.

Ant 2 Let us press on to know our God, whose going forth is sure as the dawn.

Ant 3 When Jesus saw her, he had compassion on her and said, "Do not weep."

READING

"Let us know, let us press on to know the Most High; whose appearing is as sure as the dawn; who will come to us like the showers, like the spring rains that water the earth." What shall I do with you, O Ephraim? What shall I do with you, O Judah? Your love is like a morning cloud, like the dew that goes away early.

Hos 6:3–4

RESPONSORY

From the birth of humankind, you call all people to yourself.
   —From the...
From death you raise us to new life; **—you call...**
Glory to you, Source of all Being, Eternal Word and Holy Spirit.
   —From the...

CANTICLE OF ZECHARIAH

Ant I came not to call the righteous, but sinners.

INTERCESSIONS (from Sunday, Week II, p. 51)

PRAYER: God of our history, women and men of every era tell the story of your call and your care for us. You nourish and challenge, call and direct, forgive and comfort—sheltering us in your presence every moment of our lives. Enkindle in us the faith of your prophets, the courage of your martyrs, and the love that led your Son, Jesus, to live and die for us. Let our lives continue the revelation of your goodness, you who are God forever and ever. Amen.

DAYTIME PRAYER

Ant 1 No distrust made them waver concerning the promise of God, but they grew strong in their faith as they gave glory to God.

Ant 2 Those who are well have no need of a physician, but those who are sick do.

Ant 3 How can Satan cast out Satan? If a nation is divided against itself, it cannot endure.

(Prayer as in Morning Prayer)

EVENING PRAYER II
(Psalms from Sunday, Week II, p. 53)

Ant 1 As Jesus sat at table, behold many outcasts and sinners came and sat down with him and his followers.

Ant 2 Jesus said, "I desire mercy and not sacrifice."

Ant 3 Whoever does the will of God is my brother and mother and sister.

READING

So we do not lose heart. Even though our outer nature is wasting away, our inner nature is being renewed day by day. For this slight momentary affliction is preparing us for an eternal weight of glory beyond all measure, because we look not at what can be seen but at what cannot be seen; for what can be seen is temporary, but what cannot be seen is eternal. For we know that if the earthly tent we live in is destroyed, we have a building from God, a house not made with hands, eternal in the heavens.

2 Cor 4:16–5:1

RESPONSORY

We have a building from God, a house not made with hands.
   —We have...
To last for all eternity; **—a house**...
Glory to you, Source of all Being, Eternal Word and Holy Spirit.
   —We have...

CANTICLE OF MARY

Ant   God who raised Christ Jesus will raise us also with Jesus and bring us into the presence of the Holy.

INTERCESSIONS (from Sunday, Week II, p. 55)

PRAYER: God of our history, women and men of every era tell the story of your call and your care for us. You nourish and challenge, call and direct, forgive and comfort—sheltering us in your presence every moment of our lives. Enkindle in us the faith of your prophets, the courage of your martyrs, and the love that led your Son, Jesus, to live and die for us. Let our lives continue the revelation of your goodness, you who are God forever and ever. Amen.

ELEVENTH SUNDAY IN ORDINARY TIME

EVENING PRAYER I

(Psalms and Antiphons from Sunday, Week III, p. 96)

READING

In the fashion in which life's root, placed in the ground, produces fruit in due time, and the seed cast upon the ground and decomposed, reappears multiplied by the Spirit of God which is in all things, and then those elements which in God's wisdom come to be used by [people], receiving the Word of God, become Eucharist in the body and blood of Christ, so also our bodies nourished by this Eucharist, committed to the earth and there decomposed, will rise in time because the Word of God will make them rise for the glory of God. (Irenaeus)

Mary E. Penrose, Roots Deep and Strong, p. 34, (1)

RESPONSORY

You are bountiful, O God; all of your desires for us are good. **—You are...**
Everything is a grace; **—all of...**
Glory to you, Source of all Being, Eternal Word and Holy Spirit.
   —You are...

CANTICLE OF MARY

Ant. You have shown your power; you have scattered the proud
   in their hearts' fantasy.

INTERCESSIONS and PRAYER: (from Sunday, Week III, p. 97)

MORNING PRAYER
(Psalms from Sunday, Week III, p. 98)

Ant 1 You shall be my own possession among all people.

Ant 2 So whether we are at home or away, we make it our aim to
   please our Lord Jesus Christ.

Ant 3 Jesus said to the woman, "Your faith has saved you; go in
   peace."

READING

Moses went up to God; the Most High called to him from the mountain
saying, "Thus you shall say to the house of Jacob, and tell the Israelites:
You have seen what I did to the Egyptians, and how I bore you on
eagles' wings and brought you to myself. Now therefore, if you obey my
voice and keep my covenant, you shall be my treasured possession out
of all the peoples. Indeed, the whole earth is mine, but you shall be for
me a priestly kingdom and a holy nation."

                                                              Ex 19:3–6

RESPONSORY

It is good to give thanks to you, O God, to sing praise to your name,
   Most High. **—It is...**
To declare your love in the morning; **—to sing...**
Glory to you, Source of all Being, Eternal Word and Holy Spirit.
   —It is...

CANTICLE OF ZECHARIAH

Ant We walk by faith, not by sight.

INTERCESSIONS (from Sunday, Week III, p. 100)

PRAYER: O God, Source of all good, you bless us with the revelation of yourself and risk rejection and disbelief. Bless us again with the generosity and humility to guard and nourish the seed of faith that you have planted in our hearts. Teach us how to encourage and support one another when we doubt your love and care. Our hope for salvation is in your promise. Give us the patience to await the full revelation of the mystery of your ways. May we live and die striving to be in union with you, Trinity in Unity, God forever and ever. Amen.

DAYTIME PRAYER

Ant 1 God's love is shown for us in that while we were yet sinners Christ died for us.

Ant 2 We are of good courage, and we would rather be away from the body and at home with the Lord Jesus.

Ant 3 Nathan said to David, "God has forgiven your sin; you shall not die."

(Prayer as in Morning Prayer)

EVENING PRAYER II
(Psalms from Sunday, Week III, p. 102)

Ant 1 It is no longer I who live, but Christ who lives in me.

Ant 2 When Jesus saw the crowds, he had compassion on them because they were harassed and helpless, like sheep without a shepherd.

Ant 3 With what can we compare the realm of God? It is like a grain of mustard seed.

READING

We know that a person is justified not by the works of the law but through faith in Jesus Christ. And we have come to believe in Christ Jesus, so that we might be justified by faith in Christ, and not by doing the works of the law, because no one will be justified by the works of the law. For through the law I died to the law so that I might live to God. I have been crucified with Christ; and it is no longer I who live, but it is Christ who lives in me. And the life I now live in the flesh I live by faith in the Son of God, who loved me and gave himself for me.

Gal 2:16, 19–20

RESPONSORY

You will feed your flock like a shepherd. —**You will...**
You will gather the lambs in your arms —**like a...**
Glory to you, Source of all Being, Eternal Word and Holy Spirit.
   —**You will...**

CANTICLE OF MARY

Ant We know that a person is not justified by works of the law but through faith in Jesus Christ.

INTERCESSIONS (from Sunday, Week III, p. 104)

PRAYER: O God, Source of all good, you bless us with the revelation of yourself and risk rejection and disbelief. Bless us again with the generosity and humility to guard and nourish the seed of faith that you have planted in our hearts. Teach us how to encourage and support one another when we doubt your love and care. Our hope for salvation is in your promise. Give us the patience to await the full revelation of the mystery of your ways. May we live and die striving to be in union with you, Trinity in Unity, God forever and ever. Amen.

TWELFTH SUNDAY IN ORDINARY TIME

EVENING PRAYER I

(Psalms and Antiphons from Sunday, Week IV, p. 143)

READING

When we look at the average Christian life, it would seem that the notion prevailing in the normal Christian's moral consciousness is that we have "loved our neighbor" when we have done nothing evil to him or her, and have met the objective claims he or she may justly have against us. The truth, however, is that what we are commanded by the "commandment" to love our neighbor, in its oneness with the commandment to love God, is the demolition of our own selfishness —the overthrow of the notion that love of neighbor is basically really only the rational settlement of mutual claims, that it demands only giving and taking to the mutual satisfaction of all parties. In reality, Christian love of neighbor attains its true essence only where no more accounts are kept—where a readiness prevails to love without requital—where, in the love of neighbor as well, the folly of the cross is accepted and welcomed.

Karl Rahner, The Love of Jesus and the Love of Neighbor, pp. 83–84, (2)

RESPONSORY

Lord Jesus Christ, your yoke is easy and your burden is light.
  —Lord Jesus...
In you we find rest; **—for your...**
Glory to you, Source of all Being, Eternal Word and Holy Spirit.
  —Lord Jesus...

CANTICLE OF MARY

Ant You put down the mighty from their thrones and lift up the lowly.

INTERCESSIONS (from Sunday, Week IV, p. 144)

PRAYER: Eternal God, you bless our land with flowers and fruit, and we rejoice in your goodness. But a seed has died for each thing reaped. Help us to see your creative care in our daily deaths as well as in the occasions of new life and opportunity. Help us to realize that everything is a grace. Teach us to see one another in the light of your love, living together in mutual respect and good will. Creator, Word, and Holy Spirit, make us one as you are one, now and forever. Amen.

MORNING PRAYER
(Psalms from Sunday, Week IV, p. 145)

Ant 1 In Christ Jesus you are all children of God through faith.

Ant 2 Everyone who acknowledges me before others, I also will acknowledge before God who is in heaven.

Ant 3 Jesus said to them, "But who do you say that I am?"

READING

For the love of Christ urges us on, because we are convinced that one has died for all; therefore all have died. And he died for all, so that those who live might live no longer for themselves, but for him who died and was raised for them. From now on, therefore, we regard no one from a human point of view; even though we once knew Christ from a human point of view, we know him no longer in that way. So if anyone is in Christ, there is a new creation: everything old has passed away; see, everything has become new!

2 Cor 5:14–17

RESPONSORY

Everyone who is in Christ is a new creation; the old has passed away.
  —**Everyone**...
The new has come; —**the old**...
Glory to you, Source of all Being, Eternal Word and Holy Spirit.
  —**Everyone**...

CANTICLE OF ZECHARIAH

Ant Saving your life will mean losing it, and losing your life will mean saving it.

INTERCESSIONS (from Sunday, Week IV, p. 147)

PRAYER: Eternal God, you bless our land with flowers and fruit, and we rejoice in your goodness. But a seed has died for each thing reaped. Help us to see your creative care in our daily deaths as well as in the occasions of new life and opportunity. Help us to realize that everything is a grace. Teach us to see one another in the light of your love, living together in mutual respect and good will. Creator, Word, and Holy Spirit, make us one as you are one, now and forever. Amen.

DAYTIME PRAYER

Ant 1 Sing to God; praise the Most High.

Ant 2 He died for all, that those who live might live no longer for themselves but for him.

Ant 3 God answered Job out of the whirlwind: "Who shut in the sea with doors when it burst forth from the womb?"

(Prayer as in morning prayer)

EVENING PRAYER II
(Psalms from Sunday, Week IV, p. 149)

Ant 1 Much more have the grace of God and the free gift in the grace of the Lord Jesus Christ abounded for many.

Ant 2 Who then is this, that even wind and sea obey him?

Ant 3 For you are all one in Christ Jesus.

READING

In Christ Jesus you are all children of God through faith. As many of you as were baptized into Christ have clothed yourselves with Christ. There is no longer Jew or Greek, there is no longer slave or free, there is no longer male and female; for all of you are one in Christ Jesus. And if you belong to Christ, then you are [Abraham and Sarah's] offspring, heirs according to the promise.

Gal 3:26–29

RESPONSORY

O God, I will praise you among the nations, for your love reaches to the heavens. —**O God,**...
Your faithfulness to the skies —**for your**...
Glory to you, Source of all Being, Eternal Word and Holy Spirit. —**O God,**...

CANTICLE OF MARY

Ant Why are you afraid? Have you no faith?

INTERCESSIONS (from Sunday, Week IV, p. 150)

PRAYER: Eternal God, you bless our land with flowers and fruit, and we rejoice in your goodness. But a seed has died for each thing reaped. Help us to see your creative care in our daily deaths as well as in the occasions of new life and opportunity. Help us to realize that everything is a grace. Teach us to see one another in the light of your love, living together in mutual respect and good will. Creator, Word, and Holy Spirit, make us one as you are one, now and forever. Amen.

THIRTEENTH SUNDAY IN ORDINARY TIME

EVENING PRAYER I
(Psalms and Antiphons from Sunday, Week I, p. 1)

READING

Christians have always known, in theory at least, that they can only know, make real and credible their relationship of hope and love to the incomprehensible mystery of their lives in unconditional love for their neighbor, which is the only way we can really break out of the hell of our egotism. This love for others in all the varied forms which it can take is by no means so straightforward, even without being distorted into a method of covert egotism; it is the liberating grace of God. Where this love is real, the spirit of Jesus is at work, even it if is not named, as Matthew 25 clearly teaches us. We can only say in trembling: Let us hope that the grace of God is working this miracle somewhere in ourselves! Everything depends on this, absolutely everything.

Karl Rahner, *The Practice of Faith*, p. 15, (2)

RESPONSORY

There is no limit, O God, to your love for us. **—There**...
All that you do attests **—to your**...
Glory to you, Source of all Being, Eternal Word and Holy Spirit.
   —There...

CANTICLE OF MARY

Ant This is my commandment that you love one another as I
   have loved you.

INTERCESSIONS and PRAYER: (from Sunday, Week I, p. 3)

MORNING PRAYER
(Psalms from Sunday, Week I, p. 3)

Ant 1 Christ was raised from the dead by the glory of God, that
   we, too, might walk in newness of life.

Ant 2 The woman said, "If I touch even his garments, I shall be
   made well."

Ant 3 When the days drew near for Jesus to be taken up, he set
   his face for Jerusalem.

READING

Do you not know that all of us who have been baptized into Christ Jesus were baptized into his death? Therefore we have been buried with him by baptism into death, so that, just as Christ was raised from the dead by the glory of [God], so we too might walk in newness of life. We know that Christ, being raised from the dead, will never die again; death no longer has dominion over him. The death he died, he died to sin, once for all; but the life he lives, he lives to God. So you also must consider yourselves dead to sin and alive to God in Christ Jesus.

Rom 6:3–4, 8–11

RESPONSORY

For the sake of freedom, Christ has set us free. —**For the**...
Stand fast, therefore, —**Christ has**...
Glory to you, Source of all Being, Eternal Word and Holy Spirit.
 —**For the**...

CANTICLE OF ZECHARIAH

Ant Anyone who receives you receives me, and anyone who
 receives me receives the One who sent me.

INTERCESSIONS (from Sunday, Week I, p. 5)

PRAYER: Jesus, your total trust in God through suffering and
 death is a beacon of hope for us. Protect us from deceit
 and despair that would parch our lives with fear. Turn
 our minds and hearts to the wellspring of living water,
 your Spirit within us, and let our actions bear witness
 to that Presence. Deliver us from the need to control,
 and teach us to trust in your care. So may we live in
 your peace now and forever. Amen.

DAYTIME PRAYER

Ant 1 You must consider yourselves dead to sin and alive to God
 in Christ Jesus.

Ant 2 Jesus said to the woman, "Daughter, your faith has made
 you well; go in peace."

Ant 3 As for you go and proclaim the reign of God.

(Prayer as in Morning Prayer)

EVENING PRAYER II
(Psalms from Sunday, Week I, p. 7)

Ant 1 Through love be servants of one another.

Ant 2 Do not fear, only believe.

Ant 3 If you find your life you will lose it, and if you lose your life
 for my sake you will find it.

READING

For freedom Christ has set us free. For you were called to freedom
brothers and sisters; only do not use your freedom as an opportunity for

self-indulgence, but through love become slaves to one another. For the whole law is summed up in a single commandment, "You shall love your neighbor as yourself." If, however, you bite and devour one another, take care that you are not consumed by one another. Live by the Spirit, I say, and do not gratify the desires of the flesh. For what the flesh desires is opposed to the Spirit, and what the Spirit desires is opposed to the flesh; for these are opposed to each other, to prevent you from doing what you want. But if you are led by the Spirit, you are not subject to the law.

Gal 5:1, 13–18

RESPONSORY

If we have died with Christ, we believe that we shall also live with him.
  —If we...
Death no longer has dominion over him. **—we believe**...
Glory to you, Source of all Being, Eternal Word and Holy Spirit.
  —If we...

CANTICLE OF MARY

Ant Those who put their hands to the plow and look back are not fit for the reign of God.

INTERCESSIONS (from Sunday, Week I, p. 9)

PRAYER: Jesus, your total trust in God through suffering and death is a beacon of hope for us. Protect us from deceit and despair that would parch our lives with fear. Turn our minds and hearts to the wellspring of living water, your Spirit within us, and let our actions bear witness to that Presence. Deliver us from the need to control, and teach us to trust in your care. So may we live in your peace now and forever. Amen.

FOURTEENTH SUNDAY IN ORDINARY TIME

EVENING PRAYER I

(Psalms and Antiphons from Sunday, Week II, p. 47)

READING

When one person forgives another, the change happens in the forgiving person. We say that [he or she] "relents", abandons [his or her] uptight stance. But when God forgives, it is the forgiven person's heart that is changed. Human forgiveness is the unhardening of the heart of the pardoner: divine forgiveness is the unhardening of the heart of the pardoned. This contrast is the basis of the connection between being forgiven by God and "forgiving one's [brother or sister] from the heart". For in the case of God's forgiveness, the *essence* of being forgiven is the unhardening of the heart, which is the *essence* of forgiveness of [one person] by another. That which *originates* human forgiveness, the unhardening of the heart, is *originated* by divine forgiveness.

Sebastian Moore, The Crucified Jesus Is No Stranger, p. 90, (1)

RESPONSORY

There are varieties of gifts, but the same Spirit. **—There are...**
There are varieties of service, **—but the...**
Glory to you, Source of all Being, Eternal Word and Holy Spirit.
   —There are...

CANTICLE OF MARY

Ant I will all the more boast of my weaknesses, that the power of Christ may rest upon me.

INTERCESSIONS and PRAYER: (from Sunday, Week II, p. 49)

MORNING PRAYER
(Psalms from Sunday, Week II, p. 49)

Ant 1 Let no one trouble me; for I bear on my body the marks of Jesus.

Ant 2 Many who heard Jesus were astonished, saying, "Where did this man get all this?"

Ant 3 Far be it from me to glory except in the cross of our Lord Jesus Christ.

READING

Considering the exceptional character of the revelations, therefore, to keep me from being too elated, a thorn was given me in the flesh, a messenger of Satan to torment me, to keep me from being too elated. Three times I appealed to the [Lord Jesus] about this, that it would leave me, but he said to me, "My grace is sufficient for you, for power is made perfect in weakness." So I will boast all the more gladly of my weaknesses, so that the power of Christ may dwell in me. Therefore I am content with weaknesses, insults, hardships, persecutions, and calamities for the sake of Christ; for whenever I am weak, then I am strong.

2 Cor 12:7–10

RESPONSORY

Come to me all who labor and are heavy laden, and I will give you rest.
   —Come to...
Take my yoke upon you **—and I**...
Glory to you, Source of all Being, Eternal Word and Holy Spirit.
   —Come to...

CANTICLE OF ZECHARIAH

Ant   My yoke is easy and my burden is light.

INTERCESSIONS (from Sunday, Week II, p. 51)

PRAYER: God of peace, you call us to come to you in our need, as a mother or father might beckon a distressed child. When all else may seem to betray our trust, give us the faith to turn to you with renewed hope. Your ways are mystery to us, made life-giving through the life, death, and resurrection of Jesus. In your mercy, make of us a new creation through his gospel, that our lives may praise you now and forever. Amen.

DAYTIME PRAYER

Ant 1   The one who rules shall command peace to the nations.

Ant 2   Rejoice greatly, O children of Zion.

Ant 3   The Spirit entered into me and set me upon my feet.

(Prayer as in Morning Prayer)

EVENING PRAYER II
(Psalms from Sunday, Week II, p. 53)

Ant 1   If by the Spirit you put to death your sinful addictions, you will live.

Ant 2   I am gentle and lowly in heart, and you will find rest for you souls.

Ant 3   As those who are comforted by their mother, so will I comfort you.

READING

May I never boast of anything except the cross of our Lord Jesus Christ, by which the world has been crucified to me, and I to the world.

For neither circumcision nor uncircumcision is anything; but a new creation is everything! As for those who will follow this rule—peace be upon them, and mercy, and upon the Israel of God. From now on, let no one make trouble for me; for I carry the marks of Jesus branded on my body. May the grace of our Lord Jesus Christ be with your spirit, brothers and sisters. Amen.

Gal 6:14–18

RESPONSORY

There are varieties of gifts, but the same Spirit. **—There are**...
There are varieties of service, **—but the**...
Glory to you, Source of all Being, Eternal Word and Holy Spirit.
   —There are...

CANTICLE OF MARY

Ant I will all the more boast of my weaknesses, that the power of
   Christ may rest upon me.

INTERCESSIONS (from Sunday, Week II, p. 55)

PRAYER: God of peace, you call us to come to you in our need,
   as a mother or father might beckon a distressed child.
   When all else may seem to betray our trust, give us the
   faith to turn to you with renewed hope. Your ways are
   mystery to us, made life-giving through the life, death,
   and resurrection of Jesus. In your mercy, make of us a
   new creation through his gospel, that our lives may
   praise you now and forever. Amen.

FIFTEENTH SUNDAY IN ORDINARY TIME

EVENING PRAYER I

(Psalms and Antiphons from Sunday, Week III, p. 96)

READING

When one really understands the unity of the love of God and neighbor, the latter shifts from its position as a particular demand for a delimited, verifiable achievement to a position of total fulfillment of one's life, in which we are challenged in our totality, wholly challenged, challenged beyond our capacity—but challenged in the only way in which we may gain the highest freedom: freedom from ourselves. Thus if we understand love of God and a brotherly/sisterly communion as two expressions denoting basically the same thing—and if we say "communion of brothers and sisters" rather than "love of

neighbor" because this expression is less likely than the other to be
misunderstood as a demand for a factual, neutral accomplishment that
dispenses the heart from its last obligation—then we may safely say that
with a communion of brothers and sisters, in its necessary oneness with
the love of God, we have expressed the single totality of the task of the
whole human being and of Christianity.

Karl Rahner, The Love of Jesus and the Love of Neighbor, p. 84, (2)

RESPONSORY

How great are your works, O God. Your thoughts are very deep.
   —How great...
The dull of heart will never know; **—Your thoughts...**
Glory to you, Source of all Being, Eternal Word and Holy Spirit.
   —How great...

CANTICLE OF MARY

Ant Your mercy endures through all generations.

INTERCESSIONS and PRAYER: (from Sunday, Week III, p. 97)

MORNING PRAYER
(Psalms from Sunday, Week III, p. 98)

Ant 1 I consider that the sufferings of this present time are not
worth comparing with the glory that is to be revealed in us.

Ant 2 We were chosen in Christ before the foundation of the
world, that before God we should be holy and blameless.

Ant 3 All things were created through Christ and for Christ.

READING

I consider that the sufferings of this present time are not worth
comparing with the glory about to be revealed to us. For the creation
waits with eager longing for the revealing of the children of God; for the
creation was subjected to futility, not of its own will but by the will of
the one who subjected it, in hope that the creation itself will be set free
from its bondage to decay and will obtain the freedom of the glory of the
children of God. We know that the whole creation has been groaning in
labor pains until now; and not only the creation, but we ourselves, who
have the first fruits of the Spirit, groan inwardly while we await for
adoption, the redemption of our bodies.

Rom 8:18–23

RESPONSORY

Christ Jesus is the image of the invisible God, the first-born of all creation. —**Christ Jesus**...
In him all things were created —**the first-born**...
Glory to you, Source of all Being, Eternal Word and Holy Spirit.
    —**Christ Jesus**...

CANTICLE OF ZECHARIAH

Ant You shall love God with all your heart, and with all your soul, and with all your strength, and with all your mind; and your neighbor as yourself.

INTERCESSIONS (from Sunday, Week III, p. 100)

PRAYER: Holy God, your greatness is revealed in the wonder of creation. Women and men of every race and culture tell the story of your goodness and love. Forgive us the blindness that sees the difference of color or life-style as evil. Give us the wisdom and patience to listen to one another as we share the many ways through which you call us to life. Give us the mind and heart of Jesus. This we ask in his name. Amen.

DAYTIME PRAYER

Ant 1 Turn to the Most High with all your heart and with all your soul.

Ant 2 They went out and preached that the people should repent.

Ant 3 As the rain and the snow come down from heaven, so shall my word be that goes forth from my mouth.

(Prayer as in Morning Prayer)

EVENING PRAYER II
(Psalms from Sunday, Week III, p. 102)

Ant 1 To you it has been given to know the secrets of the reign of God.

Ant 2 God destined us in love to be God's children through Jesus Christ.

Ant 3 Christ is the head of the body, the Church; he is the beginning, the firstborn from the dead.

READING

Surely, this commandment that I am commanding you today is not too hard for you, nor it is too far away. It is not in heaven, that you should say, "Who will go up to heaven for us and get it for us so that we may hear it and observe it?" Neither is it beyond the sea, that you should say, "Who will cross to the other side of the sea for us, and get it for us so that we may hear it and observe it?" No, the word is very near to you; it is in your mouth and in your heart for you to observe.

Dt 30:11–14

RESPONSORY

In Christ we have redemption through his blood, the forgiveness of our trespasses.—**In Christ**...
According to the riches of God's grace —**the forgiveness**...
Glory to you, Source of all Being, Eternal Word and Holy Spirit.
—**In Christ**...

CANTICLE OF MARY

Ant Many prophets and righteous people longed to see what you see, and did not see it, and to hear what you hear, and did not hear it.

INTERCESSIONS (from Sunday, Week III, p. 104)

PRAYER: Holy God, your greatness is revealed in the wonder of creation. Women and men of every race and culture tell the story of your goodness and love. Forgive us the blindness that sees the difference of color or life-style as evil. Give us the wisdom and patience to listen to one another as we share the many ways through which you call us to life. Give us the mind and heart of Jesus. This we ask in his name. Amen.

SIXTEENTH SUNDAY IN ORDINARY TIME
EVENING PRAYER I
(Psalms and Antiphons from Sunday, Week IV, p. 143)

READING

Both in my life and in my thinking I keep finding myself in situations of confusion which cannot be "cleared up." At first even I feel that one just has to carry on, even if one doesn't know where it's all leading. I feel that one must just keep quiet when one can't speak clearly, that carrying on in ordinary honesty is the only appropriate attitude for human beings, and the most that can be expected of us. But then I find I cannot avoid or keep silent about the question of what underlies this carrying on. What I find when I ask that question is the hope which accepts no limits as final. This hope concentrates all our experience into two words, "mystery" and "death." "Mystery" means confusion in hope, but "death" orders us not to disguise the confusion, but to endure it. I look at Jesus on the cross and know that I am spared nothing. I place myself (I hope) in his death and so hope that this shared death is the dawn of the blessed mystery.

Karl Rahner, *The Practice of Faith*, p. 17, (2)

RESPONSORY

Look upon us graciously, O God, and have mercy on us. —**Look**...
For you are our source of love; —**have**...
Glory to you, Source of all Being, Eternal Word and Holy Spirit. —**Look**...

CANTICLE OF MARY

Ant I long for you, God of my life.

INTERCESSIONS and PRAYER: (from Sunday, Week IV, p. 144)

MORNING PRAYER
(Psalms from Sunday, Week IV, p. 145)

Ant 1 I rejoice in my sufferings for your sake, and in my flesh I complete what is lacking in Christ's afflictions for the sake of his body, the Church.

Ant 2 He had compassion on them, because they were like sheep without a shepherd.

Ant 3 For Christ is our peace, who has made us one.

READING

Likewise the Spirit helps us in our weakness; for we do not know how to pray as we ought, but that very Spirit intercedes with sighs too deep for words. And God who searches the heart, knows what is the mind of the Spirit, because the Spirit intercedes for the saints according to the will of God.

Rom 8:26–27

RESPONSORY

The Spirit helps us in our weakness; for we do not know how to pray as
    we ought.—**The Spirit**...
God's own Spirit intercedes for us with sighs too deep for words.
    —for we...
Glory to you, Source of all Being, Eternal Word and Holy Spirit.
    —The Spirit...

CANTICLE OF ZECHARIAH

Ant The righteous will shine like the sun in the realm of God.

INTERCESSIONS (from Sunday, Week IV, p. 147)

PRAYER: God, our Creator, for two-thousand years the words
of your Christ have leavened our world, yet much of
humankind remains hardened and unaffected by his
life and message of love. Awaken in us the spirit of
discipleship. Help us to renew and deepen our
commitment to live the gospel. Let our lives so
radiantly reflect your own that others will long to know
and love you and your divine Son, Jesus Christ, who
lives with you and the Holy Spirit, now and forever.
Amen.

DAYTIME PRAYER

Ant 1 You have filled your children with good hope, because you
give repentance for sins.

Ant 2 In that day Judah will be saved, and Israel will dwell
securely.

Ant 3 Mary sat at Jesus' feet and listened to his teaching.

(Prayer as in Morning Prayer)

EVENING PRAYER II
(Psalms from Sunday, Week IV, p. 149)

Ant 1 The Spirit intercedes for the saints according to the will of God.

Ant 2 Thus says our God, "I will gather the remnant of my flock and they shall be fruitful and multiply."

Ant 3 Mary has chosen the good portion, which shall not be taken away from her.

READING

But now in Christ Jesus you who once were far off have been brought near by the blood of Christ. For he is our peace; in his flesh he has made both groups into one and has broken down the dividing wall, that is, the hostility between us. He has abolished the law with its commandments and ordinances, that he might create in himself one new humanity in place of the two, thus making peace, and might reconcile both groups to God in one body through the cross, thus putting to death that hostility through it. So he came and proclaimed peace to you who were far off and peace to those who were near; for through him both of us have access in one Spirit to [God].

Eph 2:13–18

RESPONSORY

Come away by yourselves to a lonely place, and rest a while.
  —**Come away**...
Jesus began to teach them many things —**rest**...
Glory to you, Source of all Being, Eternal Word and Holy Spirit.
  —**Come away**...

CANTICLE OF MARY

Ant In Christ Jesus, you who were once far off have been brought near in the blood of Christ.

INTERCESSIONS (from Sunday, Week IV, p. 150)

PRAYER: God, our Creator, for two-thousand years the words of your Christ have leavened our world, yet much of humankind remains hardened and unaffected by his life and message of love. Awaken in us the spirit of discipleship. Help us to renew and deepen our commitment to live the gospel. Let our lives so radiantly reflect your own that others will long to know and love you and your divine Son, Jesus Christ, who lives with you and the Holy Spirit, now and forever. Amen.

SEVENTEENTH SUNDAY IN ORDINARY TIME
EVENING PRAYER I
(Psalms and Antiphons from Sunday, Week I, p. 1)

READING

To come together to celebrate, rest, delight, sense the presence of God in all things, and taste the promise offered by the resurrection of Christ is to engage in profound opposition to destructive forces. In our day the humanocentrism of much of christology is expanding toward a cosmic vision of the significance of Jesus Christ. Both the example of Jesus and Spirit christologies point the way toward a new, urgently needed appreciation of the universality of reconciliation at work in our world through Christ. The promise of that redemption is meant for all the peoples of the world and for the whole cosmos itself.

Elizabeth A. Johnson, *Consider Jesus*, p. 143, (2)

RESPONSORY

I have seen the glory of God in the land of the living. —**I have**...
You are with us always; —**in the**...
Glory to you, Source of all Being, Eternal Word and Holy Spirit.
     —**I have**...

CANTICLE OF MARY

Ant Yours is the heavens and yours is the earth.

INTERCESSIONS and PRAYER: (from Sunday, Week I, p. 3)

MORNING PRAYER
(Psalms from Sunday, Week I, p. 3)

Ant 1 Father/Mother, hallowed be your name. Your kindom come.

Ant 2 There is one body and one Spirit, just as you were called to the one hope that belongs to your call.

Ant 3 You were buried with Christ in baptism, also raised with him through faith.

READING

I therefore, the prisoner in the [Lord Jesus], beg you to lead a life worthy of the calling to which you have been called, with all humility and gentleness, with patience, bearing with one another in love, making every effort to maintain the unity of the Spirit in the bond of peace. There is one body and one Spirit, just as you were called to the one hope of your calling, one Christ, one faith, one baptism, one God and [Maker] of us all, who is above all and through all and in all.

Eph 4:1–6

RESPONSORY

Lead a life worthy of the calling to which you have been called.
  —Lead a...
With all lowliness and meekness, with patience, forbearing one
  another in love; **—worthy...**
Glory to you, Source of all Being, Eternal Word and Holy Spirit.
  —Lead a...

CANTICLE OF ZECHARIAH

Ant The realm of heaven is like a merchant, who, on finding one
  pearl of great value, went and sold all and bought it.

INTERCESSIONS (from Sunday, Week I, p. 5)

PRAYER: God of truth, our needs are many, but too often our
  wants outnumber them. Give us the wisdom to discern
  one from the other. Give us a hunger for the things that
  promote goodness, truth, and justice in our daily lives.
  Protect us from dangerous and foolish directions, and
  help us to make choices that employ our time and
  energy for the good of all. So may your kindom come,
  to the praise and glory of your name. Amen.

DAYTIME PRAYER

Ant 1 The Most High appeared to Solomon in a dream by night;
  and God said, "Ask what I shall give you."

Ant 2 This is indeed the prophet who is to come into the world.

Ant 3 Every scribe who has been trained for the realm of heaven
  is like a householder who brings out of a treasure new
  things and old.

(Prayer as in Morning Prayer)

EVENING PRAYER II
(Psalms from Sunday, Week I, p. 7)

Ant 1 The realm of heaven is like a treasure hidden in a field, which a person found and covered up; who then in joy goes and sells all and buys that field.

Ant 2 There is one Christ, one faith, one baptism, one God and maker, Father/Mother, of us all.

Ant 3 Ask, and it shall be given you, seek, and you shall find, knock, and it shall be opened to you.

READING

When you were buried with Christ Jesus in baptism, you were also raised with him through faith in the power of God, who raised him from the dead. And when you were dead in trespasses and the uncircumcision of your flesh, God made you alive together with him, when [Jesus] forgave us all our trespasses, erasing the record that stood against us with its legal demands. He set this aside nailing it to the cross.

Col 2:12–14

RESPONSORY

In your mercy, O God, give your servant an understanding mind.
   —In your...
That I may discern between good and evil; **—give your**...
Glory to you, Source of all Being, Eternal Word and Holy Spirit.
   —In your...

CANTICLE OF MARY

Ant Give us each day our daily bread; and forgive us our sins.

INTERCESSIONS (from Sunday, Week I, p. 9)

PRAYER: God of truth, our needs are many, but too often our wants outnumber them. Give us the wisdom to discern one from the other. Give us a hunger for the things that promote goodness, truth, and justice in our daily lives. Protect us from dangerous and foolish directions, and help us to make choices that employ our time and energy for the good of all. So may your kindom come, to the praise and glory of your name. Amen.

EIGHTEENTH SUNDAY IN ORDINARY TIME

EVENING PRAYER I
(Psalms and Antiphons from Sunday, Week II, p. 47)

READING

...the Eucharist sets us on the way to a future we have to build. During its celebration we realize sacramentally the one body of Christ we do not yet manage to realize in the concreteness of our everyday life. Every time this celebration occurs we experience the tension between the past, the present, and the future. We remember now what happened before in view of the future to come. Our future is bound up with that past. Celebrating the Eucharist we go back to a past that we have to turn into our future. It is not without reason that the Eucharist is often called "Mass," or mission. We are on a mission.

Joseph G. Donders, *Risen Life*, p. 67, (22)

RESPONSORY

You know our frailty, O God; give us your strength; —**You**...
You fill us with hope; —**give**...
Glory to you, Source of all Being, Eternal Word and Holy Spirit.
   —**You**...

CANTICLE OF MARY

Ant Where your treasure is, there will your heart be also.

INTERCESSIONS and PRAYER: (from Sunday, Week II, p. 49)

MORNING PRAYER
(Psalms from Sunday, Week II, p. 49)

Ant 1 Let everyone who thirsts, come to the water.

Ant 2 Be renewed in the spirit of your minds, and put on the new nature created after the likeness of God.

Ant 3 Your life does not consist in the abundance of your possessions.

READING

Who will separate us from the love of Christ? Will hardship or distress, or persecution, or famine, or nakedness, or peril, or sword? No, in all these things we are more than conquerors through him who loved us. For I am convinced that neither death, nor life, nor angels, nor rulers, nor things present, not things to come, nor powers, nor height, nor depth, nor anything else in all creation will be able to separate us from the love of God in Christ Jesus our Lord.

Rom 8:35, 37–39

RESPONSORY

O God, you are my God, I long for you. **—O God**...
As in a dry and weary land without water; **—I long**...
Glory to you, Source of all Being, Eternal Word and Holy Spirit.
  —O God...

CANTICLE OF ZECHARIAH

Ant Do not labor for the food which perishes, but for the food which endures to eternal life.

INTERCESSIONS (from Sunday, Week II, p. 51)

PRAYER: O God, you challenge us to seek what eyes cannot see and ears cannot hear. Help us to keep our eyes on Jesus, to ponder his words, and to be serious about living his challenge of love. Let our words and actions be nourishment and delight for others, giving them the inspiration to love you and the courage to follow your will. So may we praise you now and in eternity. Amen.

DAYTIME PRAYER

Ant 1 You shall know that I am your God.

Ant 2 When Jesus saw the great crowd, he had compassion on them and healed their sick.

Ant 3 Set your minds on things above, not on things that are below.

(Prayer as in Morning Prayer)

EVENING PRAYER II
(Psalms from Sunday, Week II, p. 53)

Ant 1 When Christ our life appears, then we will also appear with him in glory.

Ant 2 This is the work of God, that you believe in the One whom God has sent.

Ant 3 Incline your ear, and come to me; hear, that your soul may live.

READING

Now this I affirm and insist on in the Lord Jesus: you must no longer live as the Gentiles live, in the futility of their minds. That is not the way you learned Christ! For surely you have heard about him and were taught in him, as truth is in Jesus. You were taught to put away your former way of life, your old self, corrupt and deluded by its lusts, and to be renewed in the spirit of your minds, and to clothe yourselves with the new self created according to the likeness of God in true righteousness and holiness.

Eph 4:17, 20–24

RESPONSORY

Hear my voice, O God, in your steadfast love; —**Hear my**...
In your justice preserve my life; —**in your**...
Glory to you, Source of all Being, Eternal Word and Holy Spirit.
   —**Hear my**...

CANTICLE OF MARY

Ant Here there cannot be Greek and Jew, alien, slave or free person, but Christ is all and in all.

INTERCESSIONS (from Sunday, Week II, p. 55)

PRAYER: O God, you challenge us to seek what eyes cannot see and ears cannot hear. Help us to keep our eyes on Jesus, to ponder his words, and to be serious about living his challenge of love. Let our words and actions be nourishment and delight for others, giving them the inspiration to love you and the courage to follow your will. So may we praise you now and in eternity. Amen.

NINETEENTH SUNDAY IN ORDINARY TIME
EVENING PRAYER I
(Antiphons and Psalms from Sunday, Week III, p. 96)

READING

Jesus takes on himself our guilt-entangled history, but, through his voluntary obedience and his vicarious service, gives it a new quality and establishes a new beginning. The history of disobedience, of hatred, and lying is brought to a halt in his obedience and service. Even more: in his suffering and dying on the cross, where his obedience and service reach their supreme perfection, those powers of injustice wear themselves out on him and rush to their death; since he does not respond to them, he swallows them up—so to speak—in his death. His death is the death of death, the death of injustice and lying. Jesus Christ then is not only a member of humankind, but the beginning of a new humanity.

Walter Kasper, *Jesus the Christ*, p. 218, (1)

RESPONSORY

You are the good shepherd, have compassion on us. —**You are**...
In you we find mercy; —**have**...
Glory to you, Source of all Being, Eternal Word and Holy Spirit.
   —**You are**...

CANTICLE OF MARY

Ant Be dressed for action and have your lamps lit.

INTERCESSIONS and PRAYER: (from Sunday, Week III, p. 97)

MORNING PRAYER
(Psalms from Sunday, Week III, p. 98)

Ant 1 God who is over all will be blessed forever.

Ant 2 Be kind to one another, tenderhearted, forgiving one another, as God in Christ forgave you.

Ant 3 Fear not, little flock, for it is God's good pleasure to open to you the reign of God.

READING

Do not grieve the Holy Spirit of God, with which you were marked with a seal for the day of redemption. Put away from you all bitterness and wrath and anger and wrangling and slander, together with all malice, and be kind to one another, tenderhearted, forgiving one another, as God in Christ has forgiven you. Therefore be imitators of God, as beloved children, and live in love, as Christ loved us and gave himself up for us, a fragrant offering and sacrifice to God.

Eph 4:30–5:2

RESPONSORY

Make me know your ways, O God; teach me your paths. —**Make me**...
Lead me in your truth; —**teach**...

Glory to you, Source of all Being, Eternal Word and Holy Spirit.
—**Make me**...

CANTICLE OF ZECHARIAH

Ant Lord, if it is you, bid me come to you over the water.

INTERCESSIONS (from Sunday, Week III, p. 100)

PRAYER: O God, we are no better than our ancestors, for we, too, seek you in signs and wonders. Give us the precious gift of seeing you in the ordinary events of each day—in joy and in sorrow. Help us to create a world in which there is time for all to listen for your call that leads to growth and holiness. Let the real wonder of your constant presence give us the courage to walk steadfastly in the way of faith, hope, and love. So may we truly be sisters and brothers of your son and our Lord, Jesus Christ now and forever. Amen.

DAYTIME PRAYER

Ant 1 Faith is the assurance of things hoped for, the conviction of things not seen.

Ant 2 You cannot come to me unless the One who sent me draws you; and I will raise you up on the last day.

Ant 3 If you have faith as a grain of mustard seed, nothing will be impossible to you.

(Prayer as in Morning Prayer)

EVENING PRAYER II
(Psalms from Sunday, Week III, p. 102)

Ant 1 Truly I say to you, those who believe have eternal life.

Ant 2 God, who has prepared for them a city, is not ashamed to be called their God.

Ant 3 For where your treasure is, there will your heart be also.

READING

I am speaking the truth in Christ—I am not lying; my conscience confirms it by the Holy Spirit—I have great sorrow and unceasing anguish in my heart. For I could wish that I myself were accursed and cut off from Christ for the sake of my own people, my kindred according to the flesh. They are Israelites, and to them belong the adoption, the glory, the covenants, the giving of the law, the worship, and the promises; to them belong the [patriarchs and matriarchs], and from them, according to the flesh, comes the Messiah, who is over all, God blessed forever. Amen.

Rom 9:1–5

RESPONSORY

O God, you are good and upright; you instruct sinners in your way.
   —O God...
You lead the humble in a straight path; **—you instruct...**
Glory to you, Source of all Being, Eternal Word and Holy Spirit.
   —O God...

CANTICLE OF MARY

Ant Be imitators of God, as beloved children, and walk in love, as Christ loved us and gave himself up for us.

INTERCESSIONS (from Sunday, Week III, p. 104)

PRAYER: O God, we are no better than our ancestors, for we, too, seek you in signs and wonders. Give us the precious gift of seeing you in the ordinary events of each day—in joy and in sorrow. Help us to create a world in which there is time for all to listen for your call that leads to growth and holiness. Let the real wonder of your constant presence give us the courage to walk steadfastly in the way of faith, hope, and love. So may we truly be sisters and brothers of your son and our Lord, Jesus Christ now and forever. Amen.

TWENTIETH SUNDAY IN ORDINARY TIME

EVENING PRAYER I

(Psalms and Antiphons from Sunday, Week IV, p. 143)

READING

Christian faith is of the conviction that only love for God and human beings, which is more than a commandment and obligatory exercise, brings human beings to salvation. It has the conviction that this love is the meaning of the whole of the Law and the Prophets, but that it can occur even in the humble, ordinary everyday—and that it is just there, in the everyday, unobtrusively, that the last renunciation and the last surrender to God can occur that admits us to a participation in the final deed of Jesus on the cross. A love of neighbor as one's brother and sister, a communion of brothers and sisters having a love for God both as its vehicle and as its consummation, is the highest thing of all. And this highest thing of all is a possibility, an opportunity, offered to every human being.

Karl Rahner, The Love of Jesus and the Love of Neighbor, pp. 103–104, (2)

RESPONSORY

Your love is round about me; in you I find my life.—**Your love**...
Forever I will sing your praise; —**in you**...
Glory to you, Source of all Being, Eternal Word and Holy Spirit.
  —**Your love**...

CANTICLE OF MARY

Ant Love your enemies, do good, and lend, expecting nothing in return.

INTERCESSIONS and PRAYER: (from Sunday, Week IV, p. 144)

MORNING PRAYER
(Psalms from Sunday, Week IV, p. 145)

Ant 1 I have a baptism to be baptized with; and how I am constrained until it is accomplished.

Ant 2 Address one another in psalms and hymns and spiritual songs, making melody to God with all your heart.

Ant 3 For the gifts and the call of God are irrevocable.

READING

The gifts and the calling of God are irrevocable. Just as you were once disobedient to God but have now received mercy because of their disobedience, so they have now been disobedient in order that, by the mercy shown to you, they too may now receive mercy. For God has imprisoned all in disobedience so that [God] may be merciful to all.

Rom 11:29–32

RESPONSORY

Hear my cry, O God, listen to my prayer. —**Hear my**...
From the end of the earth I call; —**listen**...
Glory to you, Source of all Being, Eternal Word and Holy Spirit.
  —**Hear my**...

CANTICLE OF ZECHARIAH

Ant I came to cast fire upon the earth, and would that it were already kindled!

INTERCESSIONS (from Sunday, Week IV, p. 147)

PRAYER: Lord Jesus, you gave yourself fully to spread the message of your Good News, but even the best of your disciples were slow to understand the meaning of it all. You rejoiced when a woman or man met you with full faith and total commitment. Lord, give us the joy of delighting you so. Give us faith that will energize us for total dedication to you and the sharing of your message. So may your word of love live on through us now and forever. Amen.

DAYTIME PRAYER

Ant 1 Keep justice, and do righteousness, for soon my salvation will come.

Ant 2 Wisdom has built her house, she has set up her seven pillars.

Ant 3 Let us run with perseverance the race that is set before us, looking to Jesus, the pioneer and the perfector of our faith.

(Prayer as in Morning Prayer)

EVENING PRAYER II
(Psalms from Sunday, Week IV, p. 149)

Ant 1 Jesus said to her, "O woman, great is your faith! Be it done for you as you desire."

Ant 2 Those who eat my flesh and drink my blood abide in me and I in them.

Ant 3 For the joy that was set before him, Jesus endured the cross, despising the shame, and is seated beside the throne of God.

READING

Therefore, since we are surrounded by so great a cloud of witnesses, let us also lay aside every weight and the sin that clings so closely, and let us run with perseverance the race that is set before us, looking to Jesus the pioneer and perfector of our faith, who for the sake of the joy that was set before him endured the cross, disregarding its shame, and has taken his seat by the side of the throne of God. Consider him who endured such hostility against himself from sinners, so that you may not grow weary or lose heart. In your struggle against sin you have not yet resisted to the point of shedding your blood.

Heb 12:1–4

RESPONSORY

I will put my Spirit within you, and you shall be my people. —**I will**...
You will live by my statutes; —**and you**...
Glory to you, Source of all Being, Eternal Word and Holy Spirit.
　　—**I will**...

CANTICLE OF MARY

Ant　The bread that I shall give for the life of the world is my
　　　flesh.

INTERCESSIONS (from Sunday, Week IV, p. 150)

PRAYER:　Lord Jesus, you gave yourself fully to spread the
　　　　　message of your Good News, but even the best of your
　　　　　disciples were slow to understand the meaning of it
　　　　　all. You rejoiced when a woman or man met you with
　　　　　full faith and total commitment. Lord, give us the joy
　　　　　of delighting you so. Give us faith that will energize
　　　　　us for total dedication to you and the sharing of your
　　　　　message. So may your word of love live on through us
　　　　　now and forever. Amen.

TWENTY-FIRST SUNDAY IN ORDINARY TIME

EVENING PRAYER I

(Psalms and Antiphons from Sunday, Week I, p. 1)

READING

No member of the Mystical Body of Christ is alive for himself or herself alone. Each has a function of service to perform for the others, even for those members who are still merely "potential"—since these too have a true, and in a way already actual, relationship, through the Incarnation and the universal salvific will of God, to those who are members of the Church in all the dimensions of their life and in all the dimensions of the Church. Thus the primary subject of full missionary authority and initiative, and of the missionary task, is the Christian as Christian.

Karl Rahner, *The Practice of Faith*, p. 102, (2)

RESPONSORY

Keep us, O God, on the path to life. —**Keep us**...
May your hand ever guide us; —**on the**...
Glory to you, Source of all Being, Eternal Word and Holy Spirit.
  —**Keep us**...

CANTICLE OF MARY

Ant Abide in me as I abide in you.

INTERCESSIONS and PRAYER: (from Sunday, Week I, p.3)

MORNING PRAYER
(Psalms from Sunday, Week I, p. 3)

Ant 1 Behold, some are last who will be first, and some are first who will be last.

Ant 2 It is the Spirit that gives life, the flesh is of no avail; the words that I have spoken to you are spirit and life.

Ant 3 To God be the glory forever, from whom and through whom and to whom all things are.

READING

O the depth of the riches and wisdom and knowledge of God! How unsearchable are [God's] judgments and how inscrutable [God's] ways! "For who has known the mind of [our God]? Or who has been [God's] counselor?" "Or who has given a gift to [God], to receive a gift in return?" For from whom and through whom and to whom all things are. To God be the glory forever. Amen.

Rom 11:33–36

RESPONSORY

My heart stands in awe of your words, as one who finds great treasure.
  —**My heart**...
I rejoice in your salvation; —**as one**...
Glory to you, Source of all Being, Eternal Word and Holy Spirit.
  —**My heart**...

CANTICLE OF ZECHARIAH

Ant Many of Jesus' companions, on hearing his words, said, "This is a hard saying; who can listen to it?"

INTERCESSIONS (from Sunday, Week I, p. 5)

PRAYER: Lord Jesus, the salvation to which you call us leads us from life, through death, to new life. Our frailty tempts us to hide from the cross and to seek an easy way. Keep us faithful to the celebration of the Eucharist and all of the mysteries of your life. Help us to build our lives on the firm foundation of your Good News, that grounded in your truth we may be worthy children of God now and forever. Amen.

DAYTIME PRAYER

Ant 1 I will place on his shoulder the key of the house of David; he shall open and none shall shut; and he shall shut, and none shall open.

Ant 2 As for me and my house, we will serve the Most High.

Ant 3 I am coming to gather all nations and tongues; and they shall come and shall see my glory.

(Prayer as in Morning Prayer)

EVENING PRAYER II
(Psalms from Sunday, Week I, p. 7)

Ant 1 Who has known the mind of God, or has given God counsel?

Ant 2 Lord, to whom shall we go? You have the words of eternal life.

Ant 3 Strive to enter by the narrow door; for many, I tell you, will seek to enter and will not be able.

READING

Endure trials for the sake of discipline. God is treating you as children; for what child is there whom a parent does not discipline? Now discipline always seems painful rather than pleasant at the time, but later it yields the peaceful fruit of righteousness to those who have been trained by it. Therefore lift your drooping hands and strengthen your

weak knees, and make straight paths for your feet, so that what is lame
may not be put out of joint, but rather be healed.

Heb 12:7, 11–13

RESPONSORY

My heart stands in awe of your words, as one who finds great treasure.
  —**My heart**...
I rejoice in your salvation; —**as one**...
Glory to you, Source of all Being, Eternal Word and Holy Spirit.
  —**My heart**...

CANTICLE OF MARY

Ant O the depth of the riches and wisdom and knowledge of God!
      How unsearchable God's judgments and how inscrutable
      God's ways!

INTERCESSIONS (from Sunday, Week I, p. 9)

PRAYER: Lord Jesus, the salvation to which you call us leads us
        from life, through death, to new life. Our frailty tempts
        us to hide from the cross and to seek an easy way.
        Keep us faithful to the celebration of the Eucharist and
        all of the mysteries of your life. Help us to build our
        lives on the firm foundation of your Good News, that
        grounded in your truth we may be worthy children of
        God now and forever. Amen.

TWENTY-SECOND SUNDAY IN ORDINARY TIME

EVENING PRAYER I

(Psalms and Antiphons from Sunday, Week II, p. 47)

READING

Pure contemplation is indescribable,...and on this account called
"secret". Not for this reason alone do we call mystical wisdom "secret"
—and it is actually so—but also because it has the characteristic of
hiding the soul within itself. Besides its usual effect, this mystical
wisdom occasionally so engulfs souls in its secret abyss that they
have the keen awareness of being brought into a place far removed from
every creature. They accordingly feel that they have been led into a
remarkably deep and vast wilderness unattainable by any human
creature, into an immense, unbounded desert, the more delightful,
savorous, and loving, the deeper, vaster, and more solitary it is.

John of the Cross, The Dark Night, II.17:5,6, (3)

RESPONSORY

You lead us into the desert and there speak to our souls; —**You lead**...
Into the depths of our hearts; —**and there**...
Glory to you, Source of all Being, Eternal Word and Holy Spirit.
   —**You lead**...

CANTICLE OF MARY

Ant I will allure you and bring you into the wilderness and there
    speak tenderly to you.

INTERCESSIONS and PRAYER: (from Sunday, Week II, p. 49)

MORNING PRAYER
(Psalms from Sunday, Week II, p. 49)

Ant 1 Do not be conformed to this world but be transformed by
    the renewal of your mind.

Ant 2 For what great nation is there that has a god so near to it
    as our God is to us, answering whenever we call.

Ant 3 For great is the might of our God who is glorified by the
    humble.

READING

I appeal to you therefore, brothers and sisters, by the mercies of God, to
present your bodies as a living sacrifice, holy and acceptable to God,
which is your spiritual worship. Do not be conformed to this world, but
be transformed by the renewing of your minds, so that you may discern
what is the will of God—what is good and acceptable and perfect.

Rom 12:1–2

RESPONSORY

With all my heart I cry to you; answer me, O God. —**With all**...
That I may observe your will; —**answer**...
Glory to you, Source of all Being, Eternal Word and Holy Spirit.
   —**With all**...

CANTICLE OF ZECHARIAH

Ant Those who exalt themselves will be humbled, and those who
    humble themselves will be exalted.

INTERCESSIONS (from Sunday, Week II, p. 51)

PRAYER: O God, our generations are blessed with length of life longed for in ancient biblical times, but it is not an unmixed blessing. Give courage and patience to the elderly and to all who experience loss, helplessness, and confusion in so many ways. Endow with compassion and ingenuity all who minister to them. Let those who care for the dying make their last days a loving preparation to meet you face to face, our God—Creator, Redeemer, and Holy Spirit, now and forever. Amen.

DAYTIME PRAYER

Ant 1 You have come to Mount Zion and the heavenly Jerusalem.

Ant 2 Present your bodies as a living sacrifice, holy and acceptable to God, which is your spiritual worship.

Ant 3 Be doers of the word, and not hearers only, deceiving yourselves.

(Prayer as in Morning Prayer)

EVENING PRAYER II
(Psalms from Sunday, Week II, p. 53)

Ant 1 For if you would save your life, you will lose it, and if you lose your life for my sake, you will find it.

Ant 2 Receive with meekness the implanted word, which is able to save your souls.

Ant 3 When you are invited, go and sit in the lowest place.

READING

You have not come to something that can be touched, a blazing fire, and darkness, and gloom, and a tempest, and the sound of a trumpet, and a voice whose words made the hearers beg that not another word be spoken to them. But you have come to Mount Zion and to the city of the living God, the heavenly Jerusalem, and to innumerable angels in festal gathering, and to the assembly of the firstborn who are enrolled in heaven, and to God the judge of all, and to the spirits of the righteous made perfect, and to Jesus, the mediator of a new covenant, and to the sprinkled blood that speaks a better word than the blood of Abel.

Heb 12:18–19. 22–24

RESPONSORY

With contrite heart and humble spirit, O God, let us be received.
—**With contrite...**
Those who trust in you cannot be put to shame; —**let us...**
Glory to you, Source of all Being, Eternal Word and Holy Spirit.
—**With contrite...**

CANTICLE OF MARY

Ant Every good endowment and every perfect gift is from above.

INTERCESSIONS (from Sunday, Week II, p. 55)

PRAYER: O God, our generations are blessed with length of life longed for in ancient biblical times, but it is not an unmixed blessing. Give courage and patience to the elderly and to all who experience loss, helplessness, and confusion in so many ways. Endow with compassion and ingenuity all who minister to them. Let those who care for the dying make their last days a loving preparation to meet you face to face, our God—Creator, Redeemer, and Holy Spirit, now and forever. Amen.

TWENTY-THIRD SUNDAY IN ORDINARY TIME

EVENING PRAYER I

(Psalms and Antiphons from Sunday, Week III, p. 96)

READING

The Christian should...be able to understand his or her earthly calling as a heavenly vocation.... All divine vocations, however they may be thought of, are summonses, vocations, to complement the descent of the eternal God into flesh. They are always vocations to earthly ordinariness and death, vocations to believe in the light shining in the darkness, to actualize love that seems to go unrewarded and unrequited, to enter into solidarity with the poor and the "shortchanged"—the brothers and sisters of Jesus Christ who are anything but the elite, and seem rather to belong to some sort of hideous, mass-produced humanity. Only through the performance of this task as a mission to "those below" does the Christian really accomplish his or her radical surrender to God's incomprehensibility as a beatifying surrender through faith, hope, and love.

Karl Rahner, *The Practice of Faith*, p. 207, (2)

RESPONSORY

Teach us to number our days that we may gain wisdom of heart.
  —**Teach**...
Let your works be manifest in us; —**that we**...
Glory to you, Source of all Being, Eternal Word and Holy Spirit.
  —**Teach**...

CANTICLE OF MARY

Ant You who are mighty have done great things for me.

INTERCESSIONS and PRAYER: (from Sunday, Week III, p. 97)

MORNING PRAYER
(Psalms from Sunday, Week III, p. 98)

Ant 1 Love is the fulfillment of the law.

Ant 2 God has chosen those who are poor in the world to be rich in faith and heirs of the realm of God.

Ant 3 If you do not bear your own cross and come after me, you cannot be my disciple.

READING

Owe no one anything, except to love one another; for the one who loves another has fulfilled the law. The commandments, "You shall not commit adultery; You shall not murder; You shall not steal; You shall not covet"; and any other commandment, are summed up in this word, "Love your neighbor as yourself." Love does no wrong to a neighbor; therefore, love is the fulfilling of the law.

Rom 13:8–10

RESPONSORY

Let your hand, O God, be on those you have chosen, those
  you make strong for yourself. —**Let your**...
Then we will never forsake you; —**those**...
Glory to you, Source of all Being, Eternal Word and Holy Spirit.
  —**Let your**...

CANTICLE OF ZECHARIAH

Ant If you do not renounce all that you have, you cannot be my disciple.

INTERCESSIONS (from Sunday, Week III, p. 100)

PRAYER: O God, we thank you for your inspired word that guides us and lights our way to you. We praise you for our own ability to speak, to communicate with one another, to establish understanding and to make peace. Help us never to abuse this precious gift. Give our words the power to comfort, heal, guide, and to tell the Good News of Jesus, sounding a song of creative love throughout the world. We ask this through the same Jesus Christ, your word and message of salvation to us all now, and forever. Amen.

DAYTIME PRAYER

Ant 1 Owe no one anything except to love one another; for by loving your neighbor, you have fulfilled the law.

Ant 2 Waters shall break forth in the wilderness, and streams in the desert.

Ant 3 Who can learn the counsel of God? Who can discern what God wills?

(Prayer as in Morning Prayer)

EVENING PRAYER II
(Psalms from Sunday, Week III, p. 102)

Ant 1 Where two or three are gathered in my name, there am I in the midst of them.

Ant 2 He has done all things well; he even makes the deaf hear and the mute speak.

Ant 3 Whatever you bind on earth shall be bound in heaven; and whatever you loose on earth shall be loosed in heaven.

READING

For who can learn the counsel of God? Or who can discern what [God] wills? For the reasoning of mortals is worthless, and our designs are likely to fail; for a perishable body weighs down the soul, and this earthly tent burdens the thoughtful mind. We can hardly guess at what is on earth, and what is at hand we find with such labor; but who has traced out what is in the heavens? Who has learned your counsel, unless you have given wisdom and sent your holy spirit from on high?

And thus the paths of those on earth were set right, and people were taught what pleases you, and were saved by wisdom.

Wis 9:13–18

RESPONSORY

Let my cry come before you, O God; give me discernment
   according to your word. —**Let my**...
Deliver me as you have promised; —**give me**...
Glory to you, Source of all Being, Eternal Word and Holy Spirit.
   —**Let my**...

CANTICLE OF MARY

Ant My brothers and sisters, show no partiality as you hold the
   faith of our Lord Jesus Christ.

INTERCESSIONS (from Sunday, Week III, p. 104)

PRAYER: O God, we thank you for your inspired word that
         guides us and lights our way to you. We praise you for
         our own ability to speak, to communicate with one
         another, to establish understanding and to make
         peace. Help us never to abuse this precious gift. Give
         our words the power to comfort, heal, guide, and to tell
         the Good News of Jesus, sounding a song of creative
         love throughout the world. We ask this through the
         same Jesus Christ, your word and message of salvation
         to us all now, and forever. Amen.

TWENTY-FOURTH SUNDAY IN ORDINARY TIME

EVENING PRAYER I

(Psalms and Antiphons from Sunday, Week IV, p. 143)

READING

Jesus Christ, Liberator, is a christological theme that evokes a new image of God, who is on the side of the oppressed with the aim to free them. It also lifts up a new image of the oppressed, of great worth, the privileged focus of God's own care. Finally, it gives us a new image of discipleship, entering into the way of Jesus with the poor, a way which has a paschal character. It carries a new answer to the question, "Who do you say that I am?" Neither passive victim nor dominating Lord, Jesus is the liberating Word of God in solidarity with the poor.

Elizabeth Johnson, *Consider Jesus.*, p. 93, (2)

RESPONSORY

O God, freedom is your gift to all, whether rich or poor. **—O God...**
You care for all peoples of the earth. **—whether**...
Glory to you, Source of all Being, Eternal Word and Holy Spirit.
    —O God...

CANTICLE OF MARY

Ant You have lifted up the powerless and filled them with good
    things.

INTERCESSIONS and PRAYER: (from Sunday, Week IV, p. 144)

MORNING PRAYER
(Psalms from Sunday, Week IV, p. 145)

Ant 1 The saying is sure and worthy of full acceptance, that
    Christ Jesus came into the world to save sinners.

Ant 2 Faith by itself, if it has no works is dead.

Ant 3 Whether we live, or whether we die, we are the Lord's.

READING

We do not live to ourselves, and we do not die to ourselves. If we live, we
live to the [Lord Jesus], and if we die, we die to the [Lord Jesus]; so
then, whether we live or whether we die, we are the Lord's. For to this
end Christ died and lived again, so that he might be Lord of both the
dead and the living.

Rom 14:7–9

RESPONSORY

In you we live and move and have our being, you are all in all.
    —In you...
Without you we can do nothing; **—you are...**
Glory to you, Source of all Being, Eternal Word and Holy Spirit.
    —In you...

CANTICLE OF ZECHARIAH

Ant Christ died and lives again, that he might be Lord of both the
    living and the dead.

INTERCESSIONS (from Sunday, Week IV, p. 147)

PRAYER: O God, strength and friend of the forsaken, we praise you in Jesus who bore the burden of our sins with a forgiving heart. Help us to walk in his spirit. We know a world of pain and anger that dots our history with war and division. Teach us how to respect our differences and to forgive as we have been forgiven. Give us the grace to realize the unity for which Jesus prayed. We ask this in his name. Amen.

DAYTIME PRAYER

Ant 1 Remember the covenant of the Most High.

Ant 2 It was fitting to make merry and be glad, for this your brother was dead, and is alive; he was lost and is found.

Ant 3 I will multiply your descendants as the stars of heaven.

(Prayer as in Morning Prayer)

EVENING PRAYER II
(Psalms from Sunday, Week IV, p. 149)

Ant 1 Remember the commandments and do not be angry with your neighbor.

Ant 2 Jesus asked them, "But who do you say that I am?" Peter said, "You are the Christ."

Ant 3 This man receives sinners and eats with them.

READING

The saying is sure and worthy of full acceptance, that Christ Jesus came into the world to save sinners—of whom I am the foremost. But for that very reason I received mercy, so that in me, as the foremost, Jesus Christ might display the utmost patience, making me an example to those who would come to believe in him for eternal life. To the [Ruler] of the ages, immortal, invisible, the only God, be honor and glory forever and ever. Amen.

1 Tim 1:15–17

RESPONSORY

With you is wisdom, O God, who knows your works.—**With you**...
And was present when you made the world, **—and who**...

Glory to you, Source of all Being, Eternal Word and Holy Spirit.
—With you...

CANTICLE OF MARY

Ant The Almighty opens my ears to hear as one who is taught.

INTERCESSIONS (from Sunday, Week IV, p. 150)

PRAYER: O God, strength and friend of the forsaken, we praise you in Jesus who bore the burden of our sins with a forgiving heart. Help us to walk in his spirit. We know a world of pain and anger that dots our history with war and division. Teach us how to respect our differences and to forgive as we have been forgiven. Give us the grace to realize the unity for which Jesus prayed. We ask this in his name. Amen.

TWENTY-FIFTH SUNDAY IN ORDINARY TIME

EVENING PRAYER I

(Psalms and Antiphons from Sunday, Week I, p. 1)

READING

While praising grace we should not forget that it does not always rush over us in a wave of victory, sweeping aside all obstacles; nor is it a simple and unhindered growth; neither does it develop our spiritual life only to the extent that we suffer all in silence, leaving everything else in the hands of God. Generally speaking, the spiritual life is grace precisely because it must be painstakingly cultivated day by day; it requires constant training and drilling. In short, the spiritual life is also (even though not exclusively or even predominantly) *work, planned exercise,* and *conscious development* of the believing, hoping, and loving life in us according to the laws of nature and grace, and according to the motives of a total dedication to God.

Karl Rahner, *The Practice of Faith*, p. 236, (2)

RESPONSORY

Those who wait for you, shall never be disappointed. **—Those**...
They shall see you face to face; **—and shall never**...
Glory to you, Source of all Being, Eternal Word and Holy Spirit.
—Those...

CANTICLE OF MARY

Ant If any want to become my followers, let them deny
themselves and take up their cross and follow me.

INTERCESSIONS and PRAYER: (from Sunday, Week I, p. 3)

MORNING PRAYER
(Psalms from Sunday, Week I, p. 3)

Ant 1 There is one mediator between God and all people, the
man Christ Jesus, who gave himself as a ransom for all.

Ant 2 Wisdom from above is first pure, then peaceable, gentle,
open to reason, full of mercy and good fruits.

Ant 3 For me to live is Christ, and to die is gain.

READING

It is my eager expectation and hope that I will not be put to shame in
any way, but that by my speaking with all boldness, Christ will be
exalted now as always in my body, whether by life or by death. For to
me, living is Christ and dying is gain. If I am to live in the flesh, that
means fruitful labor for me; and I do not know which I prefer. I am hard
pressed between the two: my desire is to depart and be with Christ, for
that is far better; but to remain in the flesh is more necessary for you.
Only live your life in a manner worthy of the gospel of Christ, so that
whether I come and see you or am absent and hear about you, I will
know that you are standing firm in one spirit, striving side by side with
one mind for the faith of the gospel.

Phil 1:20–24, 27

RESPONSORY

How great is your name, Creator God; it is chanted on the
lips of babes. **—How great...**
Your glory is above the heavens; **—it is chanted...**
Glory to you, Source of all Being, Eternal Word and Holy Spirit.
—How great...

CANTICLE OF ZECHARIAH

Ant One who is faithful in very little is faithful also in much.

INTERCESSIONS (from Sunday, Week I, p. 5)

PRAYER: Beauty, truth, and goodness are the marks of your
creation, O God. As the reality of what we have done to

the earth bears down upon us, give us the grace to do what is necessary to cooperate with your redeeming care of the cosmos. Give us the generosity and courage to do without those things that destroy earth, water, air and all that they sustain. Bless us anew that we may bless the earth with healing care, letting all the earth tell of your glory, O God—Creator, Word, and Holy Spirit. Amen.

DAYTIME PRAYER

Ant 1 Seek me, your God, while I may be found; call upon me while I am still near.

Ant 2 The righteous are God's children; God will help them.

Ant 3 God our Savior desires all to be saved and to come to the knowledge of the truth.

(Prayer as in Morning Prayer)

EVENING PRAYER II
(Psalms from Sunday, Week I, p. 7)

Ant 1 For my thoughts are not your thoughts, neither are your ways, my ways.

Ant 2 Whoever receives one such child in my name receives me, and whoever receives me, receives not me, but the One who sent me.

Ant 3 You cannot serve God and worldly possessions.

READING

First of all then, I urge that supplications, prayers, intercessions, and thanksgivings be made for everyone, for [rulers] and all who are in high positions, so that we may lead a quiet and peaceable life in all godliness and dignity. This is right and is acceptable in the sight of God our Savior, who desires everyone to be saved and to come to the knowledge of the truth. For there is one God; there is also one mediator between God and humankind, Christ Jesus, himself human, who gave himself a ransom for all—this was attested at the right time.

1 Tim 2:1–6

RESPONSORY

You have been good to your servant, O God, teach me discernment and knowledge **—You have**...

That I may keep your precepts, —**teach me**...
Glory to you, Source of all Being, Eternal Word and Holy Spirit.
—**You have**...

CANTICLE OF MARY

Ant The harvest of righteousness is sown in peace by those who make peace.

INTERCESSIONS (from Sunday, Week I, p. 9)

PRAYER: Beauty, truth, and goodness are the marks of your creation, O God. As the reality of what we have done to the earth bears down upon us, give us the grace to do what is necessary to cooperate with your redeeming care of the cosmos. Give us the generosity and courage to do without those things that destroy earth, water, air and all that they sustain. Bless us anew that we may bless the earth with healing care, letting all the earth tell of your glory, O God—Creator, Word, and Holy Spirit. Amen.

TWENTY-SIXTH SUNDAY IN ORDINARY TIME

EVENING PRAYER I
(Psalms and Antiphons from Sunday, Week II, p. 47)

READING

I'll give you one piece of advice: don't neglect his name, "Jesus." Meditate on it in your heart night and day as your personal and precious treasure. Love it more than your life. Root it in your mind. Love Jesus, because he made you and bought you at a very high price. Give your heart to him, because it is the debt you owe him. Therefore devote your love to this name "Jesus," which means "salvation." No evil thing can have any living-space in that heart where "Jesus" is faithfully kept in mind, because it chases out devils and destroys temptations and turns out all wrongful anxieties and defects, and purifies the mind. Whoever really loves it is full of God's grace and full of virtues, receives spiritual strength in this life; and when such people die, they are adopted into the orders of angels above, to behold in unending joy him whom they have loved.

Richard Rolle, *The English Writings*, pp. 150–51, (1)

RESPONSORY

At the name of Jesus every knee should bend, and every tongue
  give praise. —**At the**...
Every head should bow, —**and every**...
Glory to you, Source of all Being, Eternal Word and Holy Spirit.
  —**At the**...

CANTICLE OF MARY

Ant For you who are mighty, have made me great, most holy be
  your name.

INTERCESSIONS and PRAYER: (from Sunday, Week II, p. 49)

MORNING PRAYER
(Psalms from Sunday, Week II, p. 49)

Ant 1 Jesus said, "No one who does a mighty work in my name
  will be able soon after to speak evil of me."

Ant 2 God has highly exalted him and bestowed on him the
  name which is above every name.

Ant 3 Fight the good fight of faith; take hold of the eternal life to
  which you were called.

READING

Let the same mind be in you that was in Christ Jesus, who though he
was in the form of God, did not regard equality with God as something
to be exploited, but emptied himself, taking the form of a slave, being
born in human likeness. And being in human form, he humbled himself
and became obedient to the point of death—even death on a cross.
Therefore God also highly exalted him and gave him the name that is
above every name, so that at the name of Jesus every knee should bend,
in heaven and on earth and under the earth, and every tongue should
confess that Jesus Christ is Lord.

Phil 2:5–11

RESPONSORY

Blessed are they who dwell in your house, O God, forever
  singing your praises. —**Blessed are**...
Blessed are they who trust in you; —**forever**...
Glory to you, Source of all Being, Eternal Word and Holy Spirit.
  —**Blessed are**...

CANTICLE OF ZECHARIAH

Ant I live now, not I, but Christ lives in me.

INTERCESSIONS (from Sunday, Week II, p. 51)

PRAYER: O God, hope of all who trust in you, you created us into a world endowed with all that we need, but greed has governed our stewardship of the earth. Every year marks more clearly the division between rich and poor. Send your Holy Spirit to guide us in the way of integrity and justice. Free us to live as your children revealing your goodness and mercy. So may we glorify your name, now and forever. Amen.

DAYTIME PRAYER

Ant 1 Let each of you look to the interest of the others.

Ant 2 Would that all God's people were prophets, that the Spirit of the Most High would be upon them.

Ant 3 As for you, child of God, aim at righteousness, godliness, faith, love, steadfastness, and gentleness.

(Prayer as in Morning Prayer)

EVENING PRAYER II
(Psalms from Sunday, Week II, p. 53)

Ant 1 Truly I say to you, those who give you a cup of water to drink because you bear the name of Christ will by no means lose their reward.

Ant 2 When sinners turn away from sin to do what is right, they shall save their lives.

Ant 3 At the name of Jesus, every knee should bow, in heaven, on earth, and under the earth, and every tongue proclaim to the glory of God, Jesus Christ is Lord.

READING

But as for you, [child] of God, shun all this; pursue righteousness, godliness, faith, love, endurance, gentleness. Fight the good fight of the faith; take hold of the eternal life, to which you were called and for which you made the good confession in the presence of many witnesses.

In the presence of God, who gives life to all things, and of Christ Jesus, who in his testimony before Pontius Pilate made the good confession, I charge you to keep the commandment without spot or blame until the manifestation of our Lord Jesus Christ.

1 Tim 6:11–14

RESPONSORY

We proclaim to all nations; You, O God, are sovereign.—**We**...
You will judge the peoples with equity; —**You, O God**...
Glory to you, Source of all Being, Eternal Word and Holy Spirit.
   —**We**...

CANTICLE OF MARY

Ant What does God require of you but to do justice, and to love kindness, and to walk humbly with your God.

INTERCESSIONS (from Sunday, Week II, p. 55)

PRAYER: O God, hope of all who trust in you, you created us into a world endowed with all that we need, but greed has governed our stewardship of the earth. Every year marks more clearly the division between rich and poor. Send your Holy Spirit to guide us in the way of integrity and justice. Free us to live as your children revealing your goodness and mercy. So may we glorify your name, now and forever. Amen.

TWENTY-SEVENTH SUNDAY IN ORDINARY TIME

EVENING PRAYER I

(Psalms and Antiphons from Sunday, Week III, p. 96)

READING

Because we share the life of the resurrected Jesus, we are actually descendants of Abraham; there is no distinction between slave and free, male or felmale as far as our relationship with Christ is concerned. Paul himself did not grasp the full significance of this teaching, for he accepted the institution of slavery as a fact of life for his day. But his teaching finally brought about among Christians the realization that the institution of slavery could not be reconciled with the Christian concept of equality of all men and women who shared the life of Christ. The Church only gradually understands the fullness of the revelation of Christ. I personally am confident that the day will come when Catholics will find it just as hard to grasp how the Church once accepted the barring of women from the priesthood as it accepted the institution of slavery.

Raymond T. Bosler, *New Wine Bursting Old Skins*, pp. 96–97, (28)

RESPONSORY

O God, you are One, you love the singlehearted.—**O God...**
The pure of heart shall see you; —**you love...**
Glory to you, Source of all Being, Eternal Word and Holy Spirit.
　—**O God...**

CANTICLE OF MARY

Ant In the evening of our life we shall be judged by love.

INTERCESSIONS and PRAYER: (from Sunday, Week III, p. 97)

MORNING PRAYER
(Psalms from Sunday, Week III, p. 98)

Ant 1 Whatever is true, whatever is honorable, whatever is gracious, if there is any excellence, if there is anything worthy of praise, think about these things.

Ant 2 If you had faith as a grain of mustard seed, you could say to this sycamore, "Be rooted up and be planted in the sea," and it would obey you.

Ant 3 The peace of God, which passes all understanding, will keep your hearts and minds in Christ Jesus.

READING

Do not worry about anything, but in everything by prayer and supplication with thanksgiving let your requests be made known to God. And the peace of God, which surpasses all understanding, will guard your hearts and your minds in Christ Jesus. Finally, beloved, whatever is true, whatever is honorable, whatever is just, whatever is pure, whatever is pleasing, whatever is commendable, if there is any excellence and if there is anything worthy of praise, think about these things. Keep on doing the things that you have learned and received and heard and seen in me, and the God of peace will be with you.

Phil 4:6–9

RESPONSORY

How good and how pleasant it is, when we live together in
    unity. —**How good...**
There God gives us the blessing, life forevermore; —**when...**
Glory to you, Source of all Being, Eternal Word and Holy Spirit.
    —**How good...**

CANTICLE OF ZECHARIAH

Ant We are unworthy servants; we have only done our duty.

INTERCESSIONS (from Sunday, Week III, p. 100)

PRAYER: Lord Jesus, you blessed little children, and you give
        them into our care. Bless us now as we live the
        challenge of a wounded culture. Inspire us with new
        ways to let the little children come to you. Let our lives
        be your good news for them, guiding them to all that
        supports their growth in wisdom and goodness. Help
        them to find you in the depths of their hearts and to
        find there all that is to their peace. So may they learn
        to love and praise you, who are one with God our
        Creator and with the Holy Spirit, now and forever.
        Amen.

DAYTIME PRAYER

Ant 1 We see Jesus, who for a little while was made lower than
        the angels, crowned with glory and honor because he
        submitted to death.

Ant 2 The righteous shall live by their faith.

Ant 3 It was fitting that God, for whom and by whom all things
        exist, should make the work of our salvation perfect
        through suffering.

(Prayer as in Morning Prayer)

EVENING PRAYER II
(Psalms from Sunday, Week III, p. 102)

Ant 1 Let the children come to me, do not hinder them, for to
        such belongs the realm of God.

Ant 2 The stone which the builders rejected has become the cornerstone, and this was God's doing.

Ant 3 Whoever does not receive the realm of God like a child shall not enter it.

READING

For this reason I remind you to rekindle the gift of God that is within you through the laying on of my hands; for God did not give us a spirit of cowardice, but rather a spirit of power and of love and of self-discipline. Do not be ashamed, then, of the testimony about our [Lord Jesus] or of me his prisoner, but join with me in suffering for the gospel, relying on the power of God. Hold to the standard of sound teaching that you have heard from me, in the faith and love that are in Christ Jesus. Guard the good treasure entrusted to you, with the help of the Holy Spirit living in us.

2 Tim 1:6–8, 13–14

RESPONSORY

Rescue me from evil; guard me, O God, from my darkness.
  —Rescue me...
I know you uphold the afflicted; **—guard me**...
Glory to you, Source of all Being, Eternal Word and Holy Spirit.
  —Rescue me...

CANTICLE OF MARY

Ant Have no anxiety about anything, but in everything by prayer and supplication with thanksgiving let your requests be made known to God.

INTERCESSIONS (from Sunday, Week III, p. 104)

PRAYER: Lord Jesus, you blessed little children, and you give them into our care. Bless us now as we live the challenge of a wounded culture. Inspire us with new ways to let the little children come to you. Let our lives be your good news for them, guiding them to all that supports their growth in wisdom and goodness. Help them to find you in the depths of their hearts and to find there all that is to their peace. So may they learn to love and praise you, who are one with God our Creator and with the Holy Spirit, now and forever. Amen.

TWENTY-EIGHTH SUNDAY IN ORDINARY TIME
EVENING PRAYER I
(Psalms and Antiphons from Sunday, Week IV, p. 143)

READING

Where the one and entire hope is given beyond all individual hopes, which comprehends all impulses in silent promise,...where the bitter, deceptive and vanishing everyday world is withstood until the accepted end, and accepted out of a force whose ultimate source is still unknown to us but can be tapped by us, where one dares to pray into a silent darkness and knows that one is heard, although no answer seems to come back about which one might argue and rationalize,...where desperation is accepted and is still secretly accepted as trustworthy without cheap trust,...*there* is God and [God's] liberating grace. There we find what we Christians call the Holy Spirit of God. Then we experience something which is inescapable (even when suppressed) in life, and which is offered to our freedom with the question whether we want to accept it or whether we want to shut ourselves up in a hell of freedom by trying to barricade ourselves against it. There is the mysticism of everyday life, the discovery of God in all things.

Karl Rahner, The Practice of Faith, pp. 83–84, (2)

RESPONSORY

No one who practices deceit shall dwell in your house. —**No one**...
They who walk in the way that is blameless, —**shell dwell**...
Glory to you, Source of all Being, Eternal Word and Holy Spirit.
   —**No one**...

CANTICLE OF MARY

Ant Guide us in your truth lest we go astray.

INTERCESSIONS and PRAYER: (from Sunday, Week IV, p. 144)

MORNING PRAYER
(Psalms from Sunday, Week IV, p. 145)

Ant 1 I can do all things in the One who strengthens me.

Ant 2 The word of God is living and active, piercing to the division of soul and spirit and discerning the thoughts and intentions of the heart.

Ant 3 If we have died with him, we shall also live with him; if we endure, we shall also reign with him.

READING

On this mountain the [God] of hosts will make for all peoples a feast of rich food, a feast of well-aged wines, of rich food filled with marrow, of well-aged wines strained clear. And [God] will destroy on this mountain the shroud that is cast over all peoples, the sheet that is spread over all nations;...swallowing up death forever. Then the [Most High God] will wipe away the tears from all faces and the disgrace of the people God will take away from all the earth.

Is 25:6–8

RESPONSORY

This is the day our God has made; let us rejoice and be glad
    in it. **—This is...**
Your steadfast love endures forever; **—let us...**
Glory to you, Source of all Being, Eternal Word and Holy Spirit.
    —This is...

CANTICLE OF ZECHARIAH

Ant If we have died with Christ, we shall also live with Him.

INTERCESSIONS (from Sunday, Week IV, p. 147)

PRAYER: God and hope of every new day, our hearts are full of gratitude for your mercy. We thank you for revealing to us the way of life that is the gospel. Awaken us to its wisdom, and give us the courage to embody its message. Let nothing distract us from its call to a more conscious relationship with you and to a quality of life worthy of your children. So may we praise you for the gift of Jesus and for the call to be one with you forever. Amen.

DAYTIME PRAYER

Ant 1 It will be said on that day, "Lo, this is our God for whom we have waited, that we might be saved."

Ant 2 I prayed and understanding was given me; I called upon God and the spirit of wisdom came to me.

Ant 3 I know that there is no God in all the earth but in Israel.

(Prayer as in Morning Prayer)

EVENING PRAYER II

(Psalms from Sunday, Week IV, p. 149)

Ant 1 Go, sell what you have, and give to the poor, and you will have treasure in heaven.

Ant 2 For all things are possible with God.

Ant 3 Rise and go your way; your faith has made you well.

READING

Indeed the word of God is living and active, sharper than any two-edged sword, piercing until it divides soul from spirit, joints from marrow; it is able to judge the thoughts and intentions of the heart. And before God no creature is hidden, but all are naked and laid bare to the eyes of the one to whom we must render an account.

Heb 4:12–13

RESPONSORY

I will make my vows to you, O God, in the presence of all
   your people. —**I will**...
In the courts of your holy house, —**in the**...
Glory to you, Source of all Being, Eternal Word and Holy Spirit.
   —**I will**...

CANTICLE OF MARY

Ant If we are faithless, Christ remains faithful, for he cannot deny himself.

INTERCESSIONS (from Sunday, Week IV, p. 150)

PRAYER: God and hope of every new day, our hearts are full of gratitude for your mercy. We thank you for revealing to us the way of life that is the gospel. Awaken us to its wisdom, and give us the courage to embody its message. Let nothing distract us from its call to a more conscious relationship with you and to a quality of life worthy of your children. So may we praise you for the gift of Jesus and for the call to be one with you forever. Amen.

TWENTY-NINTH SUNDAY IN ORDINARY TIME

EVENING PRAYER I
(Psalms and Antiphons from Sunday, Week I, p. 1)

READING

All growth to fullness demands time. The seed must be buried before it germinates and grows. The earth must be plowed and permitted to lay fallow or else it will wear out. In the fall of the year nature becomes barren. Winter waits for lush and fertile springtime. We also must face the winters of our life. We lay fallow for a while. Often only then can we listen for the tiny, whispering sounds of life. Even so, waiting times can be frustrating, anxious, or boring. Instead of waiting listlessly, Louise (de Marillac) shaped her waiting with times for prayer, reflection and service. She turned to God regularly, trusting that the Holy Spirit would shed light on the next challenge of her life. Indeed, through the charitable service that Louise gave during this fallow time, God called her to the great project of her life. But Louise had to watch and wait.

Audrey Gibson and Kieran Kneaves, *Praying with Louise de Marillac,* p. 45, (42)

RESPONSORY

O God, receive our prayer which is lifted up to you. **—O God,...**
Like the fragrance of incense; **—which is...**
Glory to you, Source of all Being, Eternal Word and Holy Spirit.
   —O God,...

CANTICLE OF MARY

Ant Teach us your ways, for they are holy.

INTERCESSIONS and PRAYER: (from Sunday, Week I, p. 3)

MORNING PRAYER
(Psalms from Sunday, Week I, p. 3)

Ant 1 The cup that I drink you will drink; and with the baptism with which I am baptized, you shall be baptized.

Ant 2 God has chosen you, beloved of God, for our gospel came to you not only in word, but also in power and the Holy Spirit.

Ant 3 Whoever would be great among you must be your servant, and whoever would be first among you must be slave of all.

READING

Since, then, we have a great high priest who has passed through the heavens, Jesus, the Son of God, let us hold fast to the confession. For we do not have a high priest who is unable to sympathize with our weaknesses, but we have one who in every respect has been tested as we are, yet without sin. Let us therefore approach the throne of grace with boldness, so that we may receive mercy and find grace to help in time of need.

Heb 4:14–16

RESPONSORY

My soul pines for your salvation, O God; how long must your
    servant endure? —**My soul...**
When will you comfort me; —**how long...**
Glory to you, Source of all Being, Eternal Word and Holy Spirit.
    —**My soul...**

CANTICLE OF ZECHARIAH

Ant Since we have a great high priest who has passed through the heavens, Jesus, the Son of God, let us hold fast our confession.

INTERCESSIONS (from Sunday, Week I, p. 5)

PRAYER: God of all that is and that will be, your realm is not of this world, but you call us your children to discover it in our hearts. Give us the wisdom we need to determine our debts to Caesars and to sift through the threat of swords and slavery. Let the values of the gospel rise clearly above the call of our culture. Make us a humble people, sure of your love for every person and thing you have created. All praise to you, God, our mother and father, living one with Jesus and the Holy Spirit now and forever. Amen.

DAYTIME PRAYER

Ant 1 I am the Most High, and there is no other, besides me there is no God.

Ant 2 Continue in what you have learned and have firmly believed.

Ant 3 Let us with confidence draw near to the throne of Grace that we may receive mercy and grace in time of need.

(Prayer as in Morning Prayer)

EVENING PRAYER II
(Psalms from Sunday, Week I, p. 7)

Ant 1 For the Anointed One has come to serve, not to be served, and to give his life as a ransom for many.

Ant 2 Render therefore to Caesar the things that are Caesar's and to God the things that are God's.

Ant 3 When God's Chosen One comes, will faith be found on earth?

READING

But as for you, continue in what you have learned and firmly believed, knowing from whom you learned it, and how from childhood you have known the sacred writings that are able to instruct you for salvation through faith in Christ Jesus. All scripture is inspired by God and is useful for teaching, for reproof, for correction, and for training in righteousness, so that everyone who belongs to God may be proficient, equipped for every good work. In the presence of God and of Christ Jesus, who is to judge the living and the dead, and in view of his appearing and his kingdom, I solemnly urge you: proclaim the message; be persistent whether the time is favorable or unfavorable; convince, rebuke, and encourage, with the utmost patience in teaching.

2 Tim 3:14–4:2

RESPONSORY

May you lengthen the lives of just rulers; bid love and truth
   watch over them. —**May you**...
May they ever be enthroned before you; —**bid love**...
Glory to you, Source of all Being, Eternal Word and Holy Spirit.
   —**May you**...

CANTICLE OF MARY

Ant Take heed, and beware of all covetousness; for your life does not consist in the abundance of your possessions.

INTERCESSIONS (from Sunday, Week I, p. 9)

PRAYER: God of all that is and that will be, your realm is not of this world, but you call us your children to discover it in our hearts. Give us the wisdom we need to determine our debts to Caesar and to sift through the threat of swords and slavery. Let the values of the gospel rise clearly above the call of our culture. Make us a humble people, sure of your love for every person and thing you have created. All praise to you, God, our mother and father, living one with Jesus and the Holy Spirit now and forever. Amen.

THIRTIETH SUNDAY IN ORDINARY TIME

EVENING PRAYER I

(Psalms and Antiphons from Sunday, Week II, p. 47)

READING

If we as church are truly following our risen Lord, making his historical concerns our own and committing our lives to the coming victory of the reign of God, then we are compelled to be involved in critical peacemaking and economic issues where the *shalom* and well-being of all peoples, and indeed of the whole earth are at stake.... [This christology] begins its thinking on earth with the gospel memory of the life of Jesus, and finds there the basis for the discernment of how the risen Christ is operative in the world today.

Elizabeth Johnson, *Consider Jesus*, p. 78, (2)

RESPONSORY

You bless the peacemakers, and call them your children. **—You bless...**
You give them your spirit, **—and call...**
Glory to you, Source of all Being, Eternal Word and Holy Spirit.
    —You bless...

CANTICLE OF MARY

Ant Blessed are the peacemakers, for they shall be called
    children of God.

INTERCESSIONS and PRAYER: (from Sunday, Week II, p. 49)

MORNING PRAYER

(Psalms from Sunday, Week II, p. 49)

Ant 1 The gospel came to you not only in word, but also in power
    and in the Holy Spirit.

Ant 2 Christ did not exalt himself to be made a high priest, but was appointed by the One who said to him, "You are my Son, today I have begotten you."

Ant 3 I have fought the good fight, I have finished the race, I have kept the faith.

READING

God has chosen you because our message of the gospel came to you not in word only, but also in power and in the Holy Spirit and with full conviction; just as you know what kind of persons we proved to be among you for your sake. And you became imitators of us and of the Lord Jesus, for in spite of persecution you received the word with joy inspired by the Holy Spirit, so that you became an example to all the believers in Macedonia and Achaia. For the word of the Lord has sounded forth from you not only in Macedonia and Achaia, but in every place your faith in God has become known, so that we have no need to speak about it. For the people of those regions report about us what kind of welcome we had among you, and how you turned to God from idols, to serve a living and true God.

I Thess 1:5–9

RESPONSORY

O God you uphold all who are falling, and raise up all who are
  bowed down. **—O God**...
You are faithful in all your words; **—and raise**...
Glory to you, Source of all Being, Eternal Word and Holy Spirit.
  —O God...

CANTICLE OF ZECHARIAH

Ant If your neighbor cries to me, I will hear, for I am compassionate, says the Most High.

INTERCESSIONS (from Sunday, Week II, p. 51)

PRAYER: Lord Jesus, the blind, the lame, and sinners knew your compassion and freely confessed their need. Help us to realize that we are blind, lame, and sinful and that you look upon us with the same compassion and readiness to forgive and heal. Show us how we overlook the needs of others, how limp is our response to the challenges you offer us, and how we sin against love—love of ourselves, of others, and of the earth. You trusted in God through a difficult life and a painful death. Give us

the same total confidence in God's mercy, that we may
be a revelation of God's compassion. We ask this for
the praise and glory of your name. Amen.

DAYTIME PRAYER

Ant 1 You shall not afflict the helpless or the needy.

Ant 2 Proclaim, give praise and say, "The Most High has saved
the people and will gather them from the farthest parts of
the earth."

Ant 3 You, O God, are the judge, and with you there is no
partiality.

(Prayer as in Morning Prayer)

EVENING PRAYER II
(Psalms from Sunday, Week II, p. 53)

Ant 1 You shall love God with all your heart, and with all your
soul, and with all your mind.

Ant 2 Go your way, your faith has made you well.

Ant 3 O God, be merciful to me a sinner.

READING

For thus says the [Most High]: Sing aloud with gladness for Jacob, and
raise shouts for the chief of the nations; proclaim, give praise, and say,
"Save, O [God], your people, the remnant of Israel." See, I am going to
bring them from the land of the north, and gather them from the
farthest parts of the earth, among them the blind and the lame, those
with child and those in labor, together; a great company, they shall
return here. With weeping they shall come and with consolations I will
lead them back, I will let them walk by brooks of water, in a straight
path in which they shall not stumble; for I have become a [loving parent]
to Israel, and Ephraim is my firstborn.

                                                                Jer 31:7–9

RESPONSORY

Great peace have they who love your law, O God; nothing can
    make them stumble. —**Great peace**...
They fulfill your commandments; —**nothing**...
Glory to you, Source of all Being, Eternal Word and Holy Spirit.
    —**Great peace**...

CANTICLE OF MARY

Ant The prayers of the humble pierce the clouds.

INTERCESSIONS (from Sunday, Week II, p. 55)

PRAYER: Lord Jesus, the blind, the lame, and sinners knew your compassion and freely confessed their need. Help us to realize that we are blind, lame, and sinful and that you look upon us with the same compassion and readiness to forgive and heal. Show us how we overlook the needs of others, how limp is our response to the challenges you offer us, and how we sin against love—love of ourselves, of others, and of the earth. You trusted in God through a difficult life and a painful death. Give us the same total confidence in God's mercy, that we may be a revelation of God's compassion. We ask this for the praise and glory of your name. Amen.

THIRTY-FIRST SUNDAY IN ORDINARY TIME

EVENING PRAYER I

(Psalms and Antiphons from Sunday, Week III, p. 96)

READING

I have this hope, even if I cannot actually imagine what eternal life will really be like. I know through the good news of the Christian message and I know from Jesus Christ that the absolute, everlasting, holy, eternally good God has promised [God's self] to me as my future. And because of that, I have a good hope, an unconditional hope that is still subject to temptation as long as I am here on earth and have negative experiences with life, with society, with people, and so on. That is self-evident. But till death's door I'll hold doggedly fast, if I may say so, to the belief that there is an eternal light that will illumine me.

Karl Rahner, *I Remember*, p. 110, (2)

RESPONSORY

I will sing your praise, O God, every day of my life.—**I will**...
From sunrise to sunset, —**every day**...
Glory to you, Source of all Being, Eternal Word and Holy Spirit.
    —**I will**...

CANTICLE OF MARY

Ant In you, O God, I place my trust.

INTERCESSIONS and PRAYER: (from Sunday, Week III, p. 97)

MORNING PRAYER
(Psalms from Sunday, Week III, p. 98)

Ant 1 We thank God that when you received the word of God, you accepted it not as the word of mere creatures, but as it really is, the word of God.

Ant 2 Jesus is able for all time to save those who draw near to God through him.

Ant 3 May our God make you worthy of the call granted you, and fulfill every good resolve and work of faith by the divine power.

READING

[While we were among you] we were gentle among you, like a nurse tenderly caring for her own children. So deeply do we care for you that we are determined to share with you not only the gospel of God but also our own selves, because you have become very dear to us. You remember our labor and toil, brothers and sisters; we worked night and day, so that we might not burden any of you while we proclaimed to you the gospel of God. We also constantly give thanks to God for this, that when you received the word of God that you heard from us, you accepted it not as a human word but as what it really is, God's word, which is also at work in you believers.

1 Thess 2:7–9, 13

RESPONSORY

O God, your constant love is better than life; my lips will sing your praises. —**O God...**
I will bless you as long as I live; —**my lips...**
Glory to you, Source of all Being, Eternal Word and Holy Spirit. —**O God...**

CANTICLE OF ZECHARIAH

Ant We have one source; one God has created us.

INTERCESSIONS (from Sunday, Week III, p. 100)

PRAYER: O God, voice in the listening heart, your gifts to us are beyond measure, and your patience without limit. Receive our thanks and praise for the gift of our humanity, the consciousness and freedom that allows us to know and love you and one another. Forgive our insensitivity that lets us take you and others for granted. Teach us the reverence that graced the life of your son Jesus. So may we praise you, now and forever. Amen.

DAYTIME PRAYER

Ant 1 I am a great Ruler, says God Most High, and my name is feared among the nations.

Ant 2 Hear, O Israel, the Most High God is one God.

Ant 3 You love all things that exist, and have loathing for none of the things which you have made.

(Prayer as in Morning Prayer)

EVENING PRAYER II
(Psalms from Sunday, Week III, p. 102)

Ant 1 Those who are greatest among you shall be those who serve.

Ant 2 You shall love your neighbor as yourself.

Ant 3 I have come to seek out and save what was lost.

READING

We always pray for you, asking that our God will make you worthy of [your] call and will fulfill by [God's own] power every good resolve and work of faith, so that the name of our Lord Jesus may be glorified in you, and you in him, according to the grace of our God and the Lord Jesus Christ. As to the coming of our Lord Jesus Christ and our being gathered together to him, we beg you, brothers and sisters, not to be quickly shaken in mind or alarmed, either by spirit or by word or by letter, as though from us, to the effect that the day of the Lord Jesus is already here.

2 Thess 1:11–2:2

RESPONSORY

God has made known to us in all wisdom and insight, the
   mystery of the plan set forth in Christ.   —**God has**...
To unite all things in Christ, through —**the mystery**...
Glory to you, Source of all Being, Eternal Word and Holy Spirit.
   —**God has**...

CANTICLE OF MARY

Ant God takes delight in the people, adorning the humble with
   victory.

INTERCESSIONS (from Sunday, Week III, p. 104)

PRAYER: O God, voice in the listening heart, your gifts to us are
   beyond measure, and your patience without limit.
   Receive our thanks and praise for the gift of our
   humanity, the consciousness and freedom that allows
   us to know and love you and one another. Forgive our
   insensitivity that lets us take you and others for
   granted. Teach us the reverence that graced the life of
   your son Jesus. So may we praise you, now and
   forever. Amen.

THIRTY-SECOND SUNDAY IN ORDINARY TIME

EVENING PRAYER I

(Psalms and Antiphons from Sunday, Week IV, p. 143)

READING

The Spirit is the shaper of the new creation, dwelling at the heart of all
things and working to redeem them. In his letter to the Romans Paul
expresses this very poetically. All creation has been subjected to futility,
but it is waiting with eager longing for the glory that is to come. It will
be set free from its bondage to decay and share in the glorious liberty of
the children of God.... In other words, it is not just human beings who
are saved. We are of a piece with all creation, sharing with all creatures
a common destiny. The new heaven and the new earth for which we
hope includes the renewal of the whole universe. The dynamic power
effecting this redemption at the end and weaving webs of community
between all creatures in the interim is the Holy Spirit of the risen
Christ. In this understanding, both spirituality and ethics direct us
toward responsible stewardship of the earth.

Elizabeth Johnson, *Consider Jesus*, p. 141, (2)

RESPONSORY

Glorious are your works, God of the universe. **—Glorious**...
All creation resounds your glory; **—God of**...
Glory to you, Source of all Being, Eternal Word and Holy Spirit.
   —Glorious...

CANTICLE OF MARY

Ant   All creation cries out to you with joy.

INTERCESSIONS and PRAYER: (from Sunday, Week IV, p. 144)

MORNING PRAYER
(Psalms from Sunday, Week IV, p. 145)

Ant 1   Through Jesus, God will bring forth with him from the dead, those who have fallen asleep believing in him.

Ant 2   Christ will appear a second time, not to deal with sin but to save those who are eagerly waiting for him.

Ant 3   The Lord Jesus is faithful, he will strengthen you and guard you from evil.

READING

We do not want you to be uninformed, brothers and sisters, about those who have died, so that you may not grieve as others do who have no hope. For since we believe that Jesus died and rose again, even so, through Jesus, God will bring with him those who have died. For this we declare to you by the word of the Lord Jesus, that we who are alive, who are left until the coming of the Lord, will by no means precede those who have died. For the Lord Jesus himself, with a cry of command, with the archangel's call and with the sound of God's trumpet, will descend from heaven, and the dead in Christ will rise first. Then we who are alive, who are left, will be caught up in the clouds together with them to meet the Lord in the air; and so we will be with the Lord forever. Therefore encourage one another with these words.

1 Thess 4:13–18

RESPONSORY

Let my eyes stream with tears, night and day, without rest.
   —Let my...
For the virgin daughter of my people is smitten with a great wound; **—night and**...

Glory to you, Source of all Being, Eternal Word and Holy Spirit.
—**Let my**...

CANTICLE OF ZECHARIAH

Ant May our Lord Jesus Christ himself,...comfort your hearts
and strengthen them for every good work and word.

INTERCESSIONS (from Sunday, Week IV, p. 147)

PRAYER: Lord Jesus, in the days of your ministry, you listened
to women and followed their counsel, and you sent a
woman to tell the news of your resurrection to your
followers. Grant us the insight to let the fruits of your
Holy Spirit flow freely through every member of the
people of God, so that we may all share in the life you
have gained for us. We ask this through the
intercession of all your saints who died longing for the
coming of your reign on earth. Amen.

DAYTIME PRAYER

Ant 1 Wisdom is radiant and unfading, easily discerned by those
who love her.

Ant 2 The jar of meal shall not be spent, and the cruse of oil
should not fail, until the day that God sends rain upon the
earth.

Ant 3 The Ruler of the universe will raise us up to an everlasting
renewal of life.

(Prayer as in Morning Prayer)

EVENING PRAYER II
(Psalms from Sunday, Week IV, p. 149)

Ant 1 God is not of the dead, but of the living; for all are alive to
God.

Ant 2 Christ has appeared once for all at the end of the ages to
put away sin by the sacrifice of himself.

Ant 3 Behold the bridegroom! Come out to meet him.

READING

For Christ did not enter a sanctuary made by human hands, a mere
copy of the true one, but he entered into heaven itself, now to appear in

the presence of God on our behalf. Nor was it to offer himself again and again, as the high priest enters the Holy Place year after year with blood that is not his own; for then he would have had to suffer again and again since the foundation of the world. But as it is, he has appeared once for all at the end of the age to remove sin by the sacrifice of himself. And just as it is appointed for mortals to die once, and after that the judgment, so Christ, having been offered once to bear the sins of many, will appear a second time, not to deal with sin, but to save those who are eagerly waiting for him.

Heb 9:24–28

RESPONSORY

I was glad when they said to me: "Let us go to the house of
    God!" —**I was...**
And now our feet are standing within your gates; —"**Let us...**
Glory to you, Source of all Being, Eternal Word and Holy Spirit.
    —**I was...**

CANTICLE OF MARY

Ant Those who rise early to seek wisdom will have no difficulty,
    for they will find her sitting at their gates.

INTERCESSIONS (from Sunday, Week IV, p. 150)

PRAYER: Lord Jesus, in the days of your ministry, you listened
    to women and followed their counsel, and you sent a
    woman to tell the news of your resurrection to your
    followers. Grant us the insight to let the fruits of your
    Holy Spirit flow freely through every member of the
    people of God, so that we may all share in the life you
    have gained for us. We ask this through the
    intercession of all your saints who died longing for the
    coming of your reign on earth. Amen.

THIRTY-THIRD SUNDAY IN ORDINARY TIME

EVENING PRAYER I

(Psalms and Antiphons from Sunday, Week I, p. 1)

READING

We are united with God in Jesus by being in compassionate solidarity
with those who suffer. If God is there, resisting evil and willing life
wherever people are being damaged, then the followers of Jesus must

enter into the same solidarity. There is a traditional axiom which claims that to live a good ethical life one must "do good and avoid evil." The emphasis shifts today, slightly but very dramatically, to make us realize that this is not enough.... For in the light of the compassion of God revealed in Jesus, we must "do good and resist evil." There is a call to the Christian conscience here not to hide our face from evil, not to walk around it, or pretend it is not there; but to face its massiveness in spite of our feelings of powerlessness or insignificance and to become involved in transforming it. Suffering people are the privileged place where the God of compassion is to be found.

Elizabeth Johnson, *Consider Jesus*, p. 126, (2)

RESPONSORY

Your mercy, O God, calls us to mercy. **—Your mercy...**
It manifests your greatness, **—and calls us...**
Glory to you, Source of all Being, Eternal Word and Holy Spirit.
   —Your mercy...

CANTICLE OF MARY

Ant You have filled the hungry with good things.

INTERCESSIONS and PRAYER: (from Sunday, Week I, p. 3)

MORNING PRAYER
(Psalms from Sunday, Week I, p. 3)

Ant 1 You are not in darkness, sisters and brothers, for the day of the Lord Jesus to surprise you like a thief.

Ant 2 Those who are wise shall shine like the brightness of the firmament; and those who turn many to righteousness, like the stars forever and ever.

Ant 3 You will show me the path to life.

READING

Now concerning the times and the seasons, brothers and sisters, you do not need to have anything written to you. For you yourselves know very well that the day of the Lord Jesus will come like a thief in the night. When they say, "There is peace and security," then sudden destruction will come upon them, as labor pains come upon a pregnant woman, and there will be no escape! But you, beloved, are not in darkness, for that day to surprise you like a thief; for you are all children of light and children of the day; we are not of the night or of darkness. So then let us not fall asleep as others do, but let us keep awake and be sober.

1 Thess 5:1–6

RESPONSORY

By your word, O God, the heavens were made; your own designs
   stand forever. **—By your**...
All who live in the world stand in wonder; **—your own**...
Glory to you, Source of all Being, Eternal Word and Holy Spirit.
   —By your...

CANTICLE OF ZECHARIAH

Ant Heaven and earth will pass away, but my words will not pass
   away.

INTERCESSIONS (from Sunday, Week I, p. 5)

PRAYER: Your gift of life is a source of joy for us, O God, but the
   challenge to grow often weighs us down. Give us the
   courage to live responsibly in all of the areas of our
   lives. Inspire us with new ways to serve you and one
   another as we realize your constant presence. Let all
   that we do radiate our faith and hope in your love for
   us. Bless all who encourage us on the way, as together
   we strive for the unity that is yours, Creator, Word, and
   Holy Spirit. Amen.

DAYTIME PRAYER

Ant 1 Let us not sleep as others do, but let us keep awake and
   be sober.

Ant 2 By a single offering, Christ has perfected for all time those
   who are sanctified.

Ant 3 I will give you a mouth and wisdom which none of your
   adversaries will be able to withstand.

(Prayer as in Morning Prayer)

EVENING PRAYER II
(Psalms from Sunday, Week I, p. 7)

Ant 1 To everyone who has will more be given for their increase, but from those who have not even what they have will be taken away.

Ant 2 Heaven and earth will pass away, but my words will not pass away.

Ant 3 They will see the Anointed One coming in clouds with great power and glory.

READING

See the day is coming, buring like an oven, when all the arrogant and all evildoers will be stubble; the day that comes shall burn them up says the [Most High God], so that it will leave them neither root nor branch. But for you who revere my name the sun of righteousness shall rise, with healing in its wings.

Mal 4:1–2

RESPONSORY

When you turn back to me with all your heart, says our God,
　I am there for you. —**When you...**
I will no longer hide my face; —**I am...**
Glory to you, Source of all Being, Eternal Word and Holy Spirit.
　—**When you...**

CANTICLE OF MARY

Ant For you who fear my name, the sun of righteousness shall rise with healing in its wings.

INTERCESSIONS (from Sunday, Week I, p. 9)

PRAYER: Your gift of life is a source of joy for us, O God, but the challenge to grow often weighs us down. Give us the courage to live responsibly in all of the areas of our lives. Inspire us with new ways to serve you and one another as we realize your constant presence. Let all that we do radiate our faith and hope in your love for us. Bless all who encourage us on the way, as together we strive for the unity that is yours, Creator, Word, and Holy Spirit. Amen.

THIRTY-FOURTH SUNDAY IN ORDINARY TIME

EVENING PRAYER I
(Psalms and Antiphons from Sunday, Week II, p. 47)

READING

What Christianity really proclaims as essential is...the victory of the love of God...it points to the cross and resurrection of Jesus as to the event of this now manifest victory of God's love. This love is the cause and guarantee that our brief time, which passes away, creates an eternity which is not made up out of time. If it seems that we perish in death, since the dead do not become perceptible again anywhere where time goes on, this is merely a sign that eternity, born from time, is something other than what can readily be seen here and now.

Karl Rahner, *The Practice of Faith*, p. 312, (2)

RESPONSORY

Jesus is glorified in heaven and we have seen his glory.
    —**Jesus**...
Shining through all creation; —**we have**...
Glory to you, Source of all Being, Eternal Word and Holy Spirit.
    —**Jesus**...

CANTICLE OF MARY

Ant The reason why I came into the world is to testify to the truth.

INTERCESSIONS and PRAYER: (from Evening Prayer II, p. 433)

MORNING PRAYER
(Psalms from Sunday, Week II, p. 49)

Ant 1 Behold, I myself will search for my sheep and will seek them out.

Ant 2 I am the Alpha and the Omega, says the Most High.

Ant 3 You shall be shepherd of my people Israel, and you shall be leader over Israel.

READING

Jesus is the image of the invisible God, the firstborn of all creation; for in him all things in heaven and on earth were created, things visible and invisible, whether thrones or dominions or rulers or powers—all things have been created through him and for him. He himself is before all things, and in him all things hold together. He is the head of the body, the church; he is the beginning, the firstborn of the dead, so that he might come to have first place in everything. For in him all the fullness of God was pleased to dwell, and through him God was pleased to reconcile...all things, whether on earth or in heaven, my making peace through the blood of his cross.

Col 1:15–20

RESPONSORY

O God, you are our Sovereign, our eyes look to you. **—O God**...
Till you have mercy upon us; **—our eyes**...
Glory to you, Source of all Being, Eternal Word and Holy Spirit.
   —O God...

CANTICLE OF ZECHARIAH

Ant Give thanks to God for calling us to share in the inheritance
   of the saints in light.

INTERCESSIONS

Jesus, you washed the feet of your followers;
   —teach all civic and religious leaders how to govern with
   humility and reverence.
You did not call your disciples servants but friends;
   —help us to establish your kindom by mutual collaboration
   and loving respect.
You shared a meal with one who had betrayed you;
   —give us the desire to set aside our mistrust of one another.
Jesus, you came into the world to testify to the truth;
   —make us credible witnesses to the truth of your gospel.
You suffered at the hands of those you served;
   —enable us to serve one another selflessly without regard
   to human success.

PRAYER: God of the nations, have mercy on our divided world.
   Countries burdened with age-old hatreds struggle to
   heal wounds that would destroy them. Bless the women
   and men who serve as mediators. Heal and encourage
   those who continue to suffer the ravages of war. Teach
   us all how to be instruments of your peace, radiating
   your love to the ends of the earth. So may the reign of
   your Christ come now to our world. Amen.

DAYTIME PRAYER

Ant 1   God has delivered us from the dominion of darkness and transformed us to the realm of the beloved Son, in whom we have redemption, the forgiveness of sins.

Ant 2   Grace and peace from Jesus Christ, the faithful witness, the first born of the dead and the ruler of all on earth.

Ant 3   Christ has been raised from the dead, the first fruits of those who have fallen asleep.

(Prayer as in Morning Prayer)

EVENING PRAYER II
(Psalms from Sunday, Week II, p. 53)

Ant 1   Come, O blessed ones of God, inherit the kindom prepared for you from the foundation of the world.

Ant 2   For this I was born, and for this I have come into the world, to bear witness to the truth.

Ant 3   Truly, I say to you, today you will be with me in Paradise.

READING

That the spirit of Christ by which we are guided, is not changeable, so as once to command us from a thing as evil and again to move unto it; and we do certainly know, and so testify to the world, that the spirit of Christ, which leads us into all Truth, will never move us to fight and war against any [people] with outward weapons, neither for the kingdom of Christ, nor for the kingdoms of this world.

George Fox, *Quaker Spirituality*, p. 106, (1)

RESPONSORY

Let every tongue proclaim to the glory of God, Jesus Christ is Lord. —**Let every**...
In heaven, on the earth, and under the earth; —**Jesus Christ**...
Glory to you, Source of all Being, Eternal Word and Holy Spirit.
    —**Let every**...

CANTICLE OF MARY

Ant   My realm is not of this world.

INTERCESSIONS

Jesus, Prince of Peace;
—may those who govern seek to bring peace, that all may live in a fully human way.
Jesus, Wonderful Counselor;
—give wisdom to those who negotiate to bring about a better quality of life to all people.
Jesus, Lamb of God;
—help us to acknowledge our complicity in the suffering of others, and give us a renewed spirit that we may share in the mystery of redemption.
You are the Way, the Truth, and the Life;
—awaken in us the courage to set aside our petty ways, our half-truths that keep us divided from one another.
You prayed for the coming of the reign of God;
—may we recognize those who differ from us as our sisters and brothers sharing this one earth you came to save.

PRAYER: God of the nations, have mercy on our divided world. Countries burdened with age-old hatreds struggle to heal wounds that would destroy them. Bless the women and men who serve as mediators. Heal and encourage those who continue to suffer the ravages of war. Teach us all how to be instruments of your peace, radiating your love to the ends of the earth. So may the reign of your Christ come now to our world. Amen.

CALENDAR OF FEASTS

March 19
ST. JOSEPH

EVENING PRAYER I

Ant 1 Joseph, the husband of Mary, was a just man (alleluia). (Ps 113, p. 96)

Ant 2 Do not fear to take Mary as your wife, for that which is conceived in her is of the Holy Spirit (alleluia). (Ps 146, p. 166)

Ant 3 Joseph did as God told him and took Mary as his wife, (alleluia). (Eph 1:3–10, p. 157)

READING

In our pursuit of perfection we have St. Joseph's humble and hidden life as our model. He was highly honored as the spouse of the Immaculate Mother of God and representative of the Eternal [Father /Mother] to [the] divine Son on earth, yet he was ever humble, simple, and retiring.... In the exercise of his duties as a poor artisan he knew what real poverty was. Never was there one so poor in spirit or desire as St. Joseph, never one in whom the virtue of poverty shone with more splendor in the sight of heaven. (19 March 1893)

Bl. Mary MacKillop, RSJ, (10)

RESPONSORY

You spoke your word to Joseph, O God, and he fulfilled your will.
    —You spoke...
You blessed him with holiness, **—and he...**
Glory to you, Source of all Being, Eternal Word and Holy Spirit.
    —You spoke...

CANTICLE OF MARY

Ant Praise to you, O God, who chose Joseph to be the faithful protector and provider of Jesus, the Word made flesh, (alleluia).

INTERCESSIONS

Let us give praise for Joseph the just man, who was called the father of Jesus, the Christ:
    Blessed are those whom you choose, O God.

O God, you chose Joseph to be the guide and teacher of the child, Jesus;

—direct our minds and hearts as we strive to instruct children
in your ways.
Through the intercession of Joseph, spouse of Mary;
—give husbands and wives the grace to relate to each other
with reverence and mutual respect.
Joseph supported his family with the work of his hands;
—grant meaningful employment and an adequate wage to all.
Joseph knew the joys and sorrows of parenthood;
—bless all parents with the courage and patience to care for
their children with love and compassion.

PRAYER: O God, you gave Joseph the ineffable joy of joining
Mary in caring for the child, Jesus. Through his
intercession, grant us the grace to nurture the life of
Christ in our lives. Help us to guide and support one
another in truth and in love, and so build up the body
of your church. We ask this in the name of Jesus who
lives with you, Source of all Being, and with the Holy
Spirit. Amen.

MORNING PRAYER
(Psalms from Sunday, Week I, p. 3)

Ant 1 In a dream Joseph was told to take the child and his
mother into Egypt (alleluia).

Ant 2 Joseph rose and took Mary and Jesus at night into Egypt
(alleluia).

Ant 3 An angel appeared to Joseph in a dream telling him to
return to Israel (alleluia).

READING

I took for my advocate and lord the glorious St. Joseph and earnestly
recommended myself to him. I saw clearly...this father and lord of mine
came to my rescue in better ways than I knew how to ask for. I don't
recall up to this day ever having petitioned him for anything that he
failed to grant. It is an amazing thing the great many favors God has
granted me through the mediation of this blessed saint, the dangers I
was freed from both of body and soul. For with other saints it seems
[God] has given them grace to be of help in one need, whereas with this
glorious saint I have experience that he helps in all our needs and that
the Lord wants us to understand that just as he was subject to St.
Joseph on earth—for since bearing the title father, being the Lord's

tutor, Joseph could give the Child commands—so in heaven God does whatever he commands.

Teresa of Avila, *Life*, Ch. 6, 6, (3)

RESPONSORY

O God, you spoke your word to Joseph, and he fulfilled your will.
  — **O God,**...
You blessed him with holiness, —**and he**...
Glory to you, Source of all Being, Eternal Word and Holy Spirit.
  — **O God**...

CANTICLE OF ZECHARIAH

Ant They said of Jesus: isn't this the son of Joseph, the
    carpenter?

INTERCESSIONS

O God, you direct the life of the church through the guidance of the Holy Spirit. We have named Joseph, its guardian and protector, and so we pray:
  Help us to walk the ways of your holy ones.

In praise of Joseph we recall his humility and goodness;
  —deliver us from harmful ambition and self-seeking.
Joseph entered into the mysteries of the life of Jesus;
  —grant us the faith to recognize and follow the call of your
    Spirit in our lives.
Joseph cared for his family in an occupied land;
  —be merciful to those who are in bondage and grant them
    freedom and peace.
Joseph died knowing the love of Jesus and Mary;
  —give us the grace to die at peace with our families and with
    confidence in your mercy.

PRAYER: O God, you gave Joseph the ineffable joy of joining
    Mary in caring for the child, Jesus. Through his
    intercession, grant us the grace to nurture the life of
    Christ in our lives. Help us to guide and support one
    another in truth and in love, and so build up the body
    of your church. We ask this in the name of Jesus who
    lives with you, Source of all Being, and with the Holy
    Spirit. Amen.

DAYTIME PRAYER

Ant 1 Through Joseph and his spouse, Mary, God fulfilled the covenant promised to Abraham and Sarah, (alleluia). (Ps 120, p. 155)

Ant 2 In the hills of Nazareth, you fulfilled your plan for us in silent and hidden ways, (alleluia). (Ps 121, p. 89)

Ant 3 Joseph grew strong in faith, giving glory to God (alleluia). (Ps 122, p. 143)

(Prayer as in Morning Prayer)

EVENING PRAYER II

Ant 1 Jesus and his parents went to Jerusalem every year at the feast of Passover, (alleluia). (Ps 15, p. 14)

Ant 2 As they returned to Jerusalem, Jesus remained behind, and they searched three days for him, (alleluia). (Ps 112, p. 149)

Ant 3 The parents of Jesus found him among the teachers, listening to them and asking them questions, (alleluia). (Rev 15:3–4, p. 41)

READING

Contemporary Christians might find their way back to what is best in them if the individuality of this man [Joseph], their patron, were again producing more stature in them.... A nation needs men and women of lifelong performance of duty, of clearheaded loyalty, of discipline of heart and body. A nation needs men and women who know that true greatness is achieved only in selfless service to the greater and holy duty that is imposed upon each life.... A nation needs men and women who do not lose confidence in God's grace, even when they have to seek it as lost, as Joseph once sought the divine child. Such individuals are urgently needed in every situation and in every class.... Joseph lives...for the communion of saints is near and the seeming distance is only appearance.... We, however, will experience the blessing of his protection if we, with God's grace, open our heart and our life to his spirit and the quiet power of his intercession.

Karl Rahner, *The Great Church Year*, pp. 326–27, (2)

RESPONSORY

O God, you spoke your word to Joseph, and he fulfilled your will.
— **O God...**

You blessed him with holiness, **—and he...**
Glory to you, Source of all Being, Eternal Word and Holy Spirit.
   — O God...

CANTICLE OF MARY

Ant Jesus returned to Nazareth with his parents and was
     obedient to them, (alleluia).

INTERCESSIONS

Let us give praise for Joseph the just man, who was called the
father of Jesus, the Christ:
     Blessed are those whom you choose, O God.

O God, you chose Joseph to be the guide and teacher of the child,
Jesus;
   —direct our minds and hearts as we strive to instruct children
    in your ways.
Through the intercession of Joseph, spouse of Mary;
   —give husbands and wives the grace to relate to each other
    with reverence and mutual respect.
Joseph supported his family with the work of his hands;
   —grant meaningful employment and an adequate wage to all.
Joseph knew the joys and sorrows of parenthood;
   —bless all parents with the courage and patience to care for
    their children with love and compassion.

PRAYER: O God, you gave Joseph the ineffable joy of joining
       Mary in caring for the child, Jesus. Through his
       intercession, grant us the grace to nurture the life of
       Christ in our lives. Help us to guide and support one
       another in truth and in love, and so build up the body
       of your church. We ask this in the name of Jesus who
       lives with you, Source of all Being, and with the Holy
       Spirit. Amen.

March 25
ANNUNCIATION

EVENING PRAYER I

Ant 1 A virgin shall conceive and bear a child and the child shall
     be called Emmanuel (alleluia). (Ps 113, p. 96)

Ant 2   Sacrifice and offerings you have not desired, but a body you have prepared for me (alleluia). (Ps 147:12–20, p. 85)

Ant 3   As the rain falls from heaven and does not return until it has given growth to the seed, so shall my word accomplish my purpose (alleluia). (Phil 2:6–11, p. 96)

READING

It seems that the moment of breakthrough for Mary was also the beginning of the breakthrough of salvation for all creation....a moment came at which a unique demand was made on her.... Her response was a self-giving so total that she was, as it were, subsumed in that giving. It *was* herself. But the event we are talking about is the conception of a baby, which is above all a bodily event.... Mary, mother of the Word, had much to learn, later. She made mistakes, she did not understand, she suffered. But from that time her being, her very body, was the Being of the One to whom she had assented.

Rosemary Haughton, The Passionate God, pp. 133–34, (1)

RESPONSORY

You are the honor of our race, you are the joy of our people. **—You are**...
The promise has been fulfilled, **—you are the joy**...
Glory to you, Source of all Being, Eternal Word and Holy Spirit.
    —You are...

CANTICLE OF MARY

Ant   The angel of God declared unto Mary, and she conceived by the Holy Spirit (alleluia).

INTERCESSIONS

Mary, full of grace, is called to be the mother of Jesus. We rejoice in you, O God, as we say:
    You are the honor of your people, O blessed virgin, Mary.

Mary is blessed among women with the joy all ages have awaited;
    —through her intercession free all women who are in
      bondage and who lead lives less than human.
Mary chose freely to become the mother of the savior;
    —grant to all people the freedom to choose their way of life.
Mary rejoiced at the mystery of her motherhood;
    —grant your grace and guidance to mothers who do not want
      their children.

Mary went in haste to support and to share the mystery of new life with her cousin, Elizabeth;

—teach us how to share with others, the fruit of your Spirit in our lives.

PRAYER: O God, in the fullness of time, you called the virgin, Mary, to be the mother of Jesus. As we celebrate this mystery of the annunciation, of Mary's entrance into the mystery of redemption, grant us the grace of opening our lives to all that you would call us to be. Give us the mind and heart of Mary that we too may bear Christ to the world. We ask this through Jesus Christ, the Incarnate Word, one with you, Source of all life, and with the Holy Spirit. Amen.

MORNING PRAYER
(Psalms from Sunday, Week I, p. 3)

Ant 1 The angel Gabriel said to Mary: Hail full of grace, the Most High is with you (alleluia).

Ant 2 Favored daughter of Israel, you have found favor with God (alleluia).

Ant 3 You will give birth to Jesus who will save his people from their sins (alleluia).

READING

Oh, if you could feel in some way the quality and intensity of that fire sent from heaven, the refreshing coolness that accompanied it, the consolation it imparted; if you could realize the great exaltation of the Virgin Mother, the ennobling of the human race, the condescension of the divine majesty; if you could hear the Virgin singing with joy.... If you could see the sweet embrace of the Virgin and the woman who had been sterile and hear the greeting in which the tiny servant recognized his Lord,...then I am sure you would sing in sweet tones with the Blessed Virgin that sacred hymn: *My soul [proclaims your greatness, O my God,]* and with the tiny prophet you would exalt, rejoice and adore the marvelous virginal conception.

Bonaventure, *The Tree of Life*, p. 127, (1)

RESPONSORY

Mother of our savior, mother pierced with a lance, pray for us who trust in you. —**Mother...**

You are the cause of our joy, —**pray for**...
Glory to you, Source of all Being, Eternal Word and Holy Spirit.
    —**Mother**...

CANTICLE OF ZECHARIAH

Ant I am God's handmaid, be it done to me according to your
    word (alleluia).

INTERCESSIONS

The mercies of God endure from age to age, working marvels for
the people. With grateful hearts we pray:
        O God, holy is your name.

You blessed the holiness of Mary with the joy of your call;
    —give us the grace to persevere in faith and in prayer when our
      efforts seem fruitless.
Mary's fiat brings salvation to the world;
    —let all of our choices promote life and give you praise and
      glory.
Mary heard the word of God and entered the mystery of
redemption;
    —give us the grace to follow the lure of your call to growth.
Mary's "yes" to God brought motherhood and martyrdom of heart;
    —bless all parents who bear deep suffering in their children; be
      their refuge and strength.

PRAYER: O God, in the fullness of time, you called the virgin,
        Mary, to be the mother of Jesus. As we celebrate this
        mystery of the annunciation, of Mary's entrance into
        the mystery of redemption, grant us the grace of
        opening our lives to all that you would call us to be.
        Give us the mind and heart of Mary that we too may
        bear Christ to the world. We ask this through Jesus
        Christ, the Incarnate Word, one with you, Source of all
        life, and with the Holy Spirit. Amen.

DAYTIME PRAYER

Ant 1 I delight to do your will, O God; your law is within my
    heart (alleluia). (Ps 120, p. 155)

Ant 2 All generations shall call me blessed; most holy is your
name (alleluia). (Ps 121, p. 89)

Ant 3 You have favored the lowliness of your handmaid and have
lifted up the powerless (alleluia). (Ps 122, p. 143)

(Prayer as in Morning Prayer)

EVENING PRAYER II

Ant 1 Blessed is she who believed that God's word in her would
be fulfilled (alleluia). (Ps 110:1–5, 7, p. 53)

Ant 2 The power of the Most High overshadowed Mary, and the
Spirit came upon her (alleluia). (Ps 130, p. 143)

Ant 3 The Holy One born of you shall be called the Son of God
(alleluia). (Col 1:12–20, p. 171)

READING

...The girl prays by the bare wall
Between the lamp and the chair.
(Framed with an angel in our galleries
She has a richer painted room, sometimes a crown.
Yet seven pillars of obscurity
Build her to Wisdom's house, and Ark, and Tower.
She is the Secret of another Testament
She owns their manna in her jar.)

Fifteen years old—
The flowers printed on her dress
Cease moving in the middle of her prayer
When God, Who sends the messenger,
Meets [this] messenger in her Heart.
Her answer, between breath and breath,
Wrings from her innocence our Sacrament!
In her white body God becomes our Bread....

"The Annunciation" in *The Collected Poems of Thomas Merton*, p. 284, (16)

RESPONSORY

Blessed are you among women and blessed is the fruit of your womb.
   —Blessed...
Hail, ark of the covenant, **—blessed is...**
Glory to you, Source of all Being, Eternal Word and Holy Spirit.
   —Blessed...

CANTICLE OF MARY

Ant My spirit rejoices in God, my savior (alleluia).

INTERCESSIONS

Mary, full of grace, is called to be the mother of Jesus. We rejoice in you, O God, as we say:
You are the honor of your people, O blessed virgin, Mary.

Mary is blessed among women with the joy all ages have awaited;
—through her intercession free all women who are in bondage
and who lead lives less than human.
Mary chose freely to become the mother of the savior;
—grant to all people the freedom to choose their way of life.
Mary rejoiced at the mystery of her motherhood;
—grant your grace and guidance to mothers who do not want
their children.
Mary went in haste to support and to share the mystery of new
life with her cousin, Elizabeth;
—teach us how to share with others, the fruit of your Spirit in
our lives.

PRAYER: O God, in the fullness of time, you called the virgin,
Mary, to be the mother of Jesus. As we celebrate this
mystery of the annunciation, of Mary's entrance into
the mystery of redemption, grant us the grace of
opening our lives to all that you would call us to be.
Give us the mind and heart of Mary that we too may
bear Christ to the world. We ask this through Jesus
Christ, the Incarnate Word, one with you, Source of all
life, and with the Holy Spirit. Amen.

April 7
ST. JULIE BILLIART

MORNING/EVENING PRAYER
(Psalms from Sunday, Week I, p. 3)

Ant 1 If you would follow me, take up your cross.

Ant 2 All will go right or not; if it does not go right, the good God
will open a way for us.

Ant 3 May our good Jesus and his holy cross live in us!

READING

Julie Billiart, born in France in 1751, founded the congregation of Sisters of Notre Dame de Namur. Though afflicted by many physical sufferings and the political unrest of the French Revolution, Julie Billiart was a woman of courage with outstanding faith. She wrote: "The good God asks these very simple and easy tasks: that our soul be united to [God] by charity; that we do our duty as perfectly as possible...that we do the most common things in an uncommon manner." Julie Billiart died April 7, 1816.

Themes of Julie Billiart, p. 8, (44)

RESPONSORY

Do not be frightened, God will never fail you. —**Do not...**
In joy or adversity, — **God...**
Glory to you, Source of all Being, Eternal Word and Holy Spirit.
    —**Do not...**

CANTICLE

Ant As gold in the furnace, God proved her.

INTERCESSIONS

You use the weak ones of the earth to accomplish your works, O God, and so we pray:
    Blessed are they who suffer persecution for your sake.

O God, through the intercession of Julie Billiart;
    —may all threatened by revolutions and political unrest know
      the peace the world cannot give.
For nearly twenty years of her adult life, Julie was a cripple;
    —give courage to those who are injured and physically
      disabled.
She was a "soul of prayer" and a woman of sound common sense;
    —help us all to use our gifts of nature and grace for your glory.
Julie persevered in her dedication to your call in spite of civil, ecclesiastic, and domestic persecution;
    —comfort all who suffer misunderstanding as they follow the
      guidance of the Spirit.

PRAYER: Most loving God, you blessed your daughter, Julie, with humility and wisdom in the midst of struggle and misunderstanding. Through her, many came to know your love and concern. Bless her followers, the Sisters of Notre Dame de Namur, that they may continue the work you began in her. We ask this in the names of Jesus and his mother, Mary. Amen.

April 10
TEILHARD DE CHARDIN

MORNING/EVENING PRAYER

Ant 1 We rejoice in the works of your hands. (Ps 8, p. 92)

Ant 2 The universe reflects your glory, O God. You reveal its secrets to the wise and simple. (Ps 148, p. 99)

Ant 3 All creation sings your glory; even the stones shout for joy. (Ps 65, p. 63)

READING

Since today, Lord, I your priest have neither bread nor wine nor altar, I shall spread my hands over the whole universe and take its immensity as the matter of my sacrifice. Is not the infinite circle of things the one final Host that it is your will to transmute? The seething cauldron in which the activities of all living and cosmic substance are brewed together—is not that the bitter cup that you seek to sanctify?... Let creation repeat to itself again today, and tomorrow, and until the end of time, so long as the transformation has not run its full course, the divine saying: "This is my body."

Teilhard deChardin, The Prayer of the Universe, p. 157, p. 158, (60)

RESPONSORY

I will give thanks to God with my whole heart. —**I will**...
I will tell of all your wonders; —**with my**...
Glory to you, Source of all Being, Eternal Word and Holy Spirit.
   —**I will**...

CANTICLE

Ant Christ is the goad that urges creatures along the road of effort, of elevation, of development.

INTERCESSIONS

O Cosmic Christ, you are present in the heart of the world;
   —may we reverence you in all your works.
Unifying Center of the world, you draw all things to yourself;
   —bring all creation to the fullness of being.

Redeemer of the world;
—help us to protect our environment for future generations.
God of the heavens;
—may our ventures into space be for the good of all humankind
and in accord with gospel values.
Christ, the Alpha and the Omega;
—may all who have died enjoy the glory of resurrection and aid
us on our way.

PRAYER: We give you thanks, Creator God, for your servant,
Teilhard, and for all those who help us to see you in
your universe. May creation be continually transformed
that all may share in the life, death, and resurrection of
God become human, our Lord Jesus Christ. Amen.

April 17
ANNA DENGEL, SCMM

MORNING/EVENING PRAYER
(Psalms from Sunday, Week I, p. 3)

Ant 1 The impossible of today is the work of tomorrow.

Ant 2 I was fire and flame.... I was determined to become a
mission doctor.

Ant 3 A religious community has a task to do...to be an arm of
the Church, to reach out in the name of Christ to the
hundred and one human needs.

READING

Anna Marie Dengel was born on March 16, 1892, in Steeg, Austria. In
her late teens, she heard that women and children were dying
needlessly in another land because their customs would not allow them
to be treated by men. She responded by becoming a doctor and
eventually founding the Medical Mission Sisters, a community for whom
she obtained permission to "practice medicine in its full scope." When
Mother Dengel died in April, 1980, the Medical Mission Sisters were
serving the sick and needy on five continents, and through them the
vision of their founder continues to expand throughout the world today.

RESPONSORY

Every person has an inherent right to live a fully human life.
—**Every person...**

Justice is essential to the healing that enables all people;
   —to live...
Glory to you, Source of all Being, Eternal Word and Holy Spirit.
   —Every person...

CANTICLE

Ant All the ends of the earth have seen the saving power of God.

INTERCESSIONS

Throughout her life, Anna Dengel had a passion for possibilities;
   —O God, increase our faith.
Mother Dengel taught her sisters to be a healing presence among
people in need;
   —help us to remove anything in our lives that blocks your life-
      giving Spirit.
She dreamed of a world where no boundaries existed, where
women and men, Christian and Muslim...all people had access to
what would make them fully human;
   —Spirit of God, open our hearts and minds to the reality of
      your Presence in every person.
Her deep compassion inspired others to serve the sick in cultures
where women had formerly been left untreated;
   —Jesus our Savior, awaken us to the hidden needs of others.
To the advantage of those she taught and served, Mother Dengel
combined religious life in the Church with medical
professionalism;
   —Creator God, give us the generosity and perseverance to do all
      things well.

PRAYER: O God, Anna Dengel transformed the challenges of her
            life and the needs of others into a means of healing and
            salvation for people throughout the world. Her
            compassion and deep faith enabled her to break
            through ecclesiastic and cultural barriers to allow
            religious women to serve the needy as medical doctors.
            Through her intercession, we ask for the wisdom and
            courage we need to grant all women and men their true
            dignity in the human family. We ask this for the praise
            and glory of your name. Amen.

April 29
ST. CATHERINE OF SIENA

MORNING/EVENING PRAYER
(Psalms from Sunday, Week I, p. 3)

Ant 1 No virtue can have life in it except from love, and love is nursed and mothered by humility.

Ant 2 It was love that made you create us and give us being.

Ant 3 We are your image, and now by making yourself one with us you have become our image.

READING

Catherine was born in 1347 and as a young girl entered the Third Order of St. Dominic. She worked for peace between cities, fought for the rights of the Pope in Rome, and was a dominant figure of the fourteenth century. Though semiliterate, her experience of mystical theology was such that she has been named a Doctor of the Church. She writes: "A soul rises up, restless with tremendous desire for God's honor and the salvation of souls. She has for some time exercised herself in virtue and has become accustomed to dwelling in the cell of self-knowledge in order to know better God's goodness toward her, since upon knowledge follows love. And loving, she seeks to pursue truth and clothe herself in it. But there is no way she can so savor and be enlightened by this truth as in continual humble prayer, grounded in the knowledge of herself and of God. For by such prayer the soul is united with God, following in the footsteps of Christ crucified, and through desire and affection and the union of love he makes of her another himself. So Christ seems to have meant when he said, 'If you will love me and keep my word, I will show myself to you, and you will be one thing with me and I with you.'"*

*Catherine of Siena, *The Dialogue*, p. 25, (1)

RESPONSORY

You, O Lord Jesus, call me and I'm coming to you. —**You**...
Through your mercy, —**I'm coming**...
Glory to you, Source of all Being, Eternal Word and Holy Spirit. —**You**...

CANTICLE

Ant To love is to insert one's self in the nature of God, who is the way, the truth, and the life, who is goodness and peace.

INTERCESSIONS

O God, your daughter Catherine was a woman of great courage who challenged the Church she loved;
> —may the whole Church always be open to your grace and truth.

In her life, she was known as a woman of peace;
> —may all who are estranged be reconciled in Christ who is our peace.

Catherine was devoured by hunger for your honor O God, and the salvation of your people;
> —enkindle our desires for you and for the good of others.

Through Catherine, you called the laity and the clergy to work together as the people of God;
> —further the work of dialogue and ministry that each person's gifts may be used for the sake of the gospel.

Though a victim of slander and malicious talk, Catherine forgave those who spoke ill of her;
> —give us the grace to forgive others as we have been so graciously forgiven.

PRAYER: Loving God, you strengthened your servant, Catherine, a woman of courage and deep faith, to challenge the leaders of the Church of her day for the sake of unity and peace. Bless all those who challenge us in our complacency; give us the spirit of Jesus to truly love and reverence one another that we may be one family united in Christ. Amen.

April 30
BL. MARIE OF THE INCARNATION GUYART*

MORNING/EVENING PRAYER
(Psalms from Sunday, Week I, p. 3)

Ant 1 I could conceive nothing good or beautiful or desirable except possessing the spirit of Jesus Christ.

Ant 2 My soul was wholly lost in this great ocean of love.

Ant 3 O my Love, this house must be for Jesus, Mary, and Joseph.

READING

Born in Tours, France in 1599, Marie Guyart by the time of her death in Canada in 1572 had fulfilled the contradictory vocations of wife, mother, cloistered religious, and missionary to the New World. After seventeen years of widowhood and a series of mysterious dreams, Marie set sail with two Ursuline companions to work for the evangelization of native children, thus becoming the first woman religious in North America. She wrote: "The Spirit who has guided me so lovingly has always tended to the same goal, leading me to the practice of the virtues.... This has always been in order to have me follow the spirit of the Gospel for which, from the beginning, my soul has had a special attraction, aspiring always to that perfect possession of the spirit of Jesus Christ. He has bestowed on me that degree of perfection which has pleased him. This was accomplished by his holy actions in those successive states through which he had led me in overwhelming mercy, and to which, had I corresponded, my progress in holiness would have been very different.... I beg the God of goodness, my adorable Spouse, to cleanse all my faults in his precious blood and to have mercy on me...."*
Beatified in 1980 Marie of the Incarnation is honored not only as the founder of the Canadian Ursulines but as a patron of Canada as well.

Marie of the Incarnation: Selected Writings, pp. 177–78, (1)

RESPONSORY

Marie left her sisters and her country to bring the Gospel to the
    New World. —**Marie left**...
She lived in the Spirit of Jesus Christ, —**to bring**...
Glory to you, Source of all Being, Eternal Word and Holy Spirit.
    —**Marie left**...

CANTICLE

Ant In spirit I go round the world to bring souls to Jesus Christ.

INTERCESSIONS

As a child Marie responded to God's avowal of love by an unconditional "Yes";
    —fill us with a spirit of unswerving trust in God's unconditional
       love for us and, like Marie, let us share this grace especially
       with those whose image is of a God harsh and unforgiving.
In being faithful to God's plan for her, Marie broke through accepted social and religious conventions;

—give your church leaders and all your people clarity of vision and courage to honor the leading of the Holy Spirit even when it means breaking with time-honored conventions.

Marie, despite her fears and her apparent failure, was steadfast in her dream of bringing Jesus Christ to the people of the New World;

—at a time when the number of poor and homeless is growing daily, give courage and compassion to those called to work with the marginalized, the refugees, and the indigenous peoples of our world.

Marie recognized that it was only through a spirit of prayer that she would be strengthened for her work;

—in a world often frenetic with action deepen in your people a spirit of contemplation so that all our actions will begin and end in you who alone can sustain us.

PRAYER: God of loving kindness, you led Blessed Marie of the Incarnation to contemplate the wonder of the Trinity, and gave her the zealous heart of an apostle. By her intercession and example make us witnesses of your generosity that more may come to know, love, and serve you. Amen.

*Composed by Irene Mahoney, osu, New Rochelle, New York.

May 8
JULIAN OF NORWICH

MORNING/EVENING PRAYER
(Psalms from Sunday, Week I, p. 3)

Ant 1 You will see yourself, that every kind of thing will be well.

Ant 2 We shall rejoice only in our blessed Savior, Jesus, and trust in him for everything.

Ant 3 By contrition we are made clean, by compassion we are made ready, and by true longing for God we are made worthy.

READING

Julian of Norwich, an anonymous woman, was a fourteenth-century mystic. She lived as a recluse in a cell attached to the church of St. Julian of Norwich. Her writings have been a source of inspiration throughout the centuries, and they reveal a contemplative woman who is a reliable spiritual guide for those who follow the spiritual path. In her *Revelations* she wrote: "But often when our falling and our wretchedness are shown to us, we are so much afraid and so greatly ashamed of ourselves that we scarcely know where we can put ourselves. But then our courteous Mother [Jesus] does not wish us to flee away, for nothing would be less pleasing to him; but he then wants us to behave like a child. For when it is distressed and frightened, it runs quickly to its mother; and if it can do no more, it calls to the mother for help with all its might. So he wants us to act as a meek child, saying: My kind Mother, my gracious Mother, my beloved Mother, have mercy on me."*

*Julian of Norwich, *Showings*, p. 293, p. 301, (1)

RESPONSORY

Mercy is a sweet, gracious operation in love, mingled with plentiful
  compassion. —**Mercy**...
For mercy works, protecting us, turning everything to good for us;
  —**mingled**...
Glory to you, Source of all Being, Eternal Word and Holy Spirit.
  —**Mercy**...

CANTICLE

Ant For I saw most truly that where Jesus Christ appears, peace
  is received and wrath has no place.

INTERCESSIONS

O God of tender compassion, we trust in you at every moment. We
turn to you and pray:
  O God, have mercy upon us.

You, O God, are our true peace and safe protector;
  —may all who experience the horrors of war and violence
    find comfort in your outstretched arms.
Jesus, you have compassion on us because of our sin;
  —may all who are estranged know the peace of your
    reconciling love.
You take heed not only of great and noble things, but also in
those which are little and small;
  —may all know the joy of your providential love and care.
You invite us, O God, to be united with you in prayer;
  —in you alone, we live, and move, and have our being.
Jesus lived in the desert for forty days, praying and fasting;

—bless all women who are called to be hermits and anchorites.

PRAYER: O Compassionate One, you rejoice that you are our Father, and you rejoice that you are our Mother. Give us the faith and courage to truly believe in the absolute truth of your tender mercy for us and for all humanity. We ask this in the name of Jesus, our Savior and brother. Amen.

May 9
BLESSED THERESA OF JESUS GERHARDINGER, SSND*

MORNING/EVENING PRAYER
(Psalms from Sunday, Week I, p. 3)

Ant 1 I cannot describe my interior peace. Now I am in Jesus. May he do what he wants with me.**

Ant 2 All the works of God proceed slowly and in pain; but then, their roots are sturdier and their flowering the lovelier.**

Ant 3 God must be in all things our goal and the end and highest good, in whom we find everything that will make us content and truly happy.**

READING

Theresa Gerhardinger was born in Regensburg-Stadtamhof, Germany in 1797. Theresa believed that family life would improve only when women were educated. It was this purpose that led her to found the School Sisters of Notre Dame in 1833. In her dialog with the hierarchical church she was a witness to courage and enduring love. Through great difficulty she was named one of the first women in church history to lead a religious congregation with no male director over her. She wrote to her Sisters shortly before her death, "My dear Sisters, Our Lord has placed a limit on my days; I shall soon appear before God's judgment seat. I am urged, therefore, before I leave this world, to direct these words to you, words which fill my heart to overflowing.... My grateful thanks for all the love, the confidence you have shown me, for all your patience with my weakness. I believe I can honestly say that I meant well with every sister, and that I have treasured you all in my heart....". (Letter #5319, 1878) Theresa Gerhardinger died May 9, 1879.

RESPONSORY

In my opinion our perfection lies in the love of God. —In my...

Jesus must be the Way we walk, the Truth we follow, the Life we
  lead; —**our perfection**...
Glory to you, Source of all Being, Eternal Word and Holy Spirit.
  —**In my**...

CANTICLE

Ant His mother said to the servants, "Do whatever he tells you."

INTERCESSIONS

Creator God, you fostered in Theresa a vision of women and men
in partnership creating stronger families and a better world;
  —"Do not lose courage. Jesus Christ will be at your side and
    help you to conquer."
Christ Jesus, like the poor widow of the gospel you called Theresa
to give out of her need;
  —may we continue to give out of our own need to serve your
    people where we are sent.
Holy Spirit, you strengthened Theresa to be a prophetic voice to
the hierarchical Church;
  —may we follow her example by changing unjust structures
    through dialog and reconciliation.

PRAYER: Loving Trinity, you blessed Theresa with creative
    fidelity and Eucharistic strength. In the midst of her
    suffering she could say, "I often visualize the Blessed
    Virgin standing beneath the cross as I meditate on the
    words, 'she stood.'" Please strengthen us to stand with
    your people in the silence of contemplation and the
    struggle for justice. We ask this in Jesus' name. Amen.

*Office composed by Sr. Judith Best, SSND, St. Louis, Missouri.
**Excerpts from her letters.

May 10
BL. DAMIEN de VEUSTER of MOLOKAI

MORNING/EVENING PRAYER
(Psalms from Sunday, Week I, p. 3)

Ant 1 You, O God, preserve the simple. When I was brought low,
    you saved me.

Ant 2 My heart is moved with pity for the many.

Ant 3 I love you because you have heard my voice and my supplication.

READING

Joseph de Veuster was born in Belgium in the year 1840. When he was nineteen years of age he entered the Order of the Sacred Hearts of Jesus and Mary taking the name, Damien. He was missioned to the Hawaiian Islands and began his work with the native peoples in 1864. When apprised of the need for help with the lepers of Molokai, Damien volunteered and worked tirelessly both for their physical and spiritual well-being. After twelve years working with the lepers, he contracted the disease and wrote to the bishop of Honolulu, "I cannot come for leprosy has attacked me. There are signs of it on my left cheek and ear, and my eyebrows are beginning to fall. I shall soon be quite disfigured. I have no doubt whatever about the nature of my illness, but I am calm and resigned and very happy in the midst of my people.... I daily repeat from my heart, 'Thy Will be done.'"* He died 15 April 1889.

*John Farrow, *Damien the Leper*, p. 160, (25)

RESPONSORY

He was oppressed, and he was afflicted, yet he did not open his mouth. —**He was**...
He was cut off from the land of the living; —**yet he**...
Glory to you, Source of all Being, Eternal Word and Holy Spirit.
   —**He was**...

CANTICLE

Ant For those who would save their lives will lose them; and those who lose their lives for my sake will find them.

INTERCESSIONS

You, O God, love all that you have made;
   —give us open hearts to embrace those who are afflicted and oppressed.
Damien ministered to both the physical and spiritual well-being of the lepers he had learned to love;
   —fill us with compassion, and give us the insight to recognize the needs of our sisters and brothers.
He overcame his aversion for the disfigurement caused by the disease and served his people with reverence;
   —enable us to reverence all who are ravaged by disease, that they may know themselves as children of God.

Mother Marianne Cope and other Sisters of St. Francis of
Syracuse were the first to aid Damien in his work;
  —bless all caregivers who minister to those with incurable
    diseases, and give them the graces they need to serve with
    love and compassion.
Scientific research has enabled those with Hansen's disease to
live productively within society;
  —guide the work of scientists who continue to work to find
    cures for debilitating and incurable diseases.

PRAYER: O God, in Damien you have given us a model of one
who stood in the place of those he served. Like Damien
help us to respond to the needs of others with love born
of compassion. Comfort all who are afflicted with life-
threatening diseases and bless those who minister to
them. We ask this in the name of Jesus whose healing
presence we long to be. Amen.

May 14
VEN. MOTHER THEODORE GUÉRIN, SP

MORNING/EVENING PRAYER
(Psalms from Sunday, Week I, p. 3)

Ant 1 Be assured that in leaving the past to the mercy of God
and the future to [God's] providence, you will derive from
your offering very great peace and consolation.

Ant 2 The spirit of faith consists in doing our actions for God and
in [God's] presence.

Ant 3 Oh how good a thing is silence. It is a sovereign remedy for
nearly every kind of evil and the means to acquire a great
many virtues.

READING

Mother Theodore (Anne-Therese) Guerin was born in Etables, France,
October 2, 1798. In 1823, she joined the Sisters of Providence at Ruille-
sur-Loir. In 1840, she was chosen to establish the Sisters of Providence
at St. Mary-of-the-Woods, Indiana. This mission, carried out amid the
hardships of pioneer life, entailed labors and crosses that she bore with
invincible charity and fortitude. Her life gives testimony not only to
gifted administrative ability but also to heroic faith, profound humility,

and untiring zeal for souls. She wrote: "...we shall have; our desires for certain employments; our reputation; our health—to be sick or well, useful or useless, it will be equally indifferent to us, as it will be also to have consolation or aridity in our prayers, repose or temptations; all we shall leave sweetly to the providence of God. This will be our offering."*

*A Sister of Providence, *Life and Life-Work of Mother Theodore Guérin,* p. 429, (27)

RESPONSORY

When I am afraid, I put my trust in you, in you whose word I praise.
   —When I...
In you I trust without fear; **—in you whose...**
Glory to you, Source of all Being, Eternal Word and Holy Spirit.
   —When I...

CANTICLE

Ant Perfect abandonment of ourselves in all things for the future
   requires great courage,...but we ought to aspire to it.

INTERCESSIONS

O God, you gave the gift of holiness to your servant, Mother
Theodore;
   —grant us the light, grace, and strength we need to lead lives
      holy and blameless in your sight.
With great courage, Mother Theodore endured her crosses in
union with your son in his sufferings;
   —strengthen us as we try to learn the lessons of your love and
      the cross.
O God, through your servant you brought your gospel to your
children in a foreign land;
   —help us to respond courageously in true service to your
      people, that with them we may journey toward a world of
      justice, love, and peace.

Mother Theodore taught that love and not fear is the guiding force of education;
—bless all those dedicated to the profession of teaching; may they further God's providence through works of love as they instruct others in their academic pursuits.

Provident God, Mother Theodore found you in the forests of Indiana, offering you all that she possessed; trusting in your providential guidance; hoping that through her life and the lives of her sisters, faith and knowledge would grow.
—Once again we reach out to you, offering our lives for the continued effort of building providence in our world today.

PRAYER: O God, whose name is Providence and whose face is always turned toward our world, we thank you for your constant fidelity. Our path into the future at times seems unclear, yet we turn to you with patience and trust. Leaning upon your goodness and strength, we believe we will always be sustained and supported. Hear and answer us in Jesus' name. Amen.

May 15
ST. JOHN BAPTIST DE LA SALLE*

MORNING/EVENING PRAYER
(Psalms from Sunday, Week I, p. 3)

Ant 1 They are generous, they give to the poor, the good they have accomplished will last forever.

Ant 2 Happy are those, O God, whom you guide and teach by your law.

Ant 3 As your word is proclaimed, it enlightens and the humble understand.

READING

Born at Reims, France, 30 April 1651, into a devout and influential family, John Baptist de La Salle received the tonsure at age eleven, and was named Canon of the Reims Cathedral at sixteen, and was ordained priest on 9 April 1678. Two years later he received the doctorate in theology. Meanwhile he became tentatively involved with a group of rough and barely literate young men who wanted to establish schools for poor boys. Moved by the plight of the poor who seemed so "far from salvation" either in this world or the next, he determined to put his own talents and advanced education at the service of the children "often left to themselves and badly brought up." To be more effective, he abandoned his family home, moved in with the teachers, renounced his position as Canon and his wealth, and so formed the community that became known as the Brothers of the Christian Schools. Worn out by auterities and exhausting labors, he died at Saint Yon near Rouen early on Good Friday, only weeks before his sixty-eighth birthday.

RESPONSORY

In the heart of the wise wisdom dwells. —**In the heart**...
The wise will teach the ignorant; —**where wisdom**...
Glory to you, Source of all Being, Eternal Word and Holy Spirit.
   —**In the heart**...

CANTICLE

Ant Only one who loves can educate and guide as a parent does.

INTERCESSIONS

Lord Jesus, you gave us in St. John Baptist de La Salle a living image of your merciful love;
   —grant that we experience the gentleness of your love in those who guide us.
The establishment resented his innovative methods and his insistence on gratuity for all, regardless of their circumstances;
   —bless the creative efforts of teachers and enable them to serve all who are in need.
During his time on earth, Jesus grew in wisdom, age, and grace;
   —teach us to be patient with the time one must take to mature.
Raise up Christian educators everywhere to proclaim the good news of salvation;
   —confirm them, through the example of St. John Baptist de La Salle, in their life of faith, hope, and love.
Jesus proclaimed children to be blessed and he loved them;
   —grant that we never scandalize any of those for whom he gave his life.

PRAYER: O God, you chose St. John Baptist de La Salle for the Christian education of youth, inspire teachers who are dedicated to serve the new generation, in school and throughout life. We ask this through Jesus, who taught us the way. Amen.

*Office from Christian Brothers, Landover, Maryland.

May 25
ST. MADELEINE SOPHIE BARAT

MORNING/EVENING PRAYER
(Psalms from Sunday, Week I, p. 3)

Ant 1 It is the interior spirit that gives life and fruitfulness to everything.

Ant 2 The proof of true love is forgetfulness of self and one's own interests.

Ant 3 What difference does it make how you pray, provided your heart is seeking the One whom you love?

READING

Madeleine Sophie Barat, born at Burgundy, December 12, 1779, founded the Society of the Sacred Heart. From her earliest years, she felt called to be a nun. In spite of her personal illness and many difficulties, the Society flourished. Madeleine Sophie was known for her common sense, courage, and kindness. Her apostolic zeal and her contemplative spirituality were the cornerstones of the Society she founded. She wrote to her Sisters: "...Be pious, but with a piety which puts duty before exercises of pure devotion. Be firm against the world and human respect. Be simple and modest.... Don't judge, be kindly in thought. Don't just be good; be lovable, with that lovability which is both energetic and thoughtful of others which you will find in the strong and sweet Heart of Jesus."* Madeleine Sophie died May 25, 1865.

*Margaret Williams RSCJ, *St. Madeleine Sophie*, p. 480, (35)

RESPONSORY

O God, let us drink with joy from your life-giving waters. **—O God...**
Cleanse our hearts and our minds; **—with joy...**
Glory to you, Source of all Being, Eternal Word and Holy Spirit.
    —O God...

CANTICLE

Ant Let us have no memory but to remember, no heart but to bless, no strength but to serve.

INTERCESSIONS

O God, we pray to you as we commemorate this holy woman:
    May you be glorified in your saints.

Christ Jesus, you invited the little children to come to you;
—may all children know your love and concern by the respect
given to them.
Through the intercession of Madeleine Sophie;
—bless all those responsible for the education of children.
O God, in Madeleine Sophie, you gave us a model of leadership;
—may all administrators be given the gift of wisdom and
moderation.
O God, you gave Madeleine Sophie a great love of humility;
—let all recognize you as the source and giver of all that we
are and possess.

PRAYER: O God, we bless you for the life of Madeleine Sophie.
We thank you for all that you accomplished through
her. Bless all those who follow and are guided by her
inspiration as they continue your work in this world.
May they be faithful to her spirit and counsels. This we
ask in the name of Jesus. Amen.

June 3
POPE JOHN XXIII
(Angelo Gieuseppe Roncalli)

MORNING/EVENING PRAYER
(Psalms from Sunday, Week I, p. 3)

Ant 1 You are the chosen vessel of God; you preached the truth
throughout the whole world.

Ant 2 God's grace in me has not been without fruit; it is always
at work in me.

Ant 3 You are the shepherd of the flock, you must strengthen the
faith of your sisters and brothers.

READING

My experience during these three years as Pope,...bears witness to this
maxim and is a moving and lasting reason for me to be true to it:
absolute trust in God, in all that concerns the present, and perfect
tranquillity as regards the future. The various initiatives of a pastoral
character which mark this first stage of my papal apostolate have all
come to me as pure, tranquil, loving, I might even say silent, inspiration
from the Lord, speaking to the heart of his poor servant who, through no
merit of his own save that very simple merit of mere acquiescence and

obedience, without discussion, has been able to contribute to the honor
of Jesus and the edification of souls.

Pope John XXIII, *Journal of a Soul*, pp. 313–14, (38)

RESPONSORY

Commit your work to God, your plans will be established. **—Commit**...
God has made everything for its purpose; **—your plans**...
Glory to you, Source of all Being, Eternal Word and Holy Spirit.
    —Commit...

CANTICLE

Ant A patient man will endure until the right moment, and then
    joy will burst forth for him. He will hide his words until the
    right moment, and many will tell of his good sense.

INTERCESSIONS

O God, you send your Spirit to renew the Church, the people of
God, and call them to holiness in the world. We give you thanks
and pray:
    Grant to us, Christ Jesus, a heart renewed.

You inspired Pope John to open the windows to the breath of the
Spirit;
    —keep our hearts and attitudes open to you in the signs of
       our times.
You called your servant, Pope John, to work for Christian Unity;
    —may we continue to work for the unity that respects
       differences.
Through his leadership Pope John convened the second Vatican
Council;
    —may it continue to call us forth and seed renewal for the
       future.
Pope John honored St. Joseph by including his commemoration
in the eucharistic banquet;
    —may St. Joseph intercede for all the people of God.
Through his warmth and humor, Pope John witnessed to your
loving concern for all humankind;
    —help us to learn the wisdom of simplicity and the power
       of weakness.

PRAYER: O God, you graced your church under the leadership of
        Pope John to be a witness to the world. Bless all who

are in positions of church leadership. Make them holy and true witnesses of the gospel you gave us. May all come to know their calling to be a priestly people, that the church will be seen by the world as God's holy people. We ask this in the name of Jesus who will be with his church till the end of time. Amen.

June 5
MARGARET ANNA CUSACK*
MORNING/EVENING PRAYER

Ant 1 They took up the cry that I was interfering in politics! God help me, all the politics I cared for was to feed the hungry. p. 17* (Ps 94, p. 168)

Ant 2 If I had been assassinated, to have died for the cause of charity would have been a happy end to my troubled life. (Ps 94 II, p. 169)

Ant 3 I at last decided to withdraw from a work which it was quite evident I should not be allowed to accomplish under any circumstances. p. 58* (Ps 43, p. 62)

READING

Margaret Anna Cusack was born May 6, 1829, in Dublin, Ireland. A strict Anglican, Margaret Anna eventually entered an Anglican convent of Sisters. Influenced by the Oxford movement, Margaret Anna converted to Catholicism in 1858 and shortly thereafter entered a Poor Clare community in Ireland. She dedicated herself to writing, especially on behalf of the liberation of women and children who were victims of oppression in the Church and society. In 1874 she wrote, "Give women their rights then, for these rights are justice—justice to men as well as to women, for the interests of men and women cannot be separated. Let women have the possession and the control of their property; it is a necessary right for the rich as well as for the poor" (*Women's Work*).* To broaden the scope of her work, she founded the Sisters of St. Joseph of Peace and went to the United States to help young Irish women arriving there. Conflict with the Archbishop of New York led other bishops to reject the new community. To preserve it, Margaret Anna severed canonical connections with the Sisters of St. Joseph of Peace in 1888 and returned to England. Abandoned by the Roman Catholic Church, she died with the blessing of the Anglican Church and was buried in

Leamington cemetery. Her coffin had a simple inscription, "Margaret
Anna Cusack fell asleep, June 5th, 1899, aged 70 years."*

*Dorothy A. Vidulich, csjp, *Peace Pays a Price,* p. 15, p. 70, (58)

RESPONSORY

I have put my Spirit upon her, she will bring forth justice to
    the nations. —**I have put**...
A bruised reed she will not break nor quench the smoking flax;
    —**she will**...
Glory to you, Source of all Being, Eternal Word and Holy Spirit.
    —**I have put**...

CANTICLE

Ant Those who think it is a light matter to leave all things for
      conscience sake know little indeed what it cost me at my age,
      and in my peculiar circumstances to obey the call of God.

INTERCESSIONS

Because she chose to be practical in carrying out her Christianity,
Margaret Anna Cusack went down in the eyes of her
contemporaries as a failure, only to be recognized today as a
prophet of Church and society;
    —O God, help us to recognize and affirm the prophets that
      challenge our institutions today.
Because she criticized publicly the wealth of the Church's
hierarchy in contrast to the destitution of the poor, ecclesiastics
wanted her silenced;
    —give us ears to hear what may discomfort our ease for
      the sake of justice. Comfort those who have endured
      misunderstanding and wrongful censure.
Margaret Anna foresaw that unless women were educated to be
economically and intellectually independent, they would continue
to be victimized by society;
    —grant equal opportunities to women of every nation—
      particularly women in developing countries that deny them
      basic human rights.
"It was indeed a time of darkness and sorrow to me, and I had not
then realized the utter hopelessness of trying to carry on a work to
which the bishops were determinedly opposed, no matter what
papal sanction I might have...." p. 42*;
    —at times of alienation and rejection, help us to unite our

suffering with all the suffering in the world until we know the dawn of resurrection.

In leaving the congregation she founded, she wrote: "I have kept them ignorant of what I have done, as far as possible, not because I do not love them, but because I do love them and desire their work to prosper. I know they will not misunderstand me..." p. 58*;

—we pray for all members and those associated with the Sisters of St. Joseph of Peace, whose commitment to peace most often flows as a turbulent stream into the waters of prophetic witness.

PRAYER: O God, we thank you for the life of Margaret Anna Cusack who suffered so much for the cause of justice because she risked to speak the truth to those who did not want to hear it. Like Jesus, she endured rejection and alienation from those in authority, and like the gospel, the work that she began has continued to flourish and bring life. Bless all who work to change unjust structures, that they may have the courage and the humility to continue their efforts in spite of opposition so that all peoples of the earth may have a better quality of life. We ask this in Jesus' name. Amen.

*Quotes taken from: Dorothy A. Vidulich, CSJP, *Peace Pays a Price*, (58).

June 15
EVELYN UNDERHILL

MORNING/EVENING PRAYER
(Psalms from Sunday, Week I, p. 3)

Ant 1 While I was still young, before I went on my travels, I sought wisdom openly in my prayer.

Ant 2 I directed my soul to [wisdom], and through purification I found her.

Ant 3 Draw near to me, you who are untaught. Why are your souls so thirsty?

READING

Evelyn Underhill was born in England, December 6, 1875. She was educated at King's College for Women and married Hubert Stuart Moore in 1907. In 1911 she published *Mysticism,* and by 1925 she claimed a vocation to explain the spiritual life to people living ordinary lives in the world. She wrote: "...the germ of that same transcendent life, the spring of the amazing energy which enables the great mystic to rise to freedom and dominate [her] world, is latent in all of us; an integral part of our humanity. Where the mystic has a genius for the Absolute, we have each a little buried talent, some greater, some less; and the growth of this talent, this spark of the soul, once we permit its emergence, will conform in little, and according to its measure, to those laws of organic growth, those inexorable conditions of transcendence which we found to govern the Mystic Way. Every person, then, who awakens to consciousness of a Reality which transcends the normal world of sense—however small, weak, imperfect that consciousness may be—is put upon a road which follows at low levels the path which the mystic treads at high levels."* She was the first woman to lecture at Oxford. She gave retreats to clergy and other religious professionals. The experience of the First World War led her to become a confirmed pacifist. She died June 15, 1941. In 1988, the General Convention of the Episcopal Church in the United States voted to add her to its liturgical calendar as a mystic and a theologian.

*Evelyn Underhill, *Mysticism*, p. 445, (29)

RESPONSORY

God is spirit and those who worship God must worship in spirit
 and truth. —**God is**...
The hour is coming when the true worshipers will worship
 God; —**in spirit**...
Glory to you, Source of all Being, Eternal Word and Holy Spirit.
 —**God is**...

CANTICLE

Ant The connection between real holiness and homeliness is a
 very close one. Sanctity comes right down to and through all
 the simplicities of human life, and indeed would be of no use
 to us unless it did so.

INTERCESSIONS

Jesus, you have invited us to drink of living waters;
 —give us confidence that all are called to prayer and
 contemplation.
You always did the will of the One who sent you;
 —give us true detachment that leads to attachment to God's
 purposes.

You have revealed to the mystics the secrets of your heart;
—may we know them as friends and guides for our journey.
Your Church is experiencing the universal call to holiness;
—give wisdom and insight to those who serve in all forms of
spiritual leadership.
Evelyn struggled for spiritual and intellectual integration;
—may she inspire those who have the same struggle today.
Evelyn saw deeply into the mystery of God in the daily and the
ordinary;
—open our eyes to all that the Incarnation means.

PRAYER: O God, we pray in awe at the realization of your
presence to us. Give us the grace to be present to you.
Help us to open our minds to your guidance and our
hearts to your creative love, allowing our very being to
reveal you to the world. We ask this through Jesus who
has shown us the Way. Amen.

June 24
ST. JOHN THE BAPTIST

MORNING/EVENING PRAYER
(Psalms from Sunday, Week I, p. 3)

Ant 1 Truly I say to you, among those born of women there has
arisen no one greater than John the Baptist.

Ant 2 All the prophets and the law prophesied until John; and if
you are willing to accept it, he is Elijah who is to come.

Ant 3 John said to his disciples, "He must increase, but I must
decrease."

READING

When John heard in prison what the Messiah was doing, he sent word
by his disciples and said to him, "Are you the one who is to come, or are
we to wait for another?" Jesus answered them, "Go and tell John what
you hear and see: the blind receive their sight, the lame walk, the lepers
are cleansed, the deaf hear, the dead are raised, and the poor have good
news brought to them. And blessed is anyone who takes no offense at
me." As they went away, Jesus began to speak to the crowds about
John: "What did you go out into the wilderness to look at? A reed
shaken by the wind? What then did you go out to see? Someone dressed
in soft robes? Look, those who wear soft robes are in royal palaces. What

then did you go out to see? A prophet? Yes, I tell you, and more than a prophet. This is the one about whom it is written, 'See, I am sending my messenger ahead of you, who will prepare your way before you.'"

Mt 11:2–10

RESPONSORY

He will go before him in the spirit and power of Elijah. **—He will...**
To make ready for the Lord a people prepared, **—in the...**
Glory to you, Source of all Being, Eternal Word and Holy Spirit.
    —He will...

CANTICLE

Ant The friend of the bridegroom, who stands and hears him, rejoices greatly at the bridegroom's voice; therefore this joy of mine is now full.

INTERCESSIONS

O God, John the Baptist prepared for his mission through prayer and in solitude;
    —give us a hunger for prayer and the courage to persevere in it.
John acknowledged his call and the One who called him;
    —grant us the wisdom to know who we are and who we are not.
The greed and pride of the powerful destroyed your humble prophet;
    —help us always to employ power for your glory and the welfare of all.
John rejoiced at the sound of Jesus' voice;
    —let the words of the gospel be the foundation of our deepest joy.
John the Baptist freely sent his disciples to Jesus;
    —teach us how to decrease, that the power of your Spirit may increase in the world.

PRAYER: O God, you sent John the Baptist to prepare the way for the coming of Jesus. May his humility and total dedication to your call guide us as we endeavor to open the way to Truth for one another. Give us a share of his total trust in you. We ask this in Jesus' name. Amen.

June 29
STS. PETER AND PAUL

MORNING/EVENING PRAYER
(Psalms from Sunday, Week I, p. 3)

Ant 1 Jesus said to Simon Peter, "Simon, son of John, do you love me more than these?" He said to him, "Yes, Lord; you know that I love you." He said to him, "Feed my lambs."

Ant 2 The one who worked through Peter for the mission to the circumcised worked through Paul also for the Gentiles.

Ant 3 The Lord said to Peter, "Truly, truly, I say to you, when you were young, you girded yourself and walked where you would; but when you are old,...another will gird you and carry you where you do not wish to go."

READING

After [Jesus] had dismissed the crowds, he went up the mountain by himself to pray. When evening came, he was there alone, but by this time the boat, battered by the waves, was far from the land, for the wind was against them. And early in the morning he came walking toward them on the sea. But when the disciples saw him walking on the sea, they were terrified, saying, "It is a ghost!" And they cried out in fear. But immediately Jesus spoke to them and said, "Take heart, it is I; do not be afraid." Peter answered him, "Lord, if it is you, command me to come to you on the water." He said, "Come." So Peter got out of the boat, started walking on the water, and came toward Jesus. But when he noticed the strong wind, he became frightened, and beginning to sink, he cried out, "Lord, save me!" Jesus immediately reached out his hand and caught him, saying to him, "You of little faith, why did you doubt?" When they got into the boat, the wind ceased. And those in the boat worshipped him, saying, "Truly you are the Son of God."

Mt 14:22–33

RESPONSORY

Their message goes forth to every land, and their words to the ends of the earth. —**Their message**...
They shall remember your name, O God; —**to the ends**...
Glory to you, Source of all Being, Eternal Word and Holy Spirit.
   —**Their message**...

CANTICLE

Ant The Lord said to me, "My grace is sufficient for you, for my power is made perfect in weakness."

INTERCESSIONS

Christ Jesus, you entrusted Peter, a simple fisherman, with the preaching of the gospel;
—give us the simplicity of heart to hear your Truth wherever we may find it.
You forgave Peter over and over again;
—let us never doubt your mercy when we fail you.
Your apostle Paul labored to be all things to all people;
—give us the courage and generosity to develop our talents for the good of others.
Hardships and betrayal did not deter Paul from his mission to spread the gospel;
—awaken in us a zeal that will take us to all who need your word.
Peter and Paul became humble men in your service;
—lead us all to the truth of our littleness and our total dependence upon you.

PRAYER: O God, you have blessed the church with the noble lives of your apostles Peter and Paul. They left all to follow Jesus and lived and died telling the good news of his life, death, and resurrection. Bless the church today with leaders who are open to your Spirit, that your Word may live on in us to the praise and glory of your name now and forever. Amen.

July 2
ELIZABETH LANGE* and THERESA MAXIS DUCHEMIN**

MORNING/EVENING PRAYER

Ant 1 Open to me the gates of justice, that I may enter and give thanks. (Ps 72, p. 81)

Ant 2 God is a stronghold for the oppressed, a stronghold in times of trouble. (Ps 72 II, p. 81)

Ant 3 Open your mouth, judge righteously, maintain the rights of the poor and needy. (Ps 43, p. 62)

READING

Elizabeth Lange, a Cuban refugee born into a racially mixed marriage, organized a free school for black children in her home (about 1827). Eventually she founded the Oblate Sisters of Providence, the first congregation for women of color, and with Theresa Maxis and another Oblate, pronounced vows on July 2, 1829. As prejudice grew, threats of violence brought the community to brink of collapse. Elizabeth Lange remained in Baltimore, but Theresa Maxis responded to a request to begin a school in Michigan. There she formed a new congregation, the Sister Servants of the Immaculate Heart of Mary. Later, at the request of Bishop John Neumann of Philadelphia, she established a community in Pennsylvania and established schools.

RESPONSORY

I sent you out with sorrow and weeping, but God will bring you back
    with joy and gladness. —**I sent**...
Your children were taken away like a flock carried off by the enemy;
    —**but God**...
Glory to you, Source of all Being, Eternal Word and Holy Spirit.
    —**I sent**...

CANTICLE

Ant Whoever receives one such child in my name receives me;
    and whoever receives me, receives not me but the One who
    sent me.

INTERCESSIONS

O God, your daughters, Elizabeth and Theresa, founded the first religious community for women of color;
    —may their courage in the midst of great opposition inspire
    other women of color who must endure ridicule and rejection.
Insulted by white Catholics as well as by those who opposed Catholicism, they continued to teach children of color;
    —forgive our prejudice and narrow-mindedness.
During the cholera epidemic of 1832, all eleven members of the community cared for patients in Baltimore's almshouse;
    —bless all those who risk their own well-being to serve those
    with contagious diseases.

Lacking diocesan support and experiencing prejudice from some members of the clergy, the Sisters took in washing to keep their school going;
  —strengthen all women who are denied the support of those in authority.
Trusting completely in Divine Providence, Mother Theresa Maxis and her "Blue Sisters" established schools and sacramental programs for the immigrant pioneers, empowering many, especially young women, to break the cycles of alcoholism, abuse, and illiteracy along the frontier;
  —protect immigrants of today and inspire women and men of the Church to help them find safe refuge, direction, and the tools needed to flourish in their new worlds.
During Elizabeth's lifetime, the black Oblates were denied Catholic college education;
  —may the sins of the past sharpen our awareness of present-day discrimination toward people of other races, cultures, and nationalities.

PRAYER: O God, we praise you for the life and work of our sisters, Elizabeth and Theresa, and we ask your forgiveness for too long ignoring the accomplishments of women of different races and nationalities. Open our eyes to see the contributions of others who serve you and our world. Make us mindful of the good that is done and the grace to acknowledge it so that they may know our encouragement and support. We ask this in the name of Jesus. Amen.

*Based on Joanne Turpin, *Women in Church History*, pp. 154–63, (50). **Based on Charles De Celles, Ph.D., "A Tribute to a Pioneer Educator," (57).

July 11
ST. BENEDICT

MORNING/EVENING PRAYER
(Psalms from Sunday, Week I, p. 3)

Ant 1 God has made him the father of many nations.

Ant 2 We ought at all times so to serve [God] by means of the gifts entrusted to us.

Ant 3 Listen, my child, to the precept of your master and incline the ear of your heart.

READING

Your institute has something of the nature of spring, whereby periods of history have often been raised from the squalor of ruins to a better condition and greater prosperity. Accepting the task assigned to you, render prompt assistance, that in these troubled times you may aid with kindness and with zeal. With ancient vigor and a fresh start, make your contemporaries more gentle-minded, for by them the most grave dangers and a wholesale slaughter can be prepared for the human race, the arrogant pursuit of science not in the least hindering, but rather fostering this. By the example of your lives, by your public speaking, by the use of the pen, instruct the ignorant, bring to submission those that are intractable, call back to the service of God and the light yoke of the Gospel those that hold religion in contempt. In conclusion, may Benedict, precious to God and to [us], "whose memory is held in benediction," bless the laboring Church, whose valiant defender he was.... (Pius XII)

The Holy Rule of St. Benedict, p. xiv, (33)

RESPONSORY

Seek and you shall find; knock and it shall be opened. —**Seek**...
Ask and you shall receive; —**knock**...
Glory to you, Source of all Being, Eternal Word and Holy Spirit.
    —**Seek**...

CANTICLE

Ant They shall grow as tall as palms, like cedars they shall stand, planted firmly in their God.

INTERCESSIONS

O God, through the intercession of Benedict, endow our religious leaders with wisdom and courage;
    —that all their precepts may guide and draw us to you.
Your servant Benedict lauded the value of prayer and work;
    —give us the grace to take time for prayer and to do our work with reverence and creativity.
He taught his followers to value hospitality in a remarkable way;
    —let all who travel and all in distress, find care and solace through those they meet on the way.

Through the inspiration of Benedict, help us to walk in the way of
humility, sobriety, and prudence;
  —teach us to live by the law of love.
Bless all who derive their rule of life from Benedict;
    —keep them faithful to their calling and let them bear fruit
    in abundant life for the church.

PRAYER: O God, you have endowed your servant Benedict with
the gifts of prayer and universal charity. His life, like
the good tree planted near living water, has born fruit
in countless women and men who have embraced his
way of life. Bless your laboring church whose valiant
defender he was and whose inspiration he continues to
be. We ask this in Jesus' name. Amen.

July 14
BLESSED KATERI TEKAWITHA

MORNING/EVENING PRAYER

Ant 1 From the mouths of the innocent you have perfected
praise. (Ps 8, p. 92)

Ant 2 You have come to your people to set them free.
(Ps 65, p. 63)

Ant 3 Earth's peoples and all living creatures sing your praise.
(Ps 148, p. 99)

READING

It is believed that Kateri Tekawitha was born ca. 1656. Kateri was of the
Indian Nation of the Iroquois (Mohawks). Born of a Christian mother (an
Algonquin) who had a very good influence on her, Kateri remained
faithful to her mother's teachings even after her mother's death. She
endured many trials and afflictions in being faithful to the following of
Christ, and died April 17, 1680.

RESPONSORY

Ho! All ye of the heavens, all ye of the air, all ye of the earth:
  I bid you all to hear me! —**Ho! All ye**...
Into your midst has come a new life! —**I bid**...

Glory to you, Source of all Being, Eternal Word and Holy Spirit.
—**Ho! All ye**...

CANTICLE

Ant May our bodies, our minds, our spirits learn a new rhythm paced by the rhythmic pulse of the whole created order.

INTERCESSIONS

Bless the wisdom of the Holy One above us; bless the truth of the Holy One beneath us:
Bless the love of the Holy One within us.

God of the universe, you created the land, the seas, and the heavens;
  —give us the wisdom to respect and care for our natural resources as do our native peoples.
God of the living, you created the birds, the fish, and all the animals;
  —enable us to protect their environment and to preserve the rights of every species that shares our planet with us.
God of the holy, you reveal yourself in every time and age;
  —we give you thanks for all primitive peoples who recognized the holy in beasts, rocks, plants, and all the elements of our earth.
God of our ancestors, you revealed yourself through dreamers, seers, and prophets;
  —help us to recognize and hear the prophets who speak to us today.
God of all peoples, your loving providence extends to every race and nation;
  —give us your vision and love that we may respect the rights of all peoples, especially those indigenous to our lands.

PRAYER: O God, we have sinned against you in the oppression of our native peoples. Forgive the blindness of our past and enable us to atone for our guilt by restoring the rights of all people to live on their land in peace and with dignity. We ask this for the sake of all our native peoples who died because of our greed, and in the name of Jesus who brought us your forgiveness. Amen.

July 15
BLESSED ANNE-MARIE JAVOUHEY*

MORNING/EVENING PRAYER
(Psalms from Sunday, Week I, p. 3)

Ant 1 What can be lacking to anyone who possesses God?

Ant 2 God's light is given to us little by little.

Ant 3 In bringing relief to suffering humanity, souls can be reached.

READING

Anne-Marie Javouhey was born in Jallanges, France, on November 11, 1779. In 1807, she founded the Sisters of St. Joseph of Cluny who dedicated themselves to the care of the sick and to teaching. She wrote, "...There is so much resourcefulness in children. It is on them that I count if God wishes to use us for such a great apostolate...." Called to minister to the colonies, Anne-Marie devoted herself to the emancipation of the slaves. She died July 15, 1851.

RESPONSORY

One must try to adapt oneself to the present time so as to gain
   the world for God. —**One must**...
Making ourselves all things to all; —**so as**...
Glory to you, Source of all Being, Eternal Word and Holy Spirit.
   —**One must**...

CANTICLE

Ant They are asking sisters everywhere to educate the girls. I find
   this is a beautiful mission. Women have such an influence
   on society.

INTERCESSIONS

During the French Revolution and religious persecution, Anne-Marie Javouhey at age nineteen dedicated her life to God and promised to serve children, the poor, and the sick;
   —give courage to all those who minister to others, especially
      those who endanger their lives to do so.
Anne-Marie answered the call to serve native peoples in distant lands;

—support those who uproot themselves to serve others in
   times of trouble or in distressed areas of our world.
Distraught by witnessing slave-traffic, Anne Marie tended the
suffering captives and worked tirelessly for the liberation of
enslaved peoples;
   —free all who are still bound by our sins of prejudice,
   blindness, and indifference to the plight of others.
Falsely accused and misunderstood, Anne-Marie was deprived of
the Sacraments for a period of two years;
   —comfort all who are wrongly sanctioned by ecclesiastical
   authority and give them inner peace.
Anne-Marie balanced her leadership and organizational skills with
true humility and genuine charity;
   —help us to use our gifts and talents for the service of
   others and recognize them as your gifts to us.

PRAYER: O God, we thank you for the life of Blessed Anne-Marie
   Javouhey and for the apostolic work continued by her
   followers, the Sisters of St. Joseph of Cluny. May they
   be faithful to her spirit in their service to the young, the
   poor, the sick, and the mentally afflicted. We ask this
   in the name of Jesus whose gospel she so faithfully
   followed. Amen.

*Office based on *The Wonderful Story of a Great Missionary: Anne Marie Javouhey*, Editions Fleurus, (26)

July 22
ST. MARY MAGDALENE

MORNING/EVENING PRAYER
(Psalms from Sunday, Week I, p. 3)

Ant 1 It was not you who chose me, it was I who chose you.

Ant 2 The twelve accompanied Jesus. Among them was Mary
   Magdalene and also some women who had been cured of
   evil spirits and maladies.

Ant 3 Near the cross of Jesus stood Mary Magdalene.

READING

The last woman to appear in the Fourth Gospel is Mary Magdalene who
was also mentioned as standing under the cross of Jesus. She not only
discovers the empty tomb but is also the first to receive a resurrection

appearance. Thus in a double sense she becomes the *apostola apostolorum*, the apostle of the apostles.... While—for apologetic reasons —the post-Pauline and post-Petrine writers seek to limit women's leadership roles in the Christian community to roles which are culturally and religiously acceptable, the evangelists called Mark and John highlight the alternative character of the Christian community and therefore accord women apostolic and ministerial leadership.... The writers of Mark and John have made it impossible for the Christian church to forget the invitation of Jesus to follow him on the way to the cross. Therefore, wherever the gospel is preached and heard, promulgated and read, what the women have done is not totally forgotten because the Gospel story remembers that the discipleship and apostolic leadership of women are integral parts of Jesus' "alternative" praxis of *agape* and service. The "light shines in the darkness" of patriarchal repression and forgetfulness, and this "darkness has never overcome it."

Elizabeth Schüssler Fiorenza, In Memory of Her, p. 332, p. 334, (2)

RESPONSORY

Mary Magdalene went and announced to the disciples, "I have
    seen the Lord". —**Mary Magdalene**...
She turned around and saw Jesus standing there; —**I have**...
Glory to you, Source of all Being, Eternal Word and Holy Spirit.
    —**Mary Magdalene**...

CANTICLE

Ant Go out to all the nations and tell the good news.

INTERCESSIONS

As you sent Mary Magdalene to announce the good news of our resurrection, you continue to send forth women with messages of life for your church;
    —open the minds and hearts of your disciples who reject the
       message carried by the women you send today.
Often we prejudge, misjudge, and stereotype the character of another through our own personal biases;
    —grant us conversion of heart that we may welcome and
       befriend those who challenge us.
Mary stood at the foot of your cross—a faithful companion and disciple;

—give us the courage to stand with you when love is crucified
through oppression, aggression, abuse, war, vengeance, and
other forms of injustice.
Jesus, your loving relationship with women is shown repeatedly
in Scripture;
—may all women know and claim the dignity that is theirs
as women made in the image and likeness of God.
Mary Magdalene was your faithful friend, follower, and apostle;
—enable women called to ministry to serve you and your
Church in whatever capacity they feel called to serve.

PRAYER: Jesus, as you called Mary Magdalene, call us by name
when we stand at the tomb of ambiguity and cannot
recognize you. Like her, let us proclaim: "I have seen
the Lord!" Send us out as you sent her to be an apostle
in proclaiming through our prayer and ministry that
you are risen and live among us—that disciples will be
made of all nations—and all will come to know that you
are with us always as our Way, our Truth, and our Life.
Amen.

July 26
STS. ANNE and JOACHIM, GRANDPARENTS OF JESUS

MORNING/EVENING PRAYER
(Psalms from Sunday, Week I, p. 3)

Ant 1 The just leave an inheritance to their children's children.

Ant 2 The memory of the righteous is a blessing.

Ant 3 Wisdom has built her house and has set up her seven
pillars.

READING

"Tell the next generation that this is God, our God forever and ever"
(Ps 48:13–14). *This* is God—a God of creation and cross; and in loving
faith [a God who] is ours days without end. By focusing on experience, I
have intimated that *how* you tell the next generation that this is our
God is not so much in words as in deeds, less through abstract doctrine
than through concrete living; that for the next generation *you* are the
Church—each one of you individually, and all of you in your corporate
existence. A privilege indeed....

Walter J. Burghardt, sj, *Lovely in Eyes Not His*, pp. 114–15, (1)

RESPONSORY

Your mercy, O God, is on those who fear you, throughout all
   generations. **—Your mercy**...
Most Holy be your name; **—throughout**...
Glory to you, Source of all Being, Eternal Word and Holy Spirit.
   —Your mercy...

CANTICLE

Ant My child, keep my words and treasure up my
     commandments; keep my commandments and live.

INTERCESSIONS

O God, not in name only did blessed Anna and Joachim "grace"
their child;
   —we praise you for the blessings that come to us through
     them, Mary and Jesus.
Bless all grandparents, living and dead;
   —may their goodness and wisdom continue to inspire and
     encourage us.
Bless our children with the gift of time with their grandparents;
   —let them hear their history, the joys and sorrows of those
     who have given life to them.
Grant to those who have no grandchildren the blessing of Saint
Anne;
   —that they may "grandparent" the children of their
     neighborhoods and those who need their love.
Be merciful to all who must bear the breakup of families through
violence or for whatever reason;
   —let the Mother who stood motherless at the death of her
     Son be their strength and hope.

PRAYER: O God, we rejoice in the celebration of the grandparents
      of Jesus. Let the awareness of the influence of others in
      our lives help us to realize the unity of all people.
      Deepen our desire to fulfill the prayer of Jesus that we
      all may be one. Teach us to revere and be nourished by
      the lives of those who have given us life. We ask this in
      the name of Jesus, faithful son and grandson, hope of
      the ages. Amen.

July 31
ST. IGNATIUS OF LOYOLA
MORNING/EVENING PRAYER
(Psalms from Sunday, Week I, p. 3)

Ant 1 All for the greater honor and glory of God.

Ant 2 As you have sent me into the world, so I have sent them.

Ant 3 Here I am, O God, I come to do your will.

READING

The Holy Spirit will teach you better than anyone else the means to take to relish with affection and to put into execution with sweetness that which reason points out to be for the greater service and glory of God. It is true that reason gives us sufficient motives for seeking what is better and more perfect. And yet the will, even when this determination and execution do not precede, can easily attain it, since God...rewards the confidence we place in [God's] providence and the complete surrender of self and giving up on one's consolation, with a deep contentment and relish and all the greater abundance of spiritual consolation, especially when one does not seek it, but seeks rather [God's] glory and good pleasure alone.

Letters of St. Ignatius of Loyola, p. 417, (19)

RESPONSORY

You, O God, are my inheritance; your goodness is with me always.
  —You, O God,...
You show me the path to life; **—your...**
Glory to you, Source of all Being, Eternal Word and Holy Spirit.
  —You, O God,...

CANTICLE

Ant It is not ourselves that we preach, but Christ Jesus our
  redeemer.

INTERCESSIONS

You gave Ignatius the wisdom to be a spiritual guide for others;
  —may you continue to encourage spiritual directors to rely
    on your wisdom and to share your gifts.
You call us to be your companions and to journey together in
freedom and love;

—help us to be generous, supportive, and challenging in our
relationships with one another.
You invite us to let go of all things in order to possess you;
   —enable us to recognize that attachment to you is
commensurate with our attachment to all our sisters and
brothers.
You give us life in abundance and we return it to you;
   —assist us to nurse the sick with gentleness, to teach our
youth with kindness, and to comfort the oppressed with
compassion.
Through your servant, Ignatius, you founded a Society that has
spread your gospel message throughout the world;
   —continue to bless their endeavors that all may know the
freedom to which we are called.

PRAYER: Take, O God, receive all my liberty, my memory, my
understanding, my entire will. You have given all to me,
now I return it. All I have is yours. Dispose of it, wholly
according to your will. Give me only your love and your
grace, with these I am rich enough. I desire no more.
Amen.

August 4
ST. JOHN MARY VIANNEY

MORNING/EVENING PRAYER
(Psalms from Sunday, Week I, p. 3)

Ant 1 Learn from me, for I am gentle and lowly in heart, and you
will find rest for your souls.

Ant 2 Behold my servant whom I have chosen. He will not break
a bruised reed or quench a smoldering wick.

Ant 3 You are a priest forever, according to the order of
Melchizedek.

READING

[Monsieur Vianney, the Curé of Ars'] life suffered no change. He
continued to give sixteen or seventeen hours a day to the confessional.
He took his regular place in the pulpit near the Lady Chapel and there
spoke—by gestures mainly, since voice he had practically none, by the
expression of his face and by the tears pouring from his eyes—of the
great goodness of God. [People] thronged closer round him; a whole
world of them, dragged from their sleep by this one old man, that they

might hear his last lessons, kneel under his last blessings, that their souls might live again. The atmosphere was stifling. He, at least, never seemed to notice it. The truth was that he was hiding the extent of his sufferings. He had made up his mind to die working, since God's will had refused him the contemplative life he craved.

Henri Ghéon, *The Secret of the Curé d'Ars*, p. 201, (45)

RESPONSORY

Come to me, all who labor and are heavy laden, and I will give
   you rest for your souls. —**Come to**...
Take my yoke upon you; —**and I**...
Glory to you, Source of all Being, Eternal Word and Holy Spirit.
   —**Come to**...

CANTICLE

Ant God of heaven and earth, you have hidden these things from
   the wise and prudent and revealed them to little ones.

INTERCESSIONS

O God, you have given us John Vianney as patron of priests;
   —inspire all priests with love and gratitude for their calling.
You gave John Vianney the grace to overcome his limitations;
   —encourage and enlighten seminarians in times of difficulty
      and doubt.
You inspired John Vianney to enrich his apostolate through
penance and mortification;
   —give our priests the wisdom to entrust their lives into your
      hands.
You blessed John Vianney with a special gift for healing souls in
the sacrament of reconciliation;
   —fill our hearts with patience, understanding, and
      compassion for one another.
You have given us a sacramental church;
   —fill us with gratitude for the gifts you have given and may
      all called to the ministry of priesthood find fulfillment.

PRAYER: O God, you inspired John Vianney with the desire to
          fill up in his flesh what was wanting in the sufferings of
          Christ. His love for you and for the church drew
          multitudes to your table of forgiveness and unity.
          Through his intercession, bless our priests and all who
          aspire to this calling. Let them know your love and the

support of those whom they serve, that together we may praise you forever and ever. Amen.

August 6
TRANSFIGURATION

EVENING PRAYER I

Ant 1 The skies opened and I saw the Holy One receive from God dominion, glory and power. (Ps 113, p. 96)

Ant 2 The reign of Christ is everlasting; it shall never pass away. (Ps 117, p. 44)

Ant 3 The heavens proclaim the goodness of God; all peoples behold God's glory. (Rev 19:1, 5–7, p. 54)

READING

Heavenly glory...does not come from outside like a whirlwind to whisk us off the planet earth in a shock of wonder; rather, it is already developing within us like seed planted within mother earth still surrounded with darkness. Occasionally its inspirations and insights, its secret hopes and joys, break through and transfigure, at least momentarily, the surface doldrums of our life. These are those wonderful yet awesome moments when God summons us to leap beyond all earthly limitations and with our earthly body to perform heroic deeds. These moments are fleeting dreams come true.

Carroll Stuhlmueller, CP, *Biblical Mediations for Lent*, p. 99, (1)

RESPONSORY

You are covered with glory, O Christ; we bow down and adore you.
   —You are...
In brilliant light you stand before us; **—we bow...**
Glory to you, Source of all Being, Eternal Word and Holy Spirit.
   —You are...

CANTICLE OF MARY

Ant As Jesus stood transformed before them, the disciples were overcome with awe.

INTERCESSIONS

Jesus was transfigured before his disciples and Elijah and Moses appeared with him. In God's presence we proclaim:
                    It is good for us to be here.

Jesus, beloved of God, fulfillment of prophecy;
— help us to listen to your word spoken through the prophets of
our day.
You appeared in the splendor of a vision to your apostles;
— strengthen with the gift of prayer all who labor in your
vineyard.
You shone in glory on Mt. Tabor and descended the mount to take
up your cross;
— keep us faithful to you as we carry our own daily cross.
On Tabor you shone with a radiant light;
— let your presence in our lives be light for others as they seek
to follow you
Your transfiguration foretold your resurrection in glory;
— comfort the dying with the hope of eternal life.

PRAYER: O Christ, you gave comfort and strength to your
apostles through the vision of your transfiguration.
Have mercy on us, and show yourself to all who face
suffering and death for the cause of truth. Bless us all
with the hope of resurrection. This we ask through the
power of your name. Amen.

MORNING PRAYER
(Psalms from Sunday, Week I, p. 3)

Ant 1 Jesus received glory and praise from the Most High.

Ant 2 Jesus was transfigured in the sight of the disciples.

Ant 3 Moses and Elijah appeared with Jesus, the fulfillment of
the law and the prophets.

READING

When we make [an] ultimate act of faith, summoned from the most
hidden mysterious depths of our person, then like Jesus we are
transfigured.... Everything comes together for we are at the pith point of
all existence in ourselves and in God. In Jesus the transfiguration scene
absorbs words and ideas from the Baptism of Jesus, his agony in the
garden, the messianic confession of Peter, his death on the cross. We,
too, if we share with Jesus the same faithful consecration to [God's] will,
will find our own entire life converging. From beginning to end it will be
translucent with God's presence.

Carroll Stuhlmueller, CP, *Biblical Meditations for Lent*, p. 118, (1)

RESPONSORY

Christ Jesus was clothed in brilliance, and we saw his glory.
  —**Christ**...
Sovereign over all creation; —**and we saw**...
Glory to you, Source of all Being, Eternal Word and Holy Spirit.
  —**Christ**...

CANTICLE OF ZECHARIAH

Ant Light dawns for the upright, and joy for the pure of heart.

INTERCESSIONS

On the mountain Jesus was transfigured in glory and his apostles
were overcome with awe. With holy reverence, we proclaim:
  Jesus, you are the Chosen One of God!

Jesus, you took your faithful friends to the mountain to pray;
  —bless us with relationships that keep us faithful to you.
On the mountain you prepared for your suffering and death;
  —let all that we do make us more and more open to
    whatever life may ask of us.
You spoke with prophets from the past and with apostles of the
future;
  —open our minds and hearts to the magnitude of God's ways.
Yours are the heavens and yours is the earth;
  —bless our civic and religious leaders with the gift of wisdom.
You were bathed in light, your garments white as snow;
  —dispel from our world all that blinds us to you; make us a
    forgiving and thankful people.

PRAYER: O Christ, coming down from the mountain, the
              disciples saw "only Jesus!" Enable us to recognize the
              presence of the transcendent in the ordinary and the
              mundane, knowing that you are with us in all the
              circumstances of our lives. We ask this that we might
              give you glory in all that we do. Amen.

DAYTIME PRAYER

Ant 1 As Jesus was praying, the appearance of his face changed
           and his clothing became dazzling white. (Ps 123, p. 109)

Ant 2 Moses and Elijah appeared with Jesus and they spoke of his death in Jerusalem. (Ps 124, p. 109)

Ant 3 Peter, James, and John saw the glory of God on the Mount of Tabor. (Ps 125, p. 115)

(Prayer as in Morning Prayer)

EVENING PRAYER II

Ant 1 Jesus took with him Peter, James, and John and went up on the mountain to pray. (Ps 110:1–5, 7, p. 53)

Ant 2 As Jesus prayed, his appearance changed, and Moses and Elijah stood with him. (Ps 121, p. 89)

Ant 3 This is my Beloved, my Chosen One!

Canticle 1 Tm 3:16

Praise our Savior, all you nations.
Christ manifested in the flesh,
Christ justified by the Spirit.

Praise our Savior, all you nations.
Christ seen by the angels,—

Christ proclaimed to unbelievers.

Praise our Savior, all you nations.
Christ believed in by the world,
Christ taken up in glory.

Praise our Savior, all you nations. **Glory...**

READING

With Jesus' transfiguration hopes break the bonds of the present moment. Heavenly glory exudes from within and casts a garment of dazzling whiteness about Jesus. Jesus must have been bearing this divine glory always within himself, for such wonder to break loose unexpectedly as this. To live with such godly hopes, ideals and expectations, day by day, is bound to cause tension and frustration, far greater than Abraham's [hope in God's promise]. Yet, by such mystic experience Jesus was convinced that the future belonged to him.

Carroll Stuhlmueller, CP, *Biblical Meditations for Lent*, p. 135, (1)

RESPONSORY

Praise to you, transformed in glory; we bow down before you. **—Praise...**
Your sun has risen, O Christ, your holiness is revealed; **—we bow...**

Glory to you, Source of all Being, Eternal Word and Holy Spirit.
—**Praise**...

CANTICLE OF MARY

Ant Jesus touched the disciples and said: Arise, have no fear. When they looked up, they saw no one but Jesus.

INTERCESSIONS

On the mountain Jesus was transfigured in glory and his apostles were overcome with awe. With holy reverence, we proclaim:
Jesus, you are the Chosen One of God!

Jesus, you took your faithful friends to the mountain to pray;
—bless us with relationships that keep us faithful to you.
On the mountain you prepared for your suffering and death;
—let all that we do make us more and more open to
whatever life may ask of us.
You spoke with prophets from the past and with apostles of the future;
—open our minds and hearts to the magnitude of God's ways.
Yours are the heavens and yours is the earth;
—bless our civic and religious leaders with the gift of wisdom.
You were bathed in light, your garments white as snow;
—dispel from our world all that blinds us to you; make us a
forgiving and thankful people.

PRAYER: O Christ, coming down from the mountain, the disciples saw "only Jesus!" Enable us to recognize the presence of the transcendent in the ordinary and the mundane, knowing that you are with us in all the circumstances of our lives. We ask this that we might give you glory in all that we do. Amen.

August 8
ST. DOMINIC*

MORNING/EVENING PRAYER
(Psalms from Sunday, Week I, p. 3)

Ant 1 Dominic was a man of prayer and preacher of truth.

Ant 2 Dominic shared the fruit of his prayer by his preaching.

Ant 3 Dominic, preacher of grace, you communed with God both night and day.

READING

How beautiful upon the mountains are the feet of the messenger who announces peace, who brings good news, who announces salvation, who says to Zion, "Your God reigns."

Is 52:7

RESPONSORY

He shared the fruit of his prayer through his preaching.
   —**He shared...**
To spread the Word of God among the people; —**through**...
Glory to you, Source of all Being, Eternal Word and Holy Spirit.
   —**He shared...**

CANTICLE

Ant Jesus appointed twelve, whom he also named apostles, to be with him, and to be sent out to proclaim the message.

INTERCESSIONS

O God, your servant Dominic preached the Good News of salvation wherever he went and to whomever he met;
   —help us to know the gospel message and share it with others.
Dominic spent long hours in prayer united with Jesus and preparing for his mission of preaching;
   —call us to a deep spirit of prayer and a generosity and compassion in serving others.
He was sensitive to the Word spoken in the heart of every man and woman, especially those who were enslaved in misery and need;
   —free those enslaved by their addictions or by economic and political oppression.
Dominic was at the heart of the church in the service of the world;
   —enable all who share in that charism and his prophetic vision to proclaim the Word that the Spirit puts into their hearts.
Dominic's zeal for preaching the Word drew countless followers into his Order;
   —give us the grace to be ever faithful in our following of Jesus, serving him in the least of his sisters and brothers.

PRAYER: O God, let the holiness and preaching of St. Dominic come to the aid of your church. May he help us now with his prayers as he once inspired people by his preaching. We ask this through our Lord Jesus Christ, your Son, who lives and reigns with you and the Holy Spirit, one God, forever and ever. Amen.

*Composed by Dominican Sisters, Columbus, Ohio.

August 8
BLESSED MARY MacKILLOP*

MORNING/EVENING PRAYER
(Psalms from Sunday, Week I, p. 3)

Ant 1 Out of your infinite glory, O Christ, you give us the power through your Spirit for our hidden selves to grow strong.

Ant 2 It is those who are poor according to the world that God chooses to be rich in grace.

Ant 3 I believe that nothing can happen that will outweigh the supreme advantage of knowing Christ Jesus, my Lord.

REFLECTION/SHARING

Mary MacKillop, born of Scottish parents in Melbourne in 1842, founded with Rev. Julian Tenison Woods the Congregation of the Sisters of St. Joseph of the Sacred Heart. Their vision brought to life a new and radical form of religious life that took the sisters in small groups to live in primitive dwellings among the pioneering people of the Australian bush. A woman before her time, she was forthright, assertive, loving, simple, and intensely loyal to the Church, even when excommunicated and removed from the leadership of her Congregation. She wrote to her Sisters: "Be kind to each other, bear with one another, bear with the faulty as you hope God will bear with you. God loves us all, but [God] loves those best who help the weak to become more perfect."* Mary committed her life to the poor and destitute, establishing orphanages, refuges for women and children, and schools for the poor and isolated children. But she cautioned, "Poor houses, poor garments, etc., are all exterior show if there is not a true spirit of poverty in our hearts. It is not always the poorest dressed and the poorest housed who are the poorest before the searching eyes of God."* Mary died in 1909 and was beatified January 19, 1995.

*Bl. Mary MacKillop, RSJ, (10)

RESPONSORY

It is I, your God, who teach you what is good for you. —**It is**...
I lead you in the way you must go, —**and teach**...
Glory to you, Source of all Being, Eternal Word and Holy Spirit.
—**It is**...

CANTICLE

Ant As for me, the only thing I can boast about is the cross of our Lord Jesus Christ.

INTERCESSIONS

Most holy and loving God, your Incarnate Word, Jesus Christ, was the source and inspiration of Mary MacKillop's life. In gratitude, we pray:
We praise you, we bless you, we glorify you.

With great trust in your providence, Mary MacKillop was open and ready to meet the needs of her time;
   —grant that we may meet the challenges of today's world with faith and courage.
Mary suffered misunderstanding, calumny, and wrongful excommunication with peace and humility;
   —may we also bear with peace and humility any difficulties we meet in your service.
Mary had a deep love of your will and a readiness to embrace the cross;
   —grant us the courage to follow her in accepting all that is painful in our lives.
Mary MacKillop spent her life caring for the poor and destitute and educating the children of the poor;
   —grant that we may bring love and compassion to all whom we serve.

PRAYER: God of mercy and compassion, you called Blessed Mary MacKillop to be the founder of a religious congregation committed to the education of poor children and to the service of those in need. We thank you for all who have followed in her footsteps and for the love and concern shown to others through them. We ask you to bless them and those they serve in the name of Jesus who is our Way, our Truth, and our Life. Amen.

* Composed by the Sisters of St. Joseph, Australia.

August 9
BLESSED EDITH STEIN

MORNING/EVENING PRAYER
(Psalms from Sunday, Week I, p. 3)

Ant 1 God is truth, and whoever seeks the truth is seeking God, whether [they] know it or not.

Ant 2 "Follow me." We too are confronted with these words, and the decision they pose between light and darkness.

Ant 3 I am convinced that whenever God calls someone, it is not for the sake of that person alone.

READING

Edith Stein, born into a Jewish family, October 12, 1891, was a brilliant philosopher, who studied under Husserl and collaborated with him. Discovering the writings of St. Teresa of Avila, she converted to Catholicism and became a Carmelite Nun. Together with other Jewish Catholics, she was arrested after the Church in Holland made a formal protest against genocide. She wrote from the death camp on August 5, "All the Catholics are together and in our dormitory we have all the nuns.... We are all very calm and cheerful. Of course, so far there has been no Mass and Communion; maybe that will come later. Now we have a chance to experience a little how to live purely from within...."* Five days later she met death in an Auschwitz gas chamber on August 9, 1942.

*Edith Stein: Self-Portrait in Letters, p. 315, (3)

RESPONSORY

Where you go, I will go; where you die, I will die. **—Where**...
Your people shall be my people; **—where you die**...
Glory to you, Source of all Being, Eternal Word and Holy Spirit.
    —Where...

CANTICLE

Ant Far be it from me to glory except in the cross of our Lord Jesus Christ, by which the world has been crucified to me, and I to the world.

INTERCESSIONS

O God, the Holocaust, the crucifixion of a people, still wounds our hearts;
   —we beg for the grace to banish such evil from the world.
For the Christian there is no such thing as a "stranger." There is only the neighbor—the person most in need of our help;
   —God our Creator, help us to see that we are one human
      family.
The mystic is simply a person who has experiential knowledge that God dwells in the soul;
   —Spirit of God, help us to remember that we are your temple.
I joyfully accept in advance the death God has appointed for me.
   —O God, give us an acceptance of your will that perseveres
      to the end.
Come, Rosa. We are going for our people.
   —Jesus, grant us the love and courage to die for one another.

PRAYER: O God, through her love for truth, you led Blessed
            Edith Stein to the very core of Divine Wisdom. Her life
            of prayer and simplicity prepared her for the
            martyrdom that would bear witness to her complete
            acceptance of the mystery of faith. An angel of mercy
            to those imprisoned with her, she was light and love in
            the midst of the darkness of evil. Let the message of
            her life and the death of all victims of the Holocaust
            open us to your call to transformation of ourselves and
            of our world. We ask this in Jesus' name. Amen.

August 9
FRANZ JAGERSTATTER

MORNING/EVENING PRAYER

Ant 1 Let us love our enemies, bless those who curse us, pray for those who persecute us. (Ps 55:1–19, 22–24, p. 72)

Ant 2 Happy are they who live and die in God's love.
         (Jer 14:17–21, p. 132)

Ant 3 For love will conquer and will endure for all eternity.
         (Ps 28:1–3, 6–9, p. 39)

READING

At the hour of his death, few people knew Franz Jagerstatter, and no one who knew him supported him in his refusal to kill for the Führer. Legions of Christians told him to do his duty and to go to war like the other men. His bishop, pastor, and spiritual advisors endeavored to persuade him that his conscientious objection was a wrong and futile course. So it can be said with certitude, that when the blade of the guillotine fell at Brandenburg Prison in Berlin at 4 p.m. on August 9, 1943, Franz Jagerstatter was totally alone, almost totally unknown, and destined to be totally forgotten.... The actual movements of mind and heart that empowered Franz Jagerstatter to see what others failed to see can never be known with certainty this side of eternity.... However, we can catch a glimpse of what was going on inside of him from this prison statement which he wrote shortly before he was to die; "Just as those who believe in National Socialism tell themselves that their struggle is for survival, so must we, too, convince ourselves that our struggle is for the eternal Kingdom. But with this difference: we need no rifles or pistols for our battle, but instead, spiritual weapons—and the foremost among these is prayer."

Emmanuel Charles McCarthy, "The Man Who Chose to See", p. 2, p. 6, (36)

RESPONSORY

Let us love our enemies, bless those who curse us, pray for those
     who persecute us, for love will conquer all. **—Let us...**
The time of travail is short; **—for love...**
Glory to you, Source of all Being, Eternal Word and Holy Spirit.
     —Let us...

CANTICLE

Ant They shall beat their swords into ploughshares, and their
     spears into pruning hooks.

INTERCESSIONS

We pray for all those who encounter opposition in their work for
peace and justice.
     —sustain them and bless their efforts.
When evil masquerades as good;
     —give us discerning hearts that we may know your Truth.
Many are imprisoned for their efforts to live the Gospel;
     —comfort them and send them advocates that justice may
        prevail.
You call us to live in peace with one another;

—enable us to allow conscientious objectors to follow their consciences with dignity and respect.

Teach us the ways of non-violence;

—that your reign of justice may enable all to live in freedom.

PRAYER: Jesus, you sought the good of all, but knew rejection from your closest followers, and suffering and death from those who saw you as a threat to their social system. May those who seek to follow you along this path, experience your sustaining love even at the cost of losing their lives. Help us all to follow the way of non-violence as we seek to bring the reign of God into our world. We ask this in your name. Amen.

August 11
ST. CLARE OF ASSISI

MORNING/EVENING PRAYER
(Psalms from Sunday, Week I, p. 3)

Ant 1 The realm of heaven is promised and given by the Lord Jesus only to the poor: for those who love temporal things lose the fruit of love.

Ant 2 O blessed poverty, who bestows eternal riches on those who love and embrace her!

Ant 3 Place your mind before the mirror of eternity! Place your soul in the brilliance of glory!

READING

Clare was born in Assisi in 1193. Inspired by the preaching of Francis, she desired to live the life of holy poverty. She founded the order of Poor Clares who lived an austere life performing many works of charity. Her spirituality was totally formed by her love of poverty. She was known for her gift of healing, her kindness to her Sisters, and her love of the Eucharist. She wrote in her Rule: "...on bended knees and with all possible respect, I commend all my sisters, both those present and those to come,...by the love of the Lord who was poor as he lay in the crib, poor as he lived in the world, who remained naked on the cross, may [our Protector] always see to it that [this] little flock observe that which [our good God] has begotten in [our] holy Church by the word and example of our blessed father Francis who followed the poverty and humility of [Christ Jesus] and...[the] glorious Virgin Mother—namely, holy poverty, which we have promised God and our most blessed Father Francis."*

*Clare of Assisi, *Francis and Clare*, p. 230, (1)

RESPONSORY

Look to heaven that invites us, O dearly beloved, and take up
  the cross. —**Look to**...
Follow Christ who goes before us; —**and take**...
Glory to you, Source of all Being, Eternal Word and Holy Spirit.
  —**Look to**...

CANTICLE

Ant Place your heart in the figure of the divine substance, and
  transform your entire being into the image of the Godhead
  through contemplation.

INTERCESSIONS

O God, your daughter Clare courageously left all to follow the
gospel and became the founder of a new order;
  —bless all who follow the Franciscan way of life in their
    efforts to live the gospel as Francis and Clare enjoined
    them.
Holy poverty was Clare's treasure and delight;
  —teach us simplicity in this consumer society and help us
    to trust in your loving providence.
It was through poverty that Clare was able to be a woman of
prayer;
  —keep our hearts free from clutter so that they may be
    centered on you.
Clare wanted her sisters to grow in the likeness of Christ and to
be witnesses of sisterly charity;
  —help us to proclaim the gospel by our loving relationships
    with one another.
Though she lived in an enclosed community, Clare's light
continues to shed its rays throughout the world;
  —send your healing love to those who suffer wherever they
    may be.
Through the holy friendship Francis shared with Clare;
  —grant that our deep friendships may show us the radiant
    face of Christ ever more clearly.

PRAYER: O God, through the preaching of Francis, your daughter Clare, a woman of noble birth, embraced a life of total poverty. Trusting solely on the generosity of others and holy providence, she and her followers found happiness in austerity. Bless all throughout the world who have embraced her spirit. May they continue to be a sign of your loving care and may all who follow your gospel know the gift of true simplicity and poverty of mind and heart. We ask this in the name of the poor Christ who first showed us the way. Amen.

August 15
ASSUMPTION

EVENING PRAYER I

Ant 1 Arise, O God, go to your resting place, you and the ark of your covenant, alleluia. (Ps 113, p. 96)

Ant 2 Thanks be to God, who gives us victory over death through Jesus Christ, alleluia. (Ps 147:12–20, p. 85)

Ant 3 Blessed is the one who hears the word of God and keeps it. (Phil 2:6–11, p. 96)

READING

Thank you for your letter out of retreat and for remembering my love for the heavenly feast of the Assumption, the most perfect blending of joy and wistfulness that one can have, with the Ascension and All Saints; and I am sure that Our Lady looks with a certain wistfulness back on earth, as we shall ever do to the home of our childhood. May she draw our thoughts and longings more and more to heavenly things.

Life and Letters of Janet Erskine Stuart, p. 480, (15)

RESPONSORY

Mother of our redeemer, pray for us. **—Mother**...
You reign with Christ forever, **—pray**...
Glory to you, Source of all Being, Eternal Word and Holy Spirit.
—Mother...

CANTICLE OF MARY

Ant You have shown might and mercy; you have exalted the lowly, alleluia.

INTERCESSIONS

O God, you are blessed in your angels and saints. Most blessed are you in your daughter, Mary. In joy we proclaim:
You have lifted up the lowly.

O God, you chose Mary to be the mother of Jesus and the mother of the church;
  —bless all who follow her example and bring Christ to the world.
Mary lived the mystery of Jesus and followed him to the cross;
  —give us the faith to follow you all the days of our lives.
Mary's glory is her union with your will;
  —through her intercession may we always do what is pleasing to you.
You called Mary to be the new Eve, the gate of heaven;
  —as we ponder your word, enkindle our hearts with love for your will, that we too may attain eternal life.

PRAYER: O God, you called Mary to be the mother of Jesus and the mother of our salvation. Let the example of her fidelity inspire us to open ourselves to the fullness of your grace, that we, too, may bear your Christ to the world. Grant this in the name of the same Jesus Christ who lives with you and the Holy Spirit forever. Amen.

MORNING PRAYER
(Psalms from Sunday, Week I, p. 3)

Ant 1 A great sign appeared in heaven; a woman clothed with the sun.

Ant 2 Rejoice, O Heaven, and you that dwell therein!

Ant 3 O Mary, full of grace, you dwell with God forever.

READING

The Virgin Mary has always been proposed to the faithful by the Church as an example to be imitated not precisely in the type of life she led, and much less for the socio-cultural background in which she lived and which today scarcely exists anywhere. Rather, she is to help us as an example to the faithful for the way in which in her own particular life she fully and responsibly accepted the will of God, because she heard the word of God and acted on it, and because charity and a spirit of service were the driving force of her actions. She is worthy of imitation because she was the first and the most perfect of Christ's disciples.

Pope Paul VI, Marialis Cultus, #35, (61)

RESPONSORY

Blessed are you, O Mary, for your faith in the word of God.
  —**Blessed**...
The Most High exalts you forever, —**for your**...
Glory to you, Source of all Being, Eternal Word and Holy Spirit.
  —**Blessed**...

CANTICLE OF ZECHARIAH

Ant May your servants be clothed in holiness, O God; may they sing for joy, alleluia.

INTERCESSIONS

Mary enters heaven to the joy of all the angels and saints, and so we pray:
  You are the glory of your people.

O God, through the intercession of Mary;
  —number us among your saints in glory.
Jesus, through your mother, Mary, you learned to pray;
  —teach us to pray and to be open to your Spirit.
You changed water into wine at the request of your mother;
  —increase our faith in your care for our needs.
Your mother was your first disciple;
  —as we meditate on the words of your gospel, may it bear fruit in our lives.

PRAYER: Glory to you, O God, in the entrance to eternal life of the ever Blessed Virgin Mary. Through her intercession, may we live the gospel of Jesus with constancy and love. As we celebrate her joy, may we imitate her fidelity. We ask this in the name of Jesus, the Eternal Word, who lives with you and with the Holy Spirit, forever. Amen.

DAYTIME PRAYER

Ant 1 Blessed is Mary who believed that what was spoken to her by God would be fulfilled. (Ps 120, p. 155)

Ant 2 Hail, full of grace; God is with you forever. (Ps 121, p. 89)

Ant 3 Through all generations, your name will be blessed. (Ps 131, p. 116)

(Prayer as in Morning Prayer)

EVENING PRAYER II

Ant 1 Mary is glorified with Christ; she dwells with the Trinity in heaven. (Ps 122, p. 143)

Ant 2 Your consent, O Mary, enabled God to take on our human nature and live among us. (Ps 127, p. 122)

Ant 3 God has given good things to the hungry, and has shown compassion to the lowly. (Eph 1:3–10, p. 157)

READING

...The skies speed up to meet you, and the seas
Swim you the silver of their crests.
If you delay to come, we'll see the meteors by night,
Skimming before your way,—
Lighting the time of death's dismay
In lights as lithe as animals.
And God will blaze your pathway with the incandescent stars.

But oh! Queen of all grace and counsel,
Cause of our joy, Oh Clement Virgin, come:
Show us those eyes as chaste as lightning,
Kinder than June and true as Scripture.
Heal with your looks the poisons of the universe,
And claim your Son's regenerate world!...

"Canticle for the Blessed Virgin" in *The Collected Poems of Thomas Merton*, p. 161, (16)

RESPONSORY

The Savior dwelt within you, Holy Mother of God. **—The**...
Now you dwell with Christ forever, **—Holy**...
Glory to you, Source of all Being, Eternal Word and Holy Spirit. **—The**...

CANTICLE OF MARY

Ant God is glorified in Mary, who is taken into heaven and intercedes for us in her loving kindness.

INTERCESSIONS

O God, you are blessed in your angels and saints. Most blessed are you in your daughter, Mary. In joy we proclaim:
You have lifted up the lowly.

O God, you chose Mary to be the mother of Jesus and the mother of the church;
—bless all who follow her example and bring Christ to the world.
Mary lived the mystery of Jesus and followed him to the cross;
—give us the faith to follow you all the days of our lives.
Mary's glory is her union with your will;
—through her intercession may we always do what is pleasing to you.
You called Mary to be the new Eve, the gate of heaven;
—as we ponder your word, enkindle our hearts with love for your will, that we too may attain eternal life.

PRAYER: O God, you called Mary to be the mother of Jesus and the mother of our salvation. Let the example of her fidelity inspire us to open ourselves to the fullness of your grace, that we, too, may bear your Christ to the world. Grant this in the name of the same Jesus Christ who lives with you and the Holy Spirit forever. Amen.

August 18
ST. JANE FRANCES DE CHANTAL

MORNING/EVENING PRAYER
(Psalms from Sunday, Week I, p. 3)

Ant 1 I learned what I had never before truly understood, that one must not seek all one's consolations in creatures but in God and that the true means of being healed consists in relying upon and abandoning oneself to the divine mercy without any reservation.

Ant 2 I felt such indescribable longings to know and follow the will of God, whatever might happen.

Ant 3 Those who are in the world need [particular friendships] in order to secure and assist one another amid the many dangerous passages through which they must pass.

READING

Jane Frances was born in Dijon, France, in 1572. She was married and the mother of four children (two others having died as newborns) when her husband was killed in a hunting accident. After years of widowhood that included care of the sick and poor, she founded the Visitation Order in collaboration with St. Francis de Sales. She was a wise and gentle administrator of her Order and spiritual director to women and men. She wrote: "Show one to another a goodness and a childlike amiability, bearing with one another in charity, and never letting the faults of the community or of any one individual sister astonish you. For to be astonished at the defects of our sisters, to scrutinize them, to examine them, and to be upset by them, is the mark of a weak mind, with little charity and forbearance, and of no true insight into human misery...."* Jane Frances died December 13, 1641. Her surviving children were three daughters and one son.

*The Spirit of Saint Jane Frances de Chantal as Shown by her Letters, p. 257, (15)

RESPONSORY

My soul proclaims your greatness; my spirit has rejoiced in
   you. —**My soul**...
For your regard has blessed me; —**my spirit**...
Glory to you, Source of all Being, Eternal Word and Holy Spirit.
   —**My soul**...

CANTICLE

Ant How is it that the mother of my Lord should come to me? The moment I heard your greeting, the babe in my womb leapt for joy.

INTERCESSIONS

We must remain in the state where God puts us: in pain, we must have patience, in suffering we must endure;
   —grant that we may live the present moment and accept it
   as God's gift to us.

Ah, my dear sisters, our beloved Visitation is a tiny kingdom of charity;
—help us to live with love in our families and communities.
God has taken away from all power of any prayer...all I can do is to suffer and hold myself very simply before God...;
—give us the faith to believe, in times of darkness, that it is the Spirit who prays within us.
Never, amidst trials, lose the equanimity and peace of your heart, nor overburden it by scrutinizing your infidelities and your want of discernment;
—help us not to take ourselves too seriously, but trust in God's love and infinite mercy.
A widow, a mother, a God-seeker, founder of the Visitation Order, Jane Frances de Chantal followed the urgings of her heart to be all for God;
—help us to accept the circumstances of our life as an invitation to deeper union with the God who lures us on the way to wholeness.

PRAYER: O God, under the guidance of Francis de Sales you called Jane Frances de Chantal to a life of surrender to your love and your will. We thank you for those persons in our lives who support us on our spiritual journeys. May the Spirit of Wisdom be with all those who companion others on their way to you, and may all who follow the rule Jane Frances gave her Sisters be faithful as she was faithful. We ask this in Jesus' name. Amen.

August 30
BLESSED JEANNE JUGAN*

MORNING/EVENING PRAYER

Ant 1 The bread of the poor is the bread of God. (Ps 21:2–8, 14, p. 21)

Ant 2 Only the little ones are truly pleasing to God. (Ps 71, p. 107)

Ant 3 Go and find Jesus when your patience and strength give out and you feel alone and helpless. (Ps 71 II, p. 108)

READING

Jeanne Jugan founded the Little Sisters of the Poor to care for the sick, the homeless, and the elderly. Her humility in the face of rejection by clerical authorities was an inspiration to those who knew her and to those who followed her. She died August 30, 1879. At the cause of her beatification, Pope John Paul II, said: "...Sister Jeanne Jugan invites us to live the Gospel beatitude of poverty in the simplicity of little ones and in the joy of children of God. She invites us especially to open our heart to the elderly, so often neglected and set aside. In proclaiming this woman Blessed, the Church intends to emphasize the charism of service rendered to the aged and, in this way, to manifest honor and love to all people advanced in age, to whom such due tribute of honor and love is sometimes denied."

RESPONSORY

May Christ dwell in your hearts through faith; and charity
     be the root and foundation of your life. **—May Christ**...
That you may attain to the fullness of God; **—and charity**...
Glory to you, Source of all Being, Eternal Word and Holy Spirit.
     —May Christ...

CANTICLE

Ant   It is so beautiful to be poor, to have nothing, to await all
       from God.

INTERCESSIONS

O God, you reveal your compassion for the elderly and the poor through the work of the Little Sisters of the Poor;
     —bless them as they serve those who are so special to you.
Your daughter, Jeanne, touched the hearts of all with her humility and childlike faith;
     —free us to be singlehearted; to cherish the reality that we
       are your children.
Though Jeanne Jugan founded the Order, she was unjustly overlooked and deposed as superior by ecclesiastical authority;
     —may all who suffer unjustly know God's loving compassion
       and find meaning in their trials.
Humiliated and ignored, Jeanne Jugan continued to serve the poor and the Order with love and devotion;
     —grant that our service may always be for others and not for
       personal recognition.

Serving as a domestic for many years, the tools of her trade were a broom, a scrubbing brush, a cleaning bucket, and a kitchen knife;

—may we find our self-worth in the love with which we do our work, rather than in prestige of position and power.

PRAYER: O Loving God, we thank you for the gift of Jeanne Jugan to the church and to the world. In her, the elderly and the poor, the neglected and the homeless found an advocate and a friend. Through her daughters, the Little Sisters of the Poor, her work continues and your little ones are served. May all who work to ease the suffering of the elderly be strengthened in their task of mercy. May they know the fullness of your peace as they follow the way of your son, Jesus, who came to bring glad tidings to the poor of the world. Amen.

*Office based on *At the Service of the Elderly: Jeanne Jugan and the Little Sisters of the Poor,* Editions Fleurus, (26)

September 7
FREDERICK OZANAM
MORNING/EVENING PRAYER

Ant 1 When one looks at God through God's creation, how can one fail to realize that paradise must begin now in this world. (Ps 21:2–8, 14, p. 21)

Ant 2 How can anyone doubt that those who live with the love of God in their hearts are already enjoying here, on this earth, a foretaste of heaven? (Ps 65, p. 63)

Ant 3 The Authority that tells us we shall always have the poor amongst us is the same that commands us to do all that we can that poverty may cease to be. (Ps 25, p. 32)

READING

Frederick Ozanam was born in Milan in 1813. A brilliant student of the University of Paris, he founded the Society of St. Vincent de Paul for relief of the poor in 1833. He wrote in an article: "...we should occupy ourselves with the people whose wants are too many and whose rights are too few; who are crying out, and fairly, for a share in public affairs, for assurances of employment, and against distress; who follow bad leaders because they have no good leaders...."* By the time of his death in 1853, the society had become operative in sixteen countries. Today, there are more than 600,000 women and men who, like Frederick and Vincent, believe that service to the poor and suffering is a necessary part of our Christian calling.

*James Patrick Derum, *Apostle in a Top Hat*, pp. 201–202, (31)

RESPONSORY

If you give your bread to the hungry and relief to the oppressed,
    your light will rise in darkness. **—If you...**
And your shadows become like noon; **—your light...**
Glory to you, Source of all Being, Eternal Word and Holy Spirit.
    —If you...

CANTICLE

Ant Blessed are the poor in spirit, for theirs is the kindom of heaven.

INTERCESSIONS

O God, you endowed Frederick Ozanam with a love for the poor and the ability to help them;
    —bless all who spend themselves to serve the needs of others.
Frederick was a scholar, a teacher, a faithful husband, and a father who was totally dedicated to the poor;
    —show us ways to be available to the poor no matter what
        our state in life.
His greatest gift to the poor was the daily service of his mind and heart;
    —grant strength and perseverance to all members of the
        St. Vincent de Paul Society, and inspire others to support
        them.
Frederick bore the resentment of those who did not understand his mission;
    —let the prophets who speak for the poor be heard today.
He saw God reflected in all creatures;
    —give us the will and the ways to preserve the beauty of the
        earth and to conserve its resources.

PRAYER: O God, you filled the hearts of Frederick Ozanam and his companions with a love of the poor and inspired them to found a Society for the relief of those in need. Be praised in the dedication of your servant, Frederick, bless those dedicated to the work he has begun, and raise up leaders today to carry on the work of Christian charity. We ask this in Jesus' name. Amen.

September 14
TRIUMPH OF THE CROSS
EVENING PRAYER I

Ant 1 The cross of Christ is the power and wisdom of God to those who believe, alleluia. (Ps 147:1–11, p. 173)

Ant 2 Jesus humbled himself and became obedient unto death, even death on a cross, alleluia. (Ps 147:12–20, p. 181)

Ant 3 God has exalted Christ above every other creature, alleluia. (Phil 2:6–11, p. 143)

READING

The [one] who embraces the cross is always alone, looking up at one who is not looking down, but who is in turn looking upward towards the God who has forsaken them. This is the important thing: that he lifts our abandonment into his own greater abandonment. Those words he spoke that [God] should forgive them; that his soul is commended to God; that another will share paradise with him; that his mother is our mother; that he thirsts; that, truly, it has all been done—having meaning only because he knows what abandonment is.

Theologians Today: Hans Ur Von Balthasar, p. 121, (5)

RESPONSORY

By the cross of Christ, we have been redeemed. **—By the…**
Through Jesus' death and resurrection, **—we have…**
Glory to you, Source of all Being, Eternal Word and Holy Spirit.
   —By the…

CANTICLE OF MARY

Ant I must be lifted up so that all who believe in me may have life eternal.

INTERCESSIONS

Faithful cross, tree like no other, on you Christ triumphed over death. Let us pray:

Praise to you, Lord Jesus Christ!

Jesus, through your ignominious death on the cross;
  —give comfort and hope to those who suffer torture or
    imprisonment.
Jesus, pierced with a lance;
  —open our hearts in an outpouring of love and care for the
    poor.
Jesus, raised on high on the cross;
  —help us to rise above our petty desires and complaints.
Jesus, reviled and rejected on the cross;
  —deliver us from all forms of pride and human respect that
    would separate us from you.

PRAYER: O God, you love the world so much that you sent your
         Word Incarnate to save us and to bring us new life.
         Give us the grace to follow Jesus in humility,
         obedience, and persevering love. Let the glory of his
         cross enable us to bear the cost of discipleship and to
         remain true to you till the end. We commend our spirits
         to you this day and at the hour of our death. Amen.

MORNING PRAYER
(Psalms from Sundays, Week I, p. 3)

Ant 1 I have been crucified with Christ; I live now, not I, but
       Christ lives in me.

Ant 2 If we are crucified with Christ, we will live with Christ
       forever.

Ant 3 By the power of the cross we have been redeemed; death
       no longer has dominion over us.

READING

Where God seems not to be, where God seems to have withdrawn, there we shall find God most intensely present. This logic contradicts the logic of reason. This is the logic of the cross. The logic of the cross is a scandal to reason, and must be maintained as such. Only thus shall we have access to God. Otherwise we should never surmise it. Reason seeks the cause of suffering. Reason seeks reasons for evil. The cross seeks no causes. God is to be found in suffering, and most intensively of all. Where reason sees the absence of God, the logic of the cross sees God's full revelation.... The cross must remain the cross: the blind spot in the eye of the reasoning and the wisdom of the world.

Leonardo Boff, *Passion of Christ, Passion of the World*, p. 109, (22)

RESPONSORY

Christ is triumphant over sin and death. —**Christ is**...
By his cross, Jesus won victory, —**over**...
Glory to you, Source of all Being, Eternal Word and Holy Spirit.
   —**Christ is**...

CANTICLE OF ZECHARIAH

Ant Jesus came into the world, not to condemn us, but to reconcile us to God.

INTERCESSIONS

As the serpent was lifted up in the desert, Jesus was lifted up on the cross. In exaltation, we proclaim:
Indeed this is the Holy One of God!

Jesus, you died on the cross betrayed by your friends;
   —give us the grace to be faithful to you till death.
Jesus, crucified for us, your love reaches to the ends of the earth;
   —teach us how to proclaim your word to the world.
You forgave those who crucified you and prayed for us all;
   —sign us with the cross of reconciliation and mercy.
Obedient to death on a cross, you are the source of our salvation;
   —keep us faithful to your teaching and make us worthy of
   the healing power of your cross.

PRAYER: O God, you love the world so much that you sent your Word Incarnate to save us and to bring us new life. Give us the grace to follow Jesus in humility, obedience, and persevering love. Let the glory of his cross enable us to bear the cost of discipleship and to remain true to you till the end. We commend our spirits to you this day and at the hour of our death. Amen.

DAYTIME PRAYER
(Psalms from the current weekday in the Psalter)

Ant 1 If you wish to be my disciple, take up your cross and follow me.

Ant 2 Come to me, you who are burdened, and I will give you rest.

Ant 3 If you wish to save your life, you must lose it for my sake.

(Prayer as in Morning Prayer)

EVENING PRAYER II

Ant 1 We who were once dead because of sin, are now alive in God because of Christ's death on the cross.
(Ps 110:1–5, 7, p. 53)

Ant 2 Christ endured the cross and was raised in glory.
(Ps 116, 10–19, p. 96)

Ant 3 We praise you, O Christ, who for our sake opened your arms on the cross. (Rev 4:11; 5:9, 10, 12, p. 67)

READING

[Jesus] surrendered himself in his death unconditionally to the absolute mystery that he called his Father, into whose hands he committed his existence, when in the night of his death and God-forsakenness he was deprived of everything that is otherwise regarded as the content of a human existence: life, honor, acceptance in earthly and religious fellowship, and so on. In the concreteness of his death it becomes only too clear that everything fell away from him, even the perceptible security of the closeness of God's love, and in this trackless dark there prevailed silently only the mystery that in itself and in its freedom has no name and to which he nevertheless calmly surrendered himself as to eternal love and not to the hell of futility.... The Christian, every Christian at all times, follows Jesus by *dying* with him; following Jesus has its ultimate truth and reality and universality in the following of the Crucified.... In all these brief moments of dying in installments we are faced with the question of how we are to cope with them.... [Do] we merely protest, merely despair...become cynical and cling all the more desperately and absolutely to what has been taken from us?... [Or do] we abandon with resignation what is taken from us, accept twilight as promise of an eternal Christmas full of light, regard slight breakdowns as events of grace?

Karl Rahner, *Theological Investigations, Vol. XVIII*, p. 160, p. 165, p. 169, (2)

RESPONSORY

Jesus. Lamb of God, have mercy on us. **—Jesus,...**
You take away our sins by your holy cross, **—have**...
Glory to you, Source of all Being, Eternal Word and Holy Spirit.
    —Jesus,...

CANTICLE OF MARY

Ant Worthy is the Lamb who was slain to receive power and
    wealth, wisdom, and honor.

INTERCESSIONS

Faithful cross, tree like no other, on you Christ triumphed over
death. Let us pray:
                    Praise to you, Lord Jesus Christ!

Jesus, through your ignominious death on the cross;
    —give comfort and hope to those who suffer torture or
      imprisonment.
Jesus, pierced with a lance;
    —open our hearts in an outpouring of love and care for the
      poor.
Jesus, raised on high on the cross;
    —help us to rise above our petty desires and complaints.
Jesus, reviled and rejected on the cross;
    —deliver us from all forms of pride and human respect that
      would separate us from you.

PRAYER: O God, you love the world so much that you sent your
        Word Incarnate to save us and to bring us new life.
        Give us the grace to follow Jesus in humility,
        obedience, and persevering love. Let the glory of his
        cross enable us to bear the cost of discipleship and to
        remain true to you till the end. We commend our spirits
        to you this day and at the hour of our death. Amen.

September 17
HILDEGARD OF BINGEN

MORNING/EVENING PRAYER
(Psalms from Sunday, Week I, p. 3)

Ant 1 I prayed and understanding was given me; I called upon God and the spirit of Wisdom came to me.

Ant 2 I preferred Wisdom to scepters and thrones, and I accounted wealth as nothing in comparison with her.

Ant 3 Wisdom I loved more than health or beauty, and I chose to have her rather than light, because her radiance never ceases.

READING

Hildegard believed that God was delighted with creation, and her conviction was reflected in her lifeworks.... The emphasis in her writings was on the order and structure of the universe in all its magnificence and splendor, and the mystery revealed in the ever-unfolding drama of its history. She believed that whatever God created was bound together in cosmic interdependence.... According to Hildegard, life, the world, and God are far from boring. God is full of immeasurable glory and abundant sweetness, which are reflected in creation.

Gloria Durka, Praying with Hildegard of Bingen, p. 67, (42)

RESPONSORY

The earth forms not only the basic raw material for humankind,
  but also the substance of the incarnation of God's son.
  —The earth...
She is the mother of all that is natural, all that is human;**—but**...
Glory to you, Source of all Being, Eternal Word and Holy Spirit.
  —The earth...

CANTICLE

Ant Our God is the song of the angel throng and the splendor of secret ways hid from all humankind. But God our life is the life of all.

INTERCESSIONS

Hildegard believed that the Creator gave woman a nature deserving of respect bordering on awe;
  —may all women recognize their inherent self-worth.

She praised you, O God, in poetry and song;
   —bless all those who enrich our worship by sharing their
      gifts.
You gave us in Hildegard a model of a woman who theologized
from the depths of her experience;
   —may our theology today reflect your interaction in our lives.
Hildegard claimed that like Mary, we too can be women
overshadowed by the Holy Spirit—vessels of the Word of God;
   —illumine our minds and our hearts that your Word can be
      incarnated in us.
In her visions, Hildegard saw the resurrected Christ resplendent
in feminine form;
   —expand our images of you that we may come to know you
      in the fullness of your being.
Through her experience with chronic illnesses, Hildegard explored
holistic ways to cure herself and others;
   —enlighten all in the healing professions as they strive to
      find cures and remedies for those they tend.

PRAYER: O God, we thank you for this holy woman, shy by
nature, yet fearless when she recognized your work in
her. Grant that we may recognize your work in us, that
we too may do your work on this earth—using the gifts
you have given us. Overshadow us with your Spirit that
the Word may become flesh in us and in our world.
Amen.

September 27
ST. VINCENT DE PAUL

MORNING/EVENING PRAYER
(Psalms from Sunday, Week I, p. 3)

Ant 1 Whatever you have done for the least of these you have
done for me.

Ant 2 It is essential to continue well, because to begin is nothing.

Ant 3 Have a great affection for the poor, and take great care to
teach them the truths necessary for salvation.

READING

Jesus called disciples to follow him. Women as well as men responded, leaving their families, their homes, their jobs, and their villages. They formed a community of brothers and sisters around him, traveling with him, listening to him and being taught by him, learning his ways and even being sent on mission by him, little trial runs into ministry while he was still with them. After Jesus' death and resurrection, this band of followers formed the nucleus of the church.

Elizabeth A. Johnson, Consider Jesus, p. 54, (2)

RESPONSORY

Let the little children come to me, for of such is the kindom of
    heaven. **—Let the**...
Forbid them not; **—for of**...
Glory to you, Source of all Being, Eternal Word and Holy Spirit.
    —Let the...

CANTICLE

Ant By this shall all know that you are my disciples, if you have
    love for one another.

INTERCESSIONS

O God, Vincent de Paul heard the cry of the poor and dedicated
his life to their welfare;
    —open our minds and hearts to those in need today.
Vincent labored for a sound foundation for the clergy;
    —let the spirit of wisdom guide all who minister in the
      church.
He truly believed that no one can serve two masters;
    —grant us a share in his singlehearted dedication to you.
You endowed Vincent with the gifts of wisdom, collaboration and
courage;
    —awaken leaders after your own heart in the church and in
      civic governments.
The seed you planted in France through Vincent has grown into a
world community;
    —continue to guide them in their work of justice and charity.

PRAYER: O God, we praise you for the life of St. Vincent de Paul
    and for the gift he continues to be for the church. He
    has been salvation for the poor and an inspiration to all
    who strive to live the call of the gospel. Bless all who

embrace his legacy of love and care for those in need. We ask this in Jesus' name. Amen.

October 1
ST. THÉRÈSE OF LISIEUX

MORNING/EVENING PRAYER
(Psalms from Sunday, Week I, p. 3)

Ant 1   Love is repaid by love alone.

Ant 2   Merit does not consist in doing or in giving much, but rather in receiving, in loving much.

Ant 3   Prayer is an aspiration of the heart; it is a simple glance directed to God.

READING

...Ever since I have been given the grace to understand also the love of the Heart of Jesus, I admit that it has expelled all fear from my heart. The remembrance of my faults humbles me, draws me never to depend on my strength which is only weakness, but this remembrance speaks to me of mercy and love even more. When we cast our faults with entire filial confidence into the devouring fire of love, how would these not be consumed beyond return?

St. Thérèse of Lisieux: General Correspondence, Vol. II, pp. 1133–34, (3)

RESPONSORY

We are the body of Christ; in the heart of the Church I will be love. **—We are...**
I have found my vocation; **—in the heart...**
Glory to you, Source of all Being, Eternal Word and Holy Spirit. **—We are...**

CANTICLE

Ant   God is love and they who live in love, live in God.

INTERCESSIONS

O God, in her message, your daughter Thérèse revealed to us anew the good news that you are truly a God of gentleness and compassion;
  —may all recognize you as our Father/Mother, ever close to us.

Thérèse's life was marked by a beautiful childlike simplicity;
—bless the children of this world; have mercy on all the
abused and neglected.

She manifested a heroic trust in your loving providence;
—give us the grace to be faithful to you and to trust in your
constant care.

With childlike confidence she kept alive an ardent desire to love
as she was loved;
—we thank you for having loved us so much. Give us the grace
to love one another.

Thérèse was proclaimed patroness of the missions and of
gardeners;
—help us to proclaim by our lives your boundless love and to
rejoice in your beauty and your truth.

PRAYER: Merciful Mother/Father, in the simple message of Saint
Thérèse is revealed anew the gospel message of love,
childlike trust, and simplicity. Have mercy on all who
are burdened by the complexities and unfreedoms of
our daily life. Give us the grace to follow Jesus, who
has set us free, in whom we live and move and have
our being. Amen.

October 4
ST. FRANCIS OF ASSISI

MORNING/EVENING PRAYER
(Psalms from Sunday, Week I, p. 3)

Ant 1 I was hungry and you gave me food; a stranger and you
welcomed me.

Ant 2 Let all creatures great and small bless our God.

Ant 3 Most high, all powerful, all good God; all praise is yours,
all glory, all honor and blessing.

READING

Let us desire nothing else, let us wish for nothing else, let nothing else
please us and cause us delight except our Creator and Redeemer and
Savior, the one true God, Who is the Fullness of Good, all good, every
good, the true and supreme good. Who alone is Good, merciful and
gentle, delectable and sweet; Who alone is holy, just and true, holy and
right; Who alone is kind, innocent, pure; from Whom, and through

Whom, and in Whom is all pardon, all grace, all glory of all the penitent and the just, of all the blessed who rejoice together in heaven.

Francis of Assisi, Francis and Clare, p. 133, (1)

RESPONSORY

Yours are the praises, the glory, the honor, and all benediction;
   my God and my all. **—Yours**...
To you alone, Most High, do they belong; **—my God**...
Glory to you, Source of all Being, Eternal Word and Holy Spirit.
   —Yours...

CANTICLE

Ant Henceforth let no one trouble me; for I bear on my body the marks of Christ crucified.

INTERCESSIONS

Francis called Lady Poverty his bride;
   —free us from the lure of consumerism that we may live the simplicity to which the gospel calls us.
Francis found Jesus in the poor;
   —move us to action which seeks communion and solidarity with the poor, the humble, and the lowly.
He reverenced all creation as a reflection of the Creator;
   —may we respect all forms of life, especially those living creatures which depend on our care.
We pray for environmentalists, recyclers, and those who till, care for, and harvest the fruits of our earth;
   —may they be confirmed and supported in their efforts to preserve the earth for future generations.
Francis radiated seraphic joy born of love for you;
   —inflame our hearts, make them big enough to embrace all as our sisters and brothers.

PRAYER: Almighty, eternal, just, and merciful God, grant us the grace to do for You alone what we know You want us to do, and always to desire what pleases You. Thus, inwardly cleansed, interiorly enlightened, and inflamed by the fire of the Holy Spirit, may we be able to follow in the footprints of Your beloved Son, our Lord Jesus Christ. And by your grace alone, may we make our way to You, Most High, who live and rule in perfect Trinity and simple Unity, and are glorified God all-powerful forever and ever. Amen. (Prayer of St. Francis, p. 61, (1))

October 9
MOTHER MARY JOSEPH ROGERS, MM

MORNING/EVENING PRAYER
(Psalms from Sunday, Week I, p. 3)

Ant 1 Grow so you can give.

Ant 2 God can work miracles through your hands.

Ant 3 Where there is love, there is no labor.

READING

Mary Josephine Rogers (Mother Mary Joseph), born in 1882, was inspired by the interest of Protestant students at Smith College for the foreign missions. Her desire to organize a group of Catholic students eventually led to founding, with Father James A. Walsh, the Order of Maryknoll Sisters, the first American congregation of women dedicated to the work of the foreign missions. She encouraged her sisters: "...We have tried from the beginning to cultivate a spirit which is extremely difficult and which for a long time might have been misunderstood even by those who were nearest to us, and that is, the retention of our own natural dispositions, the retention of our own individuality, having in mind, of course, that all of these things should be corrected where radically wrong, and all of it supernaturalized.... Each one of us, in her own work, with her own particular little sweetness or attractiveness, is to be used by God as a particular tool to do particular work and to save particular souls...."* Mother Mary Joseph died October 9, 1955.

RESPONSORY

Go out into the whole world, and preach the good news. —**Go**...
Cure the sick, heal the lepers; —**and preach**...
Glory to you, Source of all Being, Eternal Word and Holy Spirit.
   —**Go**...

CANTICLE

Ant There can be no Maryknoll Sister...who is not heroically generous, generous to the very last inch of her being—generous in the giving of her time, of her talents, generous in her thoughts, generous in every possible phase of religious life.*

INTERCESSIONS

Witnessing the work of the Protestants for foreign missions convinced the young Mollie Rogers (Mother Mary Joseph) that she, too, had a work to do;
> —may our appreciation of others enable ecumenism to
>   flourish, that our united efforts may build a better world.

She cautioned her Sisters to "train yourself to go up or down, in or out, with this person or that, in any work whatsoever, and to accept these changes readily, easily and quickly."*
> —give us the humility to adapt ourselves to the situations of
>   our life that are for the good of others.

Mother Mary Joseph recognized the need for professional training for catechetical work and for evangelization;
> —bless all those who study to serve others.

Recognizing the value of contemplation, Mother Mary Joseph established the Maryknoll Cloister to complement the work of the Sisters in the missions;
> —help us to center ourselves so that the work that we do
>   is the fruit of our relationship with you.

Mother Mary Joseph encouraged and fostered the gifts of each of her Sisters;
> —help us to rejoice and affirm the gifts and talents of others.

PRAYER: O God, through Mother Mary Joseph Rogers, the first American community of women religious missionaries was founded. Since the time of its inception, the poor, the oppressed, the sick from the far corners of the earth have known your love and concern through her followers. Through the work of Maryknoll, the blind see, the lepers are cleansed, and the poor have the Gospel preached to them. We ask your blessing on all those who continue the work of Mother Mary Joseph and pray that they may be faithful to her spirit and her vision. We ask this in your name. Amen.

*Quotations used in this office are the words of Mother Mary Joseph to her Sisters, as cited in Camilla Kennedy, MM, *To the Uttermost Parts of the Earth*, p. 51, p. 52, (56).

October 15
ST. TERESA OF AVILA

MORNING/EVENING PRAYER
(Psalms from Sunday, Week I, p. 3)

Ant 1 There is nothing annoying that is not suffered easily by those who love one another.

Ant 2 All must be friends, all must be loved, all must be held dear, all must be helped.

Ant 3 Humility does not disturb or disquiet or agitate, it comes with peace, delight and calm.

READING

Teresa was born in Avila, Spain, in 1515. She entered the Carmelite Order, and, wishing to live the Primitive Rule, became one of its reformers. Her writings articulate the spiritual journey—from the beginning stages of prayer to the prayer of union. Writing on contemplation, she says: "The soul understands that without the noise of words this divine Master is teaching it by suspending its faculties, for if they were to be at work they would do harm rather than bring benefit. They are enjoying without understanding how they are enjoying. The soul is being enkindled in love, and it doesn't understand how it loves. It knows that it enjoys what it loves, but it doesn't know how. It clearly understands that this joy is not a joy the intellect obtains merely through desire. The will is enkindled without understanding how. But as soon as it can understand something, it sees that this good cannot be merited or gained through all the trials one can suffer on earth. This good is a gift from the [One who rules] earth and heaven.... What I have described is perfect contemplation."* Because of the depth of her understanding of mystical theology, she has been named a Doctor of the Church.

*Teresa of Avila, *Way of Perfection*, 25.2, (3)

RESPONSORY

Let nothing disturb you, let nothing frighten you; all things are passing. —**Let nothing...**
God alone suffices; —**all things...**
Glory to you, Source of all Being, Eternal Word and Holy Spirit. —**Let nothing...**

CANTICLE

Ant The important thing is not to think much but to love much, and so do that which best stirs you to love.

INTERCESSIONS

O God, you empowered Teresa to reform the Carmelite Order;
—bless all those who seek to reform institutions; grant that they walk before you in sincerity and truth.

Your daughter, Teresa, had a great love for the humanity of Jesus and cherished him as her friend;
—may our friendship with Jesus enable us to cherish our friendships with one another.

Teresa taught her daughters to embrace humility, detachment, and love for one another;
—help us to grow in self-knowledge, to be free of hidden expectations, and to love those with whom we work and live.

You gifted Teresa with the ability to articulate the spiritual journey and the stages of prayer;
—through her writings, may many come to a personal experience of you and be consoled when the journey seems dark and prayer is dry.

The depth of her knowledge of the spiritual life resulted in Teresa being proclaimed a Doctor of the Church;
—grant that women who study theology and spirituality may gift the church with wisdom and insight.

PRAYER: O God, in Teresa you have given us a model—a woman who was faithful to prayer, to her Sisters and friends, and to the work she was called to do. Help us to be so committed to you that our daily work fosters our life of prayer and our life of prayer enables us to live fully in the world around us—aware of its needs and concerns. Bless all who follow the charism of Teresa and grant that they may be true to her spirit and faithful to a life of prayer. We ask this through Jesus, who was ever her friend. Amen.

October 16
ST. MARGUERITE D'YOUVILLE, SGM*

MORNING/EVENING PRAYER
(Psalms from Sunday, Week I, p. 3)

Ant 1 Providence is wonderful; it has incomprehensible motives; it provides for everything. In it is all my trust.

Ant 2 Is there any joy in life greater than that of a happy home? All the goods of earth cannot approach it.

Ant 3 Crosses there must be, but love makes us strong enough to bear them.

READING

Marie Marguerite Dufrost de Lajemmerais was born at Varennes, Quebec, on October 15, 1701. Through the generosity of relatives Marguerite was educated by the Ursulines in Quebec for two years. From her earliest years her life was marked by the cross. She suffered the loss of her father when she was seven; deception and humiliation by her husband, François d'Youville; and the death of four of their six children. Widowed in 1730, Marguerite managed to pay off her husband's considerable debts and to educate her two sons, who later became priests. A pioneering woman of deep faith, ever conscious of Divine Providence, she devoted herself to the care of the most destitute. This is the woman chosen by God to found the Sisters of Charity of Montreal, "Grey Nuns," in 1737 and to direct it until her death in 1771. Her work continues through her spiritual children who form six autonomous Grey Nun congregations. In perpetuating her charism throughout the world, they bear witness to the compassionate love of God in multiple works of charity.

RESPONSORY

She reaches out her hands to the poor and extends her arms
    to the needy. —**She reaches**...
The valiant woman, who can find her? —**She extends**...
Glory to you, Source of all Being, Eternal Word and Holy Spirit.
    —**She reaches**...

CANTICLE

Ant Offer yourselves to [God] and to Jesus, and see in the poor the Christ whose members they have the honor to be.

INTERCESSIONS

Learn from the heart of [our loving God] the attitudes of love, tender concern, and compassion.
    O God, help us to grow in this knowledge.

I leave all to Divine Providence; my confidence is in it. All that will happen is pleasing to God;
    —provident God, may we learn to trust you completely.
Ask God to give us the strength to bear our crosses and to make a holy use of them. We need crosses in order to reach heaven;
    —risen Jesus, strengthen us today as we follow you.
I am sincere, upright, and incapable of any subterfuge or reservation which could disguise the truth or give double meaning;
    —Holy Spirit, give us courage as we face our adversaries.
We...consecrate ourselves, without reserve, to the service of the poor...;
    —O God, may we recognize your presence in the poor.
It has pleased God to try us by fire...but the matter is over. You must think no more of it;*
    —O God, help us to accept the difficulties in our lives, and to move on.

PRAYER: God of mercy and love, you led St. Marguerite d'Youville by the way of the cross and you willed that through her charity relief might be brought to the human miseries of her times. Grant us the courage to show compassionate love as she did, and the strength to persevere until the day when you call us to participate in the joy of all the saints. We ask this through Jesus Christ. Amen.

* Composed by the Grey Nuns of the Sacred Heart, Yardley, Pa.

October 23
FIVE ADORERS OF THE BLOOD OF CHRIST
MISSIONARIES IN LIBERIA*

MORNING/EVENING PRAYER

Ant 1 In the breaking of their bodies, they seem to transcend the limits of place and time and become teachers to the world. (Ps 94, p. 168)

Ant 2 Let us become an evermore credible witness of God's tender love, of which the blood of Jesus is vibrant sign and unending covenant pledge. (Ps 94 II, p. 169)

Ant 3 They have survived the period of trial and have been deemed worthy to be numbered among the martyrs who have given their lives and shed their blood so that others may know life and freedom. (Ps 43, p. 62)

READING

Mary Joel Kolmer, Shirley Kolmer, Kathleen McGuire, Agnes Mueller, and Barbara Ann Muttra were American Sisters of the Adorers of the Blood of Christ, province of Ruma, Illinois. They served the poor, the sick, and the powerless of Liberia, West Africa, a country ravaged by civil war. Their faithfulness to their people brought them to their deaths: two of them on October 20, 1992, while traveling to help a sick child, the other three, shot by soldiers at the convent gate on October 23, 1992. Their lives and deaths bear witness to Christ's redeeming love, which gives meaning to human suffering and death. At the commemoration of their death Archbishop James Keleher challenged the congregation: "...What these five women are telling us today is simply this—you, too, have a holy mission that comes out of your baptism; that is, out of your intimate relationship with the Spirit of Jesus who leads you where it seems to fit. Indeed if we had the eyes of faith we might have seen, might have understood, what John finally recognized; namely, that the descent of the Holy Spirit makes each one of us very special and will lead you as [the Holy Spirit] led them to mission here and there and anywhere the Spirit chooses to send you, in order that you might bring the love of God to bear on those most distant and difficult places in your own world."

RESPONSORY

They lived the liberation of the blood of Christ and died in love's service. —**They**...

They sought to be ministers of reconciliation; —**and died**...

Glory to you, Source of all Being, Eternal Word and Holy Spirit.
—**They**...

CANTICLE

Ant In memory of Jesus and by the power of his blood, we
choose to love our enemy and pray for those who have
persecuted our body and our blood.

INTERCESSIONS

Blood of Christ, courage of martyrs:
Bring us to life.

For leaders of our world and our Church;
—may they have the courage to be people of vision like Sister
Shirley.
For those in anxiety or despair;
—may they be touched by the kind of joy that characterized
Sister Mary Joel.
For people in war-torn nations;
—may the justice and peace that Sister Kathleen so desired
come to them.
For women throughout the world;
—may their personal dignity be affirmed through the
perseverance of others like Sister Agnes.
For the sick, the homeless, and the oppressed;
—may they experience care and concern ministered by
persons with the commitment of Sister Barbara Ann.

PRAYER: O great and freeing Spirit, fill us as we journey on,
walking in hope, for death has never won. The five
Adorers of the Blood of Christ, missionaries in Liberia,
walked the way before us in gospel love. They are our
strength; we, their hope. They are our seed; we, their
fruit. They are our past; we, their future. Their lives
now join the martyred of your land and we join with the
dreamers of the dream. O deep and stirring Spirit,
come be with your people, who, through suffering, turn
dreaming toward the dawn. Amen.

* Compiled by the Adorers of the Blood of Christ, Ruma, Illinois.

November 1
ALL SAINTS

EVENING PRAYER I

Ant 1 Blessed are you, O God, in all your saints. (Ps 113, p. 96)

Ant 2 A multitude that no one could count stood before the Lamb, praising God. (Ps 147:12–20, p. 85)

Ant 3 Salvation belongs to God who sits upon the throne, and to the Lamb! (Rev 19:1, 5–7, p. 103)

READING

You have just come to a hard place where the two currents meet, and you could let yourself be beaten back towards the shore; but you can, instead, bend your back to the oars and pull the boat for all you are worth across that rough bit, and it will be better when you get out of the cross-currents. Hold on and let nothing dismay you. You may have to change your means; don't change your purpose. Remember you are doing God's work and God is with you, and all [God's] saints are looking on, 'a great cloud of witnesses,' while you fight in the arena, and they too have fought and overcome.... (Janet Erskine Stuart, RSCJ)

Maud Monahan, *Life and Letters of Janet Erskine Stuart*, p. 474, (15)

RESPONSORY

These are the people that praise you, O God, and glorify your name.
   —These are...
They dwell with you forever, **—and glorify...**
Glory to you, Source of all Being, Eternal Word and Holy Spirit.
   —These are...

CANTICLE OF MARY

Ant Blessed are the poor in spirit, the reign of God is theirs.

INTERCESSIONS

God is blessed forever in the angels and in the saints. With them we pray:
   Glory and praise to you, O God!

O Christ, like good earth the saints received the seed of your word and bore fruit a hundredfold;
   —help us to draw courage and inspiration from their lives.

The saving gift of your cross enabled the martyrs to offer life for life;
   —have mercy on those who are called to suffer for you; be their strength and courage.
You gave the gift of holiness to the simple and to the great, to celibates and to those who are married;
   —may we recognize your grace in the calling we now follow.
Women and men of every time and place have longed to see your face and to serve you unreservedly;
   —each generation tells of your goodness and love.

PRAYER: O God, we praise you as we celebrate the company of martyrs and saints whose faithful witness reveals your steadfast love. May the hope that they give us nourish our longing to love and serve you more. Without you we can do nothing; remember your love, and make us worthy of the company of the blessed. This we ask in the name of Jesus, and in the names of all our loved ones who have joined the multitude singing your praise forever. Amen.

MORNING PRAYER
(Psalms from Sunday, Week I, p. 3)

Ant 1 The saints have found eternal peace in God's presence.

Ant 2 All the saints praise you, O God, and proclaim your goodness to your people.

Ant 3 Your saints, O God, are a light to the nations.

READING

The saints were "passable like ourselves," theirs was not a far-away life, but a life very like our own. They never sat down to rest flushed with success; their fighting and failures and fears and experiments went on to the day of their death.... We are apt to think childish thoughts...to think they knew they were saints, and that this made all things comparatively easy.... We see the saintly attitudes in their pictures and the aureole round their heads, and we do not see the dust of every day.... They did not escape, but they endured; and in the end, after trying and failing over and over again, they "overcame and persevered to the end," not dejected, not despairing, but standing with an even mind, resigned to the will of God, and to bear for the glory of God whatever might befall them. (Janet Erskine Stuart, RSCJ)
Maud Monahan, *Life and Letters of Janet Erskine Stuart*, p. 328, (15)

RESPONSORY

We glorify you, O God, in your saints who intercede on our behalf.
　—We glorify...
We delight in the goodness of those, **—who**...
Glory to you, Source of all Being, Eternal Word and Holy Spirit.
　—We glorify...

CANTICLE OF ZECHARIAH

Ant Blessed are the pure in heart, for they shall see God.

INTERCESSIONS

Women and men of every age rejoice with the angels in eternal glory. In joy let us pray:
Blessed be God forever!

O God, Source of all life, the saints heard your creative voice in the depths of their hearts;
　—help us to silence the distractions in our lives; complete
　the work in us that you have begun.
You inspire people of every age to walk steadfastly in the way of the gospel;
　—raise up saints in our day that your love for us may be
　revealed in their lives.
Through the lives of your saints, you continue the mission of salvation;
　—give us the grace to embrace your call with generosity
　and perseverance.

PRAYER: O God, we praise you as we celebrate the company of martyrs and saints whose faithful witness reveals your steadfast love. May the hope that they give us nourish our longing to love and serve you more. Without you we can do nothing; remember your love, and make us worthy of the company of the blessed. This we ask in the name of Jesus, and in the names of all our loved ones who have joined the multitude singing your praise forever. Amen.

DAYTIME PRAYER

Ant 1 The saints are those who have run the race and won the everlasting crown. (Ps. 120, p. 155)

Ant 2 The followers of the living God rejoice in light forever.
(Ps. 121, p. 89)

Ant 3 Those who were faithful to the end have received blessing
and reward from God, their Savior. (Ps. 122, p. 143)

(Prayer as in Morning Prayer)

EVENING PRAYER II

Ant 1 See what love God has bestowed upon us, that we should
be called children of God. (Ps. 110:1–5, 7, p. 53)

Ant 2 We have been chosen by God to follow the Lamb that was
slain and now reigns in glory. (Ps. 116:10–19, p. 96)

Ant 3 Jesus said to his followers: I have chosen you to bear
much fruit and to glorify the One who sent me.
(Rev. 4:11, 5:9, 10, 12, p. 67)

READING

Since Jesus was born, and grew to his full stature, and died, everything
has continued to move forward *because Christ is not fully formed*: he has
not yet gathered about him the last folds of his robe of flesh and of love
which is made up of his faithful followers. The mystical Christ has not
yet attained to his full growth; and therefore the same is true of the
cosmic Christ. Both of these are simultaneously in the state of being
and of becoming; and it is from the prolongation of this process of
becoming that all created activity ultimately springs. Christ is the end-
point of the evolution, even the *natural* evolution, of all beings; and
therefore evolution is holy.

Teilhard de Chardin, SJ, Hymn of the Universe, p. 133, (14)

RESPONSORY

We praise you, O God, and rejoice with those who love you.
   —We praise...
May we live with you forever, **—and rejoice...**
Glory to you, Source of all Being, Eternal Word and Holy Spirit.
   —We praise...

CANTICLE OF MARY

Ant Blessed are you who hunger and thirst for holiness, you
shall be satisfied.

INTERCESSIONS

God is blessed forever in the angels and in the saints. With them
we pray:

Glory and praise to you, O God!

O Christ, like good earth the saints received the seed of your word
and bore fruit a hundredfold;

—help us to draw courage and inspiration from their lives.

The saving gift of your cross enabled the martyrs to offer life for
life;

—have mercy on those who are called to suffer for you; be
their strength and courage.

You gave the gift of holiness to the simple and to the great, to
celibates and to those who are married;

—may we recognize your grace in the calling we now follow.

Women and men of every time and place have longed to see your
face and to serve you unreservedly;

—each generation tells of your goodness and love.

PRAYER:　O God, we praise you as we celebrate the company of
martyrs and saints whose faithful witness reveals your
steadfast love. May the hope that they give us nourish
our longing to love and serve you more. Without you we
can do nothing; remember your love, and make us
worthy of the company of the blessed. This we ask in
the name of Jesus, and in the names of all our loved
ones who have joined the multitude singing your praise
forever. Amen.

November 2
ALL SOULS DAY

MORNING PRAYER

Ant 1　From the earth you formed me, with flesh you clothed me;
Christ my Redeemer, raise me up on the last day.
(Ps. 51, p. 36)

Ant 2　May it please you to rescue me; look upon me and help
me. (Is 38:10–14, 17b–20, p. 63)

Ant 3　My soul is thirsting for you, the living God; when shall I
see you face to face? (Ps 146, p. 166)

READING

Is there not a beautiful thought connected with prayer for the dead? Were it not sad to feel that when our loved ones pass away, they are wholly separated from us? Through prayer we may still hold communion with them; by the spirit of prayer we may gather the inspiration and clothe ourselves with the mantle they were clothed with. In blessing them we receive their blessing....

Andrew Barrett, The Shakers, p. 284, (1)

RESPONSORY

I know that my Redeemer lives and on the last day I shall rise
    again.—**I know**...
My own eyes will gaze on God, — **on the**...
Glory to you, Source of all Being, Eternal Word and Holy Spirit.
    —**I know**...

CANTICLE OF ZECHARIAH

Ant I am the Resurrection and the Life. Those who live and
    believe in me I will raise up on the last day.

INTERCESSIONS

Let us pray for an increase of faith in Jesus, the Resurrection and the Life:

O God, hear us.

In death, O Christ, life is changed, not taken away;
    —open us today to your call to growth.
You wept for Lazarus and comforted his sisters;
    —show yourself to the dying and comfort those who mourn.
You bled in agony the night before you died;
    —give courage and strength to those who fear death.
Time passes swiftly; we do not know the day of death;
    —help us to cherish the lifetime given to us and to make
    each moment a preparation for our last.
You promised eternal life to all who follow your way;
    —raise up all who have died, particularly those we have
    loved and those who have loved us; grant that we may
    share eternal glory with them.

PRAYER: O God, our birth is the fruit of your love; our
    redemption, the fruit of your mercy. Help us to
    remember your goodness and make our lives a worthy

revelation of your care. Let the hour of death be a
longed-for reunion with you, and with all our loved
ones who have gone before us and share life with you,
our Creator, Savior and Sanctifier. Amen.

DAYTIME PRAYER

Ant 1 You will hear me and rescue me when I call you.
(Ps. 70, p. 121)

Ant 2 Look on the faith of your servants, and save those who
hope in you. (Ps. 85, p. 111)

Ant 3 Do not hold our sins against us; remember your saving
love. (Ps 86, p. 117)

(Prayer as in Morning Prayer)

EVENING PRAYER

Ant 1 You are my savior; all my hope is in you. (Ps. 121, p. 89)

Ant 2 I wait in hope for you, O my God; I trust in your word.
Ps. 130, p. 143)

Ant 3 Jesus died for us that we might know eternal life.
(Phil. 2:6–11, p. 143)

READING

I heard today of your mother's very sudden death, and I want to tell you
how very deeply I feel for you in what I know must be a great sorrow as
well as a dreadful shock to you.... When this grief is a little more in the
past, I am sure you, who have faith, will feel that death doesn't part
people but brings them closer, and those who see things from God's side
understand us more than even the nearest could on earth. I feel sure
that over and over again you will know that your mother's love will be
helping and guiding you....

The Letters of Caryll Houselander, p. 14, (5)

RESPONSORY

Praise to you, Christ Jesus, our redeemer; you conquered
    death for us. **—Praise**...
We will see your glory, **—you conquered**...
Glory to you, Source of all Being, Eternal Word and Holy Spirit.
    —Praise...

CANTICLE OF MARY

Ant If the grain of wheat falls to the ground and dies, it produces an abundant harvest.

INTERCESSIONS

Eye has not seen, nor ear heard, what you have prepared for those who love you, and so we pray:
O God, all our hope is in your promise.

O God, we long to see your face and to praise you forever;
—let this time of "not seeing" strengthen our faith and hope in you.
For those who fear death, for those who see you as an exacting judge;
—let our lives of trust and love be a comfort and a guide.
You sent your Christ not to judge, but that we might have eternal life;
—teach us to look forward to our death as we do the birth of a child; to new life in your presence.
O Christ, many have lived without the consolation of your gospel; many die alone and afraid;
—Heart of Jesus, once in agony, have pity on the dying.

PRAYER: O God, our birth is the fruit of your love; our redemption, the fruit of your mercy. Help us to remember your goodness and make our lives a worthy revelation of your care. Let the hour of death be a longed-for reunion with you, and with all our loved ones who have gone before us and share life with you, our Creator, Savior and Sanctifier. Amen.

November 11
VENERABLE CATHERINE McAULEY

MORNING/EVENING PRAYER
(Psalms from Sunday, Week I, p. 3)

Ant 1 Blessed are the merciful for they shall obtain mercy.

Ant 2 Teach me goodness, discipline and knowledge.

Ant 3 However painful the cross may be which you have prepared for me, I await it through your grace with entire submission.

READING

Catherine McAuley, a well-educated lady, spent most of her adult life helping the poor in the city of Dublin. At the age of forty, she dedicated herself entirely to serving the poor. She founded the Order of Sisters of Mercy in 1831. She wrote to her sisters: "...We have one solid comfort amidst this little tripping about, our hearts can always be in the same place, centered in God, for whom alone we go forward or stay back. Oh may [God] look on us with love and pity and then we shall be able to do anything [God] wishes us to do, no matter how difficult to accomplish or painful to our feelings."*

The Correspondence of Catherine McAuley 1827–1841, No. 170, p. 178, (63)

RESPONSORY

I desire only to do your will, my God. —**I desire**...
To serve you in your people, —**and to do**...
Glory to you, Source of all Being, Eternal Word and Holy Spirit.
    —**I desire**...

CANTICLE

Ant Whatever you do to the least of my people, you do to me.

INTERCESSIONS

O God, you chose Catherine McAuley to found an order dedicated to works of mercy. With grateful hearts we pray:
    We praise you; we thank you; we glorify you.

Reared in a family with different religious persuasions, Catherine experienced love and returned love;
    —grant that the differences among us may enable us to grow in respect and appreciation for one another.
You call us to mercy rather than to sacrifice;
    —give us a spirit of moderation in all that we do.
Like Mary beneath the cross, Catherine suffered the loss of many she dearly loved;
    —strengthen those who attend and serve loved ones who are dying.

In your wisdom you led Catherine to found the Sisters of Mercy;
   —grant them the graces they need to carry on your work in
   this world.

PRAYER: O God, the poor and needy are with us always. Through
   the intercession of Catherine McAuley, help us to
   recognize them in our families, our communities, as
   well as in our cities, and in places far away. May they
   know your care and concern in those who minister to
   them. This we ask of you through the mercy of Jesus,
   who died that we may live. Amen.

November 13
ST. FRANCES XAVIER CABRINI

MORNING/EVENING PRAYER
(Psalms from Sunday, Week I, p. 3)

Ant 1 How blessed the woman whose heart goes out to the poor;
   those who trust in God delight in showing mercy.

Ant 2 Go out to all nations and spread the word of the gospel.

Ant 3 You are the light of the world; a city set on a hill cannot be
   hidden.

READING

Frances Xavier Cabrini founded the Missionary Sisters of the Sacred
Heart in Codogno, Italy. She came to the United States in 1889 and
eventually became a citizen. She established schools, hospitals, and
orphanages. She wrote in one of her letters: "'The soul learns that there
is no necessity to look for her Beloved outside her own being, and that
she can find Him within herself, as in His own throne and in His
tabernacle.' In this we hear the voice of the authentic mystic, though
hers was a mysticism of a very practical sort. She preceded immediately
from prayer to action."* She died in Chicago on December 22, 1917, and
became the first citizen of the United States to be canonized.

Theodore Maynard, *Too Small a World*, p. 227, (47)

RESPONSORY

My heart is glad and my soul rejoices. **—My heart...**
You have shown me the path to life; **—and my...**
Glory to you, Source of all Being, Eternal Word and Holy Spirit.
   —My heart...

CANTICLE

Ant Jesus went about all the cities and villages, teaching in their synagogues, preaching the gospel, and healing every disease and infirmity.

INTERCESSIONS

O Christ, you commissioned your early disciples to preach your gospel to all the nations. Throughout the centuries, women have left their native lands to spread the good news to other nations and peoples, and so we pray:

Praise to you, Lord Jesus Christ!

Christ, our Redeemer, your Church has named Mother Cabrini the patron of emigrants;

—may they receive welcome and hospitality in their adopted homelands.

You came to serve the lowly and the poor;

—may the cause of justice triumph over personal and national greed.

As a child, you fled to Egypt for safety;

—protect all refugees seeking asylum from unjust oppression.

You inspired Mother Cabrini to become a citizen of her new land;

—may all exercise their citizenship responsibly according to gospel values.

Mother Cabrini served you in the sick and poor;

—may her work continue that they may know your love and your healing.

PRAYER: O God, we thank you for all the good you accomplished through the life of Mother Cabrini, and through those who have followed her example. May our country be blessed with a greater desire to embrace those seeking freedom or refuge. We ask this through Jesus Christ who lives with you, Source of all Being, and with the Holy Spirit, forever. Amen.

November 16
JESUIT and COMPANION MARTYRS OF EL SALVADOR

Ignacio Martín Baró, SJ, Ignacío Ellacuría, SJ, Amando López, SJ,
Joaquin López y López, SJ, Segundo Montes, SJ, Juan Ramón Moreno, SJ,
Elba Ramos, Celina Ramos

MORNING/EVENING PRAYER

Ant 1 God has delivered us from the power of darkness and transferred us into the realm of God's beloved son, Jesus. (Jer 14:17–21, p. 132)

Ant 2 We are witnesses to these things, and so is the Holy Spirit whom God has given to those who obey God. (Ps 72, p. 81)

Ant 3 As for me, in my justice I shall see your face; when I awake, I shall be filled with the sight of your glory. (Ps 72, II, p. 81)

READING

During the night of November 16, 1989, Salvadoran troops broke into the residence of six Jesuit priests at the University of Central America and executed them together with their housekeeper and her fifteen year old daughter who witnessed the execution. In memoriam, Jon Sobrino, SJ, wrote: "It is not easy to know how to keep on hoping and we must all answer this question in our own way. It seems that everything is against hope, but for me at least, where I see there has been great love, I see hope being born again. This is not a rational conclusion and perhaps not even theological. It is simply true: love produces hope, and great love produces great hope. From Jesus of Nazareth, with many before him and many after him, whenever there has been true love, history has gone on, sinners have been forgiven and offered a future, which, it is hoped, they will accept. Many human beings and Christians have been given that hope. And together with the great love these martyrs had, there are the faces of the poor, in which God is hidden but nevertheless present, asking us to keep going, a request we cannot ignore. The history of sin and grace continues, the history of the poor goes on, and so does the history of God. To keep going amid such darkness is not at all easy, but it is something the poor and the martyrs help us to do so that it becomes possible. It is something we owe the poor and these martyrs."

Jon Sobrino, Ignatio Elacuria, and Others, *Companions of Jesus*:
The Jesuit Martyrs of El Salvador, p. 56, (22)

RESPONSORY

O God, hear a cause that is just, attend to my cry. — **O God**...
If you should try my heart or visit me by night; **—attend**...
Glory to you, Source of all Being, Eternal Word and Holy Spirit.
     — O God...

CANTICLE

Ant "The Spirit breathes in many ways, and supreme among
        them is the disposition to give one's life for others, whether
        by tireless daily commitment or by the sacrifice of a violent
        death." (Ignacio Ellacuría, SJ)

INTERCESSIONS

Ignacio Martín Baró's main concern was to empower the laity,
especially the poor and the oppressed;
     —O God, raise up those who lift up the lives of the poor.
"Above all else, listen to your heart...but know well first what
Jesus says in the Scriptures...." (Juan Ramón Moreno)
     —Jesus, let the words of the gospel be our daily bread.
Amando López lavished affection on the simple country people to
whom he ministered;
     —O God, let our love for others heal them and draw them to
        you.
Joaquin López y López was exemplary is his self-denial, never a
trace of luxury;
     —give us the wisdom and generosity to respect every person
        and to share the world's goods and services justly.
Segundo Montes' eyes seemed to watch for God, and little children
loved to put their faces against his;
     —O God, we long to see you face to face.
We pray that Elba and Celina Ramos have not died in vain.
     —may the gift of their lives continue to enrich and inspire the
        church throughout the world.

PRAYER: O God, your Holy Spirit abides in our hearts, and in
            you we are one. Through the suffering and death of
            Jesus, through the suffering and death of the martyrs
            of El Salvador, may we come to realize our power to
            support or to destroy life. Purify our minds and our
            hearts of all that cannot be offered for the praise of

your name. Let the witness of these women and men strengthen our faith and deepen our love for you. We ask this in Jesus' name. Amen.

November 18
ST. PHILIPPINE DUCHESNE

MORNING/EVENING PRAYER
(Psalms from Sunday, Week I, p. 3)

Ant 1 Come to me, all who labor and are heavy laden, and I will give you rest.

Ant 2 Go into the world, and preach the gospel to the whole creation.

Ant 3 One who loses her life for my sake will find it.

READING

Philippine Duchesne was born at Grenoble, August 29, 1769. When her community of Visitation Sisters was dispersed during the French Revolution, she entered the Society of the Religious of the Sacred Heart. At the request of the bishop of Louisiana, she came to North America in 1818 and established sixteen houses of the Society for the education of youth. Toward the end of her life, she devoted herself to the service of Native Americans. Finding the English language difficult, she devoted herself to manual labor. She wrote: "...I long for retirement and rest, and I have no hope of finding them in this life. I should not, however, want an inactivity that would expose me to the danger of napping all day long. But everything seems to point to the fact that there is no sweet retreat ahead of me. Wherever I have been, external and distracting work has been my lot and still is, though I am about to begin my seventieth year. There is still no one else here to give the morning call, make the last visit at night, care for the garden, watch by the sick, or take care of the pantry, the linen room, etc...."*

*Louise Callan, RSCJ, *Philippine Duchesne*, p. 609, (13)

RESPONSORY

Take my yoke upon you, and learn from me; for I am gentle and
   lowly in heart. —**Take my**...
And you will find rest for your souls; —**for I**...
Glory to you, Source of all Being, Eternal Word and Holy Spirit.
   —**Take my**...

CANTICLE

Ant Pray always and never lose heart.

INTERCESSIONS

O God, St. Philippine's love for the Sacred Heart of Jesus bore fruit in her dedication to the salvation of others;
  —inspire us with ways to incarnate our love for you and to live the message of the gospel.
She left her country, family, and friends and founded houses of the Society of the Sacred Heart in America;
  —inspire us with the generosity, detachment, and humility that marked her life.
The ladder by which she made her ascent to God was the prayer of adoration and love before the Blessed Sacrament;
  —in times of dryness, enable us to persevere in prayer— to give you time.
The seeds of Philippine's holiness were planted in childhood;
  —keep us faithful to the graces of the past and attentive to your spirit active in our lives now.
Philippine persevered in faith through seemingly insurmountable obstacles;
  —give us a singlehearted dedication to you and to the mission to which we are called.

PRAYER: O God, we thank you for blessing the early years of our nation with the gift of St. Philippine Duchesne. Her heart was hollowed by detachment of every sort and opened wholly to love for you and your people everywhere. Her special care for the Native American people continued through her old age, and they knew your divine power in her life in spite of her helplessness. Bless the people of France who gave her to us, and grant us her singlehearted sense of mission. May all the world know the love of the Heart of Jesus in whose name we pray. Amen.

November 22
VENERABLE JEANNE FONTBONNE
(Mother St. John)

MORNING/EVENING PRAYER
(Psalms from Sunday, Week I, p. 439)

Ant 1 They who sow in tears shall reap in joy.

Ant 2 All my desire is that you become saints.

Ant 3 When I think that you are in a different world from me, I
am consoled by the reflection that we are all in the bosom
of our God.

READING

Jeanne Fontbonne was born in Basen-Basset, France, on March 3,
1759. She became a Sister of St. Joseph and served as superior of her
community until she was imprisoned at the outbreak of the French
Revolution. She later restored her order, sent a mission to the United
States, and eventually saw the establishment of two hundred new
communities. A benefactor of Mother St. John, Mme. de la
Rochejacquelin, wrote: "...Europe does not suffice for the ardent charity
of the Sisters of St. Joseph. They have undertaken to teach in foreign
lands the truths of our holy religion to minds and hearts hitherto
uncultivated. Those are sheep without a pastor whom you are to lead
into the fold of the Church. It is a difficult task, but the Crib and the
Cross have triumphed over everything."

Abbé Rivaux, *Life of Rev. Mother St. John Fontbonne*, pp. 250–51, (27)

RESPONSORY

Love your neighbors as yourself; love them as Christ Jesus
loves you. **—Love...**
In giving your life, **—love them...**
Glory to you, Source of all Being, Eternal Word and Holy Spirit.
—Love...

CANTICLE

Ant Rely upon God who can do all things, and that most
effectively where creatures can do nothing.

INTERCESSIONS

Most gracious God, we place our trust in you. In confidence we
pray:
That all may be one.

O God, you raised up Jeanne Fontbonne to reorganize the Sisters
of St. Joseph and to extend their services throughout the world;
  —may all missionaries be graced to walk humbly, to listen
    sensitively, and to serve justly.
You call us by name to be one with you and with one another;
  —help all teachers and ministers of your word to be living
    signs of your love.
You invite us to build our future in fidelity to your gospel
message;
  —enable all members of faith communities to work for justice
    and peace, and to alleviate the causes of oppression.
You share life with us in your banquet of love;
  —may we be faithful to our commitments, respectful of our
    differences, and one in our desire to love God.

PRAYER: O God, you have shared your bountiful love and mercy
with your servant Jeanne Fontbonne, and with the
women inspired by her as Sisters of St. Joseph. We
praise you for revealing your goodness through them,
and we thank you for the gift that their commitment is
to us. Grant those who serve us today the vitality,
courage, and generosity to continue the work that you
have begun in Jeanne Fontbonne and in them. We ask
this in the name of Jesus. Amen.

November 29
DOROTHY DAY

MORNING/EVENING PRAYER

Ant 1 When did we see you hungry and give you to eat? When
did we see you thirsty and give you to drink?
(Ps 94, p. 168)

Ant 2 Blessed are those who suffer persecution for the sake of
justice, for God is their reward. (Jer 14:17–21, p. 132)

Ant 3 If you would be perfect, give all to the poor and come
follow me. (Ps 43, p. 62)

READING

Dorothy Day co-founder (with Peter Maurin) of the Catholic Worker
Movement, had a passionate love for the poor, the outcast, and the

downtrodden. She was a radical, a suffragist, an outspoken critic of the establishment. She was considered by many to be the most influential Roman Catholic of her time. Expressing her call, she wrote: "I feel that all families should have the conveniences and comforts which modern living brings and which do simplify life, and give time to read, to study, to think, and to pray. And to work in the apostolate, too. But poverty is my vocation, to live as simply and poorly as I can, and never to cease talking and writing of poverty and destitution."* Dorothy Day died November 29, 1980.

*The Dorothy Day Book, pp. 70–71, (21)

RESPONSORY

She opens her heart to the poor, and reaches out her hand to the needy. —**She**...
She opens her mouth with wisdom; —**and reaches**...
Glory to you, Source of all Being, Eternal Word and Holy Spirit. —**She**...

CANTICLE

Ant God is in the midst of her, she shall not be moved.

INTERCESSIONS

O God, you gave us Jesus to teach us that you hear the cry of the poor and the needy. Give us hearts of flesh that we may respond with compassion as we pray:
Have mercy on us!

O Christ, you reached out to the lepers and healed them;
—help us to embrace the outcasts of our society.
You socialized with the tax collectors and sinners;
—show us how to break down the barriers that divide us.
You talked with the Samaritan woman and healed the child of the Caananite woman;
—may we learn how to cross the thresholds of prejudice.
You fed the hungry by giving them bread of wheat and the bread of your body;
—teach us how to feed each other.
You had compassion on the poor and the suffering;
—may we see you in the street people, the destitute and the hopeless.

PRAYER: O God, look with tender mercy on the needs of the poor and the alienated, and teach us to hear and answer their cries. We praise you for those who have given their lives to serve you in the poor. May they know your support and love as they follow the way of Jesus. Bless especially all who serve the poor in the Catholic Worker movement. We ask this in the name of Jesus. Amen.

Last Thursday in November
THANKSGIVING DAY

MORNING/EVENING PRAYER
(Psalms from Sunday, Week I, p. 3)

Ant 1 It is right to give you thanks and praise.

Ant 2 We praise you for the gift of your harvest.

Ant 3 You have blessed our land with your bounty; we lift our hearts in thanksgiving.

READING

Perhaps there is a need for reinterpreting Thanksgiving Day. Certainly in a society more sensitive to justice, we cannot commemorate only the Mayflower in which the red-haired English colonists came; we must remember also those other ships that delivered to America the first Catholic immigrants in 1584 or the others from which Catholics from Spain landed in Florida. But, above all, we must commemorate, with a joy mixed with pain, those numerous ships in which African men and women were transported against their will. On the other hand, we know already that the food we share at the Thanksgiving meal...is a symbol for all the other gifts we have received from God: the gift of freedom and justice, the many possibilities.... Myths and rituals remain alive to the extent to which they are open to reinterpretation.

John Manuel Lozano, *Grace & Brokenness in God's Country*, pp. 42–43, (1)

RESPONSORY

Come, let us sing to God and shout for joy. —**Come**...
Let us approach with praise and thanksgiving; —**and shout**...
Glory to you, Source of all Being, Eternal Word and Holy Spirit.
    —**Come**...

CANTICLE

Ant How can we repay you, O God, for all your goodness to us.

INTERCESSIONS

Most gracious God, you have blessed our land with more than we need;
  —increase our spirit of generosity that we may share with other lands.
You have often saved our country from the ravages of war;
  —may we never cause destruction to other nations.
You have graced our country with great natural beauty;
  —grant that we may never exploit it, but endeavor to protect it and save its natural resources.
O God, our forebears sat at table with our native Americans giving thanks for your bounty;
  —help us in our endeavors to restore the rights and dignity of our indigenous peoples.
You continually call us forward;
  —may we step into the future ever conscious of our responsibility to all humankind.

PRAYER: God, most bounteous, we are mindful that you gift us at each moment. Help us to receive all as gift and give you thanks that you are our God. Continue to grant us your favors and help us as a government and as a people to share your gifts with all in need. This we ask through Jesus, who lives with you and the Holy Spirit forever and ever. Amen.

INDEX OF PSALMS

INDEX OF FEASTS

	Ps Wk	1997	1998	1999	2000	2001	2002
Sun Cycle		B	C	A	B	C	A
Wkdy Cycle		1	2	1	2	1	2
1-Adv	1	1 Dec 96	30 Nov 97	29 Nov 98	28 Nov 99	3 Dec 00	2 Dec 01
2-Adv	2	8 Dec	7 Dec	6 Dec	5 Dec	10 Dec	9 Dec
3 Adv	3	15 Dec	14 Dec	13 Dec	12 Dec	17 Dec	16 Dec
4 Adv	4	22 Dec	21 Dec	20 Dec	19 Dec	24 Dec	23 Dec
Christmas	Proper	25 Dec	25 Dec	25 Dec	25 Dec	25 Dec	25 Dec
Holy Family	1	29 Dec	28 Dec	27 Dec	26 Dec	31 Dec	30 Dec
Moth.of God	Proper	1 Jan	1 Jan	1 Jan	1 Jan	1 Jan	1 Jan
Epiphany	2	5 Jan	4 Jan	3 Jan	2 Jan	7 Jan	6 Jan
Baptism	1	12 Jan	11 Jan	10 Jan	9 Jan	8 Jan	13 Jan
2-Ord	2	19 Jan	18 Jan	17 Jan	16 Jan	14 Jan	20 Jan
3-Ord	3	26 Jan	25 Jan	24 Jan	23 Jan	21 Jan	27 Jan
4-Ord	4	2 Feb	1 Feb	31 Jan	30 Jan	28 Jan	3 Feb
5-Ord	1	9 Feb	8 Feb	7 Feb	6 Feb	4 Feb	10 Feb
6-Ord	2	–	15 Feb	14 Feb	13 Feb	11 Feb	–
7-Ord	3	–	22 Feb	–	20 Feb	18 Feb	–
8-Ord	4	–	–	–	27 Feb	25 Feb	–
9-Ord	1	–	–	–	5 Mar	–	–
Ash Wed	4	12 Feb	25 Feb	17 Feb	8 Mar	28 Feb	13 Feb
1 Lent	1	16 Feb	1 Mar	21 Feb	12 Mar	4 Mar	17 Feb
2 Lent	2	23 Feb	8 Mar	28 Feb	19 Mar	11 Mar	24 Feb
3 Lent	3	2Mar	15 Mar	7 Mar	26 Mar	18 Mar	3 Mar
4 Lent	4	9 Mar	22 Mar	14 Mar	2 Apr	25 Mar	10 Mar
5 Lent	1	16 Mar	29 Mar	21 Mar	9 Apr	1 Apr	17 Mar
Passion Sun	2	23 Mar	5 Apr	28 Mar	16 Apr	8 Apr	24 Mar
Easter	Proper	30 Mar	12 Apr	4 Apr	23 Apr	15 Apr	31 Mar
2 Easter	2	6 Apr	19 Apr	11 Apr	30 Apr	22 Apr	7 Apr
3 Easter	3	13 Apr	26 Apr	18 Apr	7 May	29 Apr	14 Apr
4 Easter	4	20 Apr	3 May	25 Apr	14 May	6 May	21 Apr
5 Easter	1	27 Apr	10 May	2 May	21 May	13 May	28 Apr
6 Easter	2	4 May	17 May	9 May	28 May	20 May	5 May
Ascension	Proper	8 May	21 May	13 May	1 Jun	24 May	9 May
7 Easter	3	11 May	24 May	16 May	4 Jun	27 May	12 May
Pentecost	Prop	18 May	31 May	23 May	11 Jun	3 Jun	19 May
Trinity Sun	Prop	25 May	7 Jun	30 May	18 Jun	10 Jun	26 May
Corpus Christi	Prop	1 Jun	14 Jun	6 Jun	25 Jun	17 Jun	2 Jun
10-Ord	2	8 Jun	–	–	–	–	9 Jun
11-Ord	3	15 Jun	–	13 Jun	–	–	16 Jun
12-Ord	4	22 Jun	21 Jun	20 Jun	–	24 Jun	23 Jun
13-Ord	1	29 Jun	28 Jun	27 Jun	2 Jul	1 Jul	30 Jun
14-Ord	2	6 Jul	5Jul	4 Jul	9 Jul	8 Jul	7 Jul
15-Ord	3	13 Jul	12 Jul	11 Jul	16 Jul	15 Jul	14 Jul
16-Ord	4	20 Jul	19 Jul	18 Jul	23 Jul	22 Jul	21 Jul
17-Ord	1	27 Jul	26 Jul	25 Jul	30 Jul	29 Jul	28 Jul
18-Ord	2	3 Aug	2 Aug	1 Aug	6 Aug	5 Aug	4 Aug
19-Ord	3	10 Aug	9 Aug	8 Aug	13 Aug	12 Aug	11 Aug
20-Ord	4	17 Agu	16 Aug	15 Aug	20 Aug	19 Aug	18 Aug
21-Ord	1	24 Aug	23 Aug	22 Aug	27 Aug	26 Aug	25 Aug
22-Ord	2	31 Aug	30 Aug	29 Aug	3 Sep	2 Sep	1 Sep
23-Ord	3	7 Sep	6 Sep	5 Sep	10 Sep	9 Sep	8 Sep
24-Ord	4	14 Sep	13 Sep	12 Sep	17 Sep	16 Sep	15 Sep
25-Ord	1	21 Sep	20 Sep	19 Sep	24 Sep	23 Sep	22 Sep
26-Ord	2	28 Sep	27 Sep	26 Sep	1 Oc	30 Sep	29 Sep
27-Ord	3	5 Oct	4Oct	3 Oct	8 Oct	7 Oct	6 Oct
28-Ord	4	12 Oct	11 Oct	10 Oct	15 Oct	14 Oct	13 Oct
29-Ord	1	19 Oct	18 Oct	17 Oct	22 Oct	21 Oct	20 Oct
30-Ord	2	26 Oct	25 Oct	24 Oct	29 Oct	28 Oct	27 Oct
31-Ord	3	2 Nov	–	31 Oct	5 Nov	4 Nov	3 Nov
32-Ord	4	9 Nov	8 Nov	7 Nov	12 Nov	11 Nov	10 Nov
33-Ord	1	16 Nov	15 Nov	14 Nov	19 Nov	18 Nov	17 Nov
34-Ord	2	23 Nov	22 Nov	21 Nov	26 Nov	25 Nov	24 Nov

	Ps Wk	2003	2004	2005	2006	2007	2008
Sun Cycle		B	C	A	B	C	A
Wkdy Cycle		1	2	1	2	1	2
1-Adv	1	1 Dec 02	30 Nov 03	28 Nov 04	27 Nov 05	3 Dec 06	2 Dec 07
2-Adv	2	8 Dec	7 Dec	5 Dec	4 Dec	10 Dec	9 Dec
3 Adv	3	15 Dec	14 Dec	12 Dec	11 Dec	17 Dec	16 Dec
4 Adv	4	22 Dec	21 Dec	19 Dec	18 Dec	24 Dec	23 Dec
Christmas	Proper	25 Dec	25 Dec	25 Dec	25 Dec	25 Dec	25 Dec
Holy Family	1	29 Dec	28 Dec	26 Dec	30 Dec	31 Dec	30 Dec
Moth.of God	Proper	1 Jan	1 Jan	1 Jan	1 Jan	1 Jan	1 Jan
Epiphany	2	5 Jan	4 Jan	2 Jan	8 Jan	7 Jan	6 Jan
Baptism	1	12 Jan	11 Jan	9 Jan	9 Jan	8 Jan	13 Jan
2-Ord	2	19 Jan	18 Jan	16 Jan	15 Jan	14 Jan	20 Jan
3-Ord	3	26 Jan	25 Jan	23 Jan	22 Jan	21 Jan	27 Jan
4-Ord	4	2 Feb	1 Feb	30 Jan	29 Jan	28 Jan	3 Feb
5-Ord	1	9 Feb	8 Feb	6 Feb	5 Feb	4 Feb	–
6-Ord	2	16 Feb	15 Feb	–	12 Feb	11 Feb	–
7-Ord	3	23 Feb	22 Feb	–	19 Feb	18 Feb	–
8-Ord	4	2 Mar	–	–	26 Feb	–	–
9-Ord	1	–	–	–	–	–	1 Jun
Ash Wed	4	5 Mar	25 Feb	9 Feb	1 Mar	21 Feb	6 Feb
1 Lent	1	9 Mar	29 Feb	13 Feb	5 Mar	25 Feb	10 Feb
2 Lent	2	16 Mar	7 Mar	20 Feb	12 Mar	4 Mar	17 Feb
3 Lent	3	23 Mar	14 Mar	27 Feb	19 Mar	11 Mar	24 Feb
4 Lent	4	30 Mar	21 Mar	6 Mar	26 Mar	18 Mar	2 Mar
5 Lent	1	6 Apr	28 Mar	13 Mar	2 Apr	25 Mar	9 Mar
Passion Sun	2	13 Apr	4 Apr	20 Mar	9 Apr	1 Apr	16 Mar
Easter	Proper	20 Apr	11 Apr	27 Mar	16 Apr	8 Apr	23 Mar
2 Easter	2	27 Apr	18 Apr	3 Apr	23 Apr	15 Apr	30 Mar
3 Easter	3	4 May	25 Apr	10 Apr	30 Apr	22 Apr	6 Apr
4 Easter	4	11 May	2 May	17 Apr	7 May	29 Apr	13 Apr
5 Easter	1	18 May	9 May	24 Apr	14 May	6 May	20 Apr
6 Easter	2	25 May	16 May	1 May	21 May	13 May	27 Apr
Ascension	Proper	29 May	20 May	5 May	25 May	17 May	1 May
7 Easter	3	1 Jun	23 May	8 May	28 May	20 May	4 May
Pentecost	Prop	8 Jun	30 May	15 May	4 Jun	27 May	11 May
Trinity Sun	Prop	15 Jun	6 Jun	22 May	11 Jun	3 Jun	18 May
Corpus Christi	Prop	22 Jun	13 Jun	29 May	18 Jun	10 Jun	25 May
10-Ord	2	–	–	5 Jun	–	–	8 Jun
11-Ord	3	–	–	12 Jun	–	17 Jun	15 Jun
12-Ord	4	–	20 Jun	19 Jun	25 Jun	24 Jun	22 Jun
13-Ord	1	29 Jun	27 Jun	26 Jun	2 Jul	1 Jul	29 Jun
14-Ord	2	6 Jul	4 Jul	3 Jul	9 Jul	8 Jul	6 Jul
15-Ord	3	13 Jul	11 Jul	10 Jul	16 Jul	15 Jul	13 Jul
16-Ord	4	20 Jul	18 Jul	17 Jul	23 Jul	22 Jul	20 Jul
17-Ord	1	27 Jul	25 Jul	24 Jul	30 Jul	29 Jul	27 Jul
18-Ord	2	3 Aug	1 Aug	31 Jul	6 Aug	5 Aug	3 Aug
19-Ord	3	10 Aug	8 Aug	7 Aug	13 Aug	12 Aug	10 Aug
20-Ord	4	17 Aug	Assum	14 Aug	20 Aug	19 Aug	17 Aug
21-Ord	1	24 Aug	22 Aug	21 Aug	27 Aug	26 Aug	24 Aug
22-Ord	2	31 Aug	29 Aug	28 Aug	3 Sep	2 Sep	31 Aug
23-Ord	3	7 Sep	5 Sep	4 Sep	10 Sep	9 Sep	7 Sep
24-Ord	4	14 Sep	12 Sep	11 Sep	17 Sep	16 Sep	14 Sep
25-Ord	1	21 Sep	19 Sep	18 Sep	24 Sep	23 Sep	21 Sep
26-Ord	2	28 Sep	26 Sep	25 Sep	1 Oct	30 Sep	28 Sep
27-Ord	3	5 Oct	3 Oct	2 Oct	8 Oct	7 Oct	5 Oct
28-Ord	4	12 Oct	10 Oct	9 Oct	15 Oct	14 Oct	12 Oct
29-Ord	1	19 Oct	17 Oct	16 Oct	22 Oct	21 Oct	19 Oct
30-Ord	2	26 Oct	24 Oct	23 Oct	29 Oct	28 Oct	26 Oct
31-Ord	3	2 Nov	31 Oct	30 Oct	5 Nov	4 Nov	2 Nov
32-Ord	4	9 Nov	7 Nov	6 Nov	12 Nov	11 Nov	9 Nov
33-Ord	1	16 Nov	14 Nov	13 Nov	19 Nov	18 Nov	16 Nov
34-Ord	2	23 Nov	21 Nov	20 Nov	26 Nov	25 Nov	23 Nov

	Ps Wk	2009	2010	2011	2012	2013	2014
Sun Cycle		IB	C	A	B	C	A
Wkdy Cycle		1	2	1	2	1	2
1-Adv	1	30 Nov 08	29 Nov 09	28 Nov 10	27 Nov 11	2 Dec 12	1 Dec 13
2-Adv	2	7 Dec	6 Dec	5 Dec	4 Dec	9 Dec	8 Dec
3 Adv	3	14 Dec	13 Dec	12 Dec	11 Dec	16 Dec	15 Dec
4 Adv	4	21 Dec	20 Dec	19 Dec	18 Dec	23 Dec	22 Dec
Christmas	Proper	25 Dec	25 Dec	25 Dec	25 Dec	25 Dec	25 Dec
Holy Family	1	28 Dec	27 Dec	26 Dec	30 Dec	30 Dec	29 Dec
Moth.of God	Proper	1 Jan	1 Jan	1 Jan	1 Jan	1 Jan	1 Jan
Epiphany	2	4 Jan	3 Jan	2 Jan	8 Jan	6 Jan	5 Jan
Baptism	1	11 Jan	10 Jan	9 Jan	9 Jan	13 Jan	12 Jan
2-Ord	2	18 Jan	17 Jan	16 Jan	15 Jan	20 Jan	19 Jan
3-Ord	3	25 Jan	24 Jan	23 Jan	22 Jan	27 Jan	26 Jan
4-Ord	4	1 Feb	31 Jan	30 Jan	29, Jan	3 Feb	2 Feb
5-Ord	1	8 Feb	7 Feb	6 Feb	5 Feb	10 Feb	9 Feb
6-Ord	2	15 Feb	14 Feb	13 Feb	12 Feb	–	16 Feb
7-Ord	3	22 Feb	–	20 Feb	19 Feb	–	23 Feb
8-Ord	4	–	–	27 Feb	–	–	2 Mar
9-Ord	1	–	–	–	–	–	–
Ash Wed	4	25 Feb	17 Feb	9 Mar	22 Feb	13 Feb	5 Mar
1 Lent	1	1 Mar	21 Feb	13 Mar	26 Feb	17 Feb	9 Mar
2 Lent	2	8 Mar	28 Feb	20 Mar	4 Mar	24 Feb	16 Mar
3 Lent	3	15 Mar	7 Mar	27 Mar	11 Mar	3 Mar	23 Mar
4 Lent	4	22 Mar	14 Mar	3 Apr	18 Mar	10 Mar	30 Mar
5 Lent	1	29 Mar	21 Mar	10 Apr	25 Mar	17 Mar	6 Apr
Passion Sun	2	5 Apr	28 Mar	17 Apr	1 Apr	24 Mar	13 Apr
Easter	Proper	12 Apr	4 Apr	24 Apr	8 Apr	31 Mar	20 Apr
2 Easter	2	19 Apr	11 Apr	1 May	15 Apr	7 Apr	27 Apr
3 Easter	3	26 Apr	18 Apr	8 May	22 Apr	14 Apr	4 May
4 Easter	4	3 May	25 Apr	15 May	29 Apr	21 Apr	11 May
5 Easter	1	10 May	2 May	22 May	6 May	28 Apr	18 May
6 Easter	2	17 May	9 May	29 May	13 May	5 May	25 May
Ascension	Proper	21 May	13 May	2 Jun	17 May	9 May	29 May
7 Easter	3	24 May	16 May	5 Jun	20 May	12 May	1 Jun
Pentecost	Prop	31 May	23 May	12 Jun	27 May	19 May	8 Jun
Trinity Sun	Prop	7 Jun	30 May	19 Jun	3 Jun	26 May	15 Jun
Corpus Christi	Prop	14 Jun	6 Jun	26 Jun	10 Jun	2 Jun	22 Jun
10-Ord	2	–	–	–	–	9 Jun	–
11-Ord	3	–	13 Jun	–	17 Jun	16 Jun	–
12-Ord	4	21 Jun	20 Jun	–	24 Jun	23 Jun	–
13-Ord	1	28 Jun	27 Jun	–	1 Jul	30 Jun	29 Jun
14-Ord	2	5 Jul	4 Jul	3 Jul	8 Jul	7 Jul	6 Jul
15-Ord	3	12 Jul	11 Jul	10 Jul	15 Jul	14 Jul	13 Jul
16-Ord	4	19 Jul	18 Jul	17 Jul	22 Jul	21 Jul	20 Jul
17-Ord	1	26 Jul	25 Jul	24 Jul	29 Jul	28 Jul	27 Jul
18-Ord	2	2 Aug	1 Aug	31 Jul	5 Aug	4 Aug	3 Aug
19-Ord	3	9 Aug	8 Aug	7 Aug	12 Aug	11 Aug	10 Aug
20-Ord	4	16 Aug	15 Aug	14 Aug	19 Aug	18 Aug	17 Aug
21-Ord	1	23 Aug	22 Aug	21 Aug	26 Aug	25 Aug	24 Aug
22-Ord	2	30 Aug	29 Aug	28 Aug	2 Sep	1 Sep	31 Aug
23-Ord	3	6 Sep	5 Sep	4 Sep	9 Sep	8 Sep	7 Sep
24-Ord	4	13 Sep	12 Sep	11 Sep	16 Sep	15 Sep	14 Sep
25-Ord	1	20 Sep	19 Sep	18 Sep	23 Sep	22 Sep	21 Sep
26-Ord	2	27 Sep	26 Sep	25 Sep	30 Sep	29 Sep	28 Sep
27-Ord	3	4 Oct	3 Oct	2 Oct	7 Oct	6 Oct	5 Oct
28-Ord	4	11 Oct	10 Oct	9 Oct	14 Oct	13 Oct	12 Oct
29-Ord	1	18 Oct	17 Oct	16 Oct	21 Oct	20 Oct	19 Oct
30-Ord	2	25 Oct	24 Oct	23 Oct	28 Oct	27 Oct	26 Oct
31-Ord	3	All Saints	31 Oct	30 Oct	4 Nov	3 Nov	2Nov
32-Ord	4	8 Nov	7 Nov	6 Nov	11 Nov	10 Nov	9 Nov
33-Ord	1	15 Nov	14 Nov	13 Nov	18 Nov	17 Nov	16 Nov
34-Ord	2	22 Nov	21 Nov	20 Nov	25 Nov	24 Nov	23 Nov

	Ps Wk	2015	2016	2017	2018	2019	2020
Sun Cycle		B	C	A	B	C	A
Wkdy Cycle		1	2	1	2	1	2
1-Adv	1	30 Nov 14	29 Nov 15	27 Nov 16	3 Dec 17	2 Dec 18	1 Dec 19
2-Adv	2	7 Dec	6 Dec	4 Dec	10 Dec	9 Dec	8 Dec
3 Adv	3	14 Dec	13 Dec	11 Dec	17 Dec	16 Dec	15 Dec
4 Adv	4	21 Dec	20 Dec	18 Dec	24 Dec	23 Dec	22 Dec
Christmas	Proper	25 Dec	25 Dec	25 Dec	25 Dec	25 Dec	25 Dec
Holy Family	1	28 Dec	27 Dec	2 Jan	31 Dec	30 Dec	29 Dec
Moth.of God	Proper	1 Jan	1 Jan	1 Jan	1 Jan	1 Jan	1 Jan
Epiphany	2	4 Jan	3 Jan	8 Jan	7 Jan	6 Jan	5 Jan
Baptism	1	11 Jan	10 Jan	9 Jan	14 Jan	13 Jan	12 Jan
2-Ord	2	18 Jan	17 Jan	15 Jan	21 Jan	20 Jan	19 Jan
3-Ord	3	25 Jan	24 Jan	22 Jan	28 Jan	27 Jan	26 Jan
4-Ord	4	1 Feb	31 Jan	29 Jan	4 Feb	3 Feb	2 Feb
5-Ord	1	8 Feb	7 Feb	–	–	10 Feb	9 Feb
6-Ord	2	15 Feb	–	–	–	17 Feb	16 Feb
7-Ord	3	–	–	5 Feb	–	24 Feb	23 Feb
8-Ord	4	–	–	12 Feb	–	3 Mar	–
9-Ord	1	–	–	19 Feb	–	–	–
Ash Wed	4	18 Feb	10 Feb	26 Feb	14 Feb	6 Mar	22 Feb
1 Lent	1	22 Feb	14 Feb	5 Mar	18 Feb	10 Mar	1 Mar
2 Lent	2	1 Mar	21 Feb	12 Mar	25 Feb	17 Mar	8 Mar
3 Lent	3	8 Mar	28 Feb	19 Mar	4 Mar	24 Mar	15 Mar
4 Lent	4	15 Mar	6 Mar	26 Mar	11 Mar	31 Mar	22 Mar
5 Lent	1	22 Mar	13 Mar	2 Apr	18 Mar	7 Apr	29 Mar
Passion Sun	2	29 Mar	20 Mar	9 Apr	25 Mar	14 Apr	5 Apr
Easter	Proper	5 Apr	27 Mar	16 Apr	1 Apr	21 Apr	12 Apr
2 Easter	2	12 Apr	3 Apr	23 Apr	8 Apr	28 Apr	19 Apr
3 Easter	3	19 Apr	10 Apr	30 Apr	15 Apr	5 May	26 Apr
4 Easter	4	26 Apr	17 Apr	7 May	22 Apr	12 May	3 May
5 Easter	1	3 May	24 Apr	14 May	29 Apr	19 May	10 May
6 Easter	2	10 May	1 May	21 May	6 May	26 May	17 May
Ascension	Proper	17 May	8 May	28 May	13 May	2 June	24 May
7 Easter	3	24 May	15 May	4 Jun	20 May	9 Jun	31 May
Pentecost	Prop	31 May	22 May	11 Jun	27 May	16 Jun	7 Jun
Trinity Sun	Prop	7 Jun	29 May	18 Jun	3 Jun	23 Jun	14 Jun
Corpus Christi	Prop	14 Jun	5 Jun	25 Jun	10 Jun	30 Jun	21 Jun
10-Ord	2	–	–	–	–	–	–
11-Ord	3	–	12 Jun	–	17 Jun	–	–
12-Ord	4	21 Jun	19 Jun	–	24 Jun	–	–
13-Ord	1	28 Jun	26 Jun	2 Jul	1 Jul	–	28 Jun
14-Ord	2	5 Jul	3 Jul	9 Jul	8 Jul	7 Jul	5 Jul
15-Ord	3	12 Jul	10 Jul	16 Jul	15 Jul	14 Jul	12 Jul
16-Ord	4	19 Jul	17 Jul	23 Jul	22 Jul	21 Jul	19 Jul
17-Ord	1	26 Jul	24 Jul	30 Jul	29 Jul	28 Jul	26 Jul
18-Ord	2	2 Aug	31 Jul	6 Aug	5 Aug	4 Aug	2 Aug
19-Ord	3	9 Aug	7 Aug	13 Aug	12 Aug	11 Aug	9 Aug
20-Ord	4	16 Aug	14 Aug	20 Aug	19 Aug	18 Aug	16 Aug
21-Ord	1	23 Aug	21 Aug	27 Aug	26 Aug	25 Aug	23 Aug
22-Ord	2	30 Aug	28 Aug	3 Sep	2 Sep	1 Sep	30 Aug
23-Ord	3	6 Sep	4 Sep	10 Sep	9 Sep	8 Sep	6 Sep
24-Ord	4	13 Sep	11 Sep	17 Sep	16 Sep	15 Sep	13 Sep
25-Ord	1	20 Sep	18 Sep	24 Sep	23 Sep	22 Sep	20 Sep
26-Ord	2	27 Sep	25 Sep	1 Oct	30 Sep	29 Sep	27 Sep
27-Ord	3	4 Oct	2 Oct	8 Oct	7 Oct	6 Oct	4 Oct
28-Ord	4	11 Oct	9 Oct	15 Oct	14 Oct	13 Oct	11 Oct
29-Ord	1	18 Oct	16 Oct	22 Oct	21 Oct	20 Oct	18 Oct
30-Ord	2	25 Oct	23 Oct	29 Oct	28 Oct	27 Oct	25 Oct
31-Ord	3	1 Nov	30 Oct	5 Nov	4 Nov	3 Nov	1 Nov
32-Ord	4	8 Nov	6 Nov	12 Nov	11 Nov	10 Nov	8 Nov
33-Ord	1	15 Nov	13 Nov	19 Nov	18 Nov	17 Nov	15 Nov
34-Ord	2	22 Nov	20 Nov	26 Nov	25 Nov	24 Nov	22 Nov

CANTICLE OF ZECHARIAH

Blessed are you, God of Israel
for you have visited and redeemed your people,
and have raised up a horn of salvation for us
in the house of your servant.

As you spoke through the mouths
of your holy prophets from of old,
that we should be saved from our enemies,
and from the hand of all who oppress us;

to perform the mercy promised to our ancestors,
and to remember your holy covenant,

the oath you swore to Abraham and Sarah,
to grant us deliverance from evil,
that we might serve you without fear,
in holiness and righteousness
all the days of our lives.

And you, child,
will be called the prophet of the Most High,
for you will go before the Holy One
to prepare God's ways,

to give knowledge of salvation to God's people
in the forgiveness of their sins,

through the tender mercy of our God
when the day shall dawn upon us from on high

to give light to those who sit in darkness
and in the shadow of death,
to guide our feet
into the way of peace.   Glory...